Killing Men & Dying Women

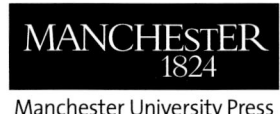

Manchester University Press

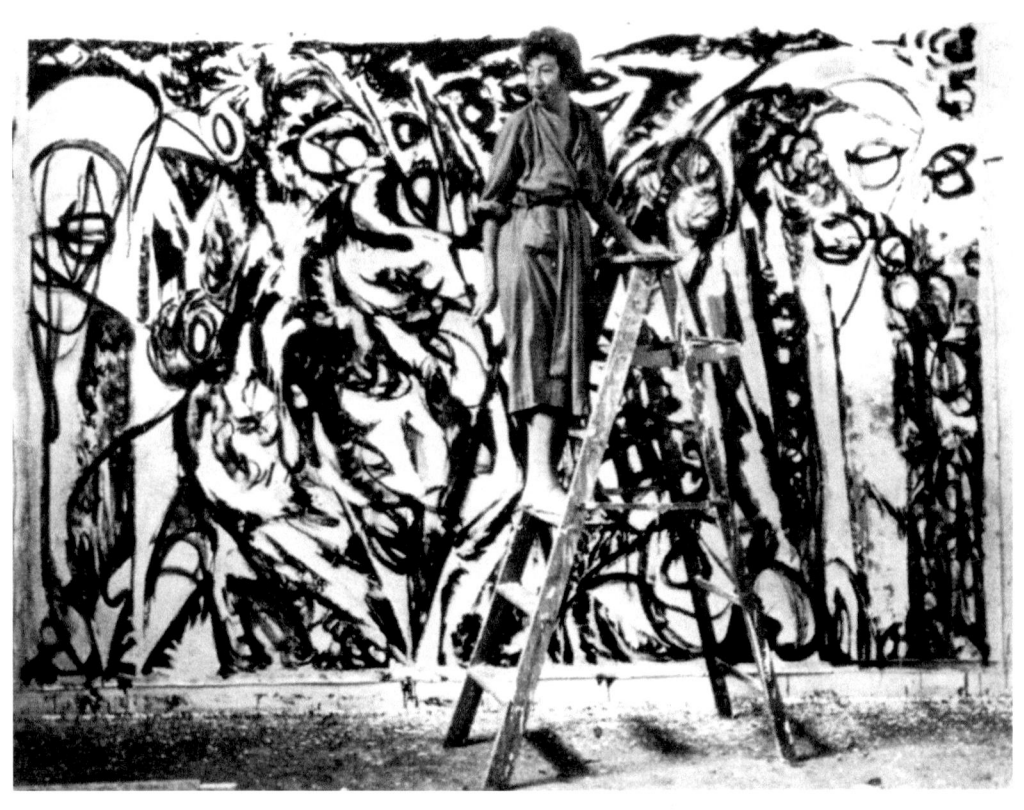

Frontispiece Halley Erskine, *Lee Krasner in her studio in front of* The Gate (*unfinished*), July–August 1959

Killing Men & Dying Women

Imagining Difference in 1950s
New York Painting

Griselda Pollock

Manchester University Press

Published by Manchester University Press
Oxford Road, Manchester M13 9PL

www.manchesteruniversitypress.co.uk

British Library Cataloguing-in-Publication Data
A catalogue record for this book is available from the British Library

ISBN 978 1 5261 6417 9 hardback
ISBN 978 1 5261 6418 6 paperback

First published 2022

Typeset
by Cheshire Typesetting Ltd, Cuddington, Cheshire
Printed in Great Britain
by Severn, Gloucester

The constant companions of my life as writer and art historian are not surprisingly those I choose to keep closest: **Antony Bryant,** *a daily interlocutor on all aspects of our endangered and unjust world;* **Hester Bloom,** *a brilliant and compassionate writer/ creator, who lightens every day with her whiplash wit and shares my delight in cinema; and* **Ben Bryant,** *a fearsome warrior against cruelty in the world who uses his sharp, analytical intelligence to hold power to account for injuries inflicted on the young and the vulnerable. Without their example and humour and warm and always supportive acceptance of my dedication to the study of art and of women as its makers, no books would ever have been written.*

This book was also written during the global pandemic of an acute respiratory syndrome: SARS-CoV-2 aka COVID-19. I salute those who developed vaccines and the health workers of all nations who went to the limit to save lives, as well as acknowledging the courage of those who have lived through anxiety, bereavement, lockdown, economic precarity and hitherto unnamed psychological conditions resulting from enforced isolation and, less critically but significantly, a lack of access to engagement with cultural forms as a fundamental social, life-enhancing and necessary activity. Our world has been shocked even as it has been bonded by the pandemic. I look forward to the artistic exploration and registration of this shock. This book is itself an oblique outcome of the sudden expulsion from the social world into the relative safety of my study.

Contents

Illustrations

Every effort has been made to obtain permission to reproduce copyright material, and the publisher will be pleased to be informed of any errors and omissions for correction in future editions.

The increasingly prohibitive cost of multiple licensing for images has prevented the inclusion of many installation shots of exhibitions critical to this study. I hope the reader might search the available internet sources to compensate for what I can simply not afford to include.

Acknowledgements

This book has emerged over many years in many conversations that began with deeply feminist discussions with Rozsika Parker during the 1970s and 1980s, while my interest in New York painting began in dialogue with Fred Orton, with whom I taught and collaboratively wrote across the 1970s and 1980s when the fields of feminist critique and the study of New York painting in the 1950s were just emerging. I have also been in conversation with artists/art historians Anthea Callen since the 1970s and Alison Rowley since the 1990s, who both, in their different ways, taught me to look at painting as materiality, process and event. Alison Rowley's writing on Helen Frankenthaler took the study of this artist's work and that of abstract painting by women to an entirely new plane and remains unsurpassed for its astute historical understanding and its theoretical subtlety. Theoretically, I am indebted to a wealth of feminist thinking including the work of artist-theorist-analyst Bracha L. Ettinger, without whose transformative theories of the matrixial feminine which released feminist thought and art writing from its anxiously filial relationship to phallocentric psychoanalysis this book would not have been imaginable.

I want to thank my editors Emma Brennan and Alun Richards at Manchester University Press for supporting this book. I appreciated enormously the three insightful reviewers whose comments enabled me see many new aspects while strengthening my experiment in writing this conceptual framework for deeper, feminist reading of what it is that painting in its abstract modes reveals to us. I want also warmly to thank Helen A. Harrison of the Pollock–Krasner Study Center and all those at Gagosian, Paul Kasmin, the Helen Frankenthaler Foundation, the Pollock–Krasner Foundation and the Willem de Kooning Foundation for their kind assistance.

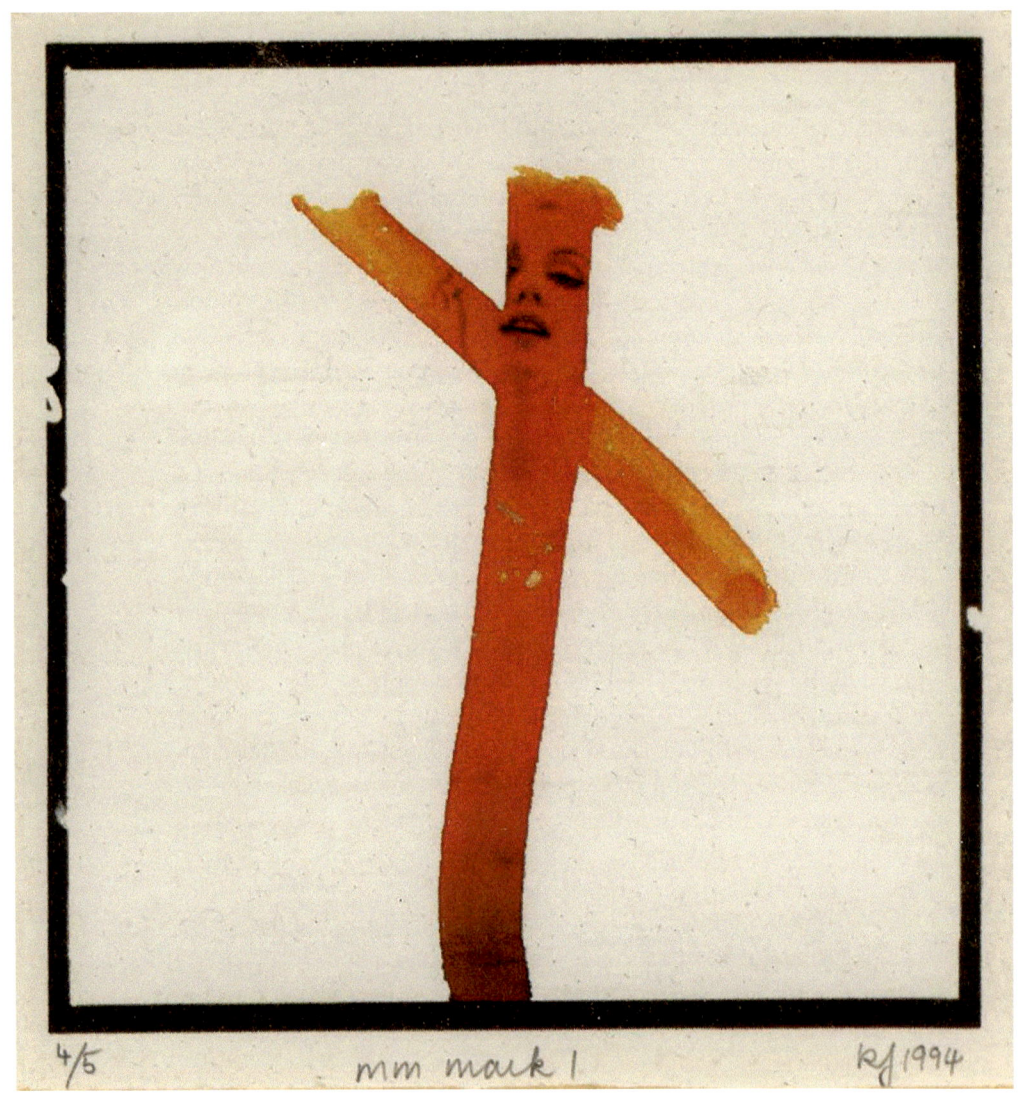

4/5   mm mark 1   kf 1994

Figure 00.1 Kerry Filer Harker, *mm Mark 1*, 1994

Preface

Lee Krasner, Marilyn Monroe and Jackson Pollock meet in the hot zone of New York painting in the 1950s

In 1994, in a series of prints titled *mm Mark 1–9*, British artist Kerry Filer Harker (b. 1971) transformed one of the defaced contact sheets from Bert Stern's photoshoot with Marilyn Monroe (1926–62) for *Vogue* in July 1962 (fig. 00.1). Monroe retained rights over her images, disfiguring shots she disliked, crossing them out with nail varnish or scratching the surface. When the negative is printed, her negation overlays the original image. Twenty years after the shoot, which yielded only a brief posthumous spread in *Vogue* (15 September 1962), Stern published 2,571 photographs of the July shoot as *Marilyn Monroe: The Last Sitting* and as *The Complete Last Sitting* in 2000.[1] He included the photographs that Monroe rejected.

Exploring this breach of trust from a feminist perspective, using early photoshop digital software, Harker isolated the negating mark, revealing Monroe's 'painterly gesture'. Her action becomes the image. Through the nail varnish's tinted transparency, the iconic pose – eyelids lowered, mouth slightly opened – hovers, endowing the abstract cipher with a gaze. The two strokes create a pose. Harker's artwork catches up the condensations and displacements that it will take the rest of this book to expand.

Is MM's mark her gestural painting, linking Marilyn Monroe with the famous Abstract Expressionists of the 1950s, the action or gestural painters who distilled the dynamic between gesture, mark and surface?[2] With whom would we align MM, given the gender exclusivity of modernist art history and of the critics writing in that moment? Abstract Expressionists? Who represents that moment when action, process and gesture became both means and content of a new kind of painting centred in New York? Probably Jackson Pollock (1912–56), himself made 'famous' by a spread in *Life* magazine in 1949 and by a film by Hans Namuth (1915–90) in 1950 (figs 2.18–2.20).[3] Overused iconic images, Namuth's film and photographs innovatively revealed the 'choreography' of Pollock's repeating movements along, around and over the supine canvases he spread unstretched on the ground. His film captured the gestures with which Pollock carved, flicked, splattered and dripped his enamel and household paint to create layered meshes, coloured skeins and added densities of solid colour.

What of the other painter resident at The Springs, East Hampton, Lee Krasner (1908–84), who often came to Pollock's studio at the end of each day from her own, to share with him the question that both had to pose after their encounters between painter, materials and canvas: 'Is this a painting? Or is it just a mess of wasted paint?' 'Does it hold as *painting* without becoming an image of anything but its own performative, if also evocative, making?' (fig. 5.1).[4] What, therefore, of the more experienced, abstractly trained painter Krasner, who sustained a brilliant career before and long after her marriage to Pollock, despite the selectively critical indifference to her work in a man-only focused artworld that, after their marriage and Pollock's early death, laid the shadow of her tragic husband over the autonomous artistic career of the widow, 'Mrs Pollock'?

If Marilyn Monroe became the icon of American Woman across popular media as much as in Willem de Kooning's painted formula of the early 1950s (fig. 6.1), and if Jackson Pollock represented the American Artist, how did Lee Krasner make sense of the duality – Woman and Artist – which modernist art history had made a contradiction?[5] How did the iconic Marilyn Monroe impinge on the cultural mythologies of gender at work and being lived and worked out in the artworld of New York in the 1950s? How would reading the *mark of MM* via her image back through the masculine artist as celebrity of that decade – Jackson Pollock – make intelligible another dimension of her body, her gestures, and body as agonized, gendered and sexual interior, not just as cosmetic surface and erotic-for-straight-men image? Would we learn to read Lee Krasner by creating a conversation between the points of a triangulation: Pollock–Monroe–Krasner? How would new questions about women, agency, creativity, sexual difference and the body come into focus? What resources would I need to mobilize to undertake such an exploration?

I arrived at my interest in the meanings of Marilyn Monroe as a cultural image from both art history and film studies. Feminist film theory was already a critical resource for the interdisciplinary, anti-canonical approach to expanded cultural studies with which I was launching *feminist interventions in art's histories*.[6] I am reversing that direction to go through Monroe's image, body and gesture to an expanded art historical inquiry. The other source was my research and teaching with artist and art historian Fred Orton from 1977 to 1980 at the University of Leeds on 'Readings in American Culture and Society in the 1950s'. At that time, teaching art that was almost contemporary – within the last twenty years – was 'un-art historical'. Time had not distilled the timeless canon. Our methods were experimental. Initiated in 1977, our art history seminar was one of the first in Britain to research and create a social art historical model for studying and teaching the painting practices, the role of institutions and the art criticism of the still recent developments in 1950s art in New York. Our second pedagogic innovation was to combine the cultural-political study of a self-consciously avant-gardist practice of New York painting with

Hollywood cinema, the other major cultural product and ideological export from the USA during the Cold War. We studied classics such as *An American in Paris*, *Invasion of the Body Snatchers*, *North by Northwest*, *The Searchers*, *Lust for Life* and *3.10 to Yuma* alongside textual study of critical writings by Clement Greenberg (1909–94) and Harold Rosenberg (1906–78), supplemented by ideological analysis of the institutional history and cultural effects of the Museum of Modern Art through readings of its exhibitions as both topic and resource. Both New York art and Hollywood cinema were shaped in the 1950s by McCarthyism (a virulent anti-communism that hounded people out of the culture industries and other national institutions through the House Committee on Un-American Activities [HUAC]), the paranoias of the Cold War and nuclear war and deep divisions within US-American capitalist, racializing and antisemitic formations around conflicting nationalist and internationalist orientations.[7]

I could not, however, easily reconcile the Marxist social history of art I had embraced – and through which Orton and I sought to counter the triumphalist and modernist art history being written for the so-called New York School of modern painting in the 1950s (Irving Sandler's *Triumph of American Painting* was published in 1970) – with feminist interventions against the racist, sexist and formalist art histories that I was developing in my parallel collaboration with Rozsika Parker on *Old Mistresses: Women, Art and Ideology* (1981), conceived and written between 1975 and 1978. My own monograph on *Mary Cassatt* (1980) was completed in 1979. As an emerging feminist art historian, I wanted to recover and to reassert the *co-creation* of modernism – from the mid-nineteenth century to the 'New American Painting', the title of a major international show in 1959 – by women working alongside men, of various ethnicities, sexualities and class backgrounds, so as to challenge the hegemonic story of modernism as a heroic, exclusively white and masculine endeavour, even when revised by Marxist social historical analysis.[8]

I had to pose, if not answer, questions not yet addressed in feminism. Does sexual difference make a difference in artistic practice? How would we theorize, analyse and interpret it without attributing innate differences to men and women in identitarian, gender categories? One pathway emerged from the fact that Orton and I were studying the cinematic Cold War, analysing the images of 'Americanness' that Hollywood projected across Westerns, musicals, thrillers, film noir and science fiction, where constructions of sexual difference and its socio-psychic dramas were systematically structural. In 1970s film studies, feminist analysis was productively coupling Marxist, semiotic and psychoanalytical theories, making the latter a major resource for many of us stranded in the straitjackets of either formalist or iconographic art history.

Fred Orton and I studied with interest director Vincente Minnelli (1903–86), whose films thematized and dramatically explored the *ordeal* of masculine creativity.[9] Since both of us were also Van Gogh scholars, one film became a focus: *Lust for Life* (dir. Minnelli, 1955–56).[10] Minnelli's reading of the Parisian artworld of the 1880s was represented in *Lust for Life* as the violent conflict between two artist-men, Paul Gauguin and Vincent van Gogh. In my own published study, I argued that Minnelli mounted a contemporary, if oblique, political, pro-modernist argument in *Lust for Life*, casting the intellectual painter Gauguin as a progressive mouthpiece for abstract art, even as the Van Gogh narrative played out Minnelli's recurring theme of the doomed creative artist through the self-destructive characterization of the suicidal, socially abused and internally tormented Dutch painter. Minnelli positioned Van Gogh as an 'old-fashioned' figurative realist. *Aesthetically* championing Gauguin's rationally articulated case for modernism and abstraction, Minnelli *cinematically* distanced his viewers from Van Gogh's unsophisticated attachment to realism – a style endorsed by anti-modernist, nationalist American art critics in the Cold War of contemporary art debate in the 1940s–1950s.[11] Creating a psychological portrait of the self-destructive Van Gogh, *Lust of Life* uncannily anticipated the tragic Jackson Pollock, killed in a car crash on 11 August 1956, just over a month before the release of Minnelli's film on 15 September 1956.[12]

As a result of this concatenation of art historical research, methodological inquiries and transdisciplinary cultural analysis, I found myself faced with another set of questions as I explored the work of Helen Frankenthaler (1928–2011) and Lee Krasner. Lee Krasner lived, created beside and outlived Jackson Pollock, the iconically tragic Minnellian figure of Americanness, Abstract Expressionism and the new type of action painter. The elective proximity of artists Krasner and Pollock, who chose to risk their own creativity in a shared commitment to the most radical adventure in modern painting, raised fascinating questions easily smothered by the conventional frames of 'husband influences wife', 'man influences woman'. Krasner sustained her long creative career across the decade that witnessed the creation of the moody Pollock's feminine cipher, the icon of another – American popular – modernism: Marilyn Monroe.

So, here is the question at the heart of this book.

What was it to be an *artist* and a *woman* – such as the brilliant painter Lee Krasner – if, in the chiasmic space of avant-garde art and popular US-American culture, to be the *artist* was iconically *Jackson Pollock* and to be a *woman* was iconically *Marilyn Monroe*?

Gender, sexuality and concepts of masculinity and femininity are complex, unstable and always contested. During the 1940–1950s, however, there was an intense politics of gender and sexuality. Officially deeply conservative, patriarchal and homophobic positions were being disrupted by emerging, contesting discourses on sexuality – Hefner's *Playboy* as much as the challenging sociological revelations about human sexual behaviour of Alfred Kinsey. Cultural practices, notably Hollywood cinema, were both charged to be and policed as conveyors of dominant ideological messages during the Cold War, through the still-active Hays Code that screened all scripts for inappropriate sexual (and politically and racially progressive) material, and through the nationalist conservatism represented by Senator Joseph McCarthy. US-American popular entertainment was domestically and internationally distributed, serving both as an instrument to disseminate ideology and, because any cinematic text *works* its ideological content in unpredictable ways, as a site of its contested renegotiation. While my question might today seem crude in its polarization – artist/woman – I argue that the *triangulation* an artist-woman faced through the iconization of her two identities, artist and woman, in such diametrically opposed yet strangely converging, even deadly ways, does open up potentially revelatory avenues for a feminist cultural and social-art historical inquiry into that moment and its continuing effects in our own.

Feminist compassion, let alone feminist theory, compels me to displace crass oppositions of high art versus popular culture, or masculinity, creativity and sexuality and energy versus femininity, performance and sex-body. Is she named 'Marilyn Monroe' only to be figured as the cinematic and photographic image produced by the publicity machine of Hollywood and the attendant popular press? What would a feminist reading of actor 'Marilyn Monroe' in a complex relation to the painter Lee Krasner, and vice versa, look like? When both are seen through a feminist lens, what oppositions might be reconfigured?

The triangulation I identified as the quandary in terms of contradictory identities offered to the artist-woman had to break down before the subtler investigations prompted by feminist analysis of the inherent instabilities in the 1950s and in American culture and society of three key elements: sexuality, subjectivity and creativity, as well as body, performance and difference. I aim to unravel my questions through *reading* just a few paintings by Lee Krasner made in the very years 1956–57 when 'Marilyn Monroe' had become a signifier across eight films made between 1953 and 1957 that made stellar a bit-part actress who had hovered at the edges of Hollywood since 1948, for reasons that my forthcoming book on *Monroe's Mov(i)es* sets out to re-examine.

My initial exploration during the 1990s became a long chapter published in a collection of writings by Fred Orton and me from our collaborative and individual work on the Euro-US-American avant-garde between 1880 and 1960.[13] My text was a collage, layering discrete episodes like an avant-garde movie whose meaning emerges only through following the fragments to their suggestive resolution. This book is the much revised, updated and considerably expanded elaboration of those exploratory reflections, which also works its experimental way, section by section. I deepen my art historical investigations through psychoanalytical theorizations of painting, subjectivity and sexual difference.

Might I discover inscriptions of *feminine sexual difference* (theorized psychoanalytically) that are historically and culturally legible while being at the same time aesthetically singular, in each artist-woman's discrete works? What would be the psycho-semiotic conditions for relations between creativity, masculinity and femininity? Are they asymmetrical? How? Why? What becomes or what evokes the phantom of the maternal body in all of this? I offer a hypothesis about the intersection of one site of creativity singularity – abstract painting and its men and women practitioners – and another – popular culture represented by the image *of* and the image produced *by* Marilyn Monroe and Hollywood cinema during the 1950s. I propose a conversation between *her* creative agency – the *mark of MM* – and its conditions of possibility and negation and those of the painter-women in abstract art, both coexisting in time and space in New York in the 1950s. Their admittedly disparate creative activities were negated by the phallocentrism that traverses the division between their respective arenas of activity.

My text is transdisciplinary and theory-rich. I think both are necessary if we are not to allow art history to fall into the realm of the financialized art market, easy consumption and light entertainment. This is even more acute now since many of the once widely taught and disseminated theoretical resources upon which I have drawn have ceased to be common currency in the academic sphere or among an interested reading public. I want to demonstrate that they enable us to recognize, think and understand what conventional – politically pacified, market-serving, entertainment-based – art history and the increasing abandon of theoretical resources is blandly effacing.

Since 1996 other feminist art historians have taken up my questions about difference in painting with, or without, due acknowledgement of my early inquiries into gender and Abstract Expressionist painting in print since 1981.[14] One interlocutor is Lisa Saltzman, who writes the following in her 'Reconsidering the Stain: On Gender and the Body in Helen Frankenthaler's Painting' (1998; revised in 2005):

> Despite the prevalence of the gendered metaphorics in the representation of abstraction, very little has been done to analyse its implications, either for New York school painting or for the interpretation of abstraction more generally. *Even in the work of the first generation of feminist art historians who*

explicitly took on questions of gender, the interpretation of abstraction was never the primary object of enquiry.[15] (my emphasis)

As one of the 'first generation of feminist art historians' who did discuss New York abstraction very much through its own formal terms as a basis for exploring questions of 'difference', I want to contest this view gently by recalling what I taught in the 1970s and published in *Old Mistresses* in 1981, when I had realized that the recovering of artist-women of the past was a necessary backstory for contemporary artist-women at risk of being marginalized:

> The move – pouring paint onto unprimed cotton duck laid on the floor – enabled Frankenthaler to assert the notion of the flatness and two-dimensionality of the surface of the painting and thus to deny the illusion of three-dimensional space. At the same time, the floating colour saturated into and, therefore, became literally part of its canvas support, creating a sense of ambiguous space through a depth of colour, the different forces of colours receding or coming forward. The paintings both conform to and undercut the notion of flatness in a way that brings the maximum number of ambiguities into play. Ambiguity was the theme Frankenthaler consciously pursued, producing, in 1957, a large canvas subsequently given the title of the leading critical study on the uses of ambiguity in literature, *Seven Types of Ambiguity* by William Empson.[16]

Frankenthaler's method transcended the banal celebration of what one critic in 1969 termed her 'bleeding-edge stain', from which alone resulted its effects and any consideration of the differences between her work and Jackson Pollock's or later Morris Louis's.[17] I argued that precisely this method and the abstraction enacted through gesture, movement and process in relation to the space of the canvas made the *body* of the artist (the locus of psycho-somatic subjectivity, not anatomy) critical to resulting *affects*. Its physicality, its gestures and the resulting *effects* must read as having been 'desired' or 'approved' by the artist.

> Unlike pre-modernist art in which how a thing was painted was subordinate to what was represented, in Abstract Expressionism the act of painting itself was emphasised and through its use of gesture, abstract form, colour and line new meanings could be produced. Despite new possibilities of meaning, the artist in Abstract Expressionism remained extremely important because the activity of painting, the materials and their effects, the gestures the artist made, became the subject of the work itself. So that rather than displacing the artist, Abstract Expressionism supremely celebrated the gestures and creativity of the maker and what one sees on an Abstract Expressionist canvas are the traces of the artist's activity … While the signifying practices opened up possibilities, particularly relevant to women, for producing new

meanings, the even more mythic status of the artist within this practice brought into headlong collision, on the field of critics' discourse on women artists, notions of the *great artist* versus the stereotypes of femininity.[18]

To undo that contradiction for artist-men and artist-women in this movement, I offered a close reading Helen Frankenthaler's *The Maud* (1963).[19] I also queried the metaphorics of gender in art criticism's account of Abstract Expressionism, when contemporary critics read the differences in terms of stereotyped interpretations of the end results; for instance, Frankenthaler's paintings were viewed as lyrical images of nature, even by those who aimed to celebrate her work. In contradiction to the premises of Abstract Expressionism, they looked at the *finished products*, the paintings, not at *how* the artist produced them.

Art historians have taken issue with my reading – where they bothered to notice it. I now engage with this expanded debate which has repeatedly addressed the potential meaning of techniques, gestures, bodies and their aesthetic inscription in a profoundly 'formal' exercise: abstract painting. The intellectual subtlety of arguments enriched by feminist theory needs to be integrated, their differences clarified and the value of each acknowledged. A consensus of interpretation is uninteresting. Differences are. What matters is both the potential of feminist analysis and the anxiety that stalks it not only in a patriarchal environment that dismisses gender let alone sexual difference theory, but also in the current feminist theoretical environment. Hostility to opposing positions and foreclosure of areas of debate or theoretical directions are not constructive.

Emerging in a cooler moment when the hot force of 'theory' and indeed cultural critique has become a remote memory or, sadly, a never-yet encountered possibility, my hope is that the tenor and intensity of feminist interventions demonstrate how much is at stake in *thinking* these big questions and in *thinking* them still and *thinking* beyond our existing orthodoxies.

Griselda Pollock
Leeds, 2021

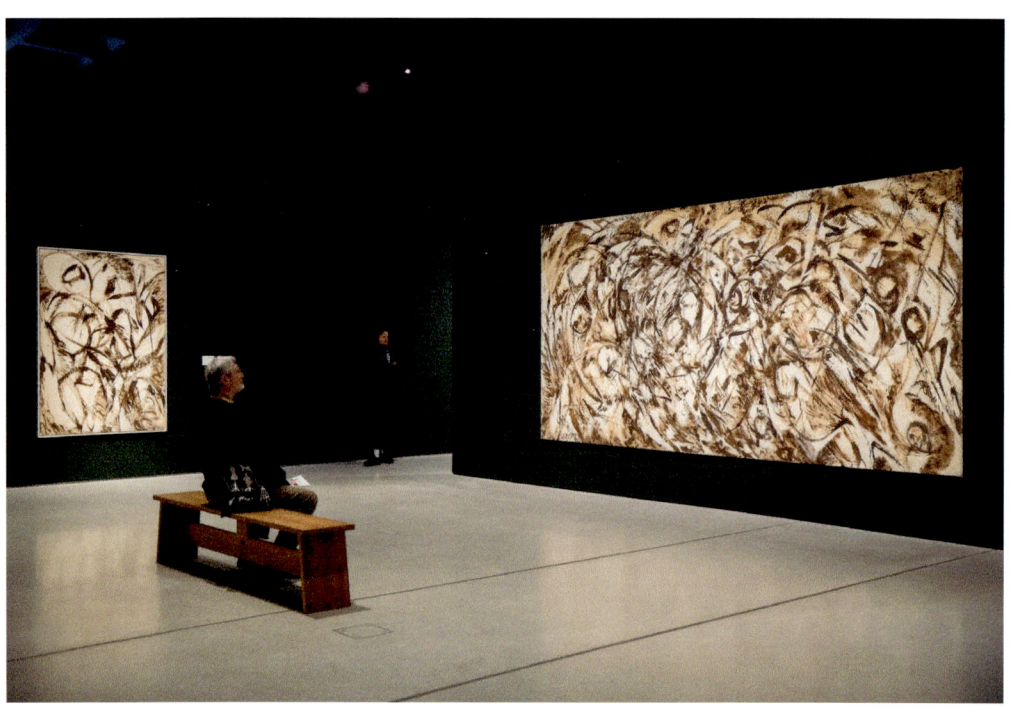

Figure 0.1 Installation view of *Lee Krasner Living Colour*, Barbican, London, 2019. Visible: *Eye is the First Circle*, 1960; *Night Watch*, 1960

Introduction

In 2021 the Centre Pompidou in Paris staged *Elles font l'abstraction: un autre histoire de l'abstraction au XXe siècle* (*She-They Made Abstraction: An Other History of Abstraction in the 20th Century*), curated by Christine Macel, which travelled to the Guggenheim Bilbao as *Women in Abstraction*. Like Camille Morineau's *elles@centrepomidou* in 2009, Macel's French title – *elles font l'abstraction* – stresses creativity 'in the feminine' by using the grammatically gendered plural, *elles*, which awkwardly translates as *She-They*, so that we hear the gender shock incited in the French. Macel's title de-universalizes – linguistically and graphically – the typical *il-he* and *ils-they* generic for artists. Highlighting artist-women (my neologism to avoid the additive and disqualifying term *woman artist*) and making visible their singular but also cumulative presence across a complexified analysis of international abstraction, Macel reframed abstraction itself. Her exhibition and catalogue offer one frame for my revisiting one moment in abstraction's history centred in New York in the 1950s.

Why a book about abstract painting in New York in the 1950s, now? Why another feminist visit to that scene of modernist artmaking? Given the quantity of documentation, exhibitions and publications on US-American modernism and even, in recent years, some admission of artist-women, why still indict art history's failures to be modern – to be inclusive and egalitarian? In recent reassessments of New York abstraction, the basic feminist call for inclusiveness is both minimal and compromised. The mere *addition* of some women's names does not yet acknowledge the *co-creation* of modern art by artist-women and artist-men. *Co-creation* is not about couples who collaborate. It signifies multiple sites and persons, genders, sexualities, ethnicities and classes sharing in the making of the modern in art. Barely going beyond basic reinsertion, revisionist art history has not integrated feminist and other challenges to the premises of the few belated 'recognitions', *feminist* signalling radically different ways of seeing and reading the artworks and art practices created by a diversity of artist-women side by side, but each differently and singularly, and with masculine peers whose stories, works and personalities have dominated an almost all-male whitewash of a complex artistic twentieth century. At what level could feminist analysis unpick the paradox of modernist art history, its systemic sexism and its systematic disinformation on the basis of gender, when gender change was itself a symptom of the modern? What concepts would we need to forge to confront these questions in relation to relatively recent, notably abstract art co-created by women and men, many of whom were still alive and creative?

Modernism is what artists, men and women, black and white, queer and straight, and from many continents, religious heritages, ethnicities, capacities variously co-created, sometimes living side by side in cheap housing, lofts or laundry boats in various cities such as Paris, New York, Buenos Aires, Barcelona, Tokyo, Ibadan, etc., in erotic partnerships or informal groupings, while each artist contributed their singular experience of race, class, gender, sexuality, embodiment, politics, artistic process and vision to the multi-threaded canvas of twentieth-century art. Challenging the limited story and narrowed vision placed before the public by art historians and museums, we demand more than token acquisitions and belated, partial integrations. Feminist, postcolonial and queer readings enrich the histories of art, and we learn to see ourselves and art's histories in complexity and diversity.

This book analyses questions of painting and sexual difference, knowingly threading theory into reading artworks. I make the case for feminist theory so that that the richness of art's histories can be saved from bland banality, hero-worship and speculative marketization of celebrity based on price tags. Art, necessarily requiring patrons and buyers, was not, however, made as entertainment, even as selling became the modern capitalist condition for earning the means to continue to make art. We owe it to the artists to grapple with the complexity of the art they make.

My focus here is a few paintings from a mid-twentieth-century community in New York at a transformative moment in Western painting and its concept of the artist. I read that moment from another historical moment – the formulation of feminist theory in the last decades of the twentieth century and still vibrant and ever more urgent in the first two decades of this century, here deployed within art history. Despite all the new shows and expensive scholarly publications and catalogues, New York painting or Abstract Expressionism remains opaque, strange and challenging to us today, precisely as one might hope art to remain.

As one of the major forms through which Western Christian and then modern culture thought itself for five centuries, painting has been displaced since the 1970s by conceptual art, performance, moving image, electronic, digital and other media, and the complex and expanded practices that constitute 'contemporary' art today. '1950s New York' painting was a kind of swansong of both Western painting and of abstraction as the dominant art language (although both continue, of course). Abstract painter Bridget Riley has argued that, when it was abruptly abandoned by so much mainstream art for the still or moving image, the text and the event, abstraction was effectively still in its infancy. Riley compared the stage of abstraction c. 1970 to the state of painting in thirteenth/fourteenth-century Italy, just beginning its adventure with oil painting, with yet five centuries of brilliance ahead.[1]

Putting two displacements, feminist theory and abstract painting, into conversation is not nostalgic. I readdress moments of art's histories to reconnect them with the effects of radical sociohistorical and cultural rupture, smoothed over by conventional linear stories of art with comforting teleologies and progressive tales of heroic masculine invention. As a double intervention into art history and feminist theory today, I propose theoretically rich methods to analyse intersections between artistic practice and cultural processes including psycho-sexual formation, subjectivity, gender and sexual difference.

I am asking: how do we *imagine* and how do we *image* difference in abstract painting?

The debate about gender and art's histories, famously reignited over half a century ago c. 1970, became hot again in the second decade of the twenty-first century around 1950s US-American abstract painting in a slew of major exhibitions: *Abstract Expressionism* (2018), *Women in Abstract Expressionism* (2018) and monographic exhibitions of the *elles*: *Lee Krasner: Living Colour* (London, 2019),[2] Perle Fine (1905–98), Bernice Bing (1936–98), Alma Thomas (1891–1978), Louise Nevelson (1899–1988) and Sonja Sekula (1918–63), to name but a few.[3] In 2018 Mary Gabriel published her mammoth collective biography, *Ninth Street Women: Lee Krasner, Elaine de Kooning, Grace Hartigan, Joan Mitchell, Helen Frankenthaler: Five Painters and the Movement that Changed Modern Art*, which at the time of writing is being made into an Amazon TV series.[4] Helen Frankenthaler's paintings featured in a solo show at the Venice Biennale in 2019 and only her second solo show, and her first major exhibition in Britain, this time of her woodcuts, is planned for the Dulwich Picture Gallery (2021–22), *Helen Frankenthaler: Radical Beauty*. In 2020 Gail Levin published *Lee Krasner: A Biography*, the same year as *Lee and Me: An Intimate Portrait of Lee Krasner* by Ruth Appelhof, while Alexander Nemerov delivered a new take on biographical writing with *Fierce Poise: Helen Frankenthaler and 1950s New York* in 2021.

In September 2020 I was solicited by a Madrid newspaper, *El País*, to write about the installation of *Lee Krasner: Living Colour* on its opening at Guggenheim Bilbao. Curated by Eleanor Nairne for the Barbican, London, as the first retrospective of the artist in London since 1965 (fig. 0.1), the show travelled to Zentrum Paul Klee, Bern, and Schirn Kunsthalle, Frankfurt (2020), before concluding in Bilbao. Invited to 'introduce' Krasner to a Spanish public unfamiliar with her name and work, I was asked to explain her *belated* recognition: Why had such a stunning artist been *overlooked?* Disheartened but delighted, I wrote*:*

> To meet Lee Krasner for the first time in 2020, in Bilbao, is to arrive very late to a party that we feminist art historians have been celebrating for more than half a century. You, we, are not *rediscovering* Lee Krasner. She was firmly part of 20th century art's history and always a major player in abstract painting.[5]

Inspired by Cindy Nemser's *Feminist Art News* article on Lee Krasner in 1975 (fig. 0.2), and later interview in *Art Talk* (1976), I began lecturing on Krasner as early as 1975–76. I only came fully to appreciate the range of her brilliance in 2000, at a retrospective at the Brooklyn Museum, New York. There I studied Krasner's works, in the flesh, decade by decade, gambit by gambit, innovation by innovation.[6] Astonished by the persistent and dynamic inventiveness sustained over a career never marked by a consolidated signature style, I was impressed by her works from the mid-1970s, hitherto unfamiliar, showing her rethinking her artistic journey by turning back to her 1930s beginnings when she excelled in both classical figure drawing and a fearless Cubist decomposition of both human form and the classical tradition itself from within. In 1976–77, Krasner sliced these early drawings and collaged their fragments on canvases titled, ironically and bitterly, with eleven tenses of the verb *to see*: *Eleven Ways To Use The Words To See* (fig. 8.5). Ghostly fragments of deconstructed geometrical figures reformed as abstract assemblages retraced Krasner's work from Cubist disruption of the figure to postmodern deconstructions of her own artistic trajectory. The title was an admonition to those who had looked at but failed to see her work. Recalling Krasner's major show of collaged paintings at the Stable Gallery in 1955, Clement Greenberg affirmed, in an interview in 1965 with Whitechapel curator Bryan Robertson, that Krasner's 1955 collage works (fig. 7.5) were the most significant moves in current abstract painting. But, as Krasner later commented in a filmed interview, *Greenberg never said so in print at the time.*[7] Critical silence sidelined Krasner from the rapidly evolving art history of New York abstract painting in the mid-1950s, even though Greenberg's high-handedness never erased her in her own lifetime. She exhibited continually, was written about, had collectors and sales, and reconfigured her practice in astonishingly creative ways.

It is, therefore, important that we are not misled into thinking that we are *rediscovering* artist-women as if they were missing from the real event, and as if some of us have now to make a special case to *introduce* them. Krasner painted in ambitious artistic conversations with predecessors and contemporaries – Mondrian, Picasso, Matisse, Jackson Pollock, Willem de Kooning, Elaine de Kooning, Helen Frankenthaler, Grace Hartigan, Alma Thomas, Hedda Sterne – the many women and men who formed

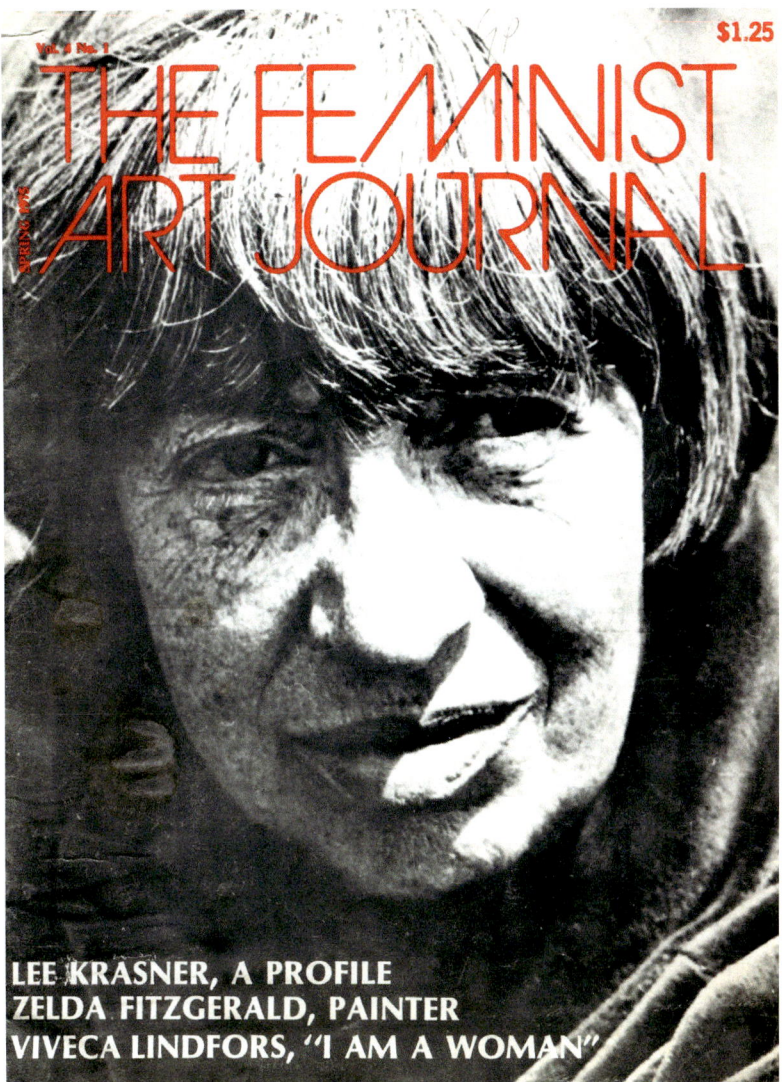

Figure 0.2 *Lee Krasner on the cover of* Feminist Art News, 1975

the dynamic artistic context for the emergence of modernist art and its multiple directions in the tiny coterie that we now collect as New York painting in the 1950s.

Beside major recent museum exhibitions, there is renewed activity on the part of commercial galleries, many taking on the estates of major but less visible mid-twentieth-century painter-women whose market value has been enhanced, not only by feminist interpretation, but by feminist agitation for at least their inclusion in the blander official histories of art. Since 2017, for instance, Paul Kasmin Gallery in New York, which had newly taken on Lee Krasner's estate, has staged a series of focused exhibitions, including a show on the collaged works of 1955 (2021) and, earlier, *Lee Krasner: Umber Paintings 1959–1962*, with a text commissioned from art historian David Anfam on her dramatic monochromatic paintings from a period of profound personal anguish and equal artistic determination (fig. 0.1).[8] His essay is particularly relevant to this book. It is indicative of art historical ambivalence.

David Anfam curated the blockbuster *Abstract Expressionism* (2016–17), which opened at London's Royal Academy, travelling to the Guggenheim in Bilbao. He included one of Lee Krasner's *Umber* series, yet his show gave neither Krasner nor the younger Abstract Expressionist painter Helen Frankenthaler the substantive space allocated to the artist-men, apart from his featuring of Joan Mitchell (1925–92), the only woman listed on the poster and given her own space in the show. Anfam was criticized for his disproportionate selectivity (see Chapter 8). Krasner and Frankenthaler, of different generations, were both positioned on wall labels as sub-Pollock artists.[9]

Writing in 2019 on Krasner's *Umber* show at Paul Kasmin, Anfam's tone had changed – a little. With one gesture, he acknowledged the achievement of the dramatic monochrome gestural paintings; with another, he preserved a masculinist hierarchy. First, he installed the younger painter, Pollock, in a position of artistic priority, situating Krasner as a late developer of her own artistic identity and only so in 'combat' with Pollock's unquestioned predominance as a ghostly, 'structuring absence':

> Paradoxically, the originality about the Umbers grew in part from engaging with another artist. The significant other was, of course, her late husband Jackson Pollock. His presence is the structuring absence that underlies the Umbers. As such they reap what literary critic Harold Bloom famously theorised as the 'anxiety of influence' whereby a creator wrestles with the powerful predecessor to become equally 'strong' themselves. Krasner's reckoning with Pollock's legacy induced a hitherto unprecedented degree of self-confidence as if she were determined to match or even trump his masculinist persona. Metaphorically couched, this is not Pollock's ventriloquism, as it were, still less is it the former muted 'Lena Krassner', but the sovereign Krasner at last speaking loud clear and often in anger. In this respect the apt titles of two Umbers resound with the fierce emotions at stake: *Uncaged* (1960) and *White Rage* (1961).[10]

Anfam references literary critic's Harold Bloom's thesis of artistic competition as an Oedipal dynamic (father-killing), structurally shaping the filial revolt of writers and artists against potent predecessors whose overpowering presence must be negotiated even as their precedence is acknowledged for the son-artist or son-writer to claim descent.

Succession is not inheritance from the predecessor but a struggle of younger poets/artists not to be artistically killed by predecessor fathers. Creatively defensive moves perpetuate the father–son rivalry as Bloom's driving force behind cultural progression. Like Freud, Bloom imagines no space for the daughter, let alone considering either daughter–mother or artist-women peer relations as equally psychologically complex and culturally interesting arenas for different creative dynamics.

Anfam's 'deadly creative struggle' takes place between a man and a woman – not the Bloomian filial competitiveness – in a marriage when both artists – Krasner and Pollock – were, in fact, peers in a shared artistic moment alongside their shared predecessors and contemporaries in the tiny New York avant-garde. Using Bloom, Anfam situates Pollock in the place of Father. He thus *daughters* Krasner, Pollock's elder, peer and partner in creative membership of the abstract art community. Reminding us also that they were husband and wife, Anfam further differentiates both as artists by setting the emboldened *Lee Krasner* – who emerges only after the dark night of battle with a Pollock-as-Father figure – against the unformed *Lena Krassner* (the artist's original family name, abandoned in the late 1940s when she adopted the artist signature *LK*). He thus locates the older and more mature abstract artist since the 1930s, Krasner, as child, daughter and wife to the dead and monumental Pollock, affirming Pollock's canonicity.

Krasner's creativity emerges only belatedly out of an uneven combat, Hamlet-like, with Pollock's haunting paternal-husband ghost.[11] Anfam produces an ambivalent frame through which Krasner's dramatic new project in the years 1959–62 is equivocally presented to the reader as a painful *coming of age*, suppressing both what would be the arena of transformation 1956–57 on which I shall concentrate in this book, as well as the critical innovations of her work in reconstituted, collaged painting in 1953–55, brilliantly analysed by Ellen G. Landau in her study of this creative period in Krasner's work when Pollock had lost his way in his own.[12] Landau probed the complex issues of co-creation in an environment of personal and artistic cohabitation that had been resolved by the mid-1950s, writing:

> Krasner reached this threshold [of transition] by reconfiguring her oppression, taking active control over the terms of *his* interjection into *her* space. Paradoxically by acknowledging literally her links to Jackson Pollock, in her collages of the early 1950s, Lee Krasner positioned her escape from marginalized status, rapidly accelerating her own artistic growth.[13]

The issue of creative struggle – *combat* is Anfam's only term – and gender has long been a topic in my own writings on art, gender and modernism. I return to study it here in terms of how much, or how little, of *feminist rethinking* of artistic agonism and non-deadly forms of creative transformation has been incorporated into our analyses of painting and sexual difference.

Furthermore, by explaining the *Umber* series (1959–62) as Krasner's grief for husband Pollock, Anfam uses biographical reductionism. Krasner affirmed that Pollock's sudden death in 1956 was devastating, but, I argue, at the level of the state *through*, not just *in*, which she painted the *Umbers*. Freud theorized the *work of mourning* as psychic working through of loss. Krasner was negotiating both the premature loss of her painter-partner in 1956 and the recent death of her mother. Each loss has different psychic resonances. Both precipitated the artist into crisis, the later loss inducing insomnia, through whose sleepless nights Krasner nevertheless painted. Unnatural light obliged her to abandon her major instrument – colour – and to find another language as she was also moving on to a vaster scale that would involve freer movements of the body, engender activity through new gestures and discover gestural rhythms within the dynamic events of monochromatic marks on this scale.

To interpret Lee Krasner's *Umber* paintings as the 'expression' of a named condition – grief – is to bypass the question: what is the *work* of mourning – the psychic struggle between loss and melancholia (the inability to resolve loss) – when it takes place through the *work of painting* in this particular moment of the *history of painting*?[14] This 'moment' in its abstract form had not only released art from figurative representation – via First Nation American, Surrealist, theosophist and Jungian ideas – but redefined painting as a staging of *psychic work* as *physical labour* on the vast, terrifyingly uncharted canvas that was also an arena of both conscious and unconscious politico-aesthetic action (Harold Rosenberg's proposition). In the light of what such painting made possible at the level of process and its interaction with subjectivity, conscious, non-conscious and unconscious, I would explore the psychic-aesthetic resonance for a woman of the life-defining moment of the passing of her mother. When both parents have orphaned us, a chill wind blows over the once-a-child's head, forcing us, the unprotected top generation, to anticipate death.

Where does *dying* meet, if at all, with psychic defence mechanisms happening to confront the masculinist model of Oedipal *killing* that Anfam introduces via Harold Bloom to place Pollock as Father-artist?[15] What psychic breaching of connectedness 'in the feminine' was Krasner processing? How does each orphaned-woman-survivor as a painter negotiate that same-sex primordial link that predates even birth, and, post-natally, is a lived-out relation between two women, and then is ruptured by death? Few myths and narratives exist in patriarchal cultures for complex feminine subjectivities in their intersection with aesthetic practices and psychic crisis. Masculine normativities are rarely questioned.

Creatively significant differences get smothered, as here, by an art history *indifferent* to the interesting, important and salient issues of psycho-sexual *difference* as they engender *specificity* through transformations in and of artistic practices.

A key moment: 1970

My questioning of bodies, gender, sexual difference and abstract painting c. 1970 was incited by three events when I was becoming both an art historian and a feminist – a project that was, I discovered, contradictory.

The first was the exhibition *New York Painting and Sculpture 1940–1970*, which opened at the Metropolitan Museum of Art in New York in 1969, curated by the museum's first curator of twentieth-century art, art historian and critic Henry Geldzahler (1935–94).[16] Showing 408 works across all 35 galleries, 43 artists were selected according to his criteria: 'My guiding principles in deciding which artists to include in the exhibition have been the extent to which their work has commanded critical attention or significantly deflected the course of recent art.'[17] In the catalogue he added: 'not even at the height of the High Renaissance, Impressionism or Cubism has anything like this number of artists seemed so crucial to the development of the art of their time. We are celebrating a fortunate era of plenitude.'[18]

Only one artist-woman was selected: Helen Frankenthaler.[19]

Did one woman alone, Helen Frankenthaler, belong to this massive band of creative artists 'deflecting' the course of art in the 'century of women' that had witnessed radical change in every area of work, education, creativity, politics and thought in terms of women as participants and women as objects of analysis; in this era of new women, suffragism and militant suffragettes, women graduates, women political leaders, women philosophers? Had only one artist-woman made New York and its abstract painters world-famous as the site of interesting art? I looked for evidence of artist-women in abstract painting in New York. I found them easily – and in abundance. They were exhibiting and being reviewed all the time, side by side with their fellow artists. The issue was that they were not being critically *positioned* alongside their masculine peers. I then asked myself what did it mean that the influential curators and authoritative art historians were effectively disappearing contemporary artists from the canon they were constructing *in the face of overwhelming evidence, and in their own lifetimes, just because they were women*? Why was I, a student of art history in the early 1970s, being offered in the last quarter of the twentieth century a history of modern/contemporary art *denuded of the women* whose very participation in all aspects of society *defined the modernity of the twentieth century*? It was their and others' existence as ambitious modern women that had fuelled my own determination, having got a university degree, to ignore advice to train as a secretary and forego the scholarship for my PhD that my academic record had won me, because, as I was told by a deputy director of the prestigious art history institution at which I was studying, 'I would waste it by soon getting married and having children' – as if loving a partner and creating children was inimical to thinking for the rest of my life.

My second life-changing event was beginning graduate studies in art history (MA and then PhD) amid the nascent Women's Movement in London that I rapidly joined as both an activist for equal rights legislation and as a tentatively *feminist* art historian. Feminist consciousness-raising not only shaped a sense of political purpose to challenge the legal and economic disadvantages still grotesquely inflicted on women as women across the world in harrowingly differential degrees. It also forced me to pose questions to art history where no artist-women were ever mentioned as having been creative, and certainly never as having 'deflected', directed or even contributed to the course of art's history (or even been present, since this avant-gardist model of an endlessly progressive history of art was itself to be questioned for its Eurocentric, Western ideology of triumphant leadership in one direction). Absent from survey and specialist textbooks, or dismissed as trivial and derivative when, rarely, a selective few were mentioned, artist-women hardly existed; we were, in effect, being taught to take that fact for granted and reconfigure our own intellects and imaginations as women to service the canonically masculine, white and Western vision of the world.

It was difficult to question this value system. Art is deemed gender-neutral and thus even asking this question of the gender of art history's writing revealed my embarrassing triviality. The tools we received narrowed our thinking to the existing disciplinary models whose terminology foreclosed questions of race and class as much as of gender and sexuality.

Defiance was resourced by US-American art historian Linda Nochlin, a highly respected social historian of art and Professor of Art History at Vassar College, with her silence-shattering article of 1971: 'Why *Are* There No Great Women Artists?' (my italics), which appeared first in a comprehensive collection of feminist studies in power and powerlessness edited as *Woman in a Sexist Society.*[20] Revised and, significantly, put into the past tense, 'Why *Have There Been* No Great Women Artists?' (as, no doubt, many contemporary artist-women had howled in exasperation), it was reprinted in *Art News.*[21] Nochlin rejected her question, prompted by an art dealer asking: 'Where *are* the great women artists?' It was the wrong question, endorsing the ideologically loaded concept of 'the great artist'. Instead, Nochlin maintained that women had historically suffered from both limiting sociological definitions of womanhood and resulting institutional exclusion from art training that inhibited their access to the means and expertise to excel in the academic artworld. Yet we, feminist-inspired art historians in 1971, easily found so many artist-women who had managed to create and were consistently recorded in the archives, histories and dictionaries of artists up to the early twentieth century. Analysing the art historical record of writing and not-writing about artist-women to write *Old Mistresses: Women, Art and Ideology* (1981), Rozsika Parker and I concluded that it was *only in the twentieth century*, in the *modernist* era, as more and more women had entered the professional art world, that gender selectivity became more and more exclusive at the levels of *art historical* writing and major *museum collections*: the twin keepers and creators of cultural memory on our behalf. This made the issue modern; an issue within the academy itself.

The third event was my graduate money-spinning experience of writing abstracts for *Art Bibliographies Modern* of articles from *Studio International* (*Studio* magazine was refounded in 1964 with editors Peter Townsend and Charles Harrison) on contemporary art. This was my extra-curricular art history education, reading critical writing on twentieth-century modern and, more terrifyingly, contemporary conceptual art. Artistic practice was, c. 1970, moving into photo-work, video, performance, installation and conceptual art. I needed both to learn the radical foundations of modernist theories of painting and sculpture, and to understand the language of its analysis in order to understand their displacement by rapidly emerging conceptualism and incipient postmodernism. Learning on the wing, amid initial bafflement – and resentment at feeling so lost – before its philosophical as well as formal and post-formal vocabularies, I became enthralled. I began to grasp cutting-edge feminist engagements with conceptual art, video and film. Yet, despite a critical discourse evolving in art criticism and exhibition catalogues, the art of the mid-twentieth century was still not yet being taught in universities.

Feminist interventions in art's histories

In my feminist art historiographical project, I create *concepts* with which to think the issues that feminism and its related postcolonial/queer critiques have launched into the world. Concepts title my books – *framing feminism, vision and difference, differencing the canon, avant-garde gambits, gender and the colour of art history, generations and geographies, the virtual feminism museum, trauma and aesthetic transformation* and, first formulated in 1988, *feminist interventions in art's histories*. I do not offer a 'feminist art history', *feminist* only signifying an appended subset, a politically motivated compartment within the empire of art history. I intervene to contest the hegemonic discursive formation, art history (the discipline rather than a domain of study – the history of art), that has produced a story, or even stories, of art that are consolidated into museal and academic canons.[22] As a discourse on art that produces both its objects and its experts, art history in the twentieth century shaped a gender-exclusive version of past and present art. As a technology of gender, it secures an asymmetrical ordering of sexual difference.[23] Ordering knowledge in a symbolic hierarchy, a selective canon affects how men and women, masculinity and femininity, as well as privileged race, class and sexuality positions are normalized, while others are suppressed. Not sexist (or racist) by purely personal prejudice on the part of individuals or by mere default, it is so structurally, if never monolithically. Art history has enacted a 'political unconscious', a systemic or institutionalized sexism, racism, homophobia and Eurocentrism so that we who participate through training in its practices absorb its selective vision of art.[24] We are shaped in its terms as we become the minds and bodies that further enact and activate these art historical technologies of race, class, gender and sexuality. To be other, to think outside its parameters, is, effectively, to cease to be recognized as an art historian.

I *pluralize* the many 'histories' of art, displacing one official story so-oft repeated, and then *intervene* rather than merely get added into the margins already prepared for others who contest the canon with so-called 'political' invasions from the politics of race, class, sexuality and gender, as if these hierarchies and differences were not already inscribed and indeed contested across the works of art conserved in the museums and celebrated or studied in the canonical art history books. Cultural forms are never isolated from the world; they negotiate, represent, explore, disrupt the riven worlds in which they and their creators are themselves formed.

In *Differencing the Canon: Feminist Desire and the Writing of Art's Histories*, I was obliged to ask: What keeps this masculinist canon in place? I concluded that there was a narcissistic investment in the ideal of masculine genius that continuously defies and quarantines feminist endeavours, that suppresses so much about what causes art to be made and about what offers us ways of thinking about its complexity, while reframing art for investment, leisure consumption and celebrity-driven entertainment. No amount of evidence alone can shift this level of theological-narcissistic attachment to the masculine ideal of the creative artist that makes woman and artist antithetical concepts. Now, more than twenty-two years on, I return again to issues that I have written about over forty years since the publication with Rozsika Parker of *Old Mistresses: Women, Art and Ideology* (republished in a new edition in 2020). This co-authored book included my initial writing on Helen Frankenthaler's painting practice, when I tentatively lectured and wrote on modern art and living artist-women – Louise Nevelson, Eva Hesse, Helen Frankenthaler, Barbara Hepworth and Lee Krasner.

My concept here is *Killing and Dying*, indulging in both wordplay and serious exploration of a recurring set of metaphors about the psychic and social violence involved in creativity and artistic competition already in play among modern theorists and commentators on art, cinema and literature in their analysis of the dynamics of artistic innovation and change. Anfam is one unconscious instance. He used the term *combat* for patricidal Oedipal rivalry. While classic art historical models deploy influence, tradition, advance and succession, in the twentieth century another mechanism appears in modernist theory: creative destruction/destructive creativity. *Killing Men* speaks to Harold Bloom's psychic model, its violence and its anxieties. It also refers to the impact of two world wars, a Cold War, militarized revolutions, fascist dictatorships, genocide, armed resistance and nuclear bombs. With *Dying Women*, I address cultural myths and psychic economies other than paternal/filial battles which must be explored if we are both to de-patriarchalize our art historical imaginaries and find ways of seeing the work created by artist-women, recognizing parallel, supplementary and differencing psychic economies also at work in creative activity that the killing/dying pair suggest. Like so many feminist cultural analysts, I denounce the persistent glorification of the trope of dying women in the myths, stories, iconographies and imaginaries of the Western European cultural traditions that are part of psychic, and too often real, femicide.[25]

Thinking difference

My original title included *imag(in)ing* as a graphic pun bonding *imaging* and *imagining* difference and inciting metaphoric evocations of both violent and non-deadly transformation in creative struggle. Thinking about difference arose from intense political revolts and social movements c. 1968 that not only swept through many societies but erupted in Euro-American universities and art studios, and was so excitingly part of the vindication and refreshing of the discipline of art history as the study of art's multiple histories. The tragedy is that such challenges to racist, heterocratic and patriarchal ways of thinking remain as urgent and necessary half a century later.

Why have we – the wider academic community as well as those generally interested in art and culture – not integrated the incredible insights and brilliant illumination of our condition offered by major twentieth-century thought into our public discourse and our understanding of who and what we are? Why does positivism remain normal while feminist, postcolonial and queer (post)structuralist thinking – the major shifts in intellectual culture in the twentieth century – are still treated as alien or are set aside, or worse, smoothed into digestible but toothless platitudes that do violence to the necessary intricacy of radical thought? How has this anti-intellectualism limited our self-understanding and capacity for critically self-aware action and for the analysis of art and other cultural forms shaped in this dialectic of bodies and psyches, of passions and repressions, of subjectivity and subjection, of desire and the Unconscious? The reverse has not been the case. Many of the major thinkers and philosophers of the twentieth century consistently studied art as a key site for their investigation – from Freud and Lacan (psychoanalysis) to Merleau-Ponty (phenomenology), Lyotard (philosophy) and Lévi-Strauss (anthropology) to Kristeva (semiotics), to name but a few. They understand art as theory, as culture and not as consumption or cultural capital.

I do not write about women artists and men artists expressing or subverting given gender identities in art. Most artist-women rightly sought to escape being 'gendered' as *women* artists under existing stereotypes even as none disowned their own lived and psycho-sexual experiences. In their work, few if any ever set out to make art *as women*. As *modernists*, they embraced the freedom that modernism promised them just to be artists and to be their own singular artist. Yet we do not, cannot, escape the complex social and psycho-sexual formations that are both defining limits and unexplored possibilities.

Moreover, differences are interesting. To want to know what women are beyond the phallocentric parameters of phallic formations of sexual difference and their social regulation is part of the rich history of centuries of women's writing, thinking, creating and imaginatively transforming the world. Some of us think, moreover, that studying potential sexual difference *not defined by phallocentrism* is an important resource for human and planetary survival.

Carrying the entangled politics of gender/class/race/sexuality/capacity, language is not a neutral vehicle for knowledge. Embedded in its terms and histories are genderings and privilegings, asymmetries and hierarchies that shape what we think and hence how we think about ourselves and others.[26] I write *artist-women* and not 'women artists'. The latter naturalizes the masculinity of the artist. Having to use *woman* adjectivally to *qualify* an artist who is not a man effectively *disqualifies* her as artist in the very act of making this qualification. I shall also write artist-men precisely to difference the term artist. This is not a trivial linguistic game. Altering our terminologies enables us to think beyond the unacknowledged, gendered frame.

So, now I come, unapologetically, to a key element of this book: theory or rather many theories – of gender, sexual difference, modernism, subjectivity, language, gesture, psychic life, painting.

The word theory derives from the verb *theorein* in Greek, meaning to look at, to contemplate, to puzzle over, although the verb also carries connotations of to divine, to discern. It suggests inquiring, thinking, asking questions. Everyone does theory. The difference is that some of us *acknowledge* that we draw on specific models for such puzzling and questioning. We explain openly which ways of thinking, posing questions or analysing we employ and explain what they help us to see and to understand.

Many scholars are, however, positivists, declaring that they have no theory and merely look at the facts and report. Stories, narratives and apparently spontaneous ways of seeing are deployed authoritatively, while those who knowingly draw upon named theories and methods are criticized for introducing alien ideas and obscurantist terminologies. Positivists do not recognize the implicit theoretical model in which they themselves operate. They do not acknowledge that treating facts as self-evident, never questioning who formed the archive or selected the data, is itself based on a theoretical assumption of the transparency of language, text or image. Other scholars are structuralist or constructivist thinkers who consider that all knowledge is *produced* and in ways that are pre-shaped by thinking systems that we, who analyse things, must learn to recognize and critically challenge or constructively make visible and acknowledge when using this theory or that method. Social structures and systems of thinking – at their most opaque and unacknowledged, we name them ideologies – predetermine what we take to be self-evident. What structures us as subjects, societies, cultures, classes, genders and social identities, and the experiences resulting from gendering, racialization and class, need to be understood. This gives rise to concepts with which to pierce the opacity of the normalized, inciting us to think critically, rippling the smooth surface of what passes as natural and inevitable, namely existing social orders and systems of power.[27]

Socially produced, all knowledge production is, therefore, *situated*.[28] Each of us must tease out and critically recognize our own assumptions arising from our social, sexual, ethnic, religious, differently embodied, geopolitical locations, privileges and predispositions, and then explain how we come to think or argue our own case as we assess the evidence that always requires a *reading*. Feminist thinking, like the critiques of racial, heterocratic thinking, challenges those who consider gender, race, class, sexuality as natural dispositions of innate differences, or as irrelevant to, or indeed destructive for, understanding the world, art or culture.

Gender, race, sexuality, sexual difference and class are classic terms from the last fifty years of radical cultural analysis with deeper roots back to the eighteenth century in Western thought and in the anti- and post-colonial rebellions and revolutions of those who have been enslaved, subordinated and exploited. They and related theoretical vocabularies have, of course, been resisted, ignored or dismissed as foreign intrusions into a neutral world produced by, and imagined in, the positivist versions of society that shield themselves behind notions of self-evidence, nature, tradition, authority and privilege. Gender, race, sexuality, sexual difference and class have not become critically part of everyday usage. Where they do enter social media discourse and activism, however, they can and have become banalized, empty signifiers weaponized for flattened, if not false, misunderstandings of the complex meanings these concepts demarcate and theorize.

These terms generate particular ways of thinking in which each term has specific dimensions, while also acquiring different meanings across disciplines and bodies of thought such as philosophy, linguistics, psychoanalysis, literary criticism, social psychology, political theory and art history, even as projects such as feminism, queer and postcolonial critique travel on transdisciplinary pathways to reveal complex entanglements of power, exploitation, suffering, creativity and transformation. These concepts are also central to the major philosophies and theories of subjectivity, sexuality and difference of the twentieth century. We can negotiate neither art nor feminism without some understanding of what cultural theories offer us as means of understanding ourselves, art and the social worlds we inhabit and sustain.

Feminism is, however, neither a theoretically nor politically, nationally, ethnically unified endeavour. I prefer to explain feminist theories and practices as a *landscape* with many different theoretical settlements, each valid, significant and productive of insight and change, and all necessary, sometimes in conflict. Yet they are distinct. There is a current tendency within this landscape to locate some theoretical settlements in the dark ages of abandoned or superseded theory, smothering their still important potentialities. Feminism also takes diverse methodological forms in the different disciplines and faces distinct challenges met by generating concepts specific to each, even as such concepts travel from their site of origination, thereby moving us beyond the boundaries of particular disciplines to work in a transdisciplinary mode with shared concepts. Feminist theory and concepts are necessarily creatively diverse and politically riven as the inevitable fissures of race, class, sexuality, motherhood or childlessness, neuro-sensory capacity, geopolitical and economic inequality and agonism dispel any illusion of a simplistically unified project, even as we share the project to save women from being killed and dying in dire social realities and in their stifled minds and silenced tongues.

Gender became a key concept in feminist theory. For feminist theory, *gender* is what *class* is to Marxism and *race* to anti-racist and postcolonial theory. Gender is not a descriptor of a personal condition or essence. It is a political-theoretical concept that articulates 1) an axis of power in social relations and 2) symbolic meanings, both producing an asymmetrical hierarchy.[29] Gender was critical for the emergence of feminism, as it shattered the idea of two given, naturally different sexes, and created a theoretical question and a site of political contestation. What is currently termed gender theory is but one settlement of feminist theory, prevalent at this point in history, particularly through feminist philosopher Judith Butler's legacy in queer and trans theory. Butler's *Gender Trouble* (1990) was, in fact, a critique of gender itself as a category. Engagement with (and misreading of) Butler's legacy has, however, put into the shade several other significant theoretical sites in the landscape of feminist theory. One of these is the concept of *sexual difference*. (See the Appendix for a theoretical elaboration.)

Sexual difference is not an affirmation of differences between two sexes. As theory and concept, sexual difference denies oppositional differentiation, while paradoxically opening up the following distinction. Difference can mean *difference from*, thus negatively relating something to its other, creating a hierarchy of two terms (x/not-x). Difference can also evoke distinct qualities, as in the specificities of x or y, thus not just an opposition between two terms. Sexual difference theory offers a critical and deconstructive examination of the psychological and linguistic processes of differentiation – *sexuation* in psychoanalytical terms – meaning the construction of the difference that designates an asymmetrical division of human subjects – based on a *produced* hierarchy signified linguistically by the opposition: masculine ($+/x$) / feminine ($-/$not-x). Sexual difference theory furthermore argues that the difference specific to what is produced as the negative, minus term, *the feminine*, remains *unexplored as a difference in the sense of specificity*. Whatever 'the feminine' might be, psychologically, linguistically, imaginatively, sexually, theoretically, is rendered unknowable even as whatever it may be being impresses its affects/effects into cultural forms and lived experience in what I have termed *inscriptions in/of/from the feminine* – awaiting our feminist methods and concepts for their decipherment.[30] This is a dialectical process.

The system that produces this hierarchy of plus/minus, man = person = human/non-man is termed phallocentric, where the Phallus refers to a symbol organizing a chain of linguistic signifiers. It is not a body part. Phallocentrism has rendered the feminine 'a dark continent' (the colonial metaphor is Freud's). As a subjectivity, 'the feminine' is, therefore, as unknown to those positioned as feminine subjects as to the phallocentric order itself, because the latter positions it as both the reflecting mirror of the sole positive term, the masculine, and the necessary if blank other that supports the (race-class-sexually privileged) masculine as the One, the Subject, the Person, the Human, the Artist etc. The system of meaning that sexuates us psychologically as its subjects also designates the feminine as the negative, the minus, the absented other that sustains the

One, the privileged race/class subject position identified as the illusory masculine position. It will be important to maintain this distinction between original and current post-Butlerian *gender theory* on the one hand, and the engagement with *sexual difference* theory on the other, for the nature of the arguments in this book.

One further explanation for the limited knowledge or currency of the wider range of feminist theory is the accessibility, or not, of its philosophical tradition, and the admittedly arcane terminology of psychoanalysis which is the foundation for sexual difference theory, and this is so even within feminist theory. There is a growing unfamiliarity with psychoanalysis despite the fact that for the last half century it has reshaped film, literary and art historical studies. Many feminists engaged with psychoanalytic theories because they offered a revealing *description* of the operation of patriarchal societies. Recognizing that patriarchy is a historical formation and not a natural order enables a critical deconstruction of how patriarchal societies operate, how their phallocentric symbolic structures recruit us culturally and produce us psychologically to be their embodiment and subjective support by inserting their laws at the deepest levels of our psyches, and by mapping our bodies – the material, sensible, sensitive locus of any form of being and feeling and thought – through their limiting, hierarchical terms. Psychoanalytical theories are necessary because I want to know what artists, working daringly at the limits of art in a creative moment of the history of painting, inscribed into culture because of the specific possibilities this painting practice opened up for *inscriptions in, of and from the feminine.*

Conjoining art and sexual difference through a range of philosophical and psychoanalytical models knowingly runs up against the current antipathy to sexual difference theory in the face of engagement with queer gender theory and the focus on intersectionality, race critique and diversity. Class issues, complex forms of ethnic and migratory diversity and the continuing significance of formations of subjectivity in relation to desire, phantasy and embodiment are, I find, being sidelined before we have adequately engaged or exhausted their political and theoretical potential for transformation. The book shows why thinking about sexual difference does not reaffirm heterocracy and is not indifferent to diversity, while also being critical to understanding what happens in the acts of creation in art forms distilled into being acts, gestures by bodies not seeking to represent but to discover forms in which subjectivity-in-the-world-and-in-a-differentiated-body might tip into visibility or legibility. I have long found psychoanalytical theories of subjectivity and aesthetics both critically invaluable and enthralling, more specifically since the blind spots and persistent phallocentrism of the practitioners and theoreticians of psychoanalysis have been challenged and displaced by feminist thinkers and practitioners. I have long drawn resources from psychoanalytically informed philosophers and film and literary theorists. I have increasingly referenced the theories of Bracha L. Ettinger, recently editing two volumes of her theoretical papers to enable a wider readership to appreciate the significance of her intervention and its relevance specifically for the study of art and aesthetics.[31]

Art history and feminism, now

Art history is facing major challenges as a school subject and a university discipline.[32] Under neoliberal rationality, the arts and humanities are being financially starved and downgraded as expensive luxuries that economies can barely afford. Our subjects are being squeezed, blended, devalued at the very moment when audiences for artistic events, attendance at museums and popular fascination with stories of art and artists is increasing. As one commentator recently asked, if art history is no longer taught at any but a few selective schools and only at privileged universities, who will be training the future curators of our cultural, material and symbolic heritages that so many love to visit? Who will direct future museums? Who will write our cultural and artistic histories? My fear is that there will be some to do so, but they will have been trained at elite institutions in ways that efface the radicalizing events of the later twentieth century as surely and complacently as the art history I was offered in 1970 had effaced the history of women and, notably in the art of that very century, their contemporaries.

Feminism is just as necessary now to agitate our cultural consciousness. No other sociopolitical movement has had the impact on society and thought in recent times as has the later twentieth-century women's movement, inheriting the 500-year history of feminist dissidence, all wrapped up in a condensed term: feminism, itself a confused and misused term for an 'issue', extraneous to the universal history of timeless art. We are now in a different historical moment, with unforeseen crises facing us through the human-caused global climate disaster that threatens planetary life and with a long-feared global pandemic that broke out in 2019 disrupting and changing every facet of daily life. Alongside these life-threatening events of the third decade of the twenty-first century, massive cultural changes are registered in the ways we communicate and indeed how we understand our hyper-mediated selves and worlds. What is the place for historical research into now remote centuries such as the twentieth, let alone beyond? What is the purpose of art historical research? Will the subject survive as a critical discipline or is it so harnessed now to both the art market and the museum as the sites of entertainment that it is no longer one of the great critical, thinking disciplines?

This book

I radically revised a polemical, experimental essay, drafted and published in 1996, into this book for two reasons. The essay was a product of my own struggle to integrate feminist and social histories of art in collaborative teaching and writing on 1950s New York painting. The issues with which this book deals – gender, sexual difference, art history, exhibition practice – have re-emerged in the last few years, but as if theoretical feminism had hardly existed, except as an irritating fly that could be regularly batted away and squashed by the sheer force of reasserting the old Geldzahler canon, still rife with conventional sexism and racism and untheorized claims for uncontested white mastery (see Chapter 8). Yet articles announce that it is 'a good time to invest in art by women', even as their prices remain relatively speaking low and account for a tiny percentage (2%) of the huge sales and profits on the art market.[33] The long neglect of women has paradoxically created a treasure trove for canny gallerists and investors who will be marketing names but with safe explanations shielded from the 'difficult' or troubling ideas touted by 'feminists'. Thus, the second reason is that the tools – the theories and methods – with which feminist thought and practice had challenged the canon, sexism, racism, under-theorization and now financialization have been airbrushed out of the present, smoothing the way for art consumption so that no difficulty need be encountered in thinking about this most complex human activity and its deep questioning. Thinking about and with art is never allowed to be complex let alone disturbing to the status quo of class, race, gender and economic power.

How, then, shall I read Lee Krasner's creative proximity to Jackson Pollock but as an ambitious and daring recognition by both artists of their abilities, an elective proximity to the fires of each other's creativity that generated their productive conversations, and which she, once he was to be mourned, was able to work through to a new gestural freedom in her own painting by a lively, abstract, gestural figuration of what I designate a *dancing space*, released from the heavy freight of modernist artist-men such as Picasso and de Kooning – but without having to kill them or Pollock, who was her peer in a risky process of co-creation and not a Father? I do so by asking a very small question: how did the abstract painter Krasner move from one traumatically figurative and menacing image that appeared in her painting in 1956 through to a series in 1957 of still semi-figurative but joyous images of life and movement? It will take seven chapters because we shall need to pass by theories of gesture, hysteria and sexual difference and acknowledge that New York painting and Hollywood formed two sides of one coin of American culture during the 1950s. The legacies of both high and popular culture of that decade persist culturally and imaginatively, as do its icons Jackson Pollock and Marilyn Monroe. Did the latter have any role in Krasner's liberation from 'deadly combat'?

The final chapter, 'Three Memories', links personal testimony, textual analysis and three encounters with paintings by Lee Krasner and Jackson Pollock in recent exhibitions. Drawing on the Marxist art writing of Harold Rosenberg, a long-term friend and interlocutor of Lee Krasner, I introduce Rosenberg's poietic-political thesis on situated action, history as biography, as a lens through which to reread Krasner's different passages through which her long-sustained abstract painting project evolved. I counter the dismissal of her work by David Anfam, whose exhibition on *Abstract Expressionism* (2016–17) was vaunted by this press release:

> Exploring an unparalleled period in American art, this long-awaited exhibition reveals *the full breadth of a movement* that will forever be associated with the boundless creative energy of 1950s New York. In the 'age of anxiety' surrounding the Second World War and the years of free jazz and Beat poetry, artists *like Pollock, Rothko and de Kooning* broke from accepted conventions to unleash a new confidence in painting.[34] (my emphases)

Let me remind the reader that only one artist-woman was named on the poster by surname, [Joan] Mitchell, while two small works and one *Umber* painting by Lee Krasner and one by Helen Frankenthaler were placed in a room of *followers* of Jackson Pollock alongside Janet Sobel (1893–1968), a self-trained artist 'furtively' admired by Pollock and Greenberg (she anticipated Pollock's method) but considered by them both as only a 'housewife' who painted. Of an exhibition of the works of Janet Sobel in 2003, art historian Gail Levin writes of Pollock:

> Returning to Pollock, one might see how, in his tacit assumption of the position of the woman – the decentered and the voiceless, the one who flows uncontrollably, the one who figures the void and the unconscious – he remained on some level, a man using his masculine authority to appropriate a feminine space.

And, she argues, a woman was there before Pollock:

> In fact, one woman had tried to articulate that space before Pollock did, in a similar way – not Krasner but Janet Sobel, who made poured, all-over compositions that unmistakably made an impact on Pollock. Greenberg recalls, 'Pollock (and I myself) admired [Sobel's] pictures rather furtively' at the *Art of This Century* gallery in 1944; 'The effect – and it was the first really "all-over" one that I had ever seen ... – was strangely pleasing. Later on, Pollock admitted that these pictures had made an impression on him.' When Sobel is mentioned at all in accounts of Pollock's development, however, she is generally

described and so discredited as a 'housewife,' or amateur, a stratagem that preserves Pollock's status as the unique progenitor, both mother and father of his art, a figure overflowing not only with semen but with amniotic fluid.[35]

Anfam's linking of Krasner and Frankenthaler with Sobel diminished all three. London art critic Adrian Searle's review of Anfam's exhibition questioned the secondariness of the artist-women to the heroic male-dominated pantheon still being put authoritatively before the new publics. His review was headlined: 'Dynamic paintings that fizz and fascinate rescue the endlessly surprising artist from her husband Jackson Pollock's shadow in this thrilling major retrospective.'[36] Searle called Anfam's self-defence perverse:

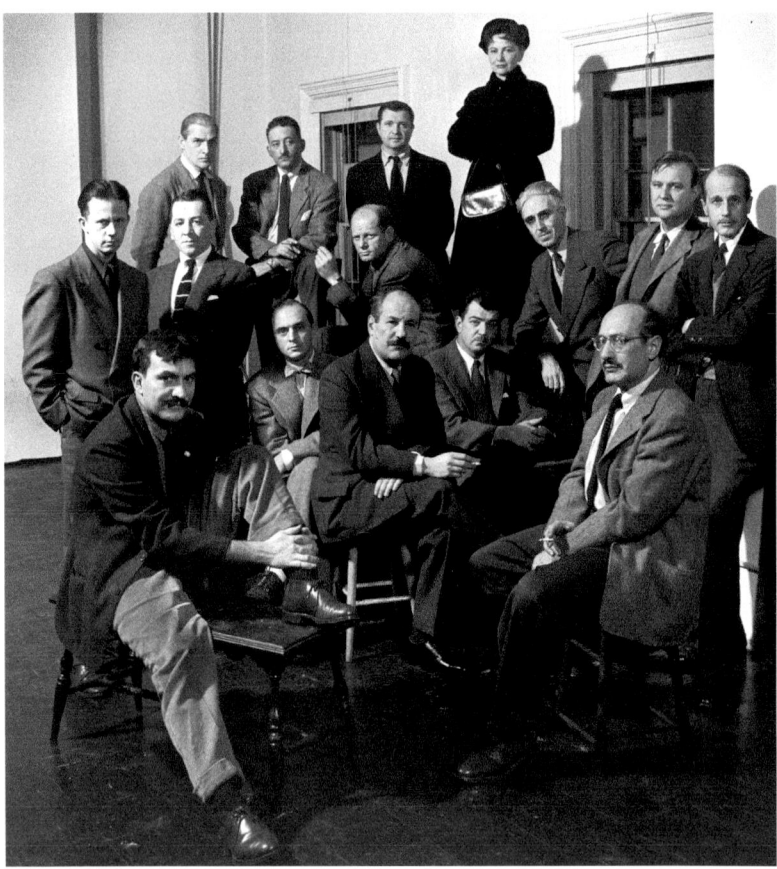

Figure 0.3 Nina Leen, *The Irascibles*, 24 November 1950. Front row: Theodore Stamos, Jimmy Ernst, Barnett Newman, James Brooks and Mark Rothko; middle row: Richard Pousette-Dart, William Baziotes, Jackson Pollock, Clyfford Still, Robert Motherwell and Bradley Walker Tomlin; back row: Willem de Kooning, Adolph Gottlieb, Ad Reinhardt; standing: Hedda Sterne

'Unfortunately', writes the show's curator, American art historian David Anfam, 'although Sterne [fig. 0.3] was a fine artist, she was not of the foremost calibre. Prejudice and other deleterious factors must be opposed when shaping any canon, yet not (*pace* some contemporary theory) at the expense of connoisseurship and quality: tokens are not fully-fledged currency, nor are quotas. As with gender, so with race.'

Searle concludes: 'This tells us a lot about the shaping of this exhibition, which makes no advances on our understanding of what Abstract Expressionism was.'[37]

In the same year, the exhibition *Women of Abstract Expressionism* (12 June–25 September 2016) was curated by Gwen F. Chanzit for the Denver Art Museum and three other venues across the United States of America (fig. 0.4). This showed the works of 42 painter-women: Mary Abbott, Ruth Abrams, Ruth Armer, Janice Bialer, Bernice Bing, Joan Brown, Jay DeFeo, Elaine de Kooning, Madeline Diamond, Amaranth Ehrenhalt, Claire Falkenstein, Lily Fenichel, Perle Fine, Helen Frankenthaler, Sonia Gechtoff, Judith Godwin, Shirley Goldfarb, Gertrude Green, Grace Hartigan, Buffie Johnson, Ida Kohlmeyer, Lee Krasner, Zoe Longfield, Mercedes Carles Matter, Joan Mitchell, Emiko Nakano, Charlotte Park, Betty Parsons, Pat Pasloff, Vita Peterson, Lil Picard, Deborah Remington, Anne Ryan, Ethel Schwabacher, Sonia Sekula, Janet Sobel, Vivian Springford, Hedda Sterne, Alma Thomas, Yvonne Thomas, Michael West and Jane Wilson. The exhibition was scheduled to come to the Whitechapel Gallery in London, but I was told that sponsorship and finance were lacking. Showing this depth of abstract painting by artist-women would have answered Anfam in no uncertain terms.[38]

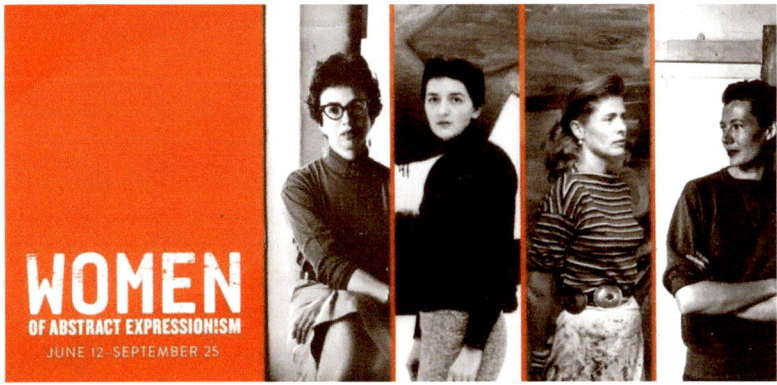

Figure 0.4 Poster for *Women of Abstract Expressionism*, Denver Museum of Art 2017. L-to-R: Photographs: Sonia Gechtoff, 1957; Judith Godwin at Betty Parsons Gallery, New York, 1959; Mary Abbott in her studio, c. 1949–50; Deborah Remington as a student at the California School of Fine Arts, San Francisco, April 1955

Anfam dismissed the attempts by African American and feminist art historians to create inclusive and historically accurate representations of this artistic moment and movement as mere tokenism, quota-setting revisionism that sacrificed the solid currency of genuine artistic value to their minority causes.[39] The blatancy of his disdain for evidence through the arrogant confidence of his connoisseurial *judgement* had already been roundly critiqued in Harold Rosenberg's analysis of what 'action painting' was and *did*. Kantian critical judgement and connoisseurship would, Rosenberg argued, never see or understand why the historic shift to painting as action and canvas as arena of action – both becoming a revelation of the historically situated and psychologically singular agent, the painter in action – was the deepest index of the nature of the social and historical conditions of their moment when revolutionary action was not possible but action was still required. Thus, the struggle I have had in order to integrate social art historical and feminist transdisciplinary theoretically expanded cultural analysis come together in a feminist appropriation and shifting of a Rosenbergian reading of Lee Krasner as action painter.

I want to share the complexity of feminist analysis of painting in the Monroe decade of the 1950s when the painters negotiated a cultural field and a psycho-social structure that played across studios and canvases and cinema screens and images. Asking what it might have meant to painters such as Lee Krasner or Helen Frankenthaler to be women and gestural painters, when the Artist was being iconized as Jackson Pollock and Woman was being given its image in a brilliant if troubling fabrication by movie-star Marilyn Monroe and the paintings of de Kooning, breaches the disciplinary walls that sacralize art even as its increasing financialization generates sales in the many millions, if never on the scale of commercial cinema.

Women and men co-created modernism side by side, despite the fact many but not all of their masculine contemporaries, critics, museum directors, dealers and critics consistently refused to acknowledge this key characteristic of modernism. We need to tear down the walls between artist-men and artist-women and explore shared if divergent psycho-social formations, as well as those between the anguishing divisions within the term *women*. These cast white Marilyn Monroe as a Pandora figure, beautiful on the surface but abjected inside, leaving no cultural recognition for the gestural painters who were women and who shared much more with her than our cultural discourses allow. In thinking about a white, working-class woman's struggle for creative agency in the face of industrial-scale sexual exploitation of her body and her labour in the movie industry in a parallel book, the questions I am posing here to abstract painting may also ironically reposition her, as Kerry Filer Harker has done (fig. 00.1), in the field of gesture, action, the body, loss and desire.

It also creates a larger field in which to consider both the artist-women and the actor-women of that decade in the diversity of their ethnicities, sexualities, race and class differences. Since this history of the art of the 1950s returns to us now in massively hyped blockbusters of paintings currently valued and traded at sometimes over 100 million dollars, my ongoing attempt to *difference the canon* is still urgent. While grand exhibitions can try to (Nairne) or may never (Anfam) offer us the primary encounter with the actual works, we know now that showing and seeing are not neutral activities.

Framed curatorially, critically and art historically in ways that, however progressive or recalcitrant in intention, must not 'frighten' the viewers with the real complexity and challenging psycho-material processes of any artmaking, we may only be learning to consume a few more artist-women, one at a time, backed by galleries. We fail to address art and sexual difference, our world and the powers that distort it, for those it disdains to admit are also artists. We are impoverished at so many levels by what we are never allowed to see and by how so much public and TV art history keeps art and its masculinist white histories celebratory, glorious, vacuously idealizing celebrity but not the work art does. Without apology, I, therefore, offer this book, which distils all the brilliant art histories I have encountered while working as much with artists as with sister and fellow thinkers, and sustains the ambition they instilled to think about art and questions that are seriously matters of life and death.

I hope to demonstrate the creative entanglement of the practices of close reading in art history with readings of theoretical texts. I want to counter passing fashions in academic activity and reveal the value of sustained fidelities to issues that current events and conditions of human vulnerability make ever more timely.

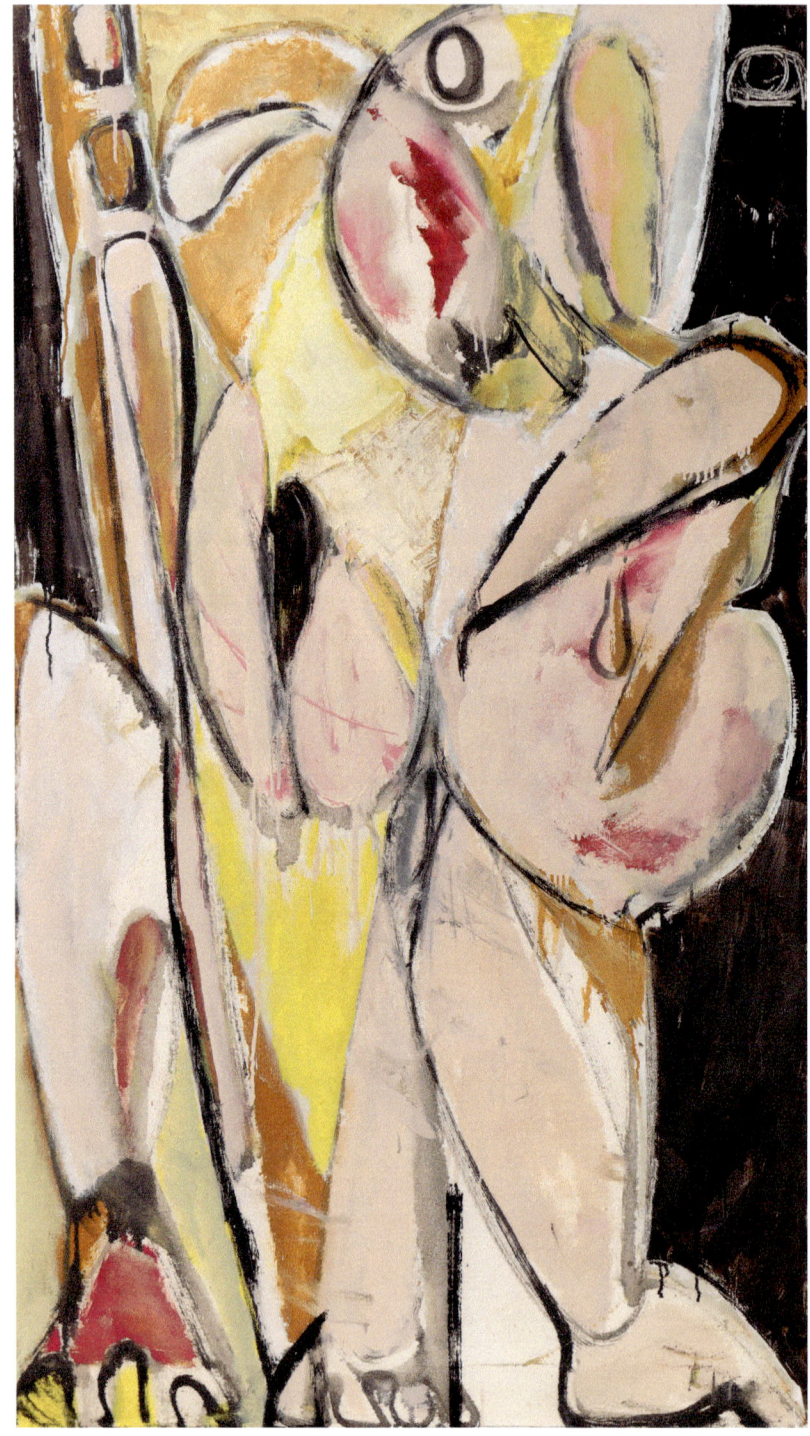

Figure 1.1 Lee Krasner, *Prophecy*, 1956

1

Prophecy, 1956

In the early summer of 1956, the American painter Lee Krasner, an advanced abstract painter since the 1930s, was unnerved when a semi-figurative painting appeared on her canvas (fig. 1.1). Her most recent show at the Stable Gallery, New York, was regarded as a decisive move in the highly competitive New York avant-garde. She had torn and cut up rejected paintings or canvas fragments to create large-scale collages with these orphaned shards of colour and strips of paint-splattered canvas. The painting, which she titled *Prophecy*, with its animalistic, Sphinx-like feet and fleshy, pink forms suggesting limbs, buttocks, pudenda and limbs, has one opaque, Cyclops eye. Another sightless eye, incised by the end of the brush as if in negative, hovers in the upper right-hand blackness that challenges and frames the ghastly pinkness of the hybrid forms with outsized, almost animal feet. It has a red but displaced mouth. It is as if the monstrous feminine Picasso had summoned in *Les Demoiselles d'Avignon* (1907) had mated with Willem de Kooning's most recent envisioning of *Woman* (1950–53, fig. 6.1) to demand a response from Krasner. In addition, the ghost of Jackson Pollock's now foregone Surrealist visions of animal-human archetypes meet up with a totemic figure that evokes the abstract standing figures of the *Personnages* by sculptor Louise Bourgeois, which had been exhibited in 1953 and 1955 in New York.[1] Pollock shared Krasner's unease about *Prophecy*, finding it nonetheless a strong if unexpected work for a hitherto abstract painter, while advising her to paint out the incised eye. The artist, rightly afraid of the surfacing of this monstrous yet hilarious vision, later stated: 'The image was there, and I had to let it out. I felt it at the time. *Prophecy* was fraught with foreboding. When I saw it, I was aware it was a frightening image.'[2] She left *Prophecy*, however, in the studio, propped up against the wall, unmodified.

On 12 July 1956 Krasner departed for a trip to Europe and a break from the worsening relations between herself and her now again alcoholic husband, the artistically inactive Pollock. Within a month she received a phone call from Clement Greenberg informing her that, on 11 August, Pollock, aged 44, had been killed with a woman passenger, with a third badly injured, when he drunkenly lost control of his car and crashed into a tree. Krasner returned to the United States, now as the artist's executor and sole heir, responsible for the management of the estate of the artist who had been proposed in an article in *Life* magazine in 1949 as 'most famous living painter in the United States' – even though his legacy would require careful curation after his inactivity over the previous few years.[3] Over the next eighteen months Krasner's painting practice became the site of an important struggle for her own artistic identity as *Lee Krasner*, now that, in her husband's permanent absence, she would be, if not more than ever, both imprisoned in and erased by her conventional social and administrative role as 'Mrs Jackson Pollock' – or rather, as 'the widow of Jackson Pollock' who is 'also a painter'.[4]

Lee Krasner had, moreover, to do battle with the painting left in her studio, *Prophecy*: 'I had to confront myself with this painting, again, and I went through a rough period in that confrontation.'[5] Over long days and nights, in a series of large paintings she later titled *Embrace* (7.6), and *Birth* (7.7), Krasner allowed hybrid creatures to come out and play on her canvases in a tangle of limbs, with leering faces, bulbous eyes and dynamic rhythms of indecipherable fleshly forms. The ghastly pallor of *Prophecy* yielded to richer hues as forms became more abstract. Out of this unexpected turn in her own work, Krasner eventually produced a series of ecstatic paintings, one of which, the vertical *Sun Woman I* (1957, fig. 1.2), will be the object of analysis in the final section of this book.[6] Was Krasner's passage from *Prophecy* to *Sun Woman* an ordeal in the classical sense, a journey into and out of the labyrinth, a psychic ordeal akin to the mysteries of Eleusis? Or was it the necessary battle of a woman, an artist, with the double jeopardy of being a woman and an artist at a radical moment in the history of painting when it was shedding the pathos formulae of the entire pantheon of the Western imaginary in order to make the ultimate wager? Could there be art in the act of creation that emerged only from the body-psyche of the artist at work with her materials as she confronted the unbound otherness of an expanse of unmarked canvas?

My art historical questions are threefold. How did Lee Krasner get from *Prophecy* to *Sun Woman I* during those months?[7] What life force enabled the transformation into colour, bold, free gestures, rhythms of movement and evocation of the face of laughter? What figuration of joy 'in the feminine' – in another sphere of culture – enabled her to escape the Sphinx-like 'idol' with its empty stare that incarnated the key icons of modern art and Western art's long histories of representation of women? A provisional and speculative answer will take up this whole book.

Did she get there by taking on – 'killing', that is, symbolically and materially battling with and thus transforming in her own, *non-destructive* terms – the powerful artists whose avant-garde gambits and generative rivalry shaped and inspired her corner of the still-tiny contemporary art world in New York: Pollock and de Kooning clearly, and behind them

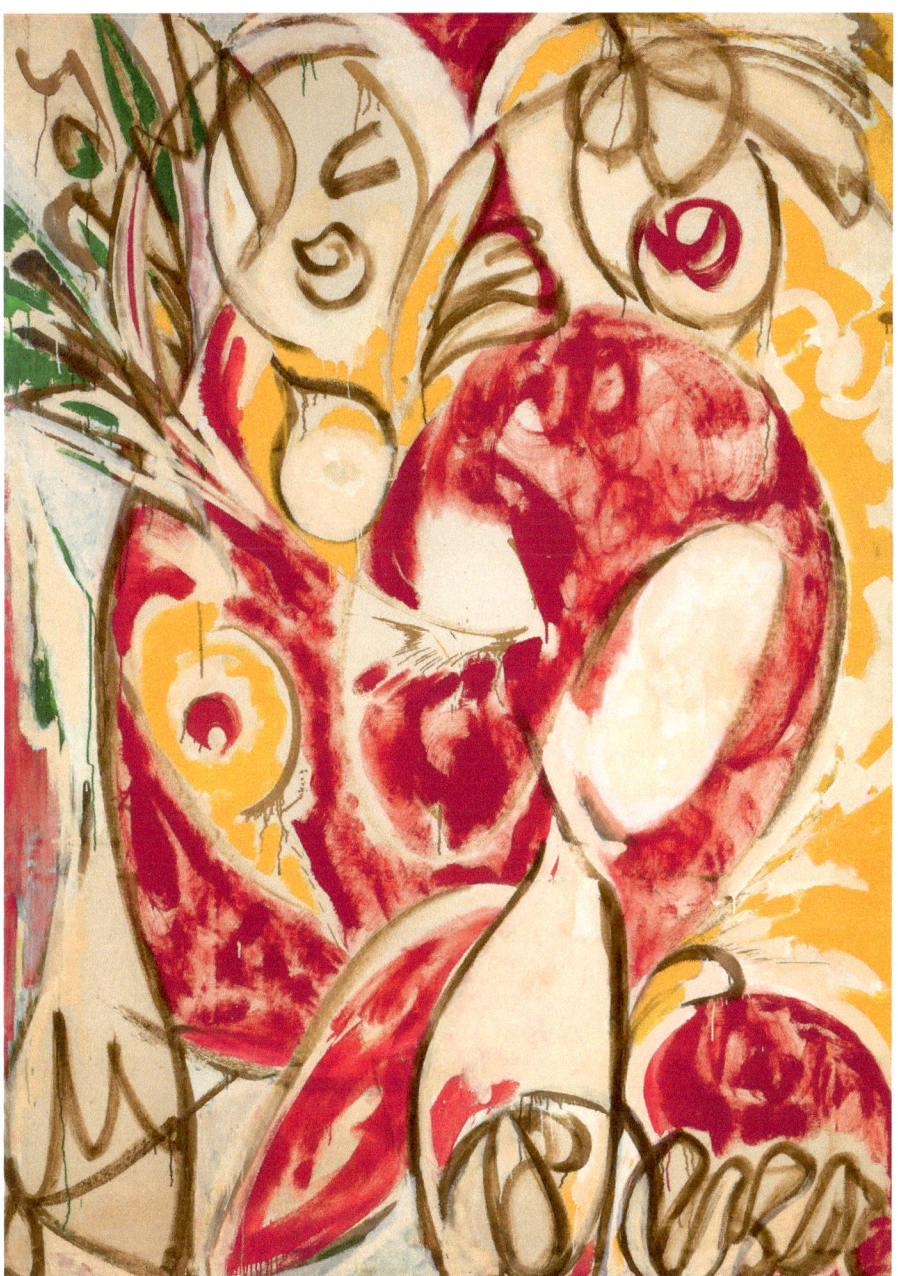

Figure 1.2 Lee Krasner, *Sun Woman I*, 1957

Picasso and Matisse, but also a number of equally significant artist-women, all engaged in the adventure of a new kind of painting and sculpture?[8] So what's new? I situate these painters and their coteries in the wider culture of cinema, music and literature in which all these artists, working side by side, participated. I show how women, not just as artists but also as icons, played a part in enabling the work of transformation that was radical painting in the 1950s in New York, because this decade was a critical moment in the discourses and imaginaries of sexuality and sexual difference. My hunch is that, both after de Kooning's funny, sad girl and before Andy Warhol's religious iconization, something of *Marilyn Monroe-ness* – a quality none of us has yet been able adequately to name – non-consciously resonated in, or even surfaced to make possible, *Sun Woman I*.[9]

La femme soleil

What are we *seeing* in *Sun Woman I*? What are we *feeling* when we see it? What are we *sensing* from the way the painting was made? Does its process impress *affects* into the world, in paint and by means of gesture, action, rhythm, movement and energy? What are the forms we perceive and what does the title suggests by the words: *Sun* and *Woman*? Do they tip us into a mythical register? Do we hear echoes of cinema and advertising?

Iconographically, there is an evocation of a body in *Sun Woman I* – the clawed or toed feet, perhaps a breast, an eye. There are curving shapes that suggest eyes crinkled in laughter perhaps, and mouths, open, singing perhaps. The mood and the dynamic of the lines and forms are, however, entirely different from what we encounter before the frontal fixity of *Prophecy*. In the former, I see and feel a joyous exuberance in the flowing lines of the paint that makes me think of arms opened and moving in space. I sense lively intensity in the rich reds that replace the ghastly, frozen stasis of the nude, fleshy pink monsters evoked in almost Egyptian monumental frontality in *Prophecy*. Is there a *jouissance* in this different evocation of a female body? Are we not sensing a creative performance and surfacing imagery that is differentiating itself from the modernist fathers now assembled in New York's Museum of Modern Art as *the story of modern art* which, as art historians Carol Duncan and Alan Wallach argued, was as much a narrative of spiritual masculine mastery over feminized matter visually staged through modernist visions of monstrous women's bodies as it was a story of stylistic innovation on the road to abstraction?[10]

Duncan and Wallach offer an iconological reading of the displays in the Museum of Modern Art, terming it a choreographed drama taking place in a space apart from daily life – the gallery – that they compare to ceremonial sites of ritual and almost mystical, psychologically transformative ordeals:

> A museum, like other ceremonial monuments, is a complex architectural phenomenon that selects and arranges works of art within a sequence of spaces. This totality of art and architectural form organises the visitor's experience as a script organises a performance. Individuals respond in different ways according to their education, culture, class. But the architecture is given and imposes the same underlying structures on everyone. By following the architectural script, the visitor engages in an activity most accurately described as a ritual. Indeed, the museum experience bears a striking resemblance to religious rituals in both form and content.[11]

In an itinerary laid out in the windowless spaces of the labyrinth of bare rooms, the visitor becomes an initiate into the mystery of modern art whose ordeal is to encounter images of the figure that haunts the battle to create a modern art – *Woman*.

> As you pass through MoMA's white, dream-like labyrinth night, the gaze of the Great Mother finds you again and again. Often, she confronts you head-on, her two eyes round and bulging, the petrifying stare, the devouring mouth of the Gorgon Medusa now before you as the awesome grotesque goddess-whores of Picasso, Kirchner, de Kooning. In the passage through Surrealism she is often a beast – a giant praying mantis. Everywhere she poses the threat of domination, sometimes as in Munch's man-killing vampire, her beauty is a snare. In Léger's sphinxes her look is frozen, her body a great steel machine. The entire labyrinth is her realm, but she is most present when you approach the threshold of a higher spiritual level – that is, moments of art historical 'breakthroughs'. Even before you enter the first Cubist room, her eyes are on you (*Les Demoiselles d'Avignon*). She intercepts you (Picasso's *Girl Before The Mirror* and *Seated Bather*), just before you reach Miró's surrealist *Creation Of The World*. You risk her gaze (de Kooning's *Woman*) as you advance towards Jackson Pollock. She personifies the dangers of the route first run by the artists themselves.[12]

They analyse sequencing and recurring presences of the opposing figures of the monstrous or the comfortingly natural Mother, showing how the competitive transformations of style were played out across images of diverse bodies of women, often of colour or otherwise othered, who emerge, precisely in modernism, as mythic figurations of what anthropology and psychology reveal as the varied form of the Great Mother.

Duncan and Wallach refute the idea that modern art abandoned 'figuration' for abstraction. Rather they present the story we encounter in the museums of modern art as a deeper struggle for masculine mastery over its other: Nature, the Body, Matter: all figured in contradictory forms of sadism, desire and terror before their feminine Other/Mother.

> Inside the labyrinth the principle of creativity is defined and celebrated as a male spiritual endeavour in which consciousness finds its identity by transcending the material, biological world and its Mother Goddess. Salvation, understood as a male norm, is alienation from the Mother and her realm. It is the integration with spirit, light, intellect. The garden [of the museum] contains reminders of the Terrible Mother of the labyrinth (e.g. Lipchitz's *Figure*) just as the images of the labyrinth occasionally echo the traits of the garden Goddesses (Matisse). In fact, both Goddess and Mother are different aspects of the Great Mother, who, in the labyrinth, emerges as dangerous. It is she who must be overcome. The way to do so is made clear by the iconography. In the labyrinth the pictures lead you along a spiritual path that rises to ever higher levels of transcendence. They do so not only through their increasingly abstract formal language, but also through their themes and subjects.[13]

Lee Krasner's struggle with this modernist genealogy of Woman (the idea and image) on canvas was clearly a battle for a place for the artist-woman in a field where Woman was already both the ground for, and object of, the art of the artist-men with whom she was in dialogue as a modernist painter. The Great Mother, the Whore and the Goddess were also present, however, in other cultural forms of this moment, notably in modern dress and in cinema's narratives and iconology.

Drawing analysis of the other America, Hollywood, into this study, I extend my question. So how did Lee Krasner's struggle with the modernist genealogy of Woman in art relate to the cultural formation and struggle of the person who, by 1953/54, represented Woman in that moment on the larger cultural and media stage of cinema: Marilyn Monroe? Can I weave together the stories of two creative women – painter Lee Krasner and actor/performer/model Marilyn Monroe – across the double but also twinned cultural sites of the United States of America during the 1950s: Hollywood/New York/popular culture/avant-garde culture?

Placing Monroe at the periphery of my art historical vision and focusing on what we might consider her cultural antithesis – the self-determining, avant-garde, New York painter-woman Krasner – I also would like to overcome these binaries that would deny agency and signifying potential to the actor named Marilyn Monroe. The name itself now connotes the *image* of the sexualized feminine circulating in popular culture in which avant-garde artists, both women and men, participated as consumers of cinema, popular music, advertising, dance. They were the ideologically interpellated viewers of the representations that iteratively produced a modelling of sexual difference shaping their imaginations and inflecting their sexual, gendered, raced and classed subjectivities from the 1930s to the 1950s. Marilyn Monroe will haunt this book. Eventually, she will converse with Lee Krasner and her paintings.[14]

To stage this meeting, I perform 'feminist interventions in art's histories' to create an expanded sense of the confluence and diversity of art's histories reconfigured by posing postcolonial, queer, feminist questions to the archive and to the practices of artmaking. Here we confront how to 'see' and be 'affected' by what *artists who are women* produce in and as part of a complex, already gender-defined universe of bodies and meanings.[15] Their works come to us, however, already 'framed' by existing, exclusionary, partial and unhistorical art historical discourses established by museum collection and display as much as by exhibition catalogues, scholarly monographs, art dealers and markets, and art criticism. The hegemonic 'ways of seeing' have established a gender-and-race-selective roster of names who alone constitute the official history of both period and movement. These names are *author-names*. Mieke Bal and Norman Bryson explain the significance of the author and the oeuvre in this kind of art history:

> The whole purpose of art historical narration is to merge the *authorized* corpus and its producer into a single entity, the totalized narrative of the-man-and-his-work, in which the rhetorical figure *author equals corpus* governs the narration down to its finest details ... The concept of 'author' brings together a series of related unities that, though assumed as given, are precisely the products and goals of its discursive operations. First is the unity of the Work. Second is the unity of the Life ... In art history, and particularly through the formula of the monograph, the narrative genre of the-man-and-his-work has exercised a hold over writing that is perhaps unparalleled in the humanities.[16]

These frames crush the potential of the works to have meaning for us as we try to relearn to see the world in its actual diversity. Making artist-women illegible or as lacking produces the valorized, white, masculine canon with its masters and their body of work that represent a life – an artist's life. Art history's key modes – catalogue raisonné, monograph and biography – create *a subject for art*, recasting complexly produced material and semiotic objects as the affirmation of artistic subjectivity that, by the exclusion of women, equates to the creative genius of a masculine, Euro-American and white subject.[17] Inscribing a heterosexual, white, masculine subjectivity in art, art historical discourse forces feminists to be perpetually reintroducing women and other others. Working against the grain of what has been validated as the unquestioned *centres* and *pinnacles* of the artistic movements already defined by its leading heroes, *rediscovery* cannot succeed. We must *difference the canon*.[18]

Differencing involves contesting interpretation of art or representation in art that does not fully acknowledge the forces shaping any representational activity, especially in artworks that themselves renounce figuration, narrative and representation itself. *Differencing* does not focus on projected and conventional differences ascribed to *men* and *women*, generally and as artists. The artworks by men and women do not differ because they are by men and women, as if these were simple, and simply different, entities with fixed characteristics, capacities, aesthetic tendencies or imaginative resources. The works by individual artist-men and artist-women who shared a specific artistic project may require us to attend as much to their shared conceptions of their practices as to the affects their specific modes of painting engendered, precisely when making processes themselves became the core and condition of their projects (as in gestural abstract painting).

Difference – defined as complicated specificities and singularities – is interesting. Difference is significant in terms of learning to see the world in complex, culturally, socially, historically diversified, non-gender-fixed, non-gender-binary, queer and decolonizing ways. To make sense of these shifts, we need to supplement, if not disown, some aspects of art history's favoured narrative of art's histories through the categories of nations (e.g. French, Italian, British, American, Indian art) periods (Baroque), movements (isms), styles and artists, and draw richly on cultural theories about art, society, subjectivity, creativity that open new ways of seeing and changing the language for the study of art's histories.

Artist-women operate in a doubled field. As ambitious painters, for instance in New York between 1930 and 1970, shaped by the formation and consciousness we call the avant-garde, they negotiated the conditions of their own artistic interventions just like any other artist of that moment and project.[19] They evolved their own gambits in the complex game of avant-garde competitiveness that I identify as *reference, deference* and *difference*.[20] The resources on which artist-women drew to do so included, however, the urgencies and pressures of social, cultural, psychological and corporeal experiences that were shaped in the formation of bodies and psyches in a historically specific context of two industrial and nuclear wars and a Cold War, in the post-Holocaust era, amid decolonization struggles, and in a phallocentric, racist and heterocratic order, even as such *formation* is often unacknowledged by a sexist-racist-heterocratic art-world within a phallocentric culture. Experience is not gendered at the level of any essential characteristics attributed to two sexes deriving from bodies and gendered minds. It is shaped by the complex formations of psycho-sexual and psycho-linguistic subjectivity in historical conditions that I am terming *sexual difference*.

Sexual difference might be assumed to define a difference between two sexes. This is not the meaning here. As a feminist concept, *sexual difference* forms part of feminist theory precisely to reveal and to value *what we do not yet know*, because phallocentric culture suppresses difference. While appearing to present Man and Woman as an opposing pair, phallic thought effectively creates one human norm, Man, and its other, that is, not-Man; the negative functions as mere prop for the positivized norm, Man. The space of that other, signified by the term (not the person) *Woman*, is at once an empty signifier while being full of projected definitions, all functioning as repetitions of the negative, the lack, the secondary, the not so good as… and so on.

At this point, I need to direct those interested readers to a theoretical digression (see Appendix) in which I explain more fully both the foundations for terms I shall be using and why it is necessary in a book about art and culture in the mid-twentieth century to use concepts from disciplines outside art history's normal vocabularies to tease out the issues of painting and abstraction in this moment. Some terms will be used in this book that may be unfamiliar, alien, even alienating because unfamiliar, unless I show clearly *what they enable us to understand about ourselves* and *what they do for us in the study of artistic practice*. In feminist theory, as in a wider range of cultural theories, we argue that our minds, thoughts, memories, phantasies and embodied sensations are profoundly and interestingly (not negatively) shaped by psycho-linguistic and psycho-sexual formation that constitutes *subjectivity* itself, a term that refers not to personal viewpoints but to the condition of being a thinking and feeling but also split subject, conscious and unconscious. My hope is that taking the time to read through – now or later – the theoretical explanation for such concepts that I have placed in the Appendix will reveal the benefit of considering sexual difference from a feminist perspective and the challenge that inheres in this term even among feminist thinkers.

How do I write of the difference of the other in ways that do not reinstate a negative effect? From French literary theory and from psychoanalysis, I draw on the concept of *the feminine/le féminin*. In conventional, everyday English, what is meant by *feminine* is not what is meant theoretically. When I use the phrase *the feminine* to discuss the work of artist-women in whose artmaking I might be seeking *the feminine/le féminin* understood as an excess, a beyond and resistance to phallocentric Law and Culture, there is a danger that readers may only hear a phallic interpretation of feminine as 'not masculine'. In phallic thinking, feminine evokes the less, the negative of agreed ideas of what is strong, powerful, creative, inventive, innovative, namely, words that positively value art, all such words being heavy with sexuated metaphors. In a phallic universe, a reader might rightly feel that suggesting an artistic practice be concerned with *the feminine/le féminin* radically undermines what should be our *indifferent* concern with the making of good art, which we think should escape all social inscription and markers because art is imagined as the very privileged locus of an unmarked individual creating universally accessible and spontaneously important cultural goods.

Why, however, would acknowledging a specificity to feminine positions as a potentially creative factor in artistic creation, *differencing the canon*, undermine the status of the art produced in dialogue with lived and socially shaped but psychic and corporeal specificity? To sniff out and identify in the artwork of women any of the *conventional* indicators that the phallic model of sexual difference (masculinity as plus and femininity as minus) creates has regularly exiled artist-women from the status of 'artist' – interpreted only as *woman*, a signifier (w-o-m-a-n) whose signified can be parsed as 'lacking the valorising and entirely convention-derived (hetero, white) masculinity'.[21]

I distinguish three concepts of sexual difference. It can be defined as a product of a specific ordering of subjectivity that produces as its terms masculinity as plus, a positive value, and femininity as lack, negative and valueless. Considered from a critical feminist perspective, as a psycho-linguistic and psycho-sexual formation of subjectivity, sexual difference incites investigation into possible, non-phallically defined meanings for *the feminine/le féminin* that are liberated from conventional meaning to become a question with as yet unknown answers but potential for transformation. Because it is cast as the negated other of the phallic masculine, feminine does not signify an inverted, now positively valued term but radically questions the basis of the phallic order of subjectivity and meaning itself, becoming a site for creativity. Thus, artistic creation, on the borders between existing meaning systems and the poeïetic – the newly created – takes its place as a potential space of such questioning. Undoing and transforming, artmaking may inscribe an unrecognized difference *emerging from* and thus not *of the feminine/le féminin* that we do not yet conceive or have never been able to acknowledge as being already inscribed in art and culture, because we have been so schooled in the phallocentric order as the only ordering of subjectivity and meaning.

Art as it is defined and art historically studied in contemporary discourse and its institutions is both an instance of the constant and iterated production of phallocentric hierarchy of sexual difference, and a representation that serves its ideological perpetuation and dissemination as both norm and nature. Art history's gender- and comparably race-selective stories of art are, therefore, *structurally*, not casually, sexist and by the same token of asymmetrical hierarchy, racist and heterocratic. Artist-women are not neglected for lack of knowledge or through sheer forgetfulness. Their consistently attributed lack of what it takes to be considered great or valued has been and is still being systematically reproduced either by silence or by selective mention marked by stereotypical language. Remember Hans Hoffman's compliment to Lee Krasner: 'This is so good you would not know it was done by a woman.'[22]

The profound paradox is this. Ignoring, effacement and stereotyping occurred more especially and consistently in the twentieth century, in modern art history and the institutions dealing with modern art. This happened despite a century of radical emancipation struggles and social changes led by women. By the same token, all our later twentieth-century feminist attempts to rectify this, through shows such as 'Women in Surrealism' or 'Women in Abstraction', while certainly making visible many remarkable artist-women and their creations, nevertheless keep these artists within the phallocentric category of the other, *women*, maintaining a separation that permits the feminists to celebrate women while the 'men' (be that men or women) continue to invest (literally as well as figuratively) in the heroic story of the great white men, untroubled by anything that would disturb their mono-gendered racialization of art.

The phallocentric regime of sexual difference is structurally an asymmetrical plus/minus hierarchy disposing value in gendered and gendering terms. Yet its bare bones are also historically clothed, hence subject to socio-economic modifiers and shaped by politico-cultural contingency. Class, ethnicity, geopolitical location and regimes of sexuality and racialization are all in complex and agonizing as well as agonistic entanglement. The theoretical analyses of the phallocentric order – in psychoanalysis and feminism, for instance – that invaded cultural discourse in the twentieth century coincided, paradoxically, with the extraordinarily arch-gender exclusivity and myths that have shaped the modernist history of art in the face of women's challenges to it. Both signify a contest in the modernist twentieth century of which the third interlocutor and indeed contestant of the other two is feminism, and specifically *feminist theory*. What might seem, therefore, like an arid turn to high theory on my part to reintroduce terms such as sexual difference, *the feminine/le féminin* and phallocentric order, is actually a product of the continuing resistance to feminist interventions in art's histories.

Using both sexual difference and *the feminine/le féminin* while focusing on the decade of the 1950s in US-American culture in New York, I explore this question. What are the contradictory relations between a *woman* (Jewish, child of immigrants, working-class, left-wing, New Yorker: Lee Krasner), an *artist* (painter, abstract), her cultural moment (New York painting in the post-war era and the Cold War) and the discursive terms available for historical analysis and interpretation of her artworks made in and beyond that moment? Art historically, my inquiry requires cultural analysis of both artist and woman, terms reshaped for that moment across an array of cultural practices that included Hollywood cinema.

In the United States of America during the 1950s, such a confrontation was framed through a newly rigidified post-war sexual division and ideological polarization of gender not witnessed since the mid-nineteenth-century promulgation of a doctrine of separate spheres for men and women. This took the form of post-war calls for women to go 'Back into the Home' and 'Out into the Suburbs' – a white, middle-class phenomenon abandoning working-class women of all communities to often impoverished conditions of labour outside as well as inside their homes. The propaganda for getting women out of the labour force that they had entered during the war years (fig. 1.3) and back into domestic labour was disseminated in typically contradictory forms through Hollywood cinema.[23] Ideologically, however, the idea was preached to all, creating the ideal woman as the sexual or domestic white woman of a certain class who would be a dedicated wife and mother and live in picket-fenced suburbia, from which would emerge Betty Friedan's feminist text, *The*

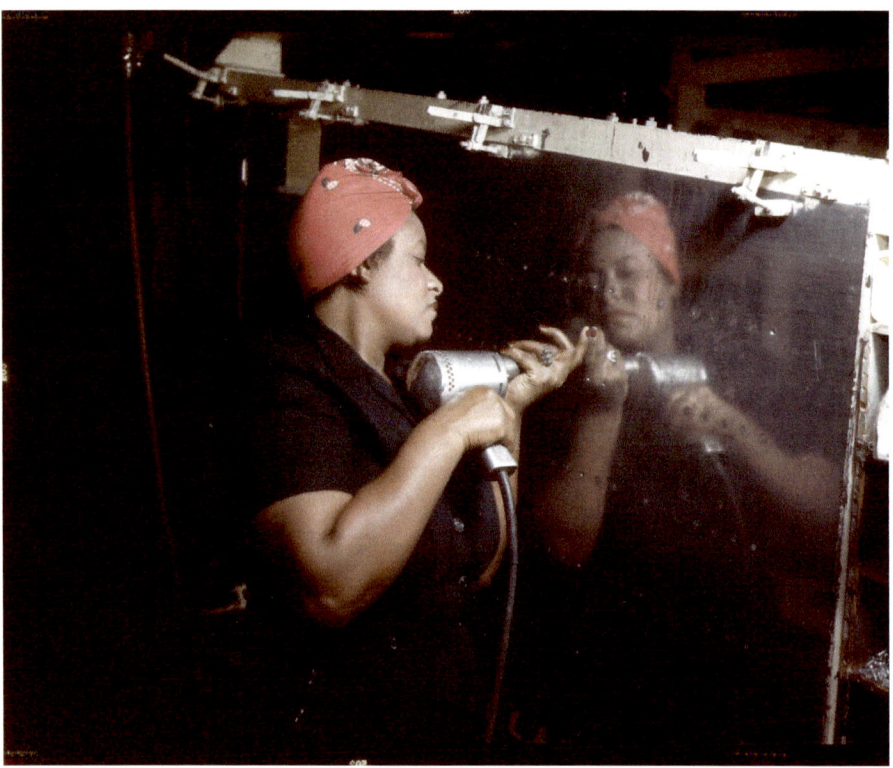

Figure 1.3 Alfred T. Palmer, *a 'Rosie the Riveter' woman worker operating a hand drill at Vultee-Nashville, Tennessee, working on an A-31 Vengeance dive bomber*, February 1943

Feminine Mystique, based on conversations with middle-class, college-educated women about their profound discontent in the later 1950s.[24]

The world war against fascism and the post-war settlement under US-American hegemony, which produced the Cold War against so-called Red fascism, not only effectively interrupted the century-long feminist historical struggle for a modernization of sexual difference that had been the major impetus for political or civil emancipation and struggles for access to education and jobs in the nineteenth and early twentieth centuries.[25] It also silenced the feminist aesthetic-cultural revolution in the generation of women from 1900 to 1939, the moment that might be epitomized by the date of publication of Virginia Woolf's *A Room of One's Own* – 1929.[26] It was not until the revolt, forty years later, of my generation of c. 1968 that a revitalized feminist movement *repoliticized* and equally *aestheticized* the suspended question of gender that mid-century high modernist culture had disavowed and placed under cultural censorship while establishing conservative bourgeois notions of masculinity and femininity.[27] While many read 1968 as the moment of feminist activism, the date also marked a second, feminist intellectual and cultural revolution that rippled through and challenged every art form and every academic discipline.

In the first decades of the twentieth century, cultural modernism offered some relief for modernizing women from the nineteenth-century ideologies of regulated and predetermined sexual differentiation between men and women, which had, as their effect, completely saturated woman as *the sex*: women's minds, bodies, emotions, art, literature and social status were publicly determined for them by Western culture's definition of women by the functions and dysfunctions of their sexual organs.[28] Poet and historian Denise Riley asked 'Does Sex Have a History?' and explored the historical temporality of changing conceptions and hence valencies of terms such as 'woman' and 'women'. Riley identifies the 'long march of the empires of gender over the entirety of the person' in relation to the historically mappable process of the ever-deeper nineteenth-century sexualization of women. This worked dialectically in relation to concurrent changes in the concept of 'Man', a white, straight, universal, class-privileged entity who became the representative human and object of analysis in the emerging disciplines of sociology, anthropology and social psychology. Riley argues that in those disciplines, this generic 'Man' was imagined as the sole agent working on the social, while the social realm itself was feminized as his field for political action.

> This was utterly different from the ways in which the concept of the social realm both encapsulated and illuminated 'women'. When this effectively feminized social was then set over and against 'man', the alignments of the sexes were conceptualized anew. It was not so much that women were omitted, *as*

that they were too thoroughly included in an asymmetrical manner. They were not the submerged opposite of 'man' in need of being fished up; they formed, rather, a continuum of sociality against which the political was set. Man in society did not undergo the same kind of immersion as did 'woman'. He faced society, rather; a society already permeated with the feminine.[29] (my emphases)

As an uncharted and dissident cultural practice, set against the conventions of 'society', posing itself as society's internal, revolting and revolutionizing force, artistic and cultural modernism under the concept of the avant-garde paradoxically appeared to promise some women a fictional space in which universals and absolutes (man versus woman, man = agent, woman = passive other identified with nature and the feminized social) could be suspended, and art could be pursued in individual freedom from the messy business of gender relations and the prison-house of 'the empire of gender' that saturated all aspects of mind and body. Many artist-women and writer-women thus embraced modernism's illusory dream of a space of freedom for creative action that was taken up as a liberation from the tyrannies of the nineteenth-century empire of gender stereotyping. Yet they and their dreams were betrayed by twentieth-century art history and its modern institutions, even as modernity itself was revealed and betrayed by the Holocaust, Hiroshima and fascism.

The creative women: artist-women

Creative modern women wanted to share in the opportunity, for instance, just to be an artist. They desired to escape being praised condescendingly as a *woman* artist – as which, in the Victorian period, they were at least mentioned and recorded in historical surveys of art past and present. Resisting being either judged or commended for making *feminine* art, modern women also aspired to make new art. This imaginary freedom articulated in avant-garde discourse and practice made modernist women, as the twentieth century wore on, often hostile to any residual or re-emerging feminist programme, as it was felt to be alien political talk unrelated to aesthetic questions, and they dismissed any discussion of gender that might reintroduce Victorian separate spheres and special sex-based characteristics in relation to artistic practice. Yet there were paradoxes.

Gallerist Peggy Guggenheim, astonished at the lack of exhibition visibility offered to the many modernist artist-women she encountered on her return to New York in 1940, created two exhibitions, *31 Women* (1943) and *The Women* (1945), at her gallery, Art of the Century. Desperate for exposure, yet afraid of being collectively seen as 'women', the artist-women struggled to decide whether to accept the invitation. Most acceded but found themselves negatively categorized just as they feared. Georgia

O'Keeffe notably refused, having already had many shows, and perhaps already knowing she would have one of the first retrospectives allocated to a woman at the Museum of Modern Art in 1946. We can thus understand the many instances of modernist avant-garde artist-women articulating resistance to the post-1968 feminist re-engagement with gender and sexual difference as a factor in art or life, while proclaiming their utter belief in art as freedom from such social ironies.[30]

Stalking their ambitions to be recognized as artists pure and simple, however, was always the dread of being once again discovered/exposed by probing patriarchal critics – still steeped in masculinist ideologies – as just a woman, then reclassified as a 'woman artist', which really meant no artist at all. The profound antagonism between the terms *woman* and *artist*, still unchanged in modernism even if publicly disavowed in the name of modernism's transcendent truths and objective purposes, played its disfiguring games during the 1940s, and especially the 1950s, in the small artworlds of New York and other art cities in ways that did not, however, prevent two generations of artists who were women from sharing in the ambitious enterprise that was US-American abstract and gestural painting in those decades.[31] There they are for us to see now and know. Yet their presence as co-creators of the modernist adventure has been systematically under-exhibited, less reported, less preserved or hardly written into history by the very men who worked with them daily and knew them and their work.

To share in the avant-garde project, the artist-women had to take a considerable risk. They had to stay close enough to the action – reference – to be part of the game, while grasping and showing that each understood the latest game-play or gambit – deference. Each had, however, to create, to difference aesthetically, to make their own particular differencing of the strategic field of the avant-garde at that moment. Each differencing resulted from the whole complex of *who* each one of them was, creatively involving class, race, gender, ethnicity, family history, politics, sexuality as well as their singular aesthetic programmes. Even here, they had endlessly to dodge the persistent curatorial imposition of what would be deadly to their desires for recognition, namely, any contaminating signs of a generic and disqualifying 'femininity', which would immediately other and devalue them.

This book also tries not to separate avant-garde painting from popular culture, art from what was the central ideological apparatus of the conservative, national, sexist and racist concept of Americanness during the 1950s. I avoid isolating different forms of women's agency and action from each other, and refuse to segregate the women from the men. Cultural and creative conversations traversed art history's imposed divisions, and this requires us to rethink the peculiar isolation of art that art history produces, quarantining artists from the world in which they lived, made art, had fun, watched movies, danced to music and believed, despite poverty, in the necessity to make paintings or sculptures. Women and men of all communites *co-created* modern art, side by side, and in dialogue with their cultures, popular, political, local, vernacular and avant-garde.

I present here a journey through the ideological thickets of the artistic avant-garde moment as it played out in the 1950s in order to be able to 'see' one or two paintings by one artist, Lee Krasner, that redesignate her place in North American painting but also in a cultural history of gender and art in the 1950s. This involves finding ways to understand how artist-women, like her, deeply admired their contemporaries – men as well as women – as much as they fiercely competed with them. Rivalry, competition, envy, those transformations of what psychoanalyst Melanie Klein took to be archaic emotions and tendencies, could function critically to drive and sustain creative practices. Hence, I shall explore a range of theories about the psychic landscape and forces of creative activity. In that landscape of modernist contradictions between the illusion of individual freedom and the resilient gender policing of access to recognition as an artist in the artworld, wider cultural discourses and representational practices constantly worked to create, stabilize, contest, reclaim and revision notions of gender and its representations, as well as those psycho-symbolic structures of sexual difference which are implanted within us as subjects in terms of phantasies, images, symbols and the unconscious.

I want to mess with the historical moment of Abstract Expressionism – the term was coined in 1946 by Robert Coates in *The New Yorker* – by coming at it from a feminist cultural analytical perspective, and taking as my focal point some paintings by Lee Krasner that may unexpectedly bear the imprint of another creative artist – Marilyn Monroe. I invoke neither the person nor even the cinematic and photographic icon. *Monroe-ness* signifies a creatively performed incarnation of a *riant, jouissant* femininity. I hope that by the end of the book, Krasner's paintings will look different, and become *visible otherwise* within a feminist vision, open to a different kind of reading. *Differencing* acknowledges the embodied and imaginary play of sexual difference to suggest how an artist such as Lee Krasner dealt with the necessary, and inevitable, confrontation with the powerful artistic figures who dominated the field in which she also wanted to be an acknowledged artistic presence. Did she do it by 'killing men'? Perhaps, but if so, she did it creatively by radical displacement of their vision. Lee Krasner certainly was neither a 'dying' nor a 'dyeing woman', even though that blonde 'Woman' was clearly haunting the works and imaginations of artists, both men and women, straight and queer, even in the moment that she made herself the brilliant star of the decade, and was not yet the mourned 'candle in the wind'.[32]

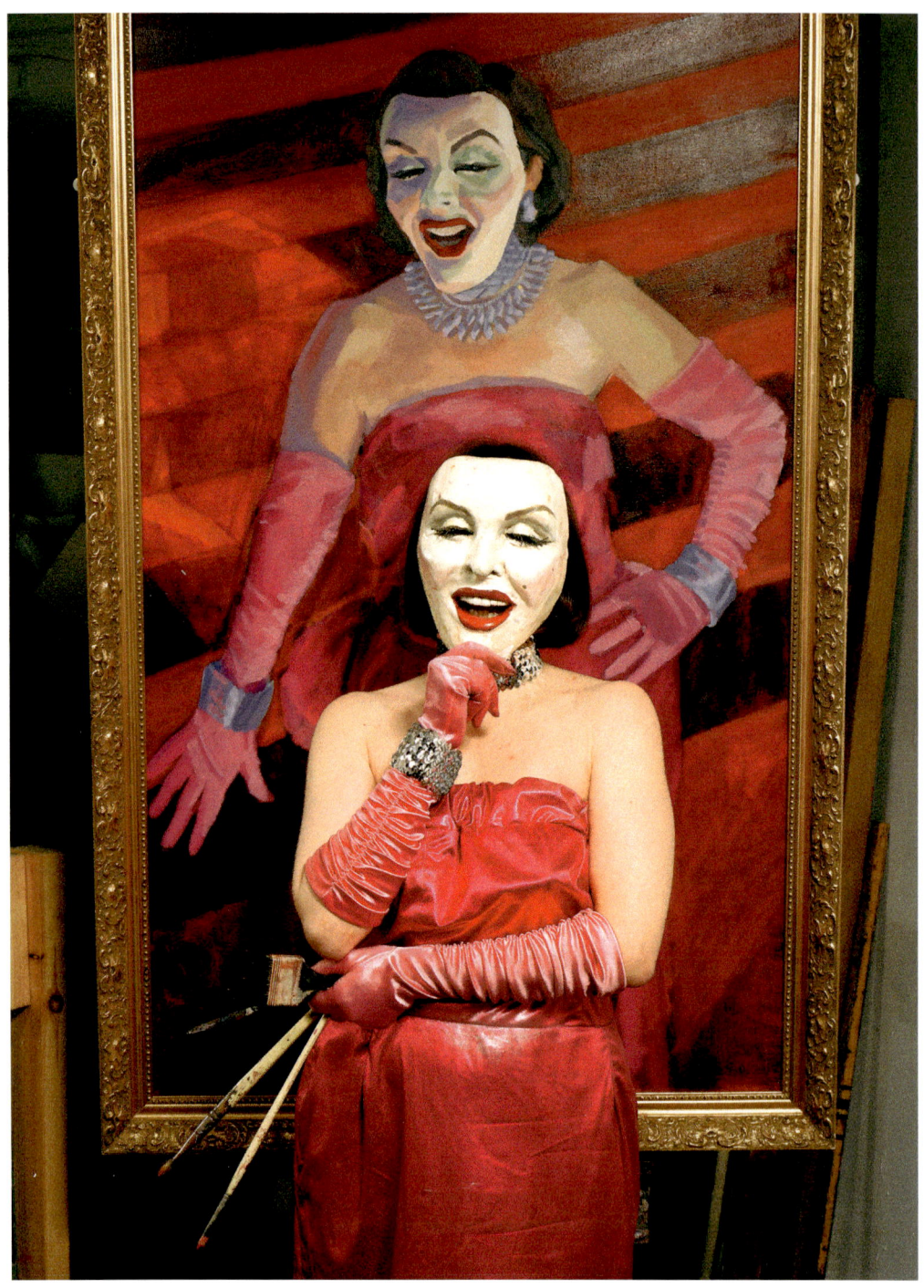

Figure 2.1 Nicky Bird, *Dressed to Paint [Marilyn Monroe]*, 1993

Five essays on sexuality (and art)

I The title

There you have it! The feminist is out in her true colours. Killing men. That's what you've always suspected about feminists. Man-haters the lot of them! With help from philosopher Jacques Derrida, I invite you to reconsider what you see when I write *Killing Men and Dying Women*. Killing men implies that men are being killed. Killing can be adjectival, qualifying men as agents of violence. Men kill. Soldiers, perhaps, or warriors in a Cold War. Similar undecidability nestles in dying women. Spoken aloud, dying is an example of Derrida's *différance*. Dying means women are meeting their deaths. Women d-i-e. It could be they are changing the colour of something, cosmetically refashioning the given body the better to conform to some schema of desirability. Women d-y-e. In the 1950s what women dyed was their hair. There was only one colour that signified dyeing because we all know that *Gentlemen Prefer Blondes*.[1] In her cultural critique and autobiographical reflection on 'Blondes', Teresa Podlesney quips: 'Gentlemen prefer blondes, but only if their roots don't show. I am determined to make mine visible.'[2]

In US-American culture of the 1950s – which was paradigmatic of modern culture internationally – dy(e)ing women met killing men and some men had to be killed – metaphorically, in paint. This is a bit more of the story of the Cold War and its cultural politics. One of the key actors is Marilyn Monroe who was made stellar by Twentieth-Century Fox's release in July 1953 of a film remake of a Broadway musical version of Anita Loos's novella *Gentlemen Prefer Blondes* (1925) (fig. 2.7). Cast as 'dumb blonde' gold-digger Lorelei Lee, Marilyn Monroe replotted a history of woman as image in cinema into that decade's glossy myth of cosmetically fashioned and dyed as well as dying femininity.[3]

The Blonde met her other in that decade in the person of the Painter – Jackson Pollock, almost himself a Method actor and, as a result of some spectacular publicity and photography, the high art version of the masculinity that Marlon Brando in his wildest role would project on screen (*The Wild One*, dir. László Benedek, 1953) (fig. 2.2).[4] Was Pollock the symbol of modern, American masculinity and a dying man?[5] Podlesney asks:

Does the blonde, characterized as mere image, mere hair colour, make possible the emergence of the 'real' man, the sensitive man of the 1950s. Because one half of the screen is so obviously and transparently constructed, the other half, reflected, can be seen as 'real', not constructed, 'natural'.[6]

The Actors Studio – to which Marilyn Monroe went in 1955 in her desire to train as a serious actor – set about naturalizing the cultural image of the man. British feminist journalist Julie Burchill defined the opposition between fake woman and authentic man: 'Masculinism started with the Method. The Method Actor looked at the Sex Doll and thought her empty and unworthy: he turned to the mirror and the other man.'[7]

They look so different: Jackson and Marilyn (figs 2.2 and 2.3). This crude juxtaposition underlines the extreme gender polarization of the 1950s when the post-war American state attempted to put the genie back in the bottle by making all the working-class 'Rosie the Riveters' of the war years (fig. 1.3) go home, while college-educated middle-class women were encouraged to find satisfaction baking brownies and raising children in the suburban dream that Betty Friedan exposed in 1963 as a nightmare: the problem with no name – *the feminine mystique*.[8]

Yet at another level, Marilyn and Jackson, icons of America in the 1950s, are disturbingly convergent. Both died unnecessary and tragic deaths: Jackson Pollock on 11 August 1956 at the age of 44 and Marilyn Monroe at 36 on 4 or 5 August 1962. Premature and sudden mortality fuels

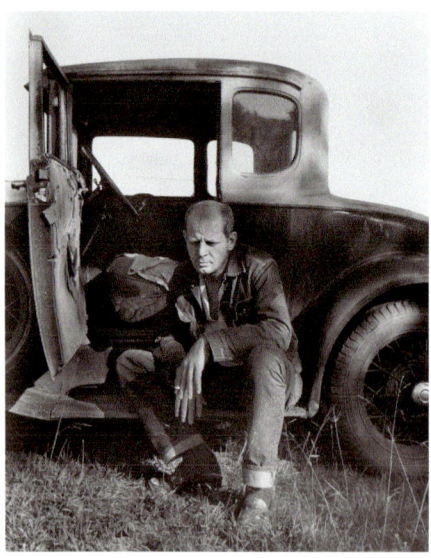

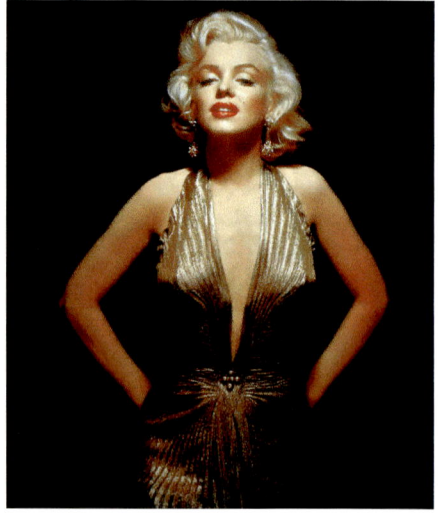

Figure 2.3 *Marilyn Monroe in the golden dress designed by Travilla for* Gentlemen Prefer Blondes, 1953

Figure 2.2 Hans Namuth, *Jackson Pollock seated in his car*, 1950

fascination with the icon when death makes the absent but famous persona become the lost object of both commercialized and academic myth.

Killing is what the culture does; premature dying is the fate of those who symbolize culture. I want to show the roots and find a livelier underside. I want to get inside the surface of the image where myth inserts itself and destabilize mythic images of masculinity and femininity in 1950s North America – a period of intense but partially obliterated creative participation by many women in the legendary period of America's accession to the cultural domination of modernism, when, as Serge Guilbaut argued, 'New York stole the avant-garde' from Paris.[9] How could you be a woman and an artist caught between the twin myths of gender and art embodied by the opposing images of Monroe – trash, popular, feminized culture – and Pollock – authentic, masculinized high art? What account of creativity 'in, of and from the feminine' could we salvage either from the heroic narratives of *The Triumph of American Painting* or from the anti-mythical exposé of 'Abstract Expressionism as Weapon of the Cold War'?[10] What has gender to do with the Cold War, with the flatness of the canvas, or all of the above with the sexuated body-psyche?

Many artist-women survived the decade, its art politics and its gender politics. Neither dyed nor dying, Lee Krasner, born in 1908, died in 1984 aged 76. Born in 1928, Helen Frankenthaler died in 2011; born in 1922, Grace Hartigan lived until 2008; Elaine de Kooning (1928–89), Joan Mitchell (1926–92), Louise Nevelson (1900–88) and Alma Thomas (1891–1978, figs 2.4a and 2.4b) all lived into old age – but barely into history, and into neither canonization nor myth. We celebrate with unabashed adulation modern masters such as Picasso or de Kooning who survived into untimely old age. There is no comparable discourse according

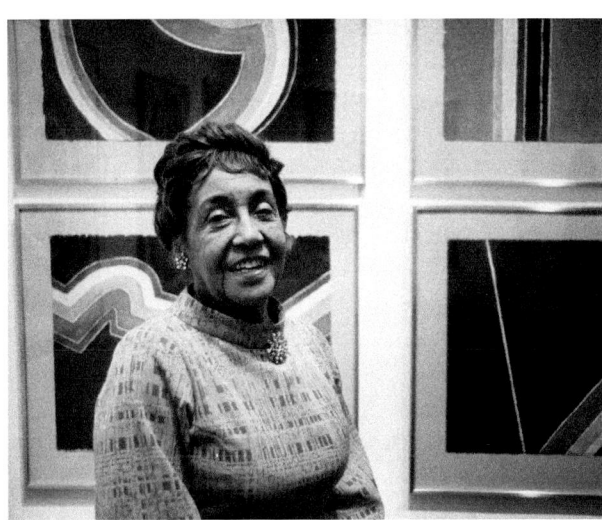

Figure 2.4a *Washington-based abstract artist Alma Thomas with her work at her retrospective at the Whitney Museum of American Art,* c. 1972

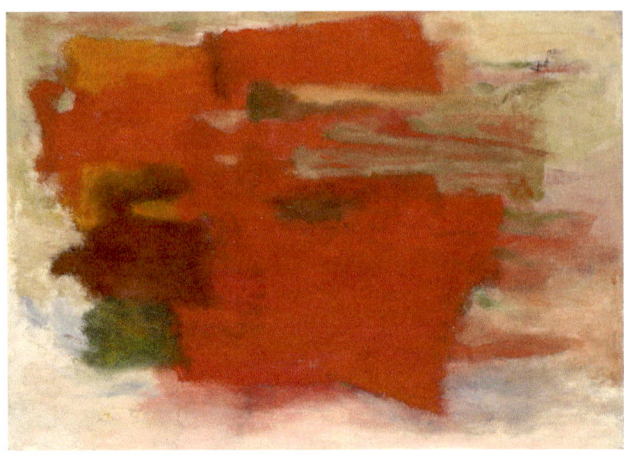

Figure 2.4b Alma Thomas,
Red Abstraction, 1959

venerated status to the long-lived artist-woman, with the exception of Louise Bourgeois (1911–2010), whereby hangs another complex tale. Until the re-emergence of the Women's Movement c. 1968, these miraculous painters scandalously received but passing notice even as they consistently created and exhibited.[11] Such artists are but witnesses to, and survivors of, the contradictions between modernity, femininity and representation.

If Nicky Bird's work asks what icons or images women artists negotiate when they are *Dressed to Paint* (fig. 2.1), do they make art by killing men rather than becoming dying women? Is creativity a necessarily sadistic, even murderous activity? This latter idea is not a feminist, man-hating thought. I derive it from canonized modernists: Clement Greenberg and Georges Bataille (1897–1962). In his essay, 'Towards a Newer Laocoon' (1940), in which he justified the logic of advanced art's purifying drive towards abstraction, Greenberg rewrote the history of modern art from Manet, with its current endpoint as its predestined outcome. The process was based on the elimination of elements extraneous to the essence of each art's medium. Assessing the nineteenth-century strategies that created modernism, Greenberg claimed that Parisian painter Edouard Manet (1832–83) had made the decisive break to liberate painting from subject matter and its dependence on literature by attacking the subject matter that painting inherited from its sister arts *on its own terrain*. In his transitional paintings of the 1860s, Greenberg argued that Manet included the traditional subjects of Western art – the nude, historical or literary themes – but he *exterminated* them, then and there, on the canvas.[12] Manet is a modernist because he took on the freight of tradition that burdened his practice and killed it stone dead in his work.

The idea of artistic advance through destruction, however, precedes Greenberg's formalist application of it. It emerges as a theme in the

Surrealist Georges Bataille's writings on art. In 1930 Bataille cited approvingly Romanian Dadaist Tristan Tzara (1896–1963) when he observed that Spanish painter Joan Miró (1929–83), in a moment of rapid reorientation of his work through the use of collage, was aiming to kill painting by its own means, a notion already in circulation through Maurice Raynal's quotation of Miró saying 'I want to murder painting.'[13] Bataille argued that modern picture making arrives when *decomposition* replaces composition – 'an intelligible totality'. This idea came to fruition in his book on Manet published in 1955.[14] Comparing Manet's strategy in paintings such as *Olympia* (1863–65, Musée d'Orsay, Paris) and *The Execution of Maximilian* (1868, Kunsthalle, Mannheim), both of which refer to an external 'text' – Baudelaire's poetry evoking prostitution in *Olympia* and a journalistic news report of a contemporary assassination in *The Execution of Maximilian* – Bataille wrote: 'In both cases what the painting *obliterates* is not the text, *but the obliteration of that text*.'[15] Bataille reads the history of modern art for these key moments of cancellation. Attempts to interpret modern painting by seeking a source, a meaning or a psychological centre for a picture are thus considered misguided. Destruction and the libidinal, sadistic impulses that drive it become the key terms of Bataille's thesis on modern art, for which he traces a trajectory, mixing the erotic and the sadistic, from Goya (1746–1828) in the eighteenth century to Delacroix (1798–1863), through Manet's critical annihilation and on to the Symbolist Gustave Moreau (1898–1926) and to Surrealism.

In 1955, and again in the 1970s, Lee Krasner made a major move in her work through collage, cutting up her own and, at times, Pollock's discarded canvases in the first instance, and subsequently, in the mid-1970s, cutting up her Cubist-inspired drawings from the 1930s.[16] Rather than reading modern art as a formalist project to hunt painting back to medium-specific two-dimensionality – the flatness of the canvas – by squeezing out all the remnants of illusory, geometric and even shallow Cubist space, an interpretation now overfamiliar to us through cheap jibes at Greenbergian formulae, Bataille works from Malraux's definition of the modern in painting as that which refuses – obliterates – all *values* foreign to painting.[17] A certain indifference to death, for instance, or absence, may result – but this not a positively created value, such as flatness was for Greenberg. Nothing replaces what has been 'murdered'. As part of the same logic, Bataille defines the role of surface in a painting quite differently from what we are accustomed to in US-American formalist (flatness) or actionist (an arena) criticism. The surface of the painting is to be imagined as a kind of lid that conceals a deadly freight just as a tombstone in a graveyard covers up a corpse. Attracting us, yet obscuring the view, the idea of a lid could also lead down a thread of associations to the Greek myth of Pandora and her box.

Pandora (Πανδώρα, meaning all gifted) was the first human woman, created on the instructions of Zeus by the blacksmith god Hephaestus (Vulcan in Roman mythology) to punish man – and indeed the human race – the first man being Prometheus, because he had stolen fire from the gods. Pandora was endowed with many gifts from the other Olympians so that she would cause suffering to humans with her seductions and guile. In a box she was given as a dowry, the gods placed all plagues and evil. She was, however, ordered never to open the box. The myth tells us that the box-woman has both an alluringly beautiful surface and a dangerous content – all the ills of the world. The box becomes both an image for the woman Pandora and the signifier of her invisible but apparently mortifying sexuality and the dangers within (fig. 2.5).

Pandora and/as her box opens up another pathway for this text. This clearly patriarchal myth of the origin of woman as the dual source of desirability and evil, causing eternal punishment for mortal ambition, conjugates danger and death with hidden interiority, linking both to the inside of the female sexual body while, at the same time, rendering feminine curiosity about a woman's own interior a deadly threat to humankind. Box, tomb, sex – these terms together with the aesthetic surface to create a chain of phantasmatic signifiers that circle around a feminine Other, sliding on to death, with secrets that mortify and an imaginary feminine body on the edge of both abjection and ecstasy.[18]

Feminist film theorist Laura Mulvey aimed to interrupt the fetishistic and voyeuristic logic of the phallocentric culture encoded in the allegory of Pandora's box by reclaiming this dark image of the dangerous beauty of woman as both a treacherous surface and a deadly, death-dealing interior.[19] She reformulates the myth to produce an epistemology and an aesthetics of feminine curiosity, a desire to know about the interiority, subjectivity and sexuality of the feminine – as yet hardly knowable under the phallic regime of meanings which attributes to woman only a negative meaning (the lacking hole) or a deadly dimension (the tomb). Mulvey imagines a feminist pleasure in knowledge of the woman's body and proposes the possibilities of feminist aesthetic practices that might explore the foreclosed domain of the feminine – body and psyche.

The blonde cinema star Marilyn Monroe was a modern incarnation of the phallocentric Pandoran fantasy – a glittering, cosmetically fashioned surface that veiled a tortured psyche and a self-destructive, or at least damaged, interior. Such fabricated images – even when this performer created the images so exquisitely – functioned, however, as a representational obstacle for women as artists. Artist-women needed to break through that excessive and fetishistically constructed carapace termed femininity and explore for themselves or release a different kind of creative interiority – corporeal and psychic – that could be imagined and

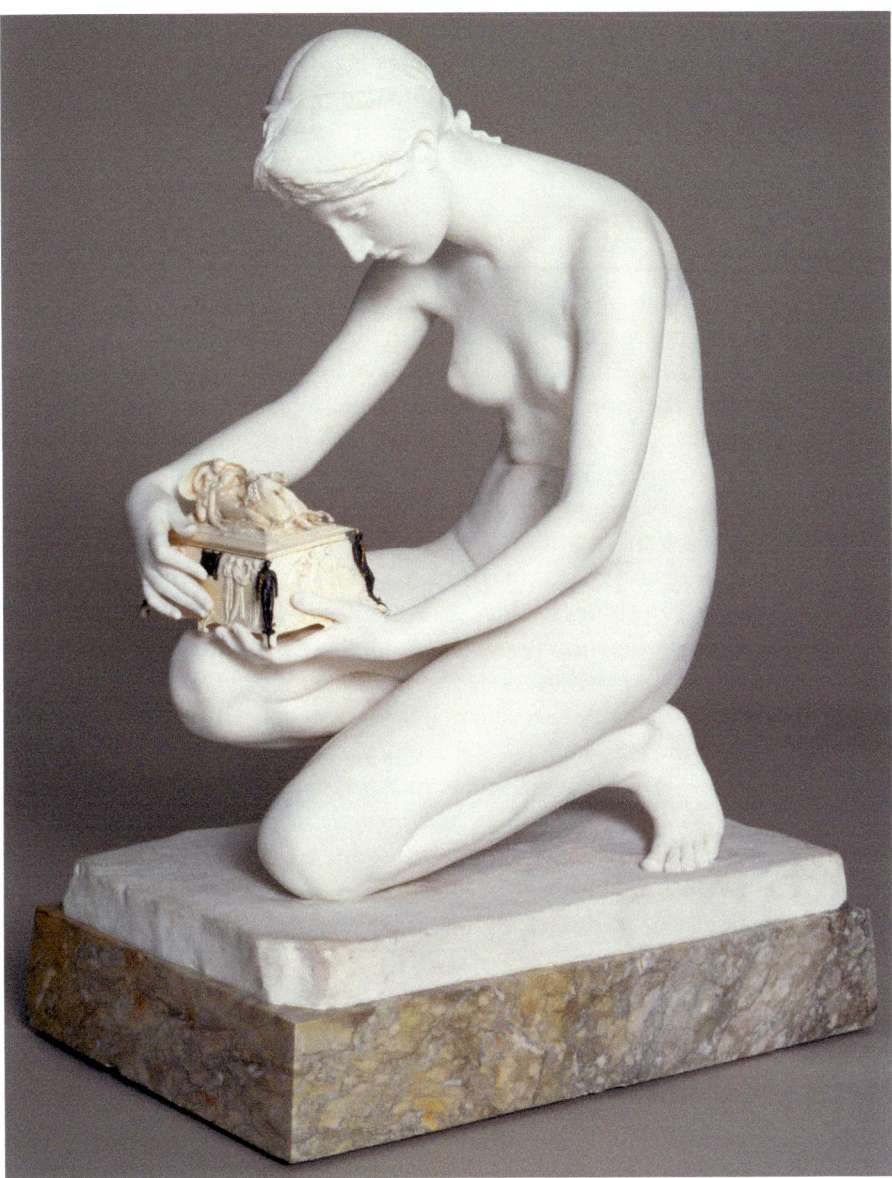

Figure 2.5 Harry Bates, *Pandora's Box*, c. 1891

enacted through the opportunities offered by post-Surrealist, abstract, gestural painting, even as such painting was mythically, at that same moment, represented only by the tragic hero – therefore, in the masculine – of a Promethean quest represented iconically by one of the several US-American painters of this tendency: Jackson Pollock. Yet, I shall suggest, artist-women were engaging via abstract painting pandorically in a strategy of feminine curiosity. Located at the heart of the modernizing enterprise in painting premised on a kind of creation through destruction, they may have had to die and to kill to gain access to it.

II The cover image

Nicky Bird's *Dressed to Paint* (1994, fig. 2.1) encapsulates, and, in part, inspired the issues addressed in this book. Stemming from a painting project exploring women, the artist-woman and cinematic images, Bird's photo-performance work features her own paintings, both speaking to the interweaving of practices, identities, memories and images linking the studio and the cinema, painting and performing.[20] She enacts a double performance – being the artist and being the image – while also negotiating a gendered relation to an image by combining visual impersonation and the act of painting in cinematic costume. Creating outfits to accompany masks she cast from her own face while building each up to resemble the iconic features of eight Hollywood divas (Garbo, Stanwick, Davis, Swanson, Hepburn, Dietrich, Crawford and Monroe), the artist dressed herself to inhabit the roles and bodies and to share the cosmetic star-faces, performing the gestures and poses of the legendary roles of actor-women who had shaped, not her childhood, but those of her British, working-class mother and grandmother who loved cinema. What had they seen at the movies? How did they negotiate glamorous images and their work experience? What pleasure did two generations of working-class British women see in the Hollywood movies that these legends created on the big screen, when cinema was a costly but regular part of precious time off. Were they lured, deceived, deluded? Or did they also see, and appreciate, working women in another industry? Bird's research was not ethnographical. It took the form of her crossing being and viewing, making and seeing, performance and painting, that the photowork of her in her studio produces as both document and artwork. Like Kerry Filer Harker (fig. 00.1), also a British, white, working-class artist-woman who shares a fascination with the image of Marilyn Monroe, Bird links painting and cinematic performance as work and creativity (figs 2.6a–c).

Dealing with non-existent bodies, screen images and indeed screen memories mediated by posed photographs, Bird told me that she had to make the outfits and masks to do the painting. She had to be *with* or *in* the image she was recreating even as she distanced the icon by masking, and through the expressionist rendering of the fixed faces from posed photographs. Thus, the artist is not painting from a mechanical image. She took *on* rather than *into* herself an other. She used her own body, recast through costume and gesture, to stage a performance of a culturally invented character, Lorelei from *Gentlemen Prefer Blondes* (1953), and thus creates an

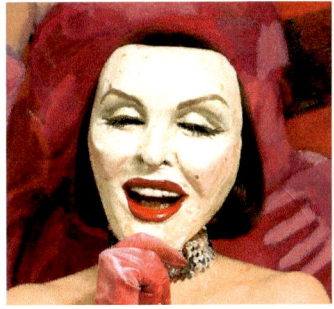
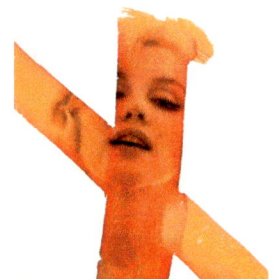
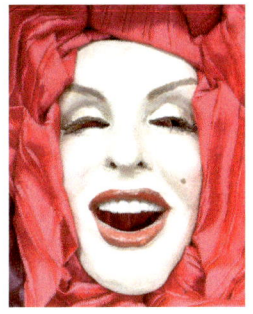

Figure 2.6a Nicky Bird, detail of mask from *Dressed to Paint [Marilyn Monroe]*, 1993

Figure 2.6b Kerry Filer Harker, detail of face from *mm Mark 1*, 1994

Figure 2.6c Nicky Bird, *Marilyn Monroe Mask*

uncanny disjunction between the cosmetically styled face turned into a physical object, the mask – making literal Barthes's idea of a face-object – and her own embodiment as she physically produces a painting. The masks have eye holes, of necessity, for Bird to paint. In the time of the painting, her eyes are implanted behind the mask, becoming a source of a doubled gaze that we, the viewers, encounter, a gaze looking back at the painter and at us even as it is the register of the painter gazing at her own masquerade.

Dressed to Paint combines, therefore, painting, photography and performance. As image, it shows an artist at work. She is, however, dressed in an evening gown, a shiny, shocking pink, strapless evening dress accessorized with long gloves and diamante jewellery. She is not very tall and has short brown hair. She is barefoot. Her face is covered. On the easel, we see the large, almost complete painting she has been making from what she apparently sees in the mirror to the left: herself posing as model. It is not just her own reflection, for we see the invisible frontal view of what we are seeing from behind, but reversed. There are now two bodies in the work, the first captured by photography, the second a photographed reflection on a mirror within the photographed space. The third body is a painting of their confrontation.

Yet the mirror does not offer a direct reflection. Mirrors reverse. The figure appears to use her right hand to hold the mask over her own face, a gesture we now return to the other figure to understand. In the mirror, the figure's left arm is outstretched, cut off by the canvas, lacking, invisible, no longer indexical. Seen from behind, the painter-figure uses her right hand, however, to press her brush into a pool of pink paint on the palette on a metal trolley. This sole gesture signifies a pause in the act of painting. There are some brushes in a tin – a planted reference perhaps to Jasper Johns's *Painted Bronze* (1960). The background of the painting also seems to invite a further speculation on Johns's *Flag* (1954–55) and his casting of body parts (1955). The brushes and studio mess add up to a statement about a studio practice: 1950s New York painting, a staged studio scene, so beloved of modernist painters. The paintbrush leads to a third image in this photograph – the painting, different in pose and gesture from both poses in the mirrored conversation. The painted mask has become dynamic, facially intense, expressive, distressingly so. The gloved hands of the painted figure are now disposed, one hand on the hip, the other out-stretched in a gesture. Both hands appear enlarged, as is the mask, which now invokes sound – someone singing, eyes half-closed and mouth open. The dress indexes Marilyn Monroe's performance of 'Diamonds are a Girl's Best Friend' in *Gentlemen Prefer Blondes* (fig. 2.7): 'It was in 1953–54

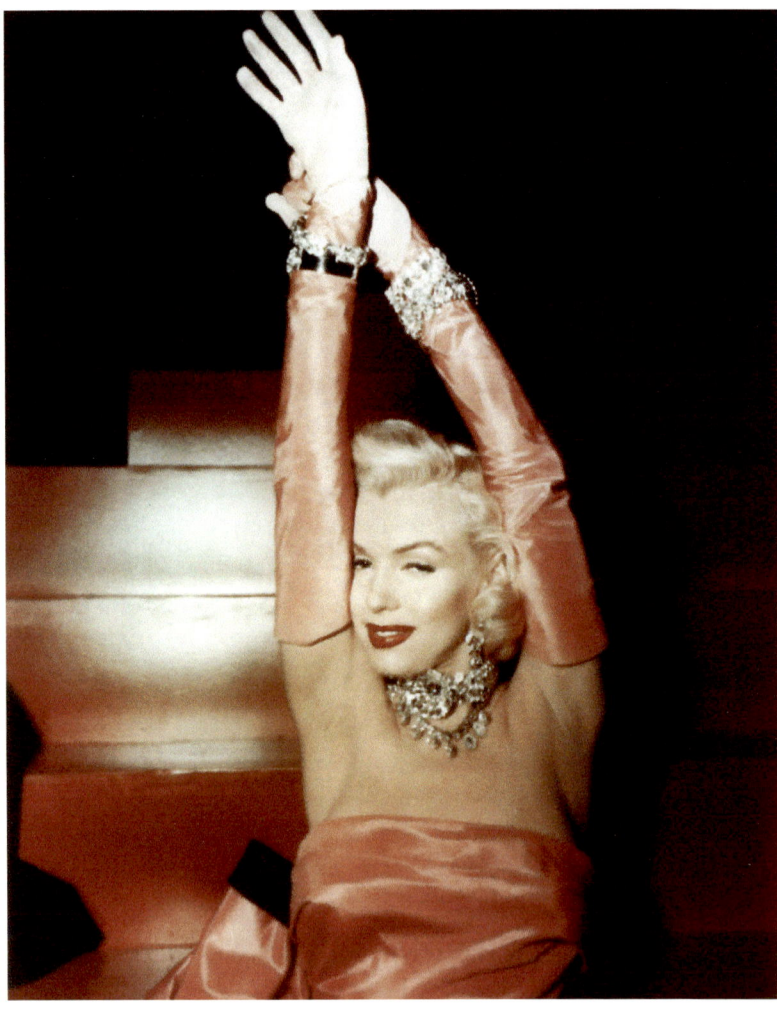

Figure 2.7 *Marilyn Monroe performing 'Diamonds are a Girl's Best Friend' from* Gentlemen Prefer Blondes, *1953*

that Monroe became indistinguishable from her image – so much so that, whatever she might do, she would never seem out of character. Three films made her the nation's number one box office attraction for 1953–54.[21]

III The year is 1953

Consider this series of conjunctions.[22]

The first issue of *Playboy* magazine featuring Marilyn Monroe on the cover appeared in December 1953 (fig. 2.8). She was also featured inside as both the first centrefold and the first ever sweetheart of the month.

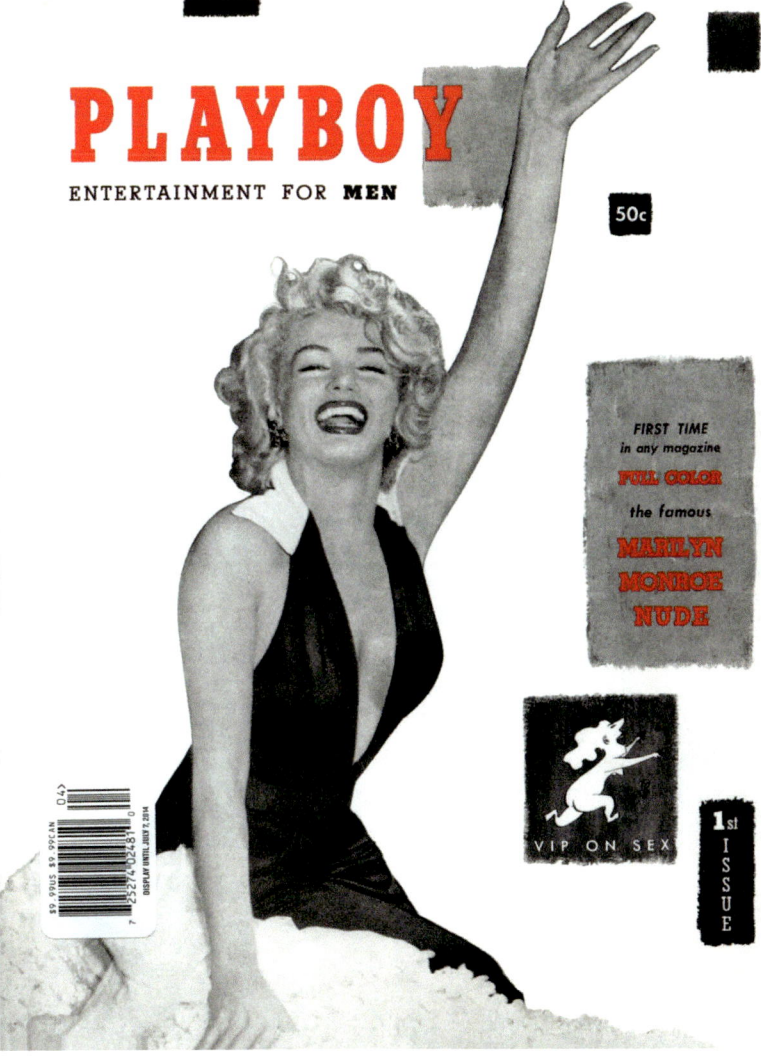

Figure 2.8 First issue of *Playboy: Entertainment for Men*, December 1953

Accompanied by the infamous nude calendar shots by Tom Kelley, the text calls her 'natural sex personified' and 'blonde all over', while remarking that 'She's as famous as Dwight Eisenhower and Dick Tracy, and she and Dr. Kinsey have so monopolised sex this year, some people in high places are investigating to make certain no anti-trust laws have been bent or broken.'[23]

The first, abridged English translation of Simone de Beauvoir's *The Second Sex* (1949) was published in 1953 (fig. 2.9). In this translation, the infamous opening sentence of Volume II, *Lived Experience* (Volume I being *Facts and Myths*), Chapter I 'Childhood', Part One, 'Formative Years', reads thus:

> One is not born, but rather becomes, a woman. No biological, psychological or economic fate determines the figure that the human female presents in society; it is civilisation as a whole which produces this creature, intermediate between male and eunuch, which is described as feminine.[24]

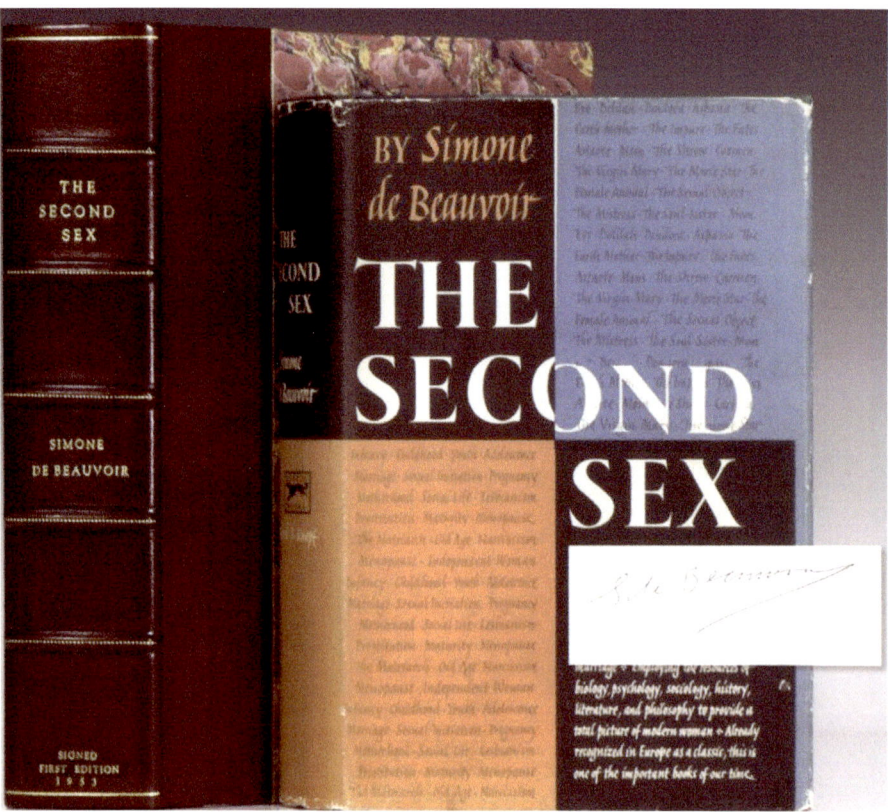

Figure 2.9 Cover of Simone de Beauvoir, *The Second Sex*, partial English translation by H. M. Parshley (New York: Alfred A. Knopf, 1953)

The 2011 translation is truer to the original French, reading:

> One is not born, but rather becomes, woman. No biological, psychical or economic destiny defines the figure that the human female takes on in society; it is civilisation as a whole that elaborates this intermediary product between the male and the eunuch that is called feminine.[25]

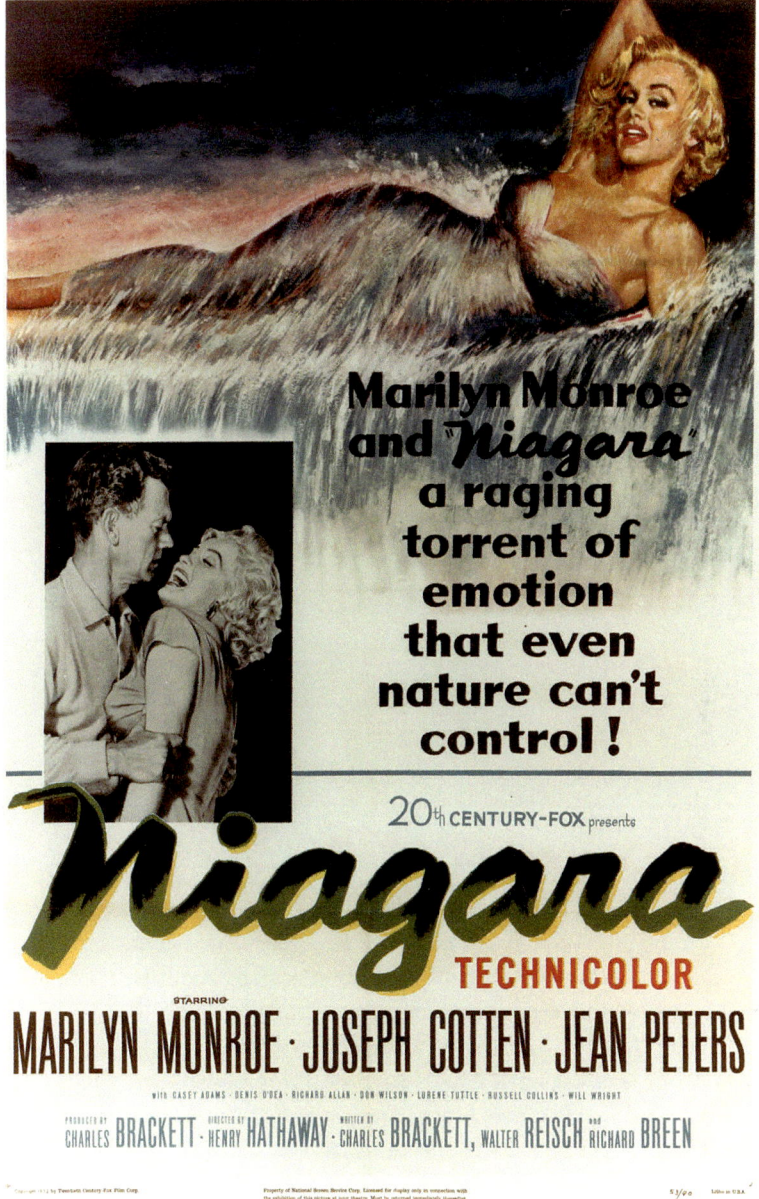

Figure 2.10 Poster for *Niagara*, released 21 January 1953

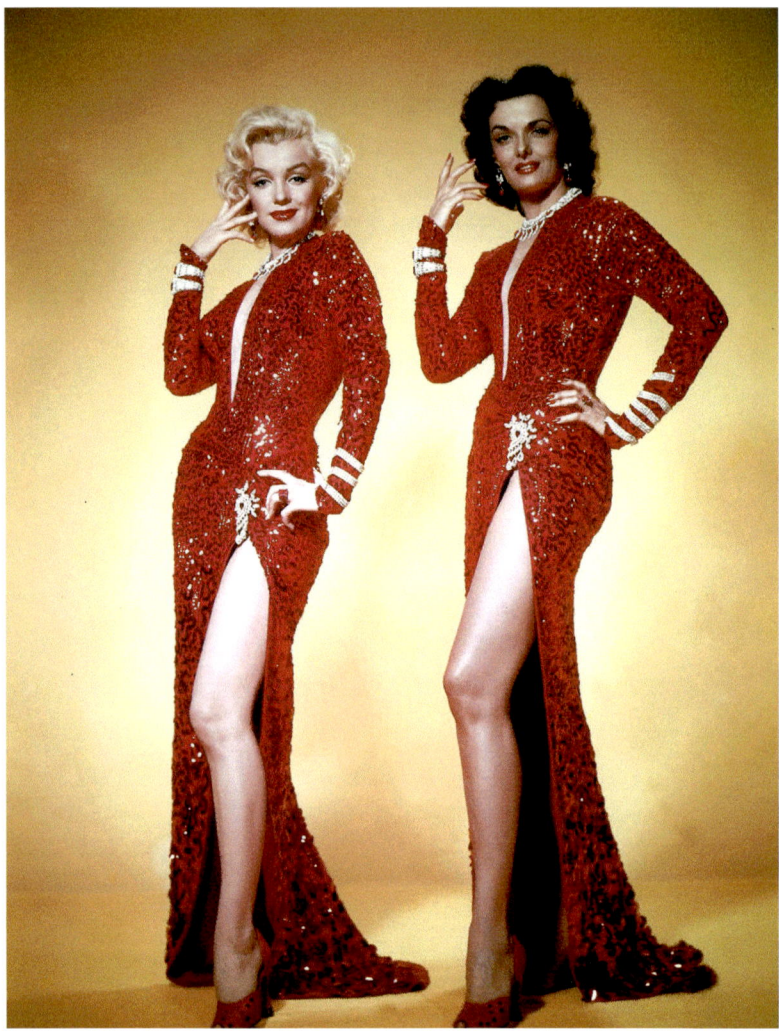

Figure 2.11 *Marilyn Monroe and Jane Russell in a publicity image for*
Gentlemen Prefer Blondes, cover, *Life magazine*, 25 May 1953

In 1953 Twentieth-Century Fox released back-to-back three films starring Marilyn Monroe: *Niagara* (January), *Gentlemen Prefer Blondes* (July)
and *How to Marry a Millionaire* (December) (figs 2.10–12). They established Monroe as the hottest and blondest star in Hollywood. From then
on her every marriage, film, illness, appearance and move was chronicled
and photographed in the popular press. In 1953 she was voted the year's
most popular actress and earned for her studio more money than any previous woman star. Monroe biographer Donald Spoto writes: 'The role of
Lorelei fixed Marilyn Monroe in the world's consciousness as the

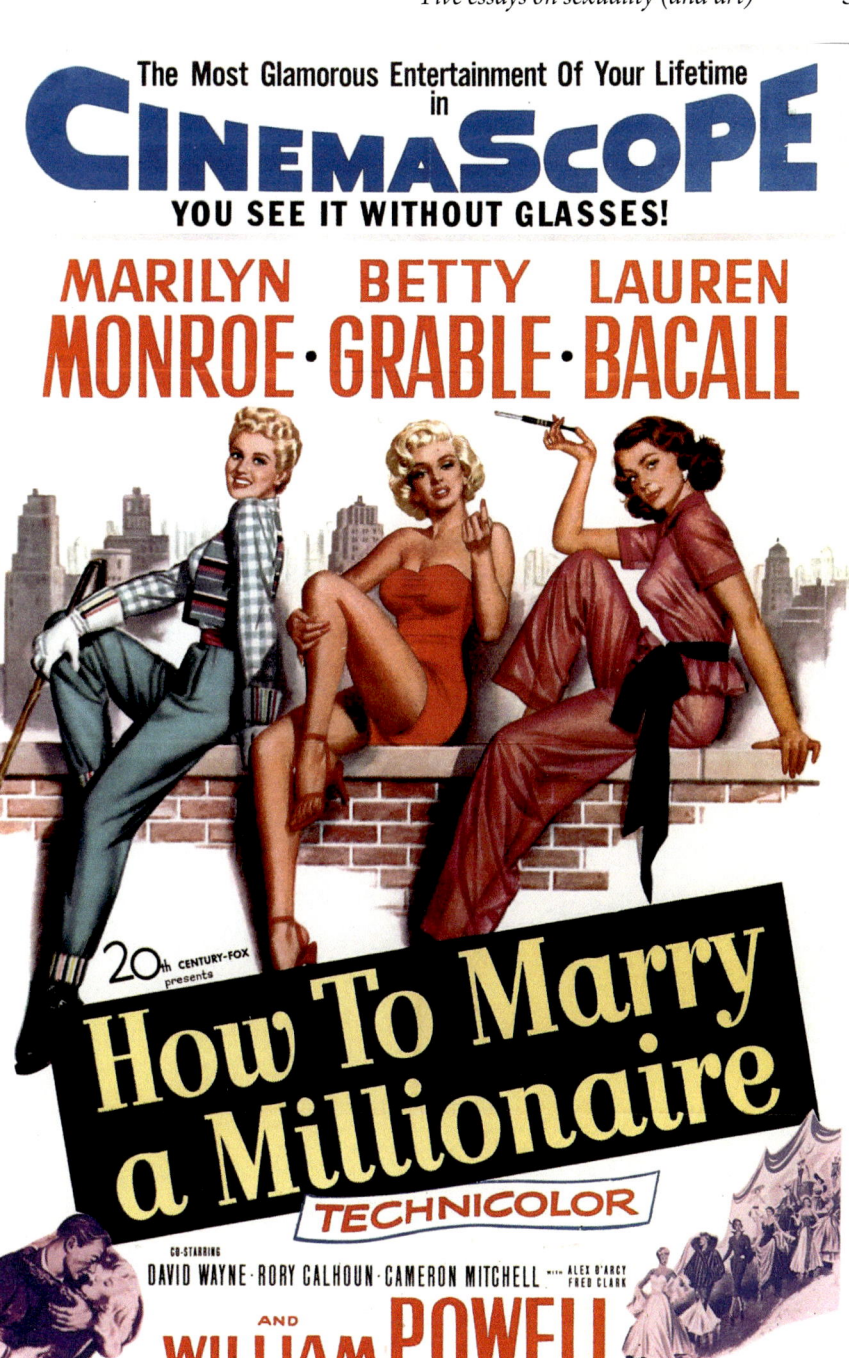

Figure 2.12 Poster for *How to Marry a Millionaire*, released 10 November 1953

exaggeratedly seductive blonde: all body; no thought; little feeling; all whispery high voice and no sensibility.'[26]

In July 1953 Dr A. C. Kinsey and his team produced their report on *Sexual Behaviour in the Human Female* (fig. 2.13). It appeared the same month as *Gentlemen Prefer Blondes* was released. Religious and civic

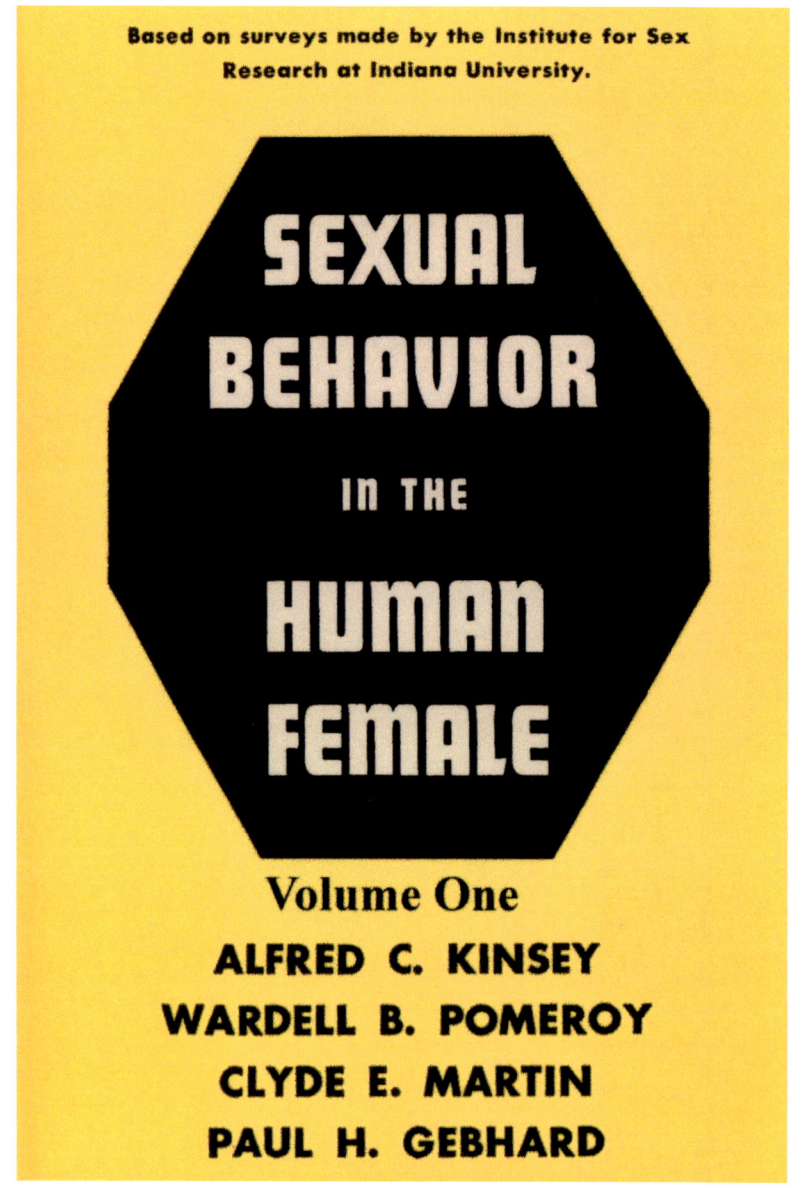

Based on surveys made by the Institute for Sex Research at Indiana University.

SEXUAL BEHAVIOR IN THE HUMAN FEMALE

Volume One
ALFRED C. KINSEY
WARDELL B. POMEROY
CLYDE E. MARTIN
PAUL H. GEBHARD

Figure 2.13 Cover of Alfred C. Kinsey, Wardell B. Pomeroy, Clyde E. Martin and Paul H. Gebhard, *Sexual Behaviour of the Human Female* (New York: W. B. Sanders, 1953)

leaders – like *Playboy* magazine – linked Monroe and Kinsey in their attacks. Kinsey's report sold 250,000 copies with its revelation that over 50 per cent of women were not virgins at marriage, over 50 per cent had had at least one homosexual relationship or experience, 25 per cent had extramarital affairs, and that the clitoris was the site of female sexual pleasure – itself a major shock of the report: women enjoyed sex.

In 1954 Dutch-American painter Willem de Kooning began a picture titled *Marilyn Monroe* (fig. 2.14), the year that the actress fled Hollywood to rebuild herself among the intellectuals, actors and poets of New York – the other America.[27] It appears as a strange, even wan epigraph to a series of extraordinarily striking paintings on the topic of *Woman* (figs 6.1 and 6.2) that had been occupying the painter since 1948 in his filial battle with the legacy of Picasso's figure of the seated woman.[28] Writing on 'The Birth of *Woman I*', art critic David Sylvester quoted de Kooning: 'They seem vociferous and ferocious. I think it had to do with the idea of the idol, the oracle and above all the hilariousness of it.'[29] Magnum photographer Eve Arnold – mistakenly I think – thought that Marilyn Monroe was the image behind the entire series.[30] Yet it is significant that she retrospectively made this connection.

Red lips float in a noseless face beneath unevenly positioned, kohl-lined eyes topped with a crop of yellow hair. The same yellow across the lower torso reflects the *Playboy* jibe: blonde all over. Between these two areas of yellow, the breasts are red, rhyming with the mouth. These clashing colours create a sublimated and yet virulent representation of the female sexual body that is shockingly at odds with the sanitized mixture of sensuality and sweetness that characterized all but *Playboy*'s writing on Marilyn Monroe.[31] Joy and vitality – key qualities of the image of Monroe – are, however, singularly absent from de Kooning's *Marilyn Monroe*. In his painting we encounter an anxious girl characterized by uneven eyes, red lips and a cosmetic, manufactured but nebulous face. The painting seems unresolved even if the application feels characteristically energetic and confident. As an image, Woman has not arrived. This image remains a child in make-up.

IV Hot lady in a cold [war] zone

Shortly after gracing the cover of the initial issue of *Playboy*, Marilyn Monroe was again in the headlines because of her marriage to all-time-famous baseball star Joe DiMaggio. In a blaze of publicity, they honeymooned in Japan. Monroe was invited to perform for the troops now guarding the frontiers of the Free World against the Red Peril on the 49th parallel in a divided Korea, a military front opened up in the so-called Cold War. When Monroe arrived, the war itself was over. A truce had been signed in

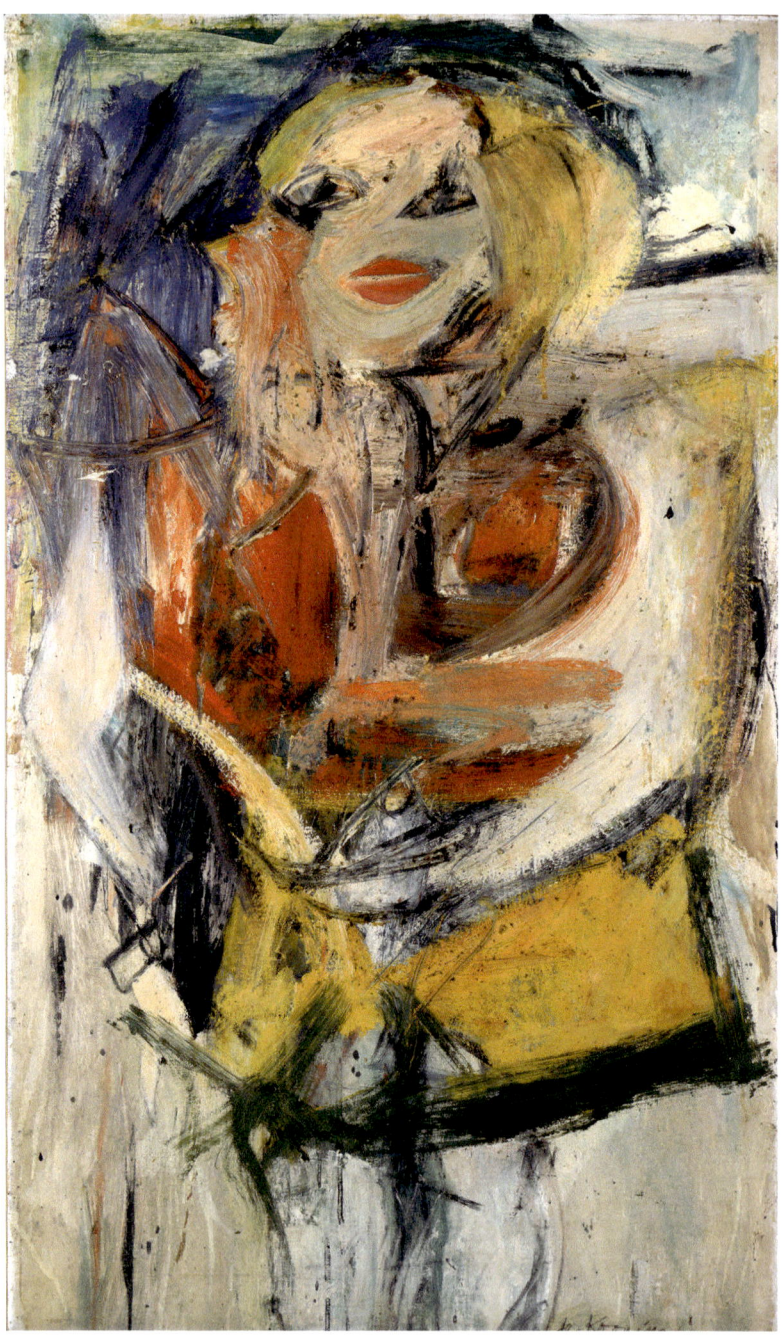

Figure 2.14 Willem de Kooning, *Marilyn Monroe*, 1954. Collection of Neuberger Museum of Art, Purchase College, State University of New York, gift of Roy R. Neuberger. Photo: Neuberger Museum

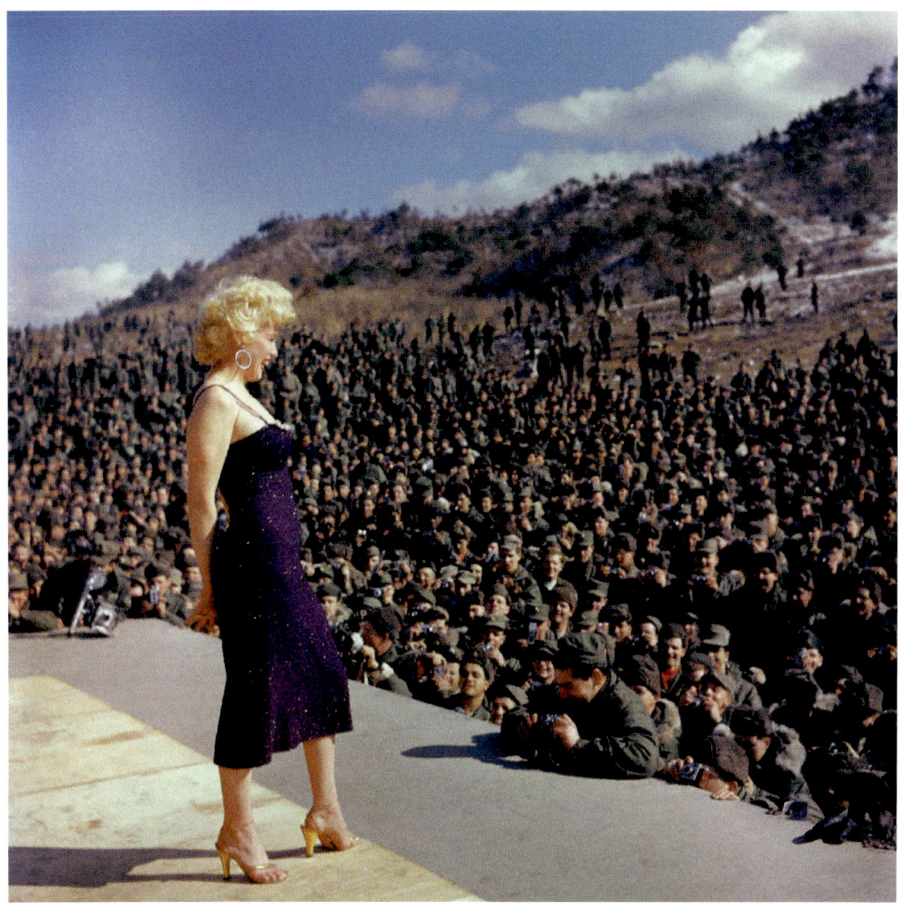

Figure 2.15 *Marilyn Monroe posing for US troops in Korea, 1954*

the summer of 1953. To entertain the troops remaining on guard on the border, Monroe agreed to put together a show based on her numbers from her 1953 box office hit *Gentlemen Prefer Blondes*. She did ten performances in four days between 16 and 20 February 1954, contracting severe pneumonia from the trip (fig. 2.15).

In sub-zero temperatures, scantily dressed in a clinging lavender dress and shoes that barely deserved the name, she sang 'Bye, Bye Baby' and 'Diamonds are a Girl's Best Friend' to a hooting, laughing and applauding male audience, who may in fact never have seen the films from which the songs came. But Monroe was already the pin-up of the American troops, extensively photographed and reproduced in magazines and calendars. A MASH team had voted her 'the girl we would most like to examine'.[32] On the final show of the tour, the troops rioted. The army launched an investigation into Monroe's activities in a Cold War zone. An unimpressed reporter for *The New York Times* referred to the concurrent hearings of the House Committee on Un-American Activities investigating the army, initiated by leading Cold War zealot Senator Joe McCarthy. The reporter bemoaned the exposure of the weakness of military morale revealed by the over-excited and indeed 'feminine' way the soldiers responded to Monroe – the reporter compared them to bobby-soxers – going on to use this episode as further support for McCarthy's domestic investigation into the Army, as well as claiming that the display would offer succour to America's 'enemies': 'their conduct must have delighted the Communists and all who hope for signs of degradation and decline in the United States'.[33]

Marilyn Monroe was sent to galvanize the troops – with what? She was an American. Was she 'American' in that political climate based on her vanilla ice-cream whiteness, for as cultural and film theorist Richard Dyer has argued, 'the ultimate embodiment of the desirable woman' was not only the white woman, 'but the blonde, the most unambiguously white you can get … Blondeness, especially platinum (peroxide) blondness is the ultimate sign of whiteness'.[34] The blonde is 'racially unambiguous'.[35] Monroe was also on offer because of sex. Dyer states: 'The Hollywood blonde body is the limit and promise constructed by the discourses of white phallo-supremacy'.[36] Where sex and race intersect, the blonde plays a role in the recirculation of the white lady/dark lady opposition, itself mapped on to oppositions of light/dark, good/evil, chaste/sexual: 'the blonde woman comes to represent not only the most desired of women but also the most womanly [read: chaste] of women'.[37] This in turn hinges upon a contradiction.

In *The Sadeian Woman*, British novelist Angela Carter argues that the 1950s blonde embodied in figures such as Marilyn Monroe contained a Sadeian paradox. Because a woman's success in Hollywood was first and foremost about sex, while a woman's success in America was first and foremost about virtue, a tension arose in the 1950s that produced 'The Good Bad Girl, the blonde buxom, sorority of Saint Justine, whose most unfortunate martyr was Marilyn Monroe'.[38] Carter discerned in Monroe a physical fragility that is the conscious disguise of masochism: perhaps too dependent on later knowledge of her life, or rather her death, this reading nonetheless makes us attend to the violence involved in putting a half-clad woman out in freezing weather to be ogled by sex-starved killing men: soldiers. A complex web of racial and sexual politics within the classic narratives of gender – men look while women watch themselves being looked at – was enacted when the Hottest Lady performed in the Coldest Zone.

She was offered to the killing men as a sex symbol. What does that mean?

She is a symbol of sex. She is not a symbol of her sex, and certainly not of her own sexuality. As Luce Irigaray has argued, in phallocentric society there is only one sex of which anyone can be a symbol. There is, Irigaray revealed through her detailed analysis of the history of Western philosophy up to and including psychoanalysis, only one sex and its other, i.e. that which is not one, not the one. The one sex is masculine. Indeed, the very idea of sex is established in the gesture that produces the masculine as the one.

In the phallic economy woman is a displaced sign of his/this one sex. Representation of the sexual in what Irigaray punningly terms *hom(m)o-sexual* logic involves the deformation and transformation of the woman's body into a commodity (exchange value) that circulates in a masculine economy of exchange secured psychically by the translation of the feminine body as a fetish for the Phallus – the one signifier that is also the signifier of the one (sex).[39] Reworked through codes of dress, hair, make-up and nowadays body sculpting through exercise, dieting and cosmetic surgery, woman's body as image, however, signifies masculine anxiety about a possible sexual difference (his misinterpretation of her body as lacking). This castration anxiety incited by the possible sight of woman is deferred through the psychic defence of fetishistic scopophilia: costuming and cosmetically covering up the danger of feminine otherness so that, remade as image, 'she' presents a perfect and reassuring surface. The beautiful mask is, however, double-edged. While allaying the fear that sexual difference inspires, fetishism continually marks the very spot of the anxiety of difference. It veils what remains menacingly hidden: displacing and yet intensifying the threat of what is concealed beneath that glossy packaging. Pandora's box suggests the oscillating movement between surface and interior, between masculine subject and that which, as its other, can never cease to provoke his anxiety and refashioning as image.

The images of Marilyn Monroe being refashioned from a pretty brunette factory worker into *the* peroxide blonde sex symbol of the 1950s are so familiar and so much part of the cultural sign systems that signify US-America in the 1950s, and feed a pervasive nostalgia for that moment, that perhaps we no longer see the violence implied in the manufacture of that beautiful image that Warhol aesthetically canonized in his pantheon of modern fame and death and that, in his painting *Woman I* (fig. 6.1), de Kooning radically eviscerated and exploded. Trained to keep her red lips lowered over her teeth so that her smile would not be too gummy, and her eyelids perpetually drooping, the actor Marilyn Monroe worked hard cosmetically to perfect the mask that would promise some ineffable pleasure from what constantly breaks through the icon as something else, what I shall term her *riant* loveliness (fig. 2.16).[40]

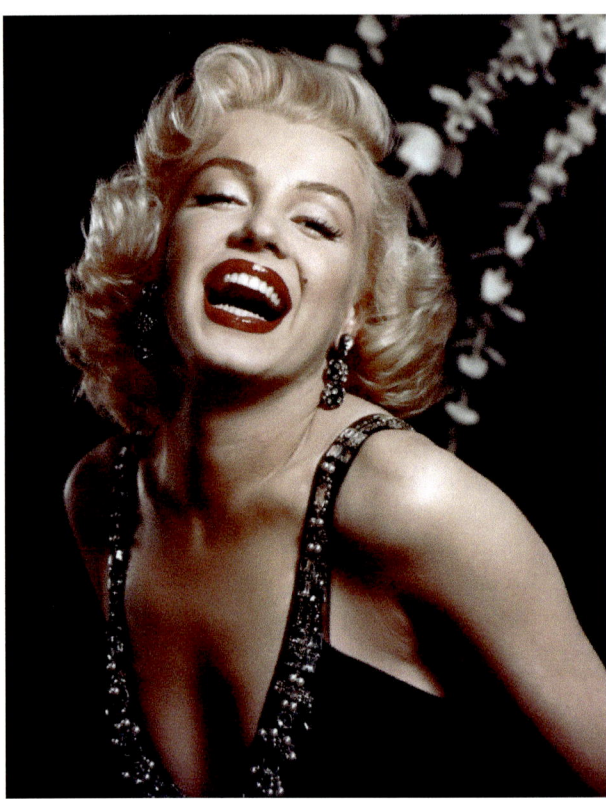

Figure 2.16 Michael Ochs,
Marilyn Monroe, c. 1953

The artifice of this modern-day Coppelia becomes more vividly out-
lined (and differentiated) in the attempted reproduction of her fabrication
by the other blondes of the 1950s. In 1959 Hollywood director Frank Tashlin made a parody of 1950s gender politics of the image in a movie-cartoon
starring a simulacrum of Marilyn Monroe: Jayne Mansfield. Mansfield
played with her role as sex symbol with knowing irony, exposing the
extremity of this artificially manufactured sexual automaton called the
blonde sex symbol, while the script brings out the utter contradiction in
which Angela Carter saw a modern version of Justine: woman as the sex
symbol and woman as domestic servant. In a famous scene set to the music
of 'The Girl Can't Help It', Mansfield, strapped into a figure-exaggerating
black suit, visits the down-and-out talent promoter whom her rich, former
crime boss boyfriend has hired to make her a star. While he recovers from
an alcoholic haze, she dons an apron and cooks the perfect breakfast, while
saying that she does not want a career but longs to be a wife and a mother –
'while everyone keeps on taking me for a sex symbol'. Tashlin's visual joke
of the busty Mansfield clutching two bottles of milk in front of her uplifted
breasts plays off the Justine/Sade that Carter identified within the Monroe
legend itself (figs 2.17a and 2.17b).

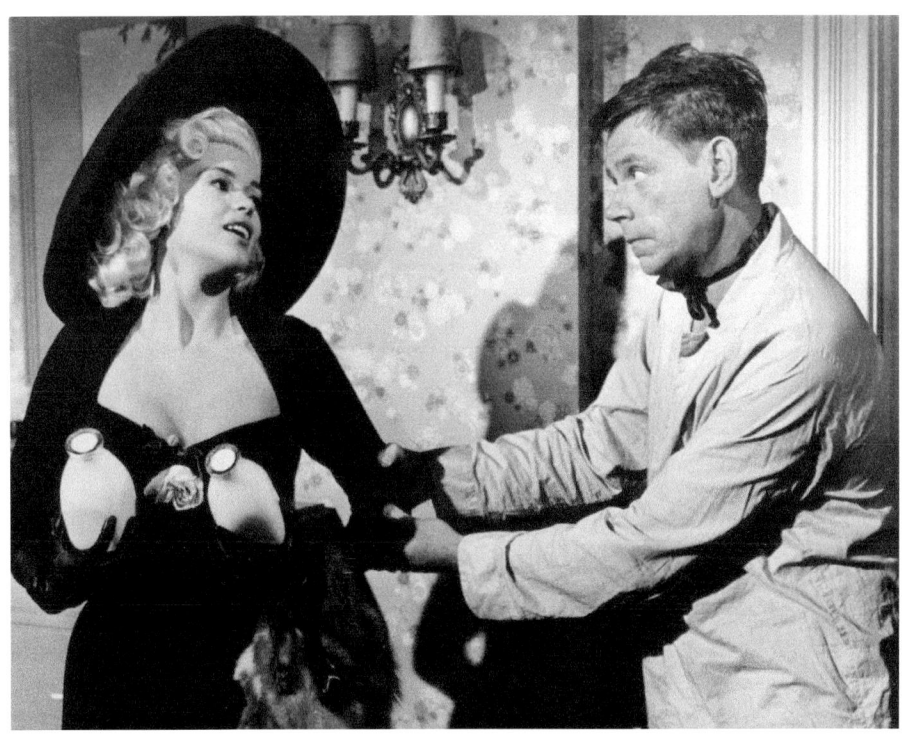

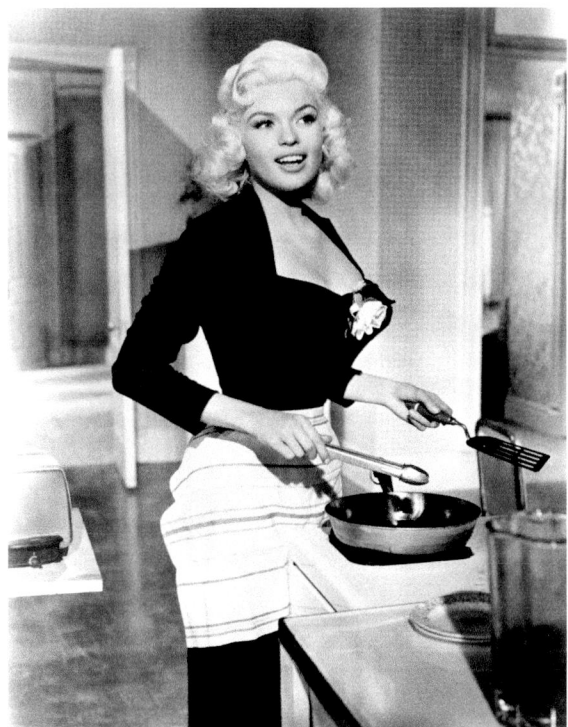

Figure 2.17a&b Jayne Mansfield
in *The Girl Can't Help It*, 1956

V The most famous living American artist

Why did the American government not send the most famous living American artist to Korea to galvanize the troops? In August 1949 *Life* magazine ran an article on Jackson Pollock under this headline, 'Is he the greatest living painter in the United States?', featuring a photograph by Arnold Newman of the artist in paint-splattered denims with a cigarette dangling from his lips, standing in front of his recently completed drip painting, *Summertime* (figs 2.18 and 8.4).[41]

Fellow New York artist Willem de Kooning commented when he saw the article: 'Look at him standing there, he looks like some guy who works at a service station pumping gas.' Abstract painter Budd Hopkins is reported as saying:

> He had everything. He was the great American painter. If you conceive of such a person, first of all, he had to be a real American, not a transplanted European. And he should have big Macho American virtues – he should be rough and tumble American – taciturn ideally – and if he is a cowboy so much the better. Certainly not an Easterner, not someone who went to Harvard. He shouldn't be influenced by the Europeans so much as he should be influenced by our own – the Mexicans, the American Indians and so on. He should come out of native soil – a man who comes up with his own thing. And he should be allowed the great American vice, the Hemingway vice, of being a drunk. It's no wonder that he had a popular *Life* magazine success, because he was so American and unique, and quirky and he had this great American face. Everything about him was right.[42]

Pollock also appeared in film and photography. Hans Namuth photographed him at work during the summer of 1950 and then began two films, with Paul Falkenberg, past associate of German directors G. W. Pabst and Fritz Lang, in the autumn of 1950, the first in black and white of Pollock painting in his cold barn at The Springs, East Hampton, and then in colour

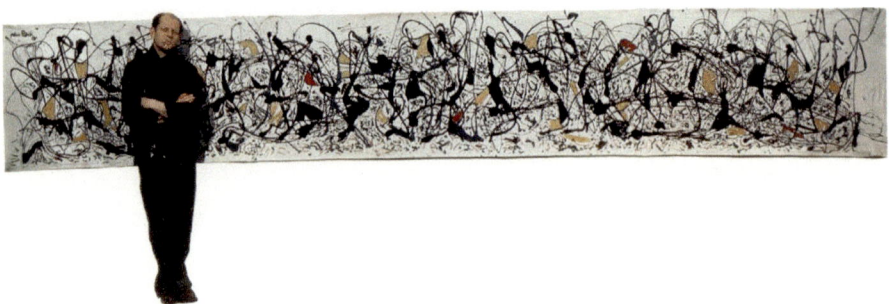

Figure 2.18 Arnold Newman, *Abstract Expressionist painter Jackson Pollock next to his painting Number 9, New York, 3 January 1949*, from *Life magazine*, 8 August 1949

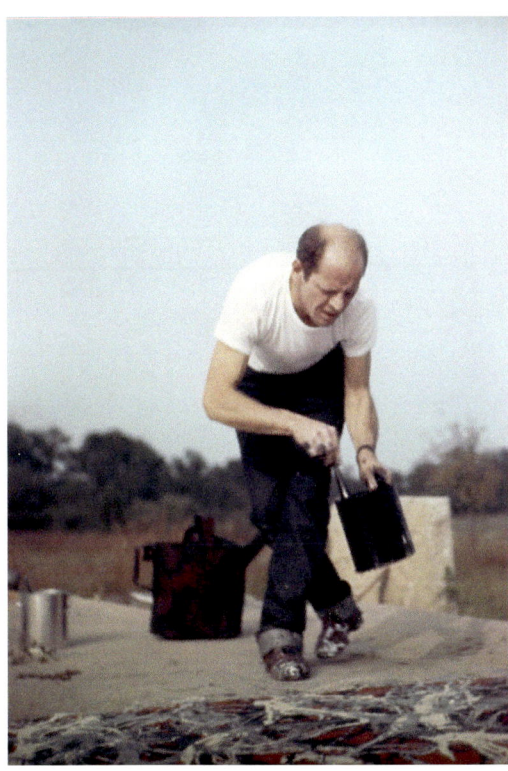

Figure 2.19 Hans Namuth, *Pollock working outside,* still from *Jackson Pollock*, film, 1950

including some famous outdoor shots (fig. 2.19).[43] The film was premiered at the Museum of Modern Art in June 1951 and at a festival in Woodstock in August of the same year. It was not well received. These images failed to present the expected iconography of the artist. Yet both films and photographs offer us a crucial kind of access to the problem of sexual difference and painting precisely in this failure to coincide with the prevailing representation of the modern artist.

As photo documentaries, Namuth's photographs locate Pollock's performance in a totally different space from that of Monroe's (fig. 2.20). It is the unheated but interior space of the converted barn studio on Pollock's and Krasner's homestead at The Springs, East Hampton, Long Island, a seemingly private place where the artist works alone with his materials. Despite contemporary critical failure, Namuth's images can be placed – if deviantly – in a significant genealogy of modern art. Indeed, they figure a key development in both modern painting itself and in supplementary writing on the artists. In early modernism, art was made visible in images of the painter at work. Art historian Carol Duncan identified as a major trope of early twentieth-century vanguardism the iconography of the artist in the studio that confirmed the artist as *symbol of art* as surely as Marilyn Monroe was made by cinema still and pin-up into a *symbol of*

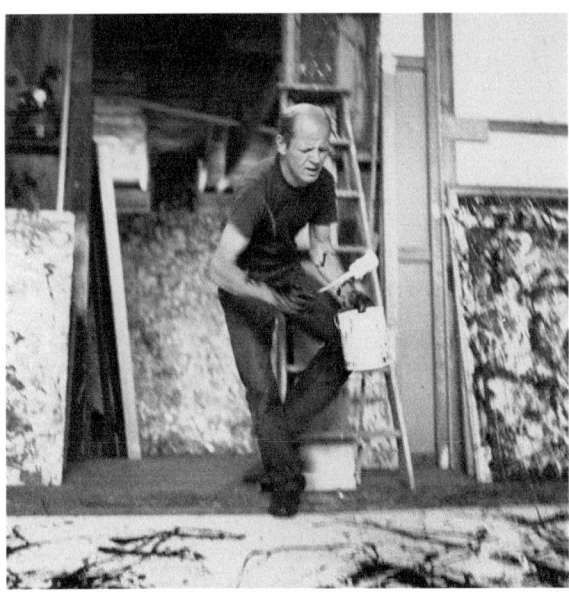

Figure 2.20 Hans Namuth,
*Pollock in his studio, The
Springs*, 1950

sex.[44] Following a genealogy from Matisse's numerous scenes of artist and
model in the studio through to Kirchner and many others, Namuth translated painting's trope into photography and film. While the model –
woman, nude, working-class or black – was a necessary element in early
twentieth-century statements of masculine artistic identity, the figuration
of the feminine seems to disappear in Namuth's images of Pollock painting. Is this just the end of figuration? Or does the feminine get translated
into other, nature, source, becoming an invisible psychic antagonist now
absorbed into/as the canvas, the space around which he moves and which
he ultimately covers/smothers with his moving, dancing body's casts of
paint and marks of his body, such as handprints?

In her identification of the politics of the representation of the artist
in the studio in early modernist painting, Duncan exposed the insistent
masculinization and sexualization of modern art at the level of its actual
practices, its key representations and painterly strategies, and its symbolic
self-representation. Iterative scenes of the artist in the studio, Duncan
argues, offered to the viewer and potential buyer bourgeois fantasies of
masculine freedom through vicarious access in the image to the unli-
censed sexuality of the artist painting the violently exposed and animal-
ized female nude. Usually the artist man is clothed, while the model,
prototypically a woman, is naked, often supine, in some gracelessly
uncomfortable position. In rare cases, such as Matisse's *The Painter in his
Studio* (1917, Centre Pompidou, Paris), the masculine nudity of the upright
artist at work signifies something different from the saturated sexuality of
the female nude. Rectitude and Apollonian intelligence and creativity are

confirmed by what is on the easel in front of the seated painter, namely his abstracting and formally decorative recreation of the brute material of the faceless female model/matter in the corner of his studio.

Such painting is a palimpsest of three orders defining Western art-making in the modern era. It generates a sexual hierarchy figured by this juxtaposition of two bodies in space – the painter's body (art) and the feminine body (its other: matter or nature). The first signifies the act of creation, the other mere matter in a creative process moving from materiality or nature to art.[45] Tradition lacks the image of *the creative woman's body at work*.

Namuth's photographs of Pollock – perhaps because these images made him *the* sign of the 'body of the painter' of the modernist century – frame his body and activity not as the studio, a social space of encounter between culture (the artist and his work) and its resource (nature/woman/other), but as an encounter with the canvas from which the other as object has apparently been banished – *eliminated* in Greenberg's theory or *obliterated* in Bataille's terms. The unframed and uncut canvas on the floor receives the flurry of his gestures that mark the artist's presence. These gestures engender a Dionysian rather than an Apollonian masculine creativity – as suggested in Matisse's prototypical modernist image. A legacy is, however, surely there in the potency and activity of the masculine body now directly mastering a field of canvas that has subsumed into its uncharted space the once necessary feminine object, the sign of painting's referent to that *from which* art is made because art is its master. Pollock patterns the canvas's displacing and condensed surface with his signature, creating an overlaying lid, screen or perhaps opaque mirror with his painted, or dripped, even for some 'urinated' inscriptions as he dances around its immense, inviting but also threatening expanse.[46]

A feature film, titled *Pollock*, directed by and starring Ed Harris in the title role was released in 2000. In its exploration of the emergence and self-destruction of the painter, there is a long scene, set in Krasner and Pollock's cramped New York apartment, after Pollock has been commissioned to create a mural by his dealer Peggy Guggenheim for her apartment. Unrolling a length of unprimed canvas, Pollock assembles the battens for its enormous stretcher. Alone for days and nights, the painter contemplates this terrifyingly vast, empty whiteness. Prolonged inactivity captures the sense of terror at beginning. Any mark on that self-contained infinity of possibilities, the canvas, could either enable or destroy any further marks or gestures. In a rush of activity after long paralysis, Pollock leaps into action by moving along the canvas making large, repeating gestures with a heavily loaded brush dipped into an industrial-sized can of black paint. These abstracted, looping standing figures take possession of the canvas along the line of his movement. The 'dance', the rhythm, the repeats of these sweeping gestures continue with different colours and densities until – the film then jump-cutting to the almost completed work – we witness Pollock painting in solid colour to fill the interstices of the intricate filaments of his layered, serial markings. This segment brilliantly, if unwittingly, represents the Bataillean psycho-drama that a 'Pollock' painting repeatedly performs.

I am not going to suggest something so crude as that the canvas now equals woman. Rather I want to suggest the possibility that the structural relations between artist–world–art involved a mediating term for which the nude female model had stood in symbolic explorations of the act of making art in the early modernist moment. This structure is both a product of, and the condition for, a historically particular ordering of sexual difference articulated through this symbolic site: the studio.[47] Abstract painting of the kind Pollock invented seemingly banished that middle term, to leave us with both a practice and a representation of that practice that sets up a dyadic reflexivity between painter and painting.

The woman's body disappears, becoming, however, a lingering trace of a structurally necessary other that was projected now, as one of many dimensions and associations, on to the space of inscription – the canvas. That surface/space becomes both *mirror* in which the artist will inscribe himself by signature mark, and *screen* that veils, but does not disappear entirely, the historic other, *Woman*. Instead of the painting registering the process of artistic transformation of something in the world, a referent of a different order – the canvas – becomes the support for marks that immediately make it, the canvas, at the same time the other to the artist's mark. The canvas-other is involved both formally (as material surface) and psychically (as virtual space) in a dialectic with the painted trace. The canvas becomes either the field of action (Rosenberg) or the support of paint (Greenberg), and the surface for semiotic inscription as much as a screen for the projection of fantasy. It plays several roles in this art of worldly renunciation. Across such registers, we need to recognize traces of the other (historically coded as feminine and once figured through the female body) that had been structural, as Carol Duncan argued, to the self-conception of the virility of modernist art in its pre-abstract stages, and that, paradoxically, becomes all the less mastered and more terrifying by disappearing into the infinite otherness of the unrolled sheet/space of the unprimed canvas.

For artist-women, the modernist genealogy of the artist-man in the studio posed, therefore, a conundrum in both its earlier figurative and later sublimated, abstract form. Women also desired to be part of the modernist adventure. They longed also to be the labouring, creative body in the discrete space of the studio and to make their mark on the canvas as the field of their other. The desire stems from, and will inevitably trace somehow, what it means to exist within the experiential parameters of a feminine body that the polarity – body of the painter (art) and feminine body (matter/nature) – cannot accommodate without a third term: the *creative woman's body*. Thus, once we include women as artists in the art history of abstract gestural painting, this ideological field becomes triangulated: the painter's body – the creative act; the feminine body – the mediating sign of art's other (figured or abstractly deferred); and the contestation of their asymmetrical duet through the emergent discourses and practices of what the modernist women's struggle in art led us to explore – 'the creative woman's psyche-soma'.

This raises the so-far unspoken question of what other, imaginary or phantasy body lies screened behind the hetero-phallocratic myth of Woman as Pandora, or Nature, or Matter, against which the creative masculine artist erects himself. Is it not the maternal-other-psyche-body that is the condition of and was once a shared space for all of us who have come into life and have been born, who all carry into post-natal existence the aesthetic-sensory legacies of the pre-natal sojourn within and with maternal body-space? These have been impressed into us both *proto-psychically* – in late pre-natality we have developed a proto-psyche through the sensed affects of an unknown but subjectivizing other – and *aesthetically* – in later pre-natality we are sensate, garnering impressions of sound, movement, rhythm and even light. These are shared by all born subjects, irrespective of later formations of gender or sexuality. Artist Bracha L. Ettinger terms this other of the late pre-natal/pre-maternal pair, the *m/Other*. Post-natally, the Mother becomes the third term in the Oedipal triangle, in which each child has to confront the question of sexual difference: who and what am I if one comes from two? Once Oedipally subjectivized and sexuated as masculine or feminine subjects by adopting one or other of the positions that gendered language and culture dictate, we relate to the Mother differently. The sameness/otherness split operates in reverse.

The question of identity and singularity for women is: who am I if I am like her; whereas for the masculinized subject it is: who am I if I am not like her? Phallocentrism's answer, for men, has been to deny any but nugatory significance to the maternal, recasting human co-becoming as the insignificant matter of biological cooking in a later abhorred and abjected interior, the womb, associated with tomb rather than with enlivening and aesthetic co-emergence and borderspacing. Oedipally, any woman as subject negotiates, later and as well, an inescapable question of the Other Woman even as both Mother and Other Woman are cast, phallically, as Other.

The project for modernist artist-women of the 1940s–1970s was to realize the third term – the creative woman's body-psyche negotiating this other woman in the field of abstract painting with gesture on canvas that would play itself out across a historically produced cultural field, bisected and overdetermined by another dissymmetry: the sex symbol and the symbol of the artist standing in and for opposing domains in culture. By the 1950s things have changed. Woman is, culturally, the symbol of sex – not the Virgin Mother – and that sex she symbolizes is not her own. As symbol of sex, Woman is definitively not Nature: the blonde bombshell was as artificial, as fabricated, and thus as fetishized as one can get. She stands as the polar opposite of that which was inversely elevated as the real, the true, the authentic, the creative – the disciplines and intensities of autogenetic modern artistic masculinity.[48]

Between, therefore, these two incommensurate icons of the 1950s, Marilyn Monroe and Jackson Pollock, structural binaries appear reified: high art and popular culture, painting and cinema, art and commodity, authenticity and artifice, masculinity and femininity. Between their opposition and iteration, which was also a structural complementarity, painting – as opposed to dying – women were caught in dilemmas and riddles posed by the gender polarities of that culture, which were inevitably the very form of these many divisions. I suggest that we dismantle the walls segregating areas of social practice to track what Foucault called the discursive regularities that constitute the formations of gender, class and race between high and low, elite and mass, because they all end up meeting in *Life* – the magazine. My question is what would it be to be a painter-woman caught in the inevitable web of these two representational scenes of diametrically opposite and yet mutually confirming symbols: a symbol of art and a symbol of sex? Both served to symbolize each element as one, and that one was the masculine. For both were symbols within a single system: a white, heterocratic, phallocentric imperializing culture that denied, however, any symbolic or representational support to the subjectivities and aesthetic inscriptions of diversely creative femininities. In the pre-1968 (if also post-1928) feminist moment that was the 1950s it was clear that to aspire to be an artist meant the total negation, not of being a woman, but of being Woman, while, at the same time, being a woman meant it was not likely that anyone would recognize you as an artist, however much or well you painted.

Marilyn Monroe played her part in the Cold War when she played to the troops in Korea. Her movies and her image, however, were also an integral part of a projected Americanism, an excruciatingly sexist, white, heterocratic, culturally imperializing world. Since the 1970s there has been plenty of evidence for Abstract Expressionism's role in the art politics of that same war, since Eva Cockcroft first called 'Abstract Expressionism [a] Weapon of the Cold War'.[49] Another instance of killing men, artists were recruited as cultural soldiers in the fight against communism. Some have argued that the ideologies that sustained abstract painting corresponded with those promoted by Cold War cultural warriors' notions of American-bred ideologies of freedom, individualism, pioneering and risk taking. Others defend the political neutrality of the art and accuse institutions such as the museums of Modern and American Art and their corporate magnate owners and backers, the Rockefellers and Whitneys, of cynically using the artists' work in their Cold War programmes to convince the Free World of the legitimate claims of American economic and cultural imperialism and the economic and political hegemony it served.

Whatever the metaphorics of interpretation which have evolved to locate this kind of work in its social and historical context, and whichever school of thought we look to, be that formalist art history or the social history of art, the issue of gender and the Cold War is rarely raised in dealing with the culture produced in the 1950s. Sealed off from its popular other, painting has been so insulated that a false universalism that is, in fact, unacknowledged masculinism has remained unquestioned. If we jump forward to the 1980s, the politics of sexual difference in the 1950s escaped the ideological freezer of the Cold War to be retrospectively revealed in the discourse of the daughters revolting against this painting. Both Cindy Sherman (b. 1954) and Barbara Kruger (b. 1945) resource their practice from not just the imagery but the very feel and sensibility of the cinematic and medial sexual politics of the 1950s, which is so vivid in its popular cultural forms: Kruger referencing the graphic design and red on black and white colour system of *Life* magazine, while Sherman explored with both pathos and discomforting ambivalence the uncanniness of the femininities of her mother's generation in the 1950s as they were figured in both US-American Hollywood and European art cinema.

None of these imaged femininities created from Cindy Sherman's wardrobe and make-up box rediscover, however, an image of *creativity in the feminine*, the position Nicky Bird sought to extract from her painting as performance (fig. 2.1). Relentlessly cinematic, Sherman's *Untitleds* confirm Laura Mulvey's analysis of woman as the very sign of cinema, and cinema as an articulation of woman as spectacle, fetish and commodity. Surface, artifice and dangerous mystery, each one seemingly different yet all ultimately the same.[50] Where is there any evidence of artist-women's sustained contribution and diverse challenges to the problematics of high modernism in that crucial decade of the 1950s? How in the era of diverted speech and repressed reference did gender signify in the Cold Zone of Hot Painting?

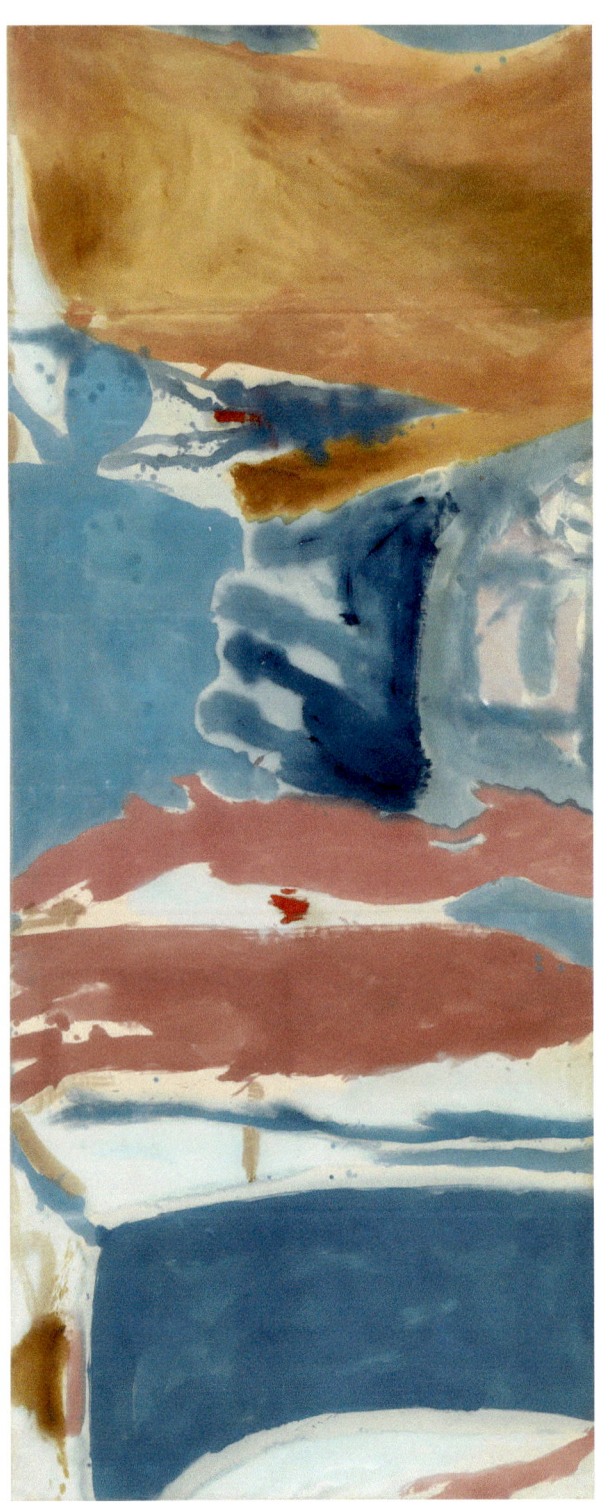

Figure 3.1 Helen Frankenthaler, *Open Wall*, 1953

What did Greenberg not say, or dare to think?

Artists continually introduce into culture all kinds of Trojan horses from the margins of their consciousness; in that way, the limits of the Symbolic are transgressed all the time by art. It is quite possible that many work-products carry subjective traces of their creators, but the specificity of works of art is that their materiality cannot be detached from ideas, perceptions, emotions, consciousness, cultural meaning, etc., and that being interpreted and reinterpreted is their cultural destiny. This is one of the reasons why works of art are symbologenic. Artists inscribe traces of subjectivity, Oedipal or not, in 'external' cultural/symbolic territories (i.e. artworks), and by analysing these inscriptions, it is possible to create and forge concepts which indicate and elaborate traces of an-other Real and to change aspects of the symbolic representation (and non-representation) of the feminine within culture.

Bracha L. Ettinger, 1992[1]

Clement Greenberg did not say anything much about artists who were women.[2] This was, and still is, pretty devastating, given his significance as one of the most articulate and influential critical voices of the US-American moment of modernism in New York between 1940 and 1970. Helen Frankenthaler (fig. 3.1) merits a passing mention in his article about Morris Louis and Ken Noland in 1960 as a bridge between Pollock and the colour field painters.[3] Lee Krasner gets a putdown in another. Georgia O'Keeffe (1887–1986) is viciously reviewed. Hedda Sterne (1910–2011) is called 'a piece of femininity' and 'nothing more than a delicate sensibility'. The Washington DC-based sculptor Anne Truitt (1921–2004) gets an article of reasonable length in *Vogue* which, however, Greenberg concludes with – ironically or seriously – a few revealing lines:

She remains less known than she should be as a radical innovator. She certainly does not 'belong'. But then how could a housewife with three small children, living in Washington belong? How could such a person fit the role of pioneer of far-out art?[4]

Greenberg did offer Lee Krasner an exhibition in 1959 – but only on the grounds of what he thought she would and should continue to paint, because he had genuinely admired the collaged paintings shown at the Stable Gallery in 1955 (fig. 7.4–7.5), considering them, though never declaring so in print, a major development in painting at the time. He did not approve of the series that she offered him in 1959 as her latest work, the *Umbers* – large-scale, gesturally expressive, monochrome, dynamic and intense (fig. 0.1). Krasner refused to exhibit on such authoritarian terms. Through Greenberg's arrogance and her justified pride in her own decisions as an artist, her work was not seen in 1959 under his imprimatur as arbiter of what constituted '"American-Type" painting'.[5] The series was instead exhibited at the Howard Wise Gallery, New York, in 1960. Greenberg's silence meant that the moves Krasner was making – which are at the heart of this book's study – did not enter into art criticism and hence art history *in their own moment*.

Greenberg's negligence was, however, being challenged at the time by the very same *Life* editor who had written about Jackson Pollock for *Life* in 1949, hailing him as 'the greatest living American painter' (fig. 2.18). Dorothy Seiberling (1922–2019) wrote an article in 1957 for *Life*, titled 'Women Artists in Ascendance' (13 May 1957), illustrated with photographs by Gordon Parks of five artists (figs 3.2 and 3.3). The opening spread showed Helen Frankenthaler demurely seated on the floor, posed *on* one of her own (possibly stretched) paintings *Blue Territory* (1955), while we can just glimpse the breakthrough painting *Mountains and Sea* (1952) on the wall to her right (fig. 3.5). She appears engulfed in her work as if it were a décor, matching the tonalities of the paintings with her soft pink and white outfit. Dressed in bold style and colour, Grace Hartigan is pictured on a windowsill beside *Orchard Street* (1957), one of her large and still abstract paintings with which her black slacks and rust-red sweater blend, while Joan Mitchell is also shown seated on the floor, almost disappearing into the energetically marked paintings that surround her. Jane Wilson (1924–2015) reclines on a chaise-longue, clothed, in a posture echoing the painting of a sprawled nude on the wall behind her. Nell Blaine is also seated in the ground, looking moodily at a work on the floor in front of her. None of them are at work. All are carefully posed in a studio that becomes a stage set in which carefully dressed women blend into their own paintings, telling us nothing about their practices. Hardly ascendant, the choice to seat all the artist-women visually inscribes their 'lowness'. To create proportions in which the set reduces the size of the artist, to colour code their clothes with their works as in a fashion spread, insistently and symptomatically undermines the apparent purpose of Seiberling's title. Pastel in tone, passive in position, the intent to present women who are artists is rerouted into creating images of young women *with* art in terms in which their ownership or creative making of such art is dissipated: a gendered/gendering political unconscious at work.

In 1977 I collaborated on a range of projects for a social history of art with my colleague Fred Orton, jointly teaching the course/seminar

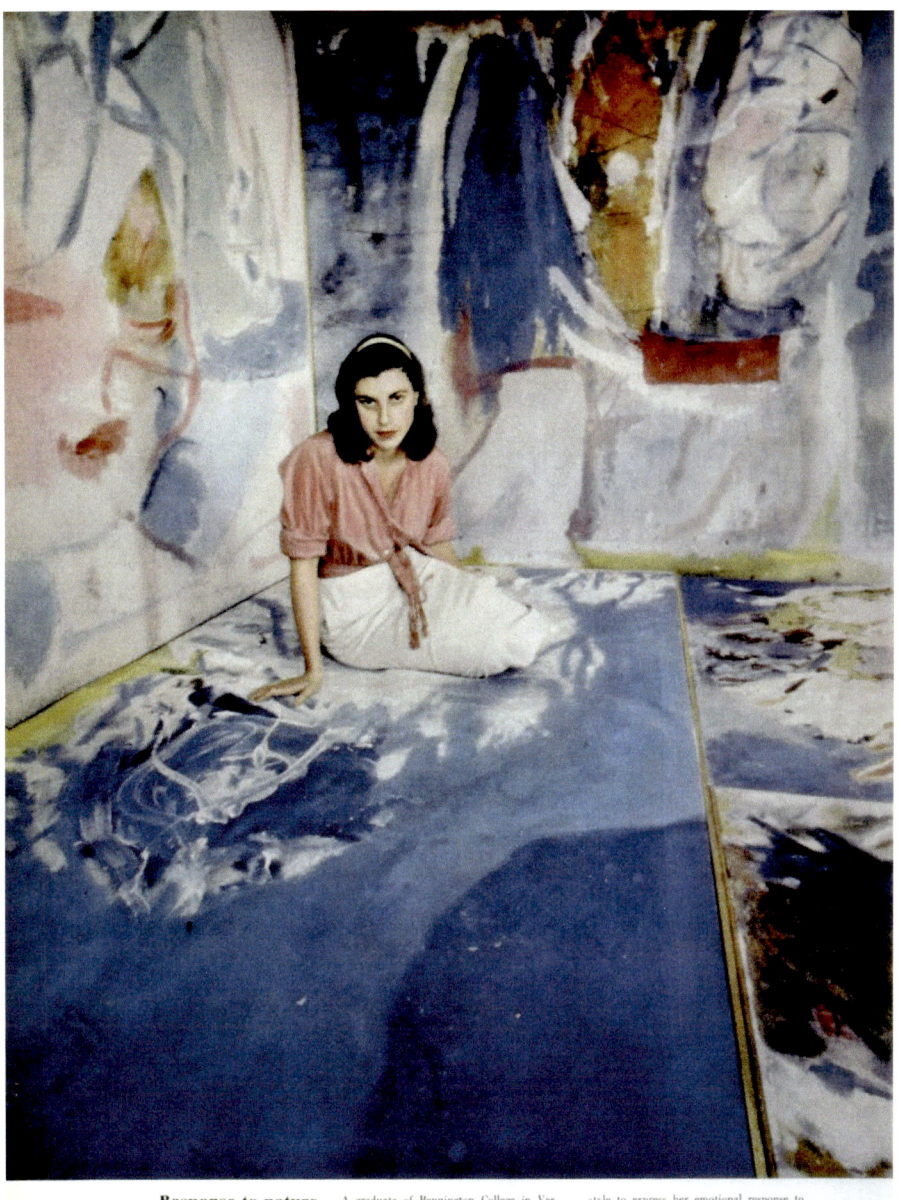

Response to nature A graduate of Bennington College in Vermont, Helen Frankenthaler started painting realistic landscapes, moved toward an abstract style to express her emotional response to nature. In New York studio she spreads painting on floor, often works in middle of it.

Figure 3.2a Gordon Parks, *Helen Frankenthaler from 'Women Artists in Ascendance', Life magazine*, 13 May 1957

Women Artists in Ascendance

YOUNG GROUP REFLECTS LIVELY VIRTUES OF U.S. PAINTING

In the art-filled centuries of the past, women rarely took up serious careers as painters or sculptors. Of the daring few who did, barely a handful achieved any lasting stature. In America, where during the 19th Century every well-bred young lady learned to while away idle moments painting pious scenes and sedate still lifes, art as a profession was left to men. Today the picture has changed. A sizable and remarkable group of young women is resolutely at work and their art is being sought by leading museums, galleries and collectors.

This movement has been building up ever since Philadelphian Mary Cassatt pioneered in the field before the turn of the century. Subsequently, artists like Georgia O'Keeffe, Loren MacIver and I. Rice Pereira earned significant reputations. But the real advance came in the 1940s when, paralleling their achievements in other professions, women in growing numbers began to distinguish themselves as artists.

On these pages LIFE presents five of the outstanding young women painters in the U.S. None over 35, they work in the varied styles that characterize the lively American art scene and have won acclaim not as notable women artists but as notable artists who happen to be women.

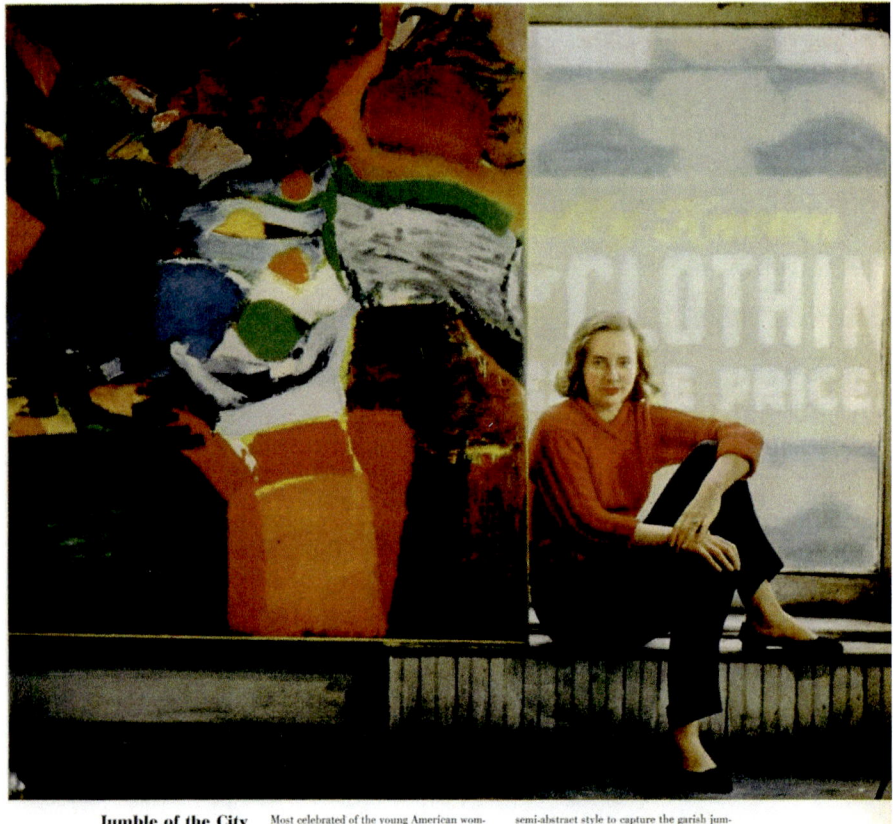

Jumble of the City   Most celebrated of the young American women painters, Grace Hartigan, who comes from Newark, N.J., has developed a brilliantly bold, semi-abstract style to capture the garish jumble and excitement of the market district of New York's lower East Side where she lives.

CONTINUED

Figure 3.2b   Gordon Parks, *Grace Hartigan from 'Women Artists in Ascendance', Life magazine*, 13 May 1957

'Readings in American Culture and Society in the 1950s'. Throughout the decade we co-taught and wrote collaboratively. Yet it never felt possible for me to integrate into this programme the feminist work I was concurrently doing in a parallel collaboration with Rozsika Parker, with whom, from 1975 to 1979, I was writing *Old Mistresses: Women, Art and Ideology*. Feminist and social histories of art ran in parallel lines without possible convergence.

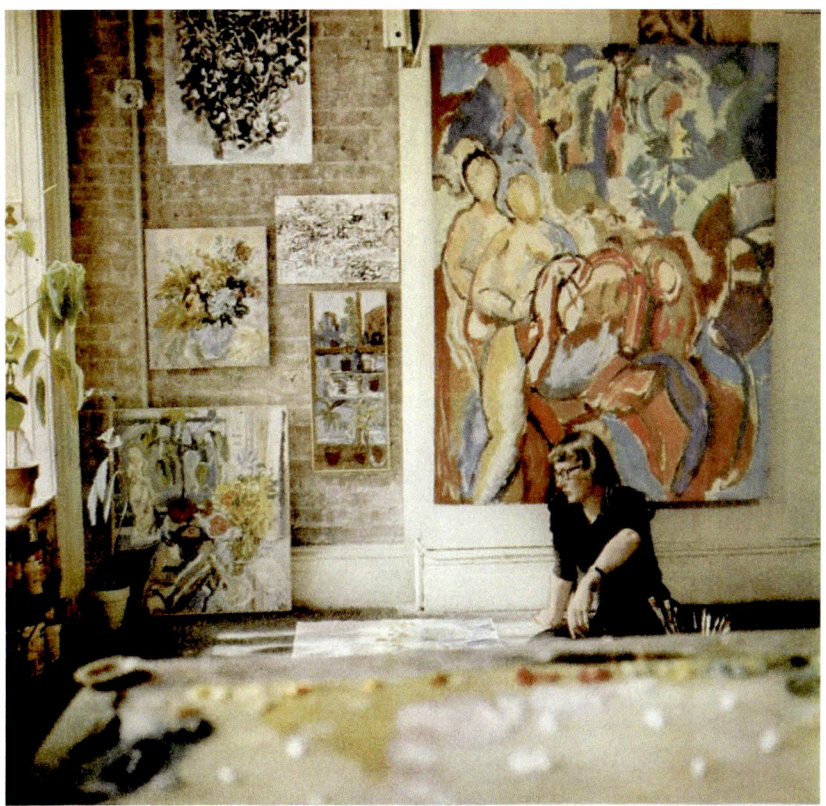

Warmth and light

Enamored of nature and, as she says, "the light around things," Nell Blaine paints outdoor scenes and still lifes at her windows with the exuberant lines and warm tones of a bouquet. From Richmond, Va., she lives in New York and supports herself by doing layout work and teaching painting.

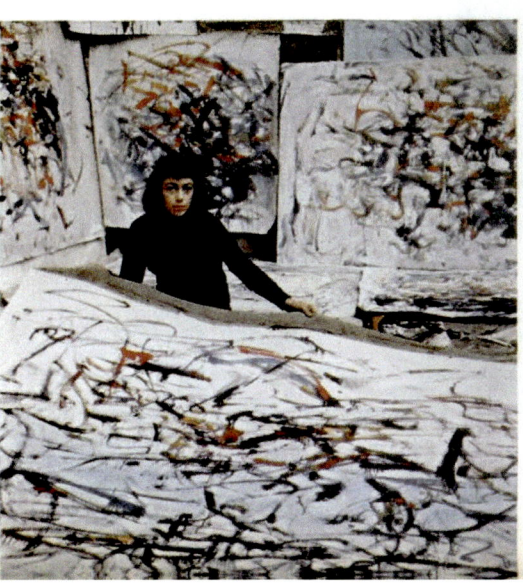

Energetic images

Born in Chicago, Joan Mitchell has become one of the leading young exponents of the abstract-expressionist school. Working in both New York and Paris, she has evolved a spontaneous, complex style to produce energetic images of "remembered landscapes which involve my feelings."

Figure 3.3a Gordon Parks, *Nell Blaine and Joan Mitchell from 'Women Artists in Ascendance', Life magazine*, 13 May 1957

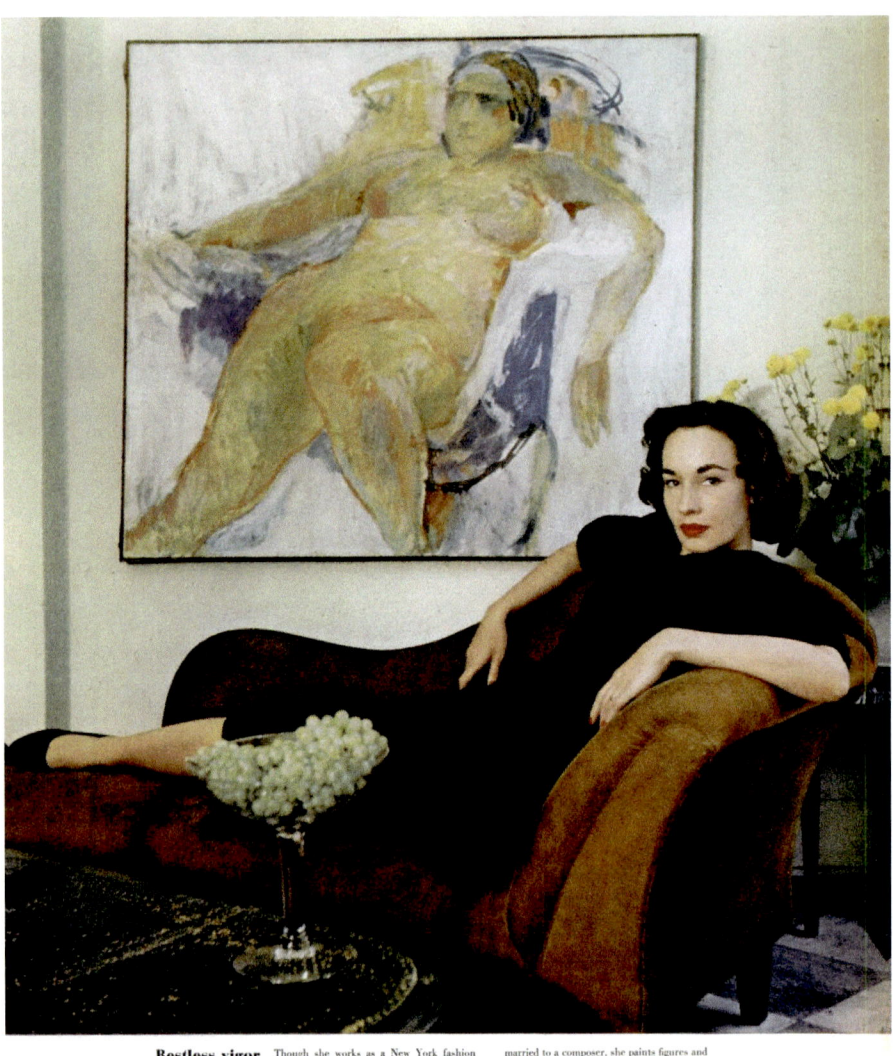

Restless vigor Though she works as a New York fashion   married to a composer, she paints figures and
model, Jane Wilson spends up to eight hours   landscapes suggesting impressionist art but
a day painting. Born in Seymour, Iowa and   with a restless, forthright vigor that is modern.

Figure 3.3b Gordon Parks, *Jane Wilson from 'Women Artists in Ascendance', Life magazine*, 13 May 1957

On 'Readings', we allocated one session on painter Helen Frankenthaler and sculptor Louise Nevelson, accommodated as the set-aside time
for me, the feminist, to talk about my special topic: 'Women in the New
York School'. Of course, the very idea of special sessions segregated the
artist-women from the main trajectory of the course/seminar, and from
the histories and debates that Orton and I were so scrupulously tracking
through the critical writings (Rosenberg and Greenberg) and exhibitions
(Peggy Guggenheim, MoMA, Betty Parsons, The Stable Gallery etc.) that
shaped the institutional accreditation of 'New American Painting' or

'American-type painting' as Abstract Expressionism was variously termed at the time. As subset, a special interest for me, artists such as Hedda Sterne, Grace Hartigan, Joan Mitchell, Elaine de Kooning, Alma Thomas, Lee Krasner, Louise Nevelson, Nell Blaine and Helen Frankenthaler, to name but a few, thus represented *sex*, not *art*. They formed a sexual otherness holding no meaning for the history of art because they were sidelined by the silence in the influential critical texts studied as primary evidence (Greenberg and other critics' writings) and by omission in subsequent museum practices (MoMA, for instance) and absence from art historians' texts (Irving Sandler's monograph *The Triumph of American Painting: A History of Abstract Expressionism*, for instance, was first published in 1970) that formed our main sources for this still very new area of research into then still almost contemporary art.

Photographs

My concurrent feminist research aimed to articulate the relations between subjectivity, art and sexual difference. I also wanted to understand how, and why, the discourses of twentieth-century art history had systematically suppressed knowledge of the modernist artist-women of this very century (let alone all preceding ones). I wanted to place artist-women in lectures on US-American art as part and parcel of their own moment in history, thus changing the all-male canon into an inclusive, diversified and more interesting as well as more faithful picture of modern creative activity. I had studied Hans Namuth's photographs of Pollock painting in 1950 (figs 2.19 and 2.20). Already in *Old Mistresses: Women, Art and Ideology* (which was begun in 1975) and in lectures in 1976 at Leicester Polytechnic before Fred Orton and I both joined the University of Leeds in 1977, I had juxtaposed Namuth's soon-to-become over-famous photographs of Pollock at work with a sequence of Helen Frankenthaler at work taken in 1969 by Ernst Haas (fig. 3.4a–e).[6]

Such photographs are more than documentation or information about how paintings got made. As *images of the painters at work*, they provide a temporal trace of what we could otherwise not see or know because it would have taken place behind closed doors in the working space of the artist, from which the finished painting would emerge to go on exhibition. It is not that the artist had never been the focus of representation before. Since the Renaissance, Western artists have portrayed themselves with or without their artistic tools before their canvases. There are also paintings of studio scenes with painters at work, amid models, students or visitors. What makes these analogue photographs of Pollock and Frankenthaler painting significant is that they index, over a sequence of shots, the *how* of the painting's making at a moment when that *how* had become painting,

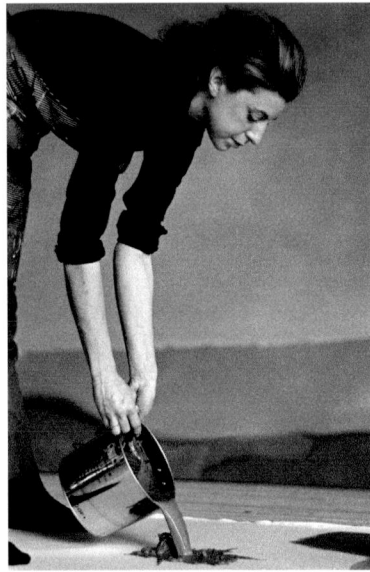
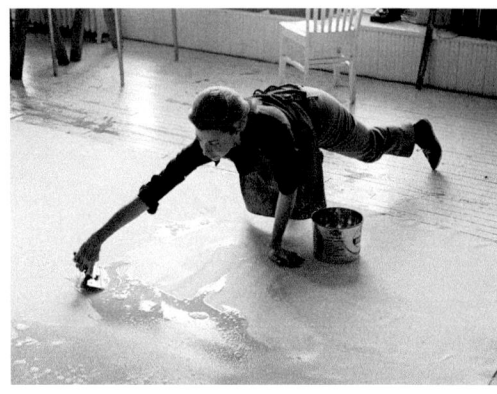
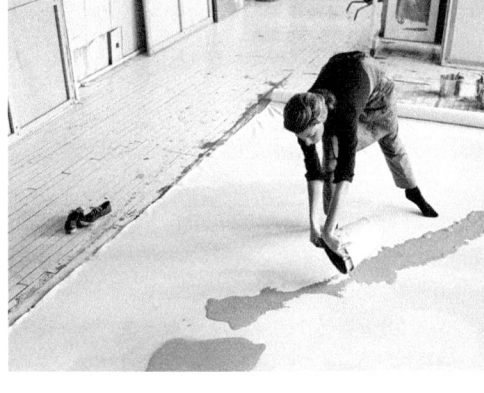
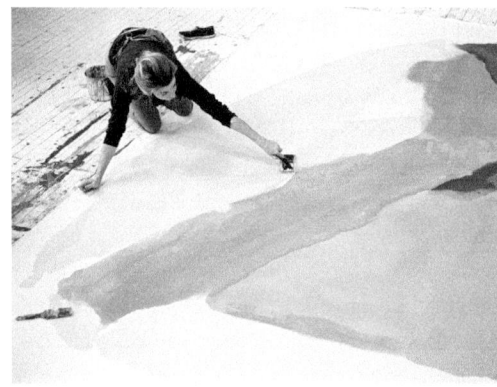
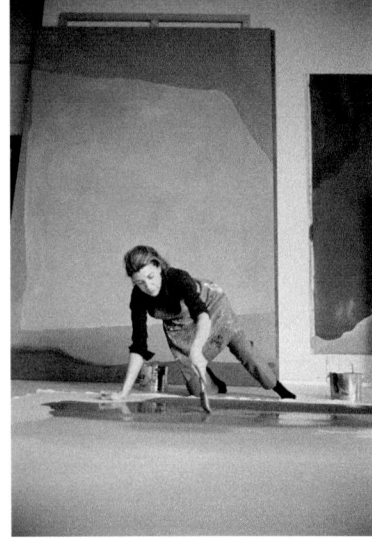

Figure 3.4a–e Ernst Haas, *Helen Frankenthaler working in her studio at East 83rd Street and Third Avenue, New York*, 1969

tout court. The photos capture *the process* by which each painting is becoming, by which each painter is making their paintings, using new procedures such as working on the floor and all over from all angles, their bodies sometimes in/on the canvas space. What we are seeing is not the backstory to the finished work, but the activity that is synonymous with the novel character of painting that their processes *enact*. Their working methods made the making and the painting synonymous at the level of ultimate effect, the effects for which we viewers will then read the paintings and, in a way, experience them as an ongoing event.

Photographs by Namuth and Haas capture the art-historically significant event in which the process of painting itself became the subject of artmaking itself. They visualize a moment in New York painting when the engagement of artist with material, support, body and gesture became the *topic* of as well as the *resource* for each painting practice. In fact, the theorization of what these formal and gestural processes involving the canvas and the body were and did determines our understanding of the movement, its having changed the meaning of artmaking, redefined the artist and extended the potential meanings to be discerned from the deepened relation between the making and both the effects and the affects of *painting*, where painting is not a representation but an event, which in due course opened the very practices of art beyond even the sphere of the unfurled sheets of canvas on and around which the artist performs.[7] Greenberg called this moment 'The Crisis of the Easel Picture'.[8]

Important as this is to grasp, it is not, however, all we are seeing in these photo-performances. In *Old Mistresses: Women, Art and Ideology*, Rozsika Parker and I used the juxtaposition of the two sets of images to pose then heretical, feminist questions. Are we *seeing* difference there because of the difference of each painter's body at work with their singular process of making? Or are we *sensing* difference when viewing the results because of what each painter has done, registering the traces of movements and effects as affects? Are we seeing difference or imposing it? What is being embodied in the very process of this new painting, because the making itself deposits traces of a subjectivized psycho-sexual body's movements and gestures as the artists approach the blank canvas, slowly, dialogically, with materials and each move, change, chance or purposed deposit? What is being brought into existence through movement, pause, gesture, reflection, seeking, touching?

We were not asking if the given and conventional gender characteristics or psychology of each artist as a man or a woman is being *expressed* and is thus *on show* according to viewer preconceptions. Nor were we suggesting that the different kinds of painting are, as a result, stylistically masculine or feminine, again on some fixed, stereotypical register of gender characteristics. We were asking questions about what could be happening in these paintings, given that these photographs enabled us to witness how each was emerging through bodies at work with materials in a radically new way. What is the significance – which I shall elaborate more theoretically in the next chapter – of the different effects of their interaction – body and materials – and the artist's gesture?

I argue that we see and sense all sorts of technical differences at the level of *how* these two sets of paintings have been made. This makes us ponder how we experience specificity before/with/through colour, space and the rhythms of the marks or gestures, and the artists' being with all of that, in a making process that has purposely suspended fully conscious control, intentionality, and does not aim at representation. That is one level where specificity and differencing come into play, as we know that Frankenthaler had a very deep grasp of what Pollock's work had done and had not done, but saw beyond it. She had noticed the impress of his paint seeping through to the reverse of his piled, unframed canvases and perceived that unprimed canvas permitted the staining and soaking of colour into the fabric, thus creating a unity of surface and medium that transcended the existing convention of oil paint *on* canvas. This dispelled canvas as passive support for paint, producing an integrity that perfectly intuited and already practised what Greenberg's thesis on squeezing out the last remnants of fictive space in painting would formally elaborate.

We could also raise this question to a psycho-sexual level by asking what are the *affects* generated by the drama and process of different creative body-psyches at work on or in a field – the canvas on the floor – with heavy paint being applied by splashes, drips and dribbles on the one hand, and on the other, with a body closer to the canvas pouring, smoothing, swiping, stilling, staining with more fluid, thinned paint that, soaking in, becomes one with its support? This is not a matter of activity versus passivity. The making of these works on this scale is a very physical, if not athletic process involving many kinds of movements, eye and hand relations and the mobility of the body around the canvas-field and on and in it. What happens as we seek the words to describe what we now encounter in the photographs and when we return to the paintings by these artists with these images of their making in mind?[9] I shall answer these questions in this chapter, looking for a way to understand difference before, in the next chapter, undermining my argument from another perspective. We need both perspectives.

So, let me pose the question, first, in the following, somewhat obvious terms: do Pollock's slashing and throwing of paint, his dance-like gyrations around or stretching over a supine canvas, enact an unconscious assault upon an imaginary feminine Other – virtually present and absent – as space and canvas? Are the traces of paint on canvas the residues of a masculine psychic performance? Is this *écriture/peinture masculine* at its most vivid?[10]

How, then, might we read Frankenthaler's pouring, pushing, smoothing gestures as she moved around the canvas, stretched across, poured or spread, or knelt near its edge on the canvas as a surface continuous with her space and her body's large, arms-spread movements, or with tiny, precise hand and finger shaping movements, long moments of watching the spread of the fluid while sensing her way to the next movement, spill or touch, as she responded not to what she had done, but to what was happening as paints flowed, stained, met, were pushed or swiped, sponged or skimmed? Does her process tempt us to suggest or even embrace a psycho-corporeally feminine modality – ways of phenomenologically and in phantasy living in a specific, sexuated, body-psyche whose resulting effects on canvas might invite the viewers to summon sexual or gendered metaphors to match to their singular and diverse sensations and perceptions?

Might Frankenthaler's processes and effects be read as *metramorphic*, a term arising from her own painting, and theorized by Bracha L. Ettinger to convey a non-phallic, matrixial modality of subjectivity, meaning and affect that involves what she terms *wit(h)ness*?[11] Ettinger defines *metramorphosis* is as a psycho-aesthetic meaning-engendering process that subverts and shifts the binary I and not-I, mark/no mark, absence/presence distinctions typical of phallocentric meaning-formation. To the phallic mode, metramorphosis would feel like an erosion of the necessary boundaries maintaining distinct identities, tipping art into chaotic formlessness. Ettinger has systematically theorized a supplementary dimension in human subjectivity that she terms the *Matrix*, which she defines as *subjectivity-as-encounter* in *shared borderspace, co-emerging* and *severality*. These are the characteristically paradoxical modes of matrixial *relating-without-relations* between I and *non*-I (rather than the I and *not*-I of the phallic mode). She writes:

> I relate the Matrix to the process I call *metramorphosis* dealing with *I* and *non*-I(*s*) in co-emergence and in co-existence, with neither symmetrical nor identical nor mirroring relationships. These are processes of change without domination. *I* and *non*-I(*s*) may relate to one another or simply turn their backs on one another, but they neither swallow nor kill one another – symbolically or in reality – while transforming in one another's presence. The borderlines between them are surpassed and transformed to become thresholds. When these transformations relate to transformations in the borderlines and in the shared spaces, *metramorphosis* may occur, creating redistribution in the shared field and a change in the common subjectivity. The borderlines between *I* and *non*-I(*s*) are surpassed and transformed to become thresholds. This is a shift aside for the Phallus, offering an-other symbolic filter.[12]

The Matrix is not feminine to the masculine Phallus. Its radicality lies in shifting aside the phallic sovereignty over sexual difference and subjectivity under its opposing plus/minus terms while, paradoxically, positing a primordial non-gendered *sexual difference* encountered by every born person that has to be understood as a *feminine* primary encounter with intimated otherness that occurs in the late pre-natal condition of *severality* with the unknown pre-maternal *partner-in-difference – the legacy of becoming human for every born person irrespective of post-natal gender or sexuality.*

To clarify the coexistence and differentiation between the phallocentric and matrixial dimensions in subjectivity where the matrixial does not distinguish between masculine and feminine but is an originary matrixial feminine, I can designate *the feminine as other*, which I have been discussing in relation to poststructuralism and phallocentric logic, as *feminine^PH* and differentiate it from the *feminine^M* radically theorized by Ettinger through a supplementary dimension of subjectivity whose symbol is the Matrix.[13] She further elaborates the aesthetics of the Matrix and its figure *metramorphosis* (recall that the figures of metaphor and metonymy characterize the phallic):

> Metramorphosis is the process of change in borderlines and thresholds *between* being and absence, memory and oblivion, *I* and *non-I*, a process of transgression and fading away. The metramorphic consciousness has no centre, cannot hold a fixed gaze – or, if it has a centre, it constantly slides to the borderline, to the margins. Its gaze escapes the margins and returns to the margins. Through this process the limits, borderlines, and thresholds conceived are continually transgressed or dissolved, thus allowing the creation of new ones.[14] (my emphasis)

Might the resulting affects – not as expressions but as materialized effects that induce in us affects (a combination of phenomenological sensations and changes of intensity in our state of feeling) – reveal a singular but shared specificity in the case here of a sexuated, psychologically embodied woman's creative activity? Do these affects generate associations with transgressed but never effaced borderspaces evoked in the sensuousness and lusciousness of the material effects of pouring paint on to unprimed canvas, making colour areas that move and merge and meet and co-transform without coalescence? What then is fluidity? Are these aesthetically sought and materially generated affects the effect of a technique that is making the paint indissoluble from its support, cotton duck or canvas, while engendering perceptual ambiguity, loosening the binary logic of figure and ground, mark and support, hence becoming metramorphic and soliciting a matrixial gazing?[15]

I shall return to elaborate these suggestive formulations later in the chapter as they also informed the writing on Frankenthaler by Alison Rowley, who carefully builds the pathway between this radical challenge to phallocentrism and Frankenthaler's painting, irrespective of her being woman or engaged in any concern with psychoanalysis, on the basis of what matrixial theory and metramorphosis tell us about painting and colour.[16] To get to Rowley's arguments, we need to pass through an earlier theorization of sexual difference that also gives us purchase on painting 'in, of and from the feminine'.

Feminist philosophy: Luce Irigaray

I turn to writings by a Belgian philosopher of sexual difference, Luce Iriga-ray, who has argued that the metaphors she identifies in the persistent phallocentrism of Western philosophical discourse and culture consistently favour and make dominant the representation of the phallic/masculine – often made explicitly male in terms of embodiment – psychic and corporeal experience. She searched for other terms that might catch up the invisibilized and 'missing' feminine – indeed female in terms of embodiment – psychic and corporeal specificity so as to draw it into cultural representation differently, and thus reshape women's now mutilated self-understanding and cultural representation. Irigaray argues that women-subjects live in exile in the desert country of the phallocentric. Thus, she proposed a revaluing of touch over sight, the haptic over the specular, and a mechanics of fluidity, mucosity and doubling over those of solids and unicity.[17]

In 'The Mechanics of Fluids' (1977), Irigaray explores mathematics and physics, revealing the difference, in the representation of the world, of the metaphors arising from solids and fluids.

> What consequences does this have for 'science' and psychoanalytical practice? And if anyone objects that the question, put this way, relies too heavily on metaphors, it is easy to reply that the question in fact impugns the privilege granted to metaphor (a quasi-solid) over metonymy (which is much more closely allied to fluids). Or – suspending the status of truth accorded to the essentially metalinguistic 'categories' and 'dichotomous oppositions' – to reply that in any event all language is (also) metaphorical, and that, by denying this, language fails to recognize the 'subject' of the unconscious and precludes inquiry into subjection, still in force, of that subject to a symbolization that grants precedence to solids.[18]

Irigaray argues that general philosophy and science understand the world in a metaphysical discourse. This tends not, however, to recognize the unconscious at work shaping, or acknowledge the political effect of, the metaphors the writers use, imagining instead that their language is transparent, directly accessing what simply *is*. As philosopher and psychoanalyst, Irigaray also argues that no one can escape the metaphoric if they do not also acknowledge how language is overdetermined from 'the other scene', the Unconscious, which Freud revealed through the study of dreams and jokes as producing meaning through *metaphor* and its figurative partner *metonymy*, displacement and condensation. If the Symbolic order, a phallocentric order, does not examine its own subjection to sym-bolization in that system through its inevitably metaphoric and uncon-sciously predetermined discourse, Irigaray argues that it continuously repeats and reinstalls a primacy of solids over fluids, form over mediation, clarity over fluency that makes the feminine identifiable with the latter set of terms, nothing but what is *not* the masculine valued terms. Women thus know nothing of themselves and are indeed afraid to ask the question of what else they might be, for fear of reinforcing the phallic logic through inversion of the valuation of the terms in which that logic exiles them. Thus, these questions of sexual difference are immensely tricky, if not treacherous. That is no reason not to open them up.

Closely examining Irigaray's theory of the mechanics of solids versus fluids as they operate in philosophical discourses that iterate a hierarchy of gender, art historian Hilary Robinson effectively deduced an aesthetic the-ory implicit, if never articulated, in Irigaray's writings that she then deployed to analyse artworks by contemporary artist-women, notably Louise Bourgeois, Bridget Riley, Jenny Saville, Rachel Whiteread, Laura Godfrey-Isaacs, Hannah Wilke, Frances Hegarty, Cynthia Mailman and Yolanda Lopez.[19] Robinson was, in fact, the first scholar to create an index of the concepts in Irigaray's many published papers. This enabled her to trace the genealogy of the concepts in the philosopher-psychoanalyst's evolving thought. She was thus able to plot out Irigaray's creation of key concepts such as *lips, morphology* and *mucous (le muqueux)*.[20] As concepts, they have specific relevance to our discussion here of the increasing focus on materiality, materials and the creative processes of the acting, gesturing body and the paint itself that, in abstract painting in the mid-twentieth century, become the topic of artmaking beyond their being mere medium or technique.

Robinson explains that morphology, from the Greek word *morphe*, shape, is not to be understood anatomically, but in terms of linguistics, where it refers to the patterns and syntax in language. Originally a scholar of linguistics, Irigaray analysed the logic of phallocentric order in language, the latter being where we think and understand ourselves through words that mediate our bodies to us. Beyond the phallocentric logic of bodies and meaning, Irigaray proposes a different logic hitherto imprisoned in phallo-logic not only at work in language, the Symbolic, but also in terms of modes of understanding the relation of bodies to psyches and words.

> Thus, for women, the issue is to learn to discover and inhabit a different kind of magnetism and the morphology of a sexualised body, particularly of the mucous particularities and qualities of that body. But women's flesh (and is not mucous in great measure the matter of which flesh is made?) is still ignored, often imagined as chaos, abyss, or rebus. Whether as prime matter

or as creation's reject, woman has yet to find her forms, yet to spread roots and bloom. She has yet to be born to her own growth, her own subjectivity. The female has yet to develop its own morphology. Forced into the maternal role, reduced to being a womb or a seductive mask, the female has served only as the means of conception, growth, birth, and rebirth of the *forms* of the other.[21] (original emphasis)

I highlight the words *discover, find, develop* to insist on a work in progress. Irigaray does not presuppose a given truth. She incites an uncharted discovery – a creation – bringing into knowledge what, being rendered unknowable by phallo-logic, may exist to have but cannot yet have effects on its potential subjects – women. I stress this because it relates to my question: do I see any difference when I watch the painting activities of Pollock and Frankenthaler? The essentialist argument would be that one artist is a man and the other is a woman; hence they deposit what they are via predetermined, different gendered methods of painting. But this is not my answer.

I argue that the question is an open one. New modes of painting made possible, for the first time, the discovery, in both their actions and our reactions to the traces of their actions, the emergence of what we need to grasp as *différance*. This means not only the linguistic unsettling of any fixed identities, *man* and *woman*, as they, both the artists, opened themselves *by these protocols of painting* to discoveries of psychic complexity not yet bounded by nominations – man and woman, masculine and feminine. It also involves the revelation of possibilities for aesthetically sensing and indexing *embodiment* differently, particularly for the phallocentrically exiled woman-body-psyche that exceeds any existing understanding of gender as an identity. Furthermore, the way each painter might be escaping socially assumed gender identities, man/woman, or even phallocentric psycho-linguistic positionalities as masculine and feminine, will itself be asymmetrical. As either social identities – man and woman – or as psycho-sexual subjectivities – masculine and feminine – they are in an asymmetrical position in relation to what these terms mean, imply, impose. Man, masculine imprison their men-subjects in already existing terms and identities, but without the structurally negative and socially disadvantaged implications that phallocentrism imposes on that which, *as the feminine*, it others.

Irigaray is proposing a process of research, not an affirmation of any existing essence. In an interview with literary scholar Alice Jardine in 1987, titled 'Writing as a Woman', Irigaray was asked if she thought, as she did in 1974, writing in her major assault on the sexed metaphorics of Western philosophy in *Speculum of the Other Woman*, that introducing 'the female body into the male corpus is an essential strategy'.[22] To this the philosopher replied that the very question misunderstands her philosophy entirely.

Thus, *Speculum* cannot suggest getting the 'female body' to enter into the male corpus, as the female body has always figured in the male corpus – not always in philosophy, it's true, although it can be found there as well. *Speculum* criticises the exclusive right of the use(s), exchange(s), representation(s) of one sex by the other. This critique is accompanied by the beginnings of a woman's phenomenological elaboration of the auto- affection and auto-representation of her body: Luce Irigaray, signatory to the book. What this implies is that the female body is not to remain the object of men's discourse or their various arts, but it is to become the object of female subjectivity experiencing and identifying itself. Such research attempts to suggest to women a morpho-logic that is appropriate to their bodies. It's aimed at the male subject, too, inviting him to redefine himself as a body with a view to exchanges between sexed subjects.[23]

The body in this statement is not a source of meaning. The body has to become known to the feminine subject in terms *adequate* and *specific* to her, as psychological and embodied, speaking subject in lieu of being a spoken, colonized, used and exchanged body-object. Questioning, opening up issues, puzzling out what I sensed when I looked at certain paintings, I found such a theory valuable as I had as yet no terms fully to articulate this 'affection: being affected' in ways that would escape the prison-house of phallo-logic.

Irigaray proposes the concept of *lips*, fundamentally two, as opposed to the single graspable form whose symbolic image is the Phallus. 'The lips' lack of one-ness; they do not have a graspable, unitary form; to give this morphology a name at present would revert to phallocentric practice, to place it in patriarchal limits.'[24] One form, one-ness, is now countered not by void or formlessness, but by the concept of 'two-ness' that is perplexing to phallic binary logic.[25] Yet there it is: at once vulval, labial, oral. Irigaray writes:

This organ which has nothing to show for itself also lacks a form of its own. And if woman takes pleasure [*jouit*, from *jouissance* – evoking intensity of feeling both pain and pleasure that can also be orgasmic] precisely from the incompleteness of form which allows her organ to touch itself over and over again, indefinitely, by itself, that pleasure is denied by civilization that privileges phallomorphism. The value granted to only definable form excludes the one that is in play in female auto-eroticism. The one form, of the individual, of the (male) sexual organ, of the proper name, of the proper meaning … supplants, while separating and dividing, that contact of at least two (lips) which keeps woman in touch with herself, but without any possibility of distinguishing what is touching from what is touched. Whence the mystery that woman represents in a culture claiming to count.[26]

Hilary Robinson identifies another feature of Irigaray's intervention with the proposition of a *morpho-logic of the mucous/mucosity* (*le muqueux*) which 'mediates a woman to herself, and also mediates her in her difference and specificity to her lover ... The lips are, morphologically, a threshold; ajar but touching; not skin (surface closure), not flayed (internal made external), not a unitary form of flesh (non-mediating), but rather the site of mediation.'[27] Robinson also clarifies the meaning she reads from this suggestive term *le muqueux*: 'Instead of symbolizing the mucous [i.e. making it a symbolic term], we need to recognize in it the play of *différance* and its morphological patterns, and develop from that site morphologies of mediation, and, contiguously, of another syntax in the Symbolic.'[28]

In aesthetic terms, these suggestions for imagining sexually specific embodiment and the plural imaginaries that it might induce can help us to escape the domination of our current imagination(s) by certain oppositions that in and of themselves create a hierarchy of value: bold and hesitant, strong and weak, sharp and blurred, hard and soft, fixed and unbounded, formed and formless, external and internal. The second terms in these sets not only tend to have been valued negatively, but they are also metaphorically feminine. Indeed, the feminine (in phallo-morphic logic) is the condensation of all the second terms, all *lacking* the qualities vis-à-vis the first terms, which, themselves affirm form, meaning, identity, calculable distinction. Irigaray's writing mimics, in order to expose and thus undo, implicit or explicit gendering of value, forms, concepts in what she reveals as Western thought's insistent phallo-logic and phallo-morphism in which her sense of the potential importance of sexual difference is rendered invisible, unthinkable, unspoken. For Irigaray, difference is not *of* woman *from* man, but is all that unsettles the fixing of such effectively mono-sexual distinctions that define the phallocentric Symbolic.

On a psycho-linguistic level, Robinson argues that Irigaray's concepts of *le muqueux* and the *lips* anticipate and extend Derrida's also linguistical thesis on *différance* (the play of deferral of meaning in the linguistic chain of signifiers that produces and unsettles the difference on which the illusion of distinct entities is precariously built), endlessly at work undoing the illusion of fixed meaning. This might be one example of what I shall shortly introduce as Alice Jardine's critique of poststructuralist writing of *woman-into-discourse* by men-thinkers because, with *différance*, Derrida was also pointing to the inherent instability of what he defined as *phallologocentrism*, a combination of phallocentrism and a primacy attributed to language, the *logos*. Yet in doing so, for him and his philosophy, *woman/Woman* remains a pure figure of this logic, identified with the 'differencing', as it were, but not allowed to become a different difference, and a differencing, in my terms, of a more radical kind that, as feminist-thinker, I explore.

Luce Irigaray refuses to allow *woman/Woman* to remain a mere philosophical or linguistic figure. Flesh and body, women are subjects relating, however, to the world, to their own bodies and to other subjects intersubjectively through a morpho-logic of mediation, touching – but also as singularity: 'no woman has the morphology of another'.[29] This means that Woman, as Other within the phallomorphic logic, yields to diversely embodied, sexual *subjects-women*, exploring the undiscovered range of feminine *subjectivities, embodiments, pleasures and creativities* through poetic, aesthetic, linguistic, psychoanalytical and philosophical processes.

The issue of sexual difference, therefore, is not difference *from*, but difference *within* each woman-subject-body, and then between women-subjects-bodies, and finally in dissident relation to the phallocentric Symbolic that lords it over the universe of meaning and bodies under its solitary sign: the One. It is under such a problematic that Irigaray will speak of men and women.

This has led to widespread misunderstanding of her thought and a frequent rejection of it from certain philosophers of current gender theory, who fearfully misrecognize in this thesis a dangerously heterocratic, heteronormative and, most dreadful of all in their view, *essentializing* tendency. Countering this misreading, philosophers Elizabeth Grosz and Pheng Cheah argue:

> It may indeed be the case (as, for instance, Judith Butler and Drucilla Cornell suggest) that Irigaray is guilty of reducing all modes of alterity to the model of the heterosexual couple. Alternatively, Irigaray's concept of sexual difference may also be more enigmatic and complex than received understandings of sexual difference. This much at the very least is suggested by her comment that the recognition of alterity of the other across sexual difference can offer a concrete model and substantive practical logic for respecting all other forms of alterity.[30]

This also enables us to address the way the abstract painting practices, captured photographically, register different modes of exploratory embodiment and revelatory subjectivity, prompting questions of non-essential but psycho-morphological sexual difference.

Feminist art history meets French theory: Lisa Saltzman, Alice Jardine and Shoshana Felman

Not yet equipped with the richness of these feminist philosophies and psychoanalyses, such as those offered by Irigaray in the 1970s–1980s or Ettinger after 1992, in 1981 Rozsika Parker and I were the first feminists to ask questions about Frankenthaler's stain and soak technique as an index of what I later (1996) termed 'inscriptions in, of and from the feminine' in artistic practice.[31] We are not, however, the only feminist art historians to enter this inquiry into sexual difference, language and art. The most sustained analysis is in a monograph by Alison Rowley on Helen Frankenthaler's first major painting, *Mountains and Sea* (1952, fig. 3.5). I shall come to her argument shortly. First, I need to mention two other texts from the 1990s.

Art historian Lisa Saltzman tells us that she first approached *Mountains and Sea* and the stain in 1989 in a graduate seminar on French feminist literary theory in which she was exploring the writings of French thinkers, literary critics, philosophers and psychoanalysts, Julia Kristeva, Hélène Cixous, Michèle Montrelay, Sarah Kofman and Luce Irigaray, in her studies with US-American literary theorist Alice Jardine, author of a recent book *Gynesis: Configurations of Women and Modernity* (1986).[32] This means she was also approaching the question from philosophical and theoretical feminist investigations such as Irigaray had already introduced. Alice Jardine (the interviewer of Irigaray introduced above) was performing a trans-Atlantic 'translation' of the concepts *woman* and *le féminin*, which had been semi-banned in or dismissed from US-American feminism even as they had become widespread in both leading Parisian theoretical circles and French feminist politics, in ways that were distinct from Anglo-American political and academic feminist discourse, whose key terms were, and had remained, *women* and *gender*.[33] The 'modernity' in Jardine's title is *modernité*, which, confusingly, is what French intellectuals then termed postmodernism, or rather, poststructuralism. Under the umbrella of *modernité* nestled Jacques Derrida's deconstruction, Michel Foucault's theses on discourse, madness, sexuality and power, Jacques Lacan on the Phallus and *jouissance*, Julia Kristeva's literary thesis on the semiotic and the *chora* and Luce Irigaray's theory of *sexual difference*.

Gynesis is Jardine's neologism to name a trend – 'the putting into discourse of *woman*' – that was the key theoretical feature of poststructuralism.[34] Characterizing the overall project of French poststructuralist theory as a critique of 'the master narratives of the West' such as humanism, anthropomorphism and [Man's] truth, Jardine identified a 'vast self-exploration, questioning, turning back upon their own discourse, in an attempt to create a new *space or spacing within themselves*' and also an exploration of what had been 'engulfed' in master narratives as a kind of 'non-knowledge', an undiagnosed excess, an unspoken supplement. This 'other-than-themselves is almost always a space of some kind (over which the narrative has lost control), and this space is coded as *feminine*, as *woman*'.[35] Both terms stand not for women as a gender or as gendered people as understood in everyday parlance, but for what is the Other in, and what is made meaningless and unthinkable by, Western master narratives, and what thus becomes a poetic otherness that destabilizes the solidity, fixity and binary logic that has structured phallocentric Western thought. *Différance*, again? Perhaps, but is the poststructuralist *woman* anything but a linguistic, philosophical effect? What is the relation, on any plane, between this *woman* and women who might paint, write or think as women or a *woman* otherwise configured or imagined?

Reading art, literature or philosophy for the *woman* or *the feminine* is not, then, a positive activity celebrating *women's* voices and experiences as opposed to *men's*, important as this has been tactically. It concerns attentiveness to the rhythms or affects (semiotics) or a relation to meaning (thought) of a *differing* of the phallocentric order, undoing its fixed parameters and oppositions, releasing that which it represses and leaves unthought. Of particular significance to the *feminist* reader is our seeking to pierce the carapace of the phallocentric logic for what it has 'engulfed', folded out of sight, rendered the 'nothing' it nonetheless constantly evokes as the consolidating but empty Other for its one-ness. So, Jardine is not hunting for essences, but effects (and I am adding *affects*).

> This *gynema* is a reading effect, a woman-in-effect that is never stable and has no identity. Its appearance in a written text is perhaps noticed only by the feminist reader – either when it is becomes insistently 'feminine' when women (as defined metaphysically, historically) seem magically to reappear within the discourse.[36]

Reading takes place in a world, even at the critical edge of theory that is still, however, problematically shaped by asymmetrical phallological sexual difference. In *modernité*, the key theorists were often men, claiming to be male feminists even, yet not quite able to disown their own master status.[37] Jardine continues:

> This tear in the fabric produces in the feminist reader a state of uncertainty and sometimes distrust – especially when the faltering narrative in which it is embedded has been articulated by a man from within a nonetheless still existent discipline. When it appears in women theorists' discourse, it would seem to be less troubling. The still existing slippages in signification amongst *feminine, woman, women* and what I am calling *gynesis* and *gynema* are dismissed, at least in the United States and increasingly by male feminist critics, as irrelevant *because* a woman is speaking.[38]

Jardine is here pointing out how the politics of sexual difference distorted the very moment when poststructuralism seemed to be writing the *woman-in-effect* into its discourse, and how it became a new kind of master discourse in a poststructuralism enunciated by certain key thinker-men such as Derrida, who, however, taking charge of it, mastered it. Then, if not outrightly dismissive of women asking where actual women who speak and write were in this *woman-effect-in-discourse*, they were condescending to the specific contribution to the larger question of deconstruction, for instance, when articulated by feminist thinker-women, who, by combining their own designation as women with the desire to 'put woman into discourse', sought to unfold what literary theorist Shoshana Felman termed 'women's missing autobiography', thus daring to challenge the new authoritative mode even as they, we, were part of its making.[39]

As a leading feminist poststructuralist and Lacanian theorist, Felman explored the question of reading and sexual difference by asking: 'What consequences might such attempts at engendering a self-analytical female discourse have for the possibilities of reading, writing thinking, analysing, living, of women *and* men?'[40] She based her project on the question that Sigmund Freud bravely dared to ask but admitted failing to answer: 'What does a woman want?'[41] What is feminine desire? Acknowledging that the psycho-sexual specificity of the feminine subject was a closed book to Freud and his theory – so far – Felman presents her practice, feminism, 'as an enabling inspiration, not a theoretical orthodoxy or as a new authorizing institutionalization'.[42] This constitutes an ethics that Felman draws from Simone de Beauvoir's *The Second Sex*, published in 1949, undertaken because its philosopher-woman-author, planning to write her autobiography, realized that the terms for understanding who *she* was were 'missing'. How could de Beauvoir write her autobiography as a woman, when she knew not what she, designated by others as woman, was except through the mirror of a culture whose science, psychology, mythology, philosophy, literature, theology and art announced what 'woman is'? Felman notes: '*The Second Sex* is thus engendered by an impulse and a quest that the writing process carries out but that the author does not at first own.'[43]

De Beauvoir's book combined an investigation into what myth, science, psychoanalysis and other cultural texts have said *Woman is* with her detailed study of how a child *becomes* a Girl and a Woman, drawing on fictional and other autobiographical accounts by women writers and artists.[44] Felman offers a commentary on this very complex process of displacing a fixed, imposed ontology – *woman is* this or that kind of being according to master narratives – by slowly discovering how a subject is formed and becomes what culture defines as woman or feminine. Here is de Beauvoir's definition: 'No biological, psychical or economic destiny defines the figure that the human female takes on in society; it is civilisation as a whole that elaborates this intermediary product between the male and the eunuch that is called feminine.'[45]

Felman, however, dismisses any notion that autobiography is telling our own story:

> I will suggest that none of us, as women, has as yet, precisely, an autobiography. Trained to see ourselves as objects and to be positioned as the Other, estranged to ourselves, we have a story that by definition cannot be self-present to us, a story, that in other words, is not a story, but *must become* a story.[46]

This requires a reading of the story, just as de Beauvoir's book required others to read it for its author to know who and what she had become. This demands others who read:

> it cannot become a story except through the bond of reading, that is, to the *story of the Other* (the story told by other women, the story of other women, the story of women told by others), insofar as this story of the Other, as *our own* autobiography, *has as yet precisely to be owned*.[47]

This wordplay is necessary to keep in play *becoming* in a relation created between a single woman-subject and other women-subjects, real or fictional, told or read, through which a story (i.e. any creative, poetic, painted or sung inscription) of our lived selves might emerge, intersubjectively at the level or reading and writing – or painting and reading painting – and encountering the hospitality of relevant interpretation and acknowledgement. It also needs theory, poetics, creative work:

> Rather, I will propose here that we might be able to engender, or to access our story only indirectly – *by conjugating literature, theory, and autobiography* together with the act of reading and by reading, thus, into the texts of culture, at once our sexual difference and our autobiography as missing.[48] (my emphasis)

Subsumed under the imposed nomination *Woman*, we, as women in all our singularity, diversity and even agonistic conflict across relations of race and class, power and economic precarity, lack the means of articulating each singularity – *autos* in Greek means self. Felman invokes a 'we' but not as a given. She writes *to* women and reads *with* singular women, and from her own singular journey which revealed to her that 'my own autobiography is missing, and why this missing of my own autobiography appears today to be characteristic of the female condition'.[49] Women's stories – 'inscriptions in, of and from the feminine' – are impressed into culture despite their not being recognized by a phallocentric world or even being intelligible to women, schooled only in the logic of the phallocentric. Like a Rosetta stone, they are full of writing, but we do not, within the present order, yet have the ciphers to decode the scripts. We might say that the project of feminist theory and cultural analysis is the search for such codes to unlock other meanings.

Irigaray, Jardine and Felman clarify what it means to ask about difference, sexual difference, when studying the painting practices and paintings of artists, women and men, in a specific historical and aesthetically theorized reconfiguration of painting, as a singular act of an embodied, psychological person. What we can 'read' as a painting is an inscription or even an affective impression that is not the expression of the conscious thoughts of a self-possessed, self-possessing, self-knowing subject. What we encounter is the possibility of discovering something not yet known through open engagement with a novel experiment in 'modes' of the visual arts.

Painting and difference

In her Jardine-prompted study of stain, gender and the body in abstract painting, Lisa Saltzman argues that difference and the body were already present in the American modernist critics' interpretations of New York painting of the 1950s as an art that was being produced by the embodied subject. Thus, the artist becomes effectively both the subject (i.e., agent) of the painting practice and the content of the resulting painting. A painting by Pollock *is* Pollock. Saltzman also argues that this abstract, all-over, all-paint painting without figuration was being read as diffusing solidity, destabilizing fixed positions. It could thus be interpreted, Saltzman suggests, in cultural terms, as enacting a creative dissolution of gender polarities even as that was unsettling to a conservative American society at the time that sought to fix gender, racial, sexual and other hierarchies.

> That is, if the language of emergent formalist criticism is taken at its word, criticism would seem to have found in these purportedly autonomous, self-reflexive, and hermetic paintings not pure abstraction but a legible subject – namely, the artistic self and, more pointedly, the artist's body. As such the gendered language of emergent formalist criticism would seem to echo in its response to the radically dispersed, diffuse, all-over surfaces of New York School painting something of a broader societal anxiety about the dissolution of gender boundaries in postwar America.[50]

Despite the engagement with Jardine and French theory of difference, Saltzman's terminology here returns us to *gender* rather than *sexual difference*, the key psychoanalytical term in French philosophical and literary theory. Moreover, she is arguing that the critical invocation of gendered terms in the critics' language in terms of the undoing of boundaries might be a reflex of social anxieties about post-war gender destabilization. Saltzman questions, then explains, why this issue had not been taken up so far by feminist writers; perhaps as a literary scholar she was curiously unaware of Parker's and my *Old Mistresses: Women, Art and Ideology*, published in 1981, as well as the earliest incarnation of the present book in

1996. Thus, she wrongly argues that early feminist art history only focused on figuration, content shall we say, rather than abstraction, which was the domain of a modernist orthodoxy that had been silent about artists who were women.

> Despite the prevalence of the gendered metaphorics in the representation of abstraction, very little has been done to analyse its implications, either for New York school painting or for the interpretation of abstraction more generally. Even in the work of the first generation of feminist art historians who explicitly took on questions of gender, the interpretation of abstraction was never the primary object of enquiry.[51]

Saltzman under-represents the emerging relation between certain feminist writers and artists and the radical shift occasioned by conceptual art theory and practice leading to aesthetic-political analysis of meaning systems, conscious and unconscious, through semiotics and psychoanalysis.[52]

Some clarification of concepts: the feminine (and back to the photographs)

I follow neither Saltzman nor Jardine entirely. So, I need to clarify what can easily become a confusing array of terms. In French theory, the term *le féminin/the feminine* signifies nothing in and of itself. It is derived from neither bodies nor anatomies nor gendered brains nor sexual organs. It marks the spot of the recalcitrant issue – for Western thought – of sexual difference in which we confront the riddles of how those, named *women* under phallocentrism, live the place we are allocated, while acting as both excess to it and as a structuring negative that keeps the system and its phallically privileged term in place. How then do we create as artists and write as thinkers, within its unsettled and contradictory psycho-linguistic and socio-ideological formations?

When I use the term *the feminine* in this context, it is important, therefore, to distinguish it from the pejorative term of abuse employed by contemporary critics to discount the art of women – what Rozsika Parker and I named 'the feminine stereotype' in which art by women is typically dismissed, or even praised, as lyrical, weak, sentimental, influenced, personal, pretty, sentimental, derivative and so forth, that is, with gendered and gendering qualifiers. *The feminine* is not an essential (of the essence, innate or anatomically derived) condition or attribute of all women. I propose *the feminine* as a complex of positional difference (the lack/minus position in the Oedipal triangle and in language) and each person's singular psycho-corporeal history, their journey to becoming a subject with all its traumas. We can also reclaim what is philosophically the *negativity* of the feminine – being positioned structurally as the other of the *phallic masculine* so that, as yet not fully known, the difference of *the feminine* becomes a resource, an uncharted excess for refusal and even renovation of the current orders of meaning and society, its ethics, politics and aesthetics. This is the position of structurally revolutionary negativity argued by Julia Kristeva.[53] This enables productive excavation of the relations between psychoanalytic hypotheses about the otherness of the other – the feminine as the *not* of phallocentrism – and cultural conventions of the 1950s that anxiously manufactured (in the face of a century of feminist protest and real social change for women) an excess of feminine masquerade in a culture with a massive ideological project to naturalize a fixed division of gender identities and attendant heterosexuality.

To raise the spectre of *the feminine* in discussion of the effects perceived in the works of a painter who is a woman is, therefore, to tangle dangerously with a complex historical legacy of unstable terms that, of course, the artist-woman personally had to, and often energetically did, disavow in order to be considered an artist *tout court*.[54] I understand entirely why these modernist artist-women kept any suggestion of femininity or feminism at bay. Yet we can rethink their resistance. Sexual difference is a conundrum that we cannot avoid as historians or as feminists. As the record has shown, nor could the artist-women, since its phallic form engulfed them and placed them at the margins, if at all, of the history of the art of their own moment.

Let me now return to the photographs (figs 2.19 and 3.4). There it is, posing itself as a question when we look at two painters at work, two bodies labouring on their own creations where the making process becomes an opened pathway to the unconscious, or at least to a less actively conscious set of actions and gestures, responses and states of mind while painting. Pollock himself spoke of working in a trance state. Precisely because the Namuth and Haas photographs of two painters at work abandon the formal iconography of artistic (self-)portraiture for the seemingly mundane record of painting, as both a formal *activity* and as an existential *action*, I suggest that these gestures of labouring, painting bodies index and trace into art profoundly different ways of being in a body, of acting from a *differentiated*, psychically imagined corporality in that actual, as well as symbolic or phantasmatic, space – the canvas in the studio.

The outcome of that process carries within it the duration and the gestures of its making. Later, different viewers might *read* both according to either prevailing cultural signs of gendered sexuality (dripping and ejaculating or urinating as opposed to spreading and bleeding) or according to their own openness to affects and meanings that the physical making initiated. I would argue that there is an aesthetically staged sexual politics right there in the most formal, and even technical, processes of high modernist gestural painting. They are historically raised to a level of transparency and exposed to us by the very dedicated abstractness and novel primacy of the materiality and process of painting. Yet, holding on to Jardine's insights about the feminine as a destabilizing otherness to the phallic that is not at the level of bodies and individuals, both these artists might be creating practices that not only unsettle the gender positions of man and woman, but also reveal the inherent fiction of a polarity of masculinity and femininity created by the phallocentric order. Are there ever really men and women? Are these positions ever stable, socially or psychically? Was the abstract painting of a certain moment that was made possible by its novel mode of practice more susceptible to such creative and psycho-sexual instability as play – open to *the feminine* as a beyond for *both* painters, Pollock and Frankenthaler (and Krasner), but still affectively *different and specific* in the paintings' effects that we, I, may still want to understand?

We require terms to counter fixed sexual difference as something derived from some organs or from nature or even as a socially constructed *gender*: man/woman (as opposed to the phallic and *the feminine* of French theory). The danger is that because, within phallocentrism, there is only one sex, the only difference permitted to what is not the dominant sex, the phallic masculine, is negative: that which is *not* the one, *is not*. It signifies simply the lack of what is positively endorsed. The term *feminine* is often abused to signal simply negative difference, not-man, not-masculine. Helen Frankenthaler's work was, therefore, relationally, 'after Pollock', 'sub-Pollock', 'less good' than 'Pollock', more feminine than 'Pollock', or as it was inscribed into the art historical literature, 'forming the bridge between Pollock and what was possible'.[55] Accustomed culturally to read art through the normative significations of the (white, heterosexual) masculine, anything that betrays signs of difference offers nothing but that lack of what is expected (and desired). This argument is as true for racialized societies in which the *not* is the black other. Or, the positive reading is made, such as Greenberg's on Frankenthaler as bridge, placing her as a useful artist, making a breakthrough after Pollock only to become the minor artistic intermediary between Pollock and the next masters 'in the course of art's history' – the colour field painters Morris Louis and Kenneth Noland.

We lack an openness to what a sexual difference of *the feminine*, plural and diverse, might bring to the world. Feminist theory provides the terms with which to imagine what the othernesses of diverse artist-women might discover, *other* than being the consolidated *Other* to the One-Man, which furthermore hides the diversity and agonistic relations and woundings of class or race or sexuality between women. Difference is not categorical, homogeneous. The purpose of art is to allow each artist to speak as a complex singularity, to articulate *who* she is, rather than to consolidate the category of *what* she is named by phallocentric culture. Yet who we are is formed by that culture's determination of what we can be, as class, race, gender, geopolitical location and sexuality act to define our field of action and our sense of self.[56]

Is this argument reductive?

In an article written in 2010, drawn from her doctoral dissertation, 'Helen Frankenthaler's Modernism: Embodiment and Pictorial Ambiguity 1950–1965' (2004), Bett Schumacher refers to Parker's and my initial work on Frankenthaler in *Old Mistresses*, when we first noted the often stereotypically gendered metaphors invoked by art critics in their deeply ambiguous yet admiring response to Frankenthaler's paintings.[57] Discussing the first incarnation of the present argument, she argues against my reading of the photographs by Ernst Haas of Frankenthaler painting. Schumacher is, however, working with a concept of *gender* as an attribute of the person, gender being, she suggests, what Frankenthaler sought to disown and displace, confirmation of which Schumacher also finds in what might call gender-indifferent universalizing commentaries on the paintings by both men and women critics. She argues that my concept of the third body, the 'creative woman's body' (the artist's body and art's body-woman being the other two), and the idea of *differentiation* remain trapped in the very *gendered* terms I was actually contesting. I posed this term to triangulate the existing dyad: artist-man-creative body and woman-as-art's-body. The third term, creative woman's body, which alleviates this opposition *m/f*, is a dialectical space that perversely (in the system's terms) conjugates creativity (art and thought) with a woman as subject at a moment when the body of the artist as actor, agent, subjective locus of 'artist' became such a critical component of the event, the effect, the outcome, that it was then adjudged at a certain point to be indeed a *painting*. For Schumacher, furthermore, I missed the *forcefulness* of Frankenthaler's painting gestures and the *athleticism* of Frankenthaler's body at work, contrasting both to my suggestion of the painter kneeling and smoothing. She misrepresents my position: 'I believe that while the Haas photographs indeed suggest that Frankenthaler envisioned something like a creative woman's body for her practice, they do not do so by invoking an essentialist relation of woman painter to canvas as Griselda Pollock maintains.'[58]

I contest strongly that my argument proposes an *essentialist* relation of woman painter to canvas, even as I do consider the psychic and material condition of being embodied and sexuated. Essentialist ideas about gender and fixed oppositional structures are precisely what the entire architecture of my text – there and again here – was built to inhibit and displace, without allowing the questions of difference, corporeality (Ettinger) and embodiment (Merleau-Ponty) and phantasy or desire (Freud etc.) to be foreclosed from discussion precisely via the specificities of abstract painting in that moment when gesture, the painting body in action, materiality and psychic space, became the arena of action whose *effects* solicit a reading. My practice involves displacing the individualist, expressive hypothesis that regularly smuggles back in fixed notions of gender identity: men and women. Psychoanalysis radically destabilizes the concept of gender by its theorization of the traumatic formations of subjectivity articulated through identifications which are phantasmatic relations to other bodies and pre-existing images. Linked to aesthetic practice at that time, psychoanalytical thinking opens up works of art to readings for conscious, unconscious and non-conscious inscriptions of dimensions of embodiment and phantasy, unknowable before the event of working, which emerged in the process of painting itself, each one painting a question posed to painting. It is precisely to elaborate the complexity of the relations between subjectivity, psycho-sexual difference and the unpredictable process of abstract gestural painting that I 'read' the photographs as witnesses to an event of unforeseen becoming, and not as documents of a known, given person's *gender or de- or re-gendering*. I perceive a momentary capture of the process of making effects, not the expressing of a pre-given, defined and labelled self.

Schumacher continues:

> Rather, the photographs indicate the presence of something like a creative woman's body in the way they revealed to us the *ambiguity* of Frankenthaler's bodily relation to her work. Thus, while I see value in Griselda Pollock's concept of the 'creative woman's body' as situated in relation to both women artists' own femininity and to the corporeality evoked in the painting of others, both male and female, I disagree with Pollock's specific claims for Frankenthaler, above all their fixity – their failure to account for variations, ambiguities and identifications in both the production and reception of her work. Additionally, in contrast to Pollock's suggestion that Frankenthaler's painting is a meditation on *differentiation* which happens psychically through procedures of identifications, I see that engagement happening within Frankenthaler's paintings themselves.[59]

I had thought that my entire argument was indeed premised on the idea that the painting is *the event*, the trace of a becoming, the product of a journey into uncharted spaces accompanied by materials, the action and gestures of the body, a thoughtful but also intuiting body-psyche that does not predetermine the event but is the condition for an occurrence, *artworking*, leaving traces that we are challenged to interpret and feel as affect, if we desire so to do, for more than what is typically encompassed in formalist readings and art historical classification. Rather than reading for predefined notions of female *gender* as attribute of the artist outside the arena of the painting work, I have been arguing instead for the recognition of the disclosure that occurs, that is as much a surprise, an event, for the maker over the duration of the making as for the potential viewer of a painting. This refers to the process as genesis shaped by aesthetic decisions along the way that renders the painting the dynamic tracing of what happens in the working/making. I have consistently argued against the equation that the term *woman painter* produces: woman in conventional terms as much revealed in the stereotypical reception of her work as lyrical or pastoral etc., as in the critical reading that foreswears any idea of 'inscription' or imprint from a sexuated singularity that inhabits a world through embodiments that are psychically as much as socially charged, and hence become semiotic: generative of the unforeseen that then we might read, in order to learn from, as ciphers in an emerging language that this new kind of painting made possible.

This set of signs exceeds the fixity of gendered critical appreciation while also reminding us of the creative significance of enfleshed consciousness (Merleau-Ponty) and phantasmatic and unconscious corporeality (psychoanalysis). I contest that our options are limited to seeing Frankenthaler performing or resisting a pre-given gender identity. My argument has no truck with essentialism. Equally I am not afraid of the specificity of the body as a site of phantasies and memories, habits and creative, sensuous, active physicality. We are corporeal beings. I also contest the feminist argument that the only way beyond essentialist oppositions, male/female, masculine/feminine, men/women, is poststructuralist ambiguity, unsettlement, deconstruction. What this forecloses is the possibility that we might learn from *inscriptions in, of and from the feminine* not only as the as-yet-illegible other of the phallocentric order that serves merely to agitate and destabilize that order at its margins, but as a resource for learning to imagine difference(s). Difference is not *difference from…* a given norm. It signals the *plurality* that Hannah Arendt postulated non-psychoanalytically as the characteristic of the human condition (note: not human nature).

The trick is to see what I define as an active and unpredictable, contingent process – the *differencing* of/by the multiple femininities as a result of both the intensity of the artist's engagement with the central problematics of this art historical moment called Abstract Expressionism, and the possibilities it offered for something in excess of what the critics have so far seen and celebrated in their selective vision, that we might invoke as a dimension of the specificities of *the feminine*, the mediating *muqueux* and the *metramorphic*.

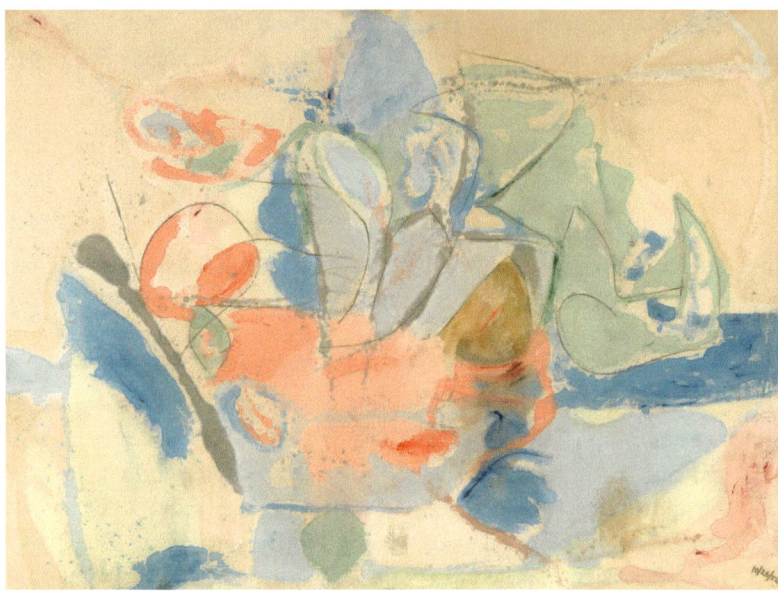

Figure 3.5 Helen Frankenthaler, *Mountains and Sea*, 1952

Alison Rowley on *Mountains and Sea* (1952)

The art historical account, such as it is, has placed Helen Frankenthaler as a second-generation Abstract Expressionist who first saw Pollock's dripped canvases at his shows in 1950 (where he showed the drip paintings *Lavender Mist*, *Autumn Rhythm* and *One: Number 31*) and 1951 (where he showed the black and white paintings) at Betty Parsons Gallery. She was then directed by Clement Greenberg to visit Pollock's studio at The Springs, East Hampton, in 1951. She found the encounter 'a clinching point of departure' from her then current evolution through her engagements with Cubism, Wassily Kandinsky, Arshile Gorky and Willem de Kooning:

> I felt I could stretch more in the Pollock framework. I found that in Pollock I also responded to a certain Surreal element … You could become a de Kooning disciple or satellite or mirror, but you could depart from Pollock.[60]

The artist spent the summer of 1952 painting the dramatic rocky coastline of Nova Scotia and came back to New York to produce the enormous canvas, *Mountains and Sea* (1952, fig. 3.5). Echoing Cézanne's famous statement, 'The landscape thinks itself in me. I am its consciousness', Frankenthaler stated: 'I know the landscape was in my arms as I did it.'[61] We can read this as a phenomenological statement in which the otherness of the world is experienced in the physical body of the painter who transposes this experienced and felt being in the world through her method, not as an image (a painting of a landscape) but through the sensations and affects of a world the body has inhabited, perceived, remembered, performed in so far as a painting process can engender such affective memories and un-cognized sensations. This involves an understanding of what Cézanne had done in his moment of modernist painting. This fundamental insight is what we find in the writings of painter and art historian Alison Rowley, to whose work on Frankenthaler I now come back.

Rowley's book on Frankenthaler's *Mountains and Sea* – while also offering a close reading of *Eden* (1956) – challenged the major art historical accounts of the making of *Mountains and Sea* in which writers have to link the painting to Pollock in order to keep in place the canonical genealogy of modern American painting, to maintain Pollock's master role and locate Frankenthaler as an admittedly innovative but follower 'daughter of the master'. Rowley's book opens with a chapter titled '*Mountains and Sea:* Cézanne's Country in New York and Nova Scotia'. Her purpose is to bring back into view a critically important encounter for Frankenthaler, and indeed for Clement Greenberg, who painted on their shared trip to Nova Scotia, with the work of the French painter Paul Cézanne (1839–1906) just at that critical point in New York artmaking and its debates c. 1950. Rowley brilliantly bypasses the accumulated and obscuring 'truths' about Frankenthaler's 'breakthrough' by concluding:

> On May 25, 1960 *Mountains and Sea* entered the art historical canon as a 'bridge between Pollock and what was possible' [Greenberg's interview with Morris Louis] but on 26 October, 1952 [the date it was signed] it was an astonishing picture of what Cézanne's Country offered a young, ambitious, American painter who happened to be a woman, profoundly involved in her own project 'to depart from Pollock'.[62]

In my early research on Helen Frankenthaler in 1975, I analysed the language of the reviews of the artist's work, in which I noted a recurring, stereotypical association of her paintings with European landscape painting of the eighteenth century, focused mainly on the pastoral *fêtes galantes* of Watteau or Goya, for instance, which prompted a recurrent use of terms such as lyrical or pastoral for Frankenthaler's paintings that clearly tipped the register of her work into the feminine, associated already with art history's appraisal of these eighteenth-century painters' chosen themes and the femininity of the Rococo itself.[63] There is no doubt an important art historical case to be made for the reference to landscape orientation as a means of shifting mid-twentieth-century abstract painting's relation to the historical legacies that had to be purified as part of the continuing job of the modernization of painting. Extended horizontality was one of the ways of escaping the tradition of easel painting and the humanocentric orientation of the vertical. If Pollock's ultimate expansion of scale and use of the horizontal format drew on his inspiration from see-ing First Nation sand painting and Mexican mural art, Frankenthaler's invites reference to landscape, but not of the eighteenth century. Through primary research, Rowley firmly established Cézanne's impact as a resource for what happened in 1952 in Frankenthaler's studio by closely studying both amateur painter and critic Greenberg's and professional painter Frankenthaler's responses to an important and revelatory exhibi-tion of watercolours by Cézanne in New York in 1952 at the Metropolitan Museum of Art.

Rowley's comment, 'a painter who happens to be a woman', was not, however, left hanging. In her second chapter, 'Other Countries, Other Cézannes', Rowley redirects the open question – what an artist-woman could be doing in 'Cézanne's Country' – by exploring another modernist 'Cézanne Country' not shaped by Greenberg's criticism and from a moment several decades earlier. Rowley introduces British painter and art historian Roger Fry (1866–1934) and his initiation of a formalist inter-pretation of Cézanne in 1927.[64] Fry initially considered emotions as the driver of form, but came then to discover that form incited the emotions' experience with art.

> I very early became convinced that our *emotions* before works of art were of many kinds and that we failed as a rule to distinguish the nature of the mix-ture and I set to work by introspection to discover what the different ele-ments of these compound emotions might be and to try to get at the most constant, unchanging, and therefore I suppose fundamental emotion. I found that this 'constant' had to do always with the contemplation of form … It also seemed to me that the emotions resulting from the contemplation of form were more universal (less particularized and coloured by the individual history), more profound and more significant spiritually than any of the emotions which had to do with life … I therefore assume that the contem-plation of form is a peculiarly important spiritual exercise …[65]

Fry's work on Cézanne opens a path for Rowley to the novel that Fry's biographer, Virginia Woolf, was concurrently writing – *To the Light-house* (1927). Woolf was the sister of painter Vanessa Bell, and witness to the massive impact of Desmond MacCarthy's and Roger Fry's exhibition of *Manet and the Post-Impressionists* in London in 1910–1911. In her novel about painting and mourning, Woolf's deep understanding of Fry's think-ing about the emotion made possible by form and the form of emotion in painting is enacted by, creatively embodied in and reflected upon by a key character, an artist-woman named Lily Briscoe, who struggles to find a way to compose and paint her *sense of*, and *longing for*, the central figura-tion of *the feminine* in this novel, Mrs Ramsay, who is the locus for Woolf's processing, formalizing, her own, long-unmourned grief for her mother,

Julia Stephen, who had died in 1895 when the author was 13 years old. Adding a close reading of Fry's text on *The Artist and Psychoanalysis* (1924) to the journal entries and other memoirs of Woolf as she conceived and began *To the Lighthouse*, Rowley reminds us that formalism, in Fry's terms, was always infused with psychic affects. Fry called for an investigation of 'the psychic structures underpinning the source of satisfaction derived from the contemplation of certain systems of formal design'.[66] Already in this community of painters, writers and thinkers, affects, emotions, psychic processes and form are entwined and examined, so that we are not straying out of formalism to read art with psychoanalysis, whose object of analysis is the psyche.

The brilliance of Rowley's argument lies in offering both a close analysis of Freud's texts and a detailed textual reading, as a painter, of Woolf's subtle and profound account of a painter, Lily Briscoe, making her paintings. In the novel, by means of an interior monologue as Briscoe paints, Woolf captures both the *emotions* of the artist in the dangerous journey of struggling with two paintings, one a failure and one providing the pleasure of its resolution, and the formal means by which the psychic freight beyond those known emotions and impulses, desire and loss, are played out by the formal and material battle with marks, emptiness, colour, arrangement of elements in colour and on the canvas as an imaginary space. What is critical is Rowley's reading of Woolf's own narrative *formulation* of mother-loss and grief and its *formulation* through the account of a painting practice deeply engaged with formal questions of how an abstract painting is resolved by finding an arrangement and a placement of elements in tension and dialogue that are adequate on an affective level and indissoluble from the aesthetic one.

In concluding, Rowley speaks to the key question that this chapter has been exploring: difference, sexual difference and differencing culture through such a psycho-aesthetic-formal understanding of modernist painting. Rowley introduces two concepts from Freud: the topography of the psyche and the theory of the death drive and repetition figured in a child's game that he named *fort/da.* In his first topography of the psyche (UCS, unconscious; PCS, pre-conscious; CS, conscious), Freud theorized different modes of our beginning to make sense of the world. He argued that there is a difference between how the unconscious works – with thing-representations that are largely visual – as opposed to word-presentations that operate in the pre-conscious and the conscious mind. Rowley poses this question to the fictional painter negotiating an image she longs to capture in paint, Mrs Ramsay and her child, and the purple triangle the modernist artist paints to move from figuration to form, but which in the end fails to satisfy. Lily Briscoe's first painting does not work.

> Can we, then, *theorize* Woolf's representation of what happens when Lily Briscoe paints in terms of Freud's first topography as activity fundamentally connected to the pre-conscious domain where there is a relation between thing-presentation and word-presentation in which we might equate the essentially visual and unconsciously rooted thing-presentation with the associated pressure Lily Briscoe refers to as 'these emotions of the body': the pressure of preverbal, affective, material below the level of consciousness?[67]

What we need then to grasp, Rowley suggests, is that beyond the specific, if fictional, embodiment who, dying, is then missing – Mrs Ramsay – is a structural, psychic loss, for all subjects, of closeness to the maternal body, which Freud identified in the game he witnessed his grandson playing when his mother left his side. (I will examine this in more detail in the next chapter.)

> For now, suffice it to say that in general Woolf's narrative appears to parallel Freud's observation [for the *fort-da* game] that it is *the absence of the maternal body* that motivates the activity of symbolic substitution, in terms both of object symbols – the painting, and language – and the fantasy scenarios that accompany the activity. But if Woolf did know something of Freud's ideas in 'Beyond the Pleasure Principle' [1920; English translation in 1922 by Ernest Jones] (even not from actually reading it herself) and explores them in fiction through the character of Lily Briscoe, *she has already made a significant transposition from a masculine to a feminine player. Does this difference make any difference?*[68] (my emphases)

I would like to take up Woolf's evocative phrase 'emotions of the body' (which might be termed *affects* in current, Bergsonian and Deleuzian parlance as well as in Freudian terms) and Freud's thesis about our use of things, words, symbols and actions that emerge to negotiate all subjects' loss of, separation from, the maternal body, in order to return to the body, *her body at work in virtual space*, signalled by Frankenthaler's revealing comment about *Mountains and Sea*. Is Rowley forging a link between Lily Briscoe's/Virginia Woolf's 'emotions of the body' and Frankenthaler's suggestion of feeling the landscape in her arms, which suggests that the body mediates between the phenomenological experience of being in space and the process of painting from that body-memory of once being in a place?[69] Using Woolf (and indirectly Fry), we can reapproach the questions of the paintings of Pollock and Frankenthaler and working through emotion, body-memory and unconscious psychic processes at the level of form, form making, form becoming in ways that are inextricable from the material processes of painting, in ways that were not yet available to the post-Impressionist, Fry-ist Lily Briscoe or Vanessa Bell, Woolf's painter sister.

Underlying and veiled by Freud's intuition that the *fort/da* game concerns the child's negotiation of the absence of his mother is a deeper loss that birth itself inflicts, while we who are born carry traces of our pre-natal becoming. Painter, analyst and aesthetic theorist Bracha L. Ettinger argues that the space and place of human becoming and being originates *with/within a body* that is in effect two bodies in a shared matrixial 'borderspace' – Ettinger's key concept. Long before the post-natal, Oedipally legislated process of progressively being separated and ultimately exiled from the post-natal Mother's body (birth, loss of the breast, the gaze, the voice and the body), which may engender a grief exacerbated, in Virginia Woolf's case, by the premature loss of the actual mother's presence through her early death, there is a prolonged pre-natal condition that is proto-subjectivizing via metramorphic aesthesis. This Ettinger terms *the Matrix* and it this that painter Alison Rowley recognizes in painting.

The painting body moves between resource and outcome, which does not, however, become a representation and does not really reference anything but its own process of becoming a painting in this manner by this painter. The painting body accomplishes its role as if it were itself both the instrument of the psyche and of the painter, whose labour and gestures replace the brush or stick and replicate the look or feel of being in the world, once touched in art through representation and landscape. Something different must occur if the painter who paints with such a body is, in fact, a woman painting from (or to find) 'the creative woman's body', a site of her own formation in the feminine and a phantasmatic feminine relation to the other body, the mother's, like hers, but also her mother's, who has died. Actual bereavement exacerbates early separation but, following Ettinger's proposition of the Matrixial, it also agitates the even deeper trauma of birth that represents expulsion from the prolonged matrixial co-emergence with an intimate other in the shared borderspace of the later months of pre-natality.

Theorizing *the maternal-feminine* that has been introduced by the novel, while forging a bridge between Merleau-Ponty's phenomenology and Freudian psychoanalysis, Rowley then shows how the theoretical concepts forged by Ettinger – also an interlocutor with Merleau-Ponty – *Matrix* and *metramorphosis* illuminate what is happening in Frankenthaler's painting once we allow this other dimension of subjectivity its place in our complex psychic formation.

Difficult to think and difficult to write, I have absolutely no problem understanding the concept of the *Matrix* and its operational mode, *metramorphosis* from experience with the materials and processes of painting. I have argued that the technical procedures and processes of painting are inextricably caught up in the binary logic of *fort/da*. That is to say, painting can only

> proceed as a temporal/spatial play of the material there/not thereness, mark/no mark, form/no form, of the figure/ground relation.[70]

So, this has to be clear. But this is not all.

> Yet also fundamental to painting as the articulation of material substance is its instability. At the most obvious level there is a capacity of paint on canvas to flip between a presence as material, and material by means of which an image of something in the world, or from the imagination, is transmitted.[71]

The shifting element is not material, but colour:

> Colour, because of its function as a relation, is the most unstable of all elements of painting, and thus has the capacity for spatial negotiation and adjustment of the utmost subtlety. To which Frankenthaler introduces another level of ambiguity when she soaks colour into the weave of un-primed canvas further blurring the distinction between figure and ground.[72]

Rowley invokes fellow painter Ettinger's concept of *metramorphosis* that I introduced earlier as a creative, generative meaning-process characterized by operations paradoxical to phallo-logic and the phallocentric order:

> *Relations-without-relating* with the other – based on a tuning of *distance-in-proximity* (and not on and either fusion or repulsion) – reflecting and creating differentiation-in-co-emergence and accompanied by shared and diffused and minimal pleasure/displeasure matrixial aspects of silent alertness open a within–with-out space. They induce instances of co-emergence of meaning.[73]

Beautifully plotted through the psychoanalytical territory through whose terms Ettinger planted her original theory of matrixial sexual difference into aesthetics and psychoanalysis, Rowley brings us back to Frankenthaler's painting. It is not the work *of a woman*, but *painting* whose process, so baffling to her contemporaries even as they realized it was a radical transformation of painting beyond any so far seen, yet so eruditely grounded in the history of painting from Titian to Cézanne and Pollock, is not about destabilizing gender, as Saltzman suggested, but rather is already metramorphic and matrixial.

> I suggest the traces of a *matrixial* subjectivizing stratum, a *matrixial* knowledge, are inscribed in *Mountains and Sea* at every level of the painting and that it is why it is so difficult to 'see' from the perspective of dominant phallically determined art-critical knowledge. And I mean difficult to see not only, indeed not even, in the sense of the painting's literal quality of not-quite-focused visuality. The painting is difficult to 'read' semiotically from within the frame of the conventions of dominant art critical knowledge

in its specific manifestation in 1952, precisely because the aspect of the matrixial *objet a* inscribed in the painting troubles the terms upon which the clarity of that discourse depends.[74]

Grounded in a theoretical journey through Lacan, and Ettinger's reading of Lacan, the latter's *objet a* is, according to Ettinger, 'the trace of the part-object [gaze, touch, breast, voice] and in my view, of the archaic Other/mother, both of which are linked to pre-Oedipal impulses and are considered forever unattainable', and hence the site of unassuaged longing.[75] Ettinger's *matrixial objet a* is, Rowley suggests, 'a *movement*, the process of co-emerging-co-fading that Ettinger calls metamorphosis'. She adds:

> in the Matrix the libidinal investment is different. Not determined as specific erogenous zones connected with the body's actual openings onto the world, it functions as 'eroticized aerials of the psyche' [Ettinger]. With this image Ettinger captures the sense of the libido as both an extension out from and between a relational and all-over subjectivizing, that is to say *signifying*, erotic effect of the most intimate exteriority. As *matrixial fantasy* Frankenthaler's statement about making *Mountains and Sea* 'I *know* the landscapes were in my arms as I did it', quite literally makes sense.[76] (original emphases)

For Fry, form sustained our psycho-aesthetic pleasure. Dis- or unpleasure would arise from lack of form. Frankenthaler's staining and soaking does not deliver form and is not fluid in Irigaray's sense either. Nor is it formless. It offers pleasure on a different register, to articulate which Rowley turns to Ettinger's matrixial to introduce a non-phallic, non-either/or operation that sustains a movement between absence and presence, forming/unforming, through the constant attunement of the co-emerging partial elements whose psychic affects are not melancholy contemplations or denials of loss, but dispersed traces of the almost-but-never-completely lost traces of this archaic severality, that is feminine in its condition, but shared by all who are born, irrespective of what, post-natal, Oedipalization will demand and impose as *m/f* psycho-sexual positions.

This is not to drag in an essentialist idea about what that body or that subject, masculine or feminine, *is*. As theorist Julia Kristeva stated, in adamant poststructuralist terms, in an interview with *Psycho & Po* published in *Tel Quel* in 1974 titled 'La femme, ce n'est jamais ça': 'woman *is* not; woman cannot *be*'. By this she means that Woman is not in the order of being.[77] My statement – that something different must occur if the painter who paints with such a body is, in fact, a woman painting from (or to find) 'the creative woman's body' – presumes nothing at the level of content, having no truck with the expressive fallacy, painting as a woman. Yet, as feminists, concerned to pose the repressed question of what the sexual difference might be outside of a phallocentric, monosexual regime that told us what woman is while suppressing knowledge of what the Lily Briscoes and Virginia Woolfs of the world might have offered to our missing auto-biographies (Felman), we must allow a space of possibility for the specificity of the feminine as both effect and as a specific arrangement of drives, impulses, locations, pleasures, repressions, fantasies, losses and so forth.[78] The difference arises between the binary notion of opposites – man/woman – and the deconstructing move that allows itself to imagine a differentiating difference that is marked by the politics and indeed the aesthetics of *the feminine* as a process of both negation and transformation without reproducing fixed meaning; specifically, when this is enacted in formal artistic practices that themselves have altered their relation between predetermined figuration and representation and made the process itself open to pressures of 'emotions of a sexuated, psycho-sexual body' and its affects via a direct self-opening to less conscious, if not the impress of unconscious, processes.

Ironically, in the very spaces of the highest of abstract modernist painting, from which had been evacuated the signs and symbols of the continuing legacy of nineteenth-century culture's invidious division of the human subject into violently polarized genders, and in the name of an abstract universalism – 'serious art or ambitious painting' – there emerged the possibility of experimentation with a practice open to what French philosopher Jacques Derrida announced in 1963, and elaborated in 1982: *différance* – which I have mentioned but not yet fully explained.[79]

Derrida is indicating a dimension in text and language because two words in French, *différence* and *différance*, cannot be distinguished when spoken, only when written. This extends to a large principle because the words contain two senses, to *differ from* and to *defer to*, indicating that meaning is produced and unfixed in the same process, disallowing the idea that words have fixed meaning and that writing produces stable signification. Indeed, the deferral at work in any text that seeks to establish meaning by seemingly positing two distinct entities reveals their co-dependence and co-implication. Derrida uses this French anomaly to argue that all meaning works not only by difference (we hear distinct sounds or read distinct letters and thus recognize different words and their meanings), but by deferral within and between terms. M-a-n is distinct from t-a-n. Yet M-a-n differs from W-o-m-a-n on a different register, that of deferral, that is, the meaning of Man defers to what can be expressed as Man (+)/Woman (−). These words do not represent real entities. They are combinations of signifiers in a system based on difference and deferral in which the signification of Man relies on its not-Man other to stabilize its meaning, while the not-Man other, Woman, does not have a reciprocal stabilizer. This is an asymmetrical hierarchy of difference/deferral in phallocentric logic. It partly explains why in the pair artist/woman artist, the latter simply conveys *not artist* rather than one of several types of artist. Thus, the very abstraction and formalism of the Greenbergian view of the purified practice of modernist painting as completely 'steeped in its own cause' – the phrase is the French poet Mallarmé's from 1876 – paradoxically opens up the space of painting to the process of *différance* in every gesture, relation, effect and affect.[80]

Difference: the body as painter

American art historian Barbara Rose pointed out that the use of the stain and soak technique, which Helen Frankenthaler evolved in response to what she saw when she was drawn as a point of creative departure to the effects on the backs of Pollock's canvases into which the excess oil paint had seeped, was not entirely without precedent in the history of *à la prima* painting. Frankenthaler's significance lies in much more than inventing a painting technique that enabled paint and colour to become inseparable from the unprimed cotton duck, thus annihilating the distinction between medium and support, the distinction Greenberg determined as the major modernist process: 'For the first time in the history of art, the painterly was completely dissociated from the loaded brush' – or stick for that matter.[81] This displacement of the phallic brush is almost too obviously suggestive.

Frankenthaler also used thinned paints that almost mimicked watercolour washes, and she often rejected the strident colours of the Fauvist tradition as well as the monochromes of both Pollock's then current work, and before him, the still influential Cubist palette. These moves allowed her to resolve some of the tensions between pictorial space created by any marking of the canvas and absolute fidelity to the two-dimensionality of the canvas, which were, according to Greenberg's formulations at the time, the shibboleths that were the cutting edge issues for advanced post-Cubist painting. Through staining colour on to unprimed cotton duck, the artist effectively made surface and image, support and space, literally one yet always not-identical, thus allowing the optical ambiguities of colour densities to create the immaterial 'push and pull' which was so critical to the tension that such painting strove to create, and then contain, by its own logic, in lieu of the coherence created by traditional composition or the armature of drawing. 'Decomposition' – Bataille's favoured move – undermines composition but *matrixially*, even as a new aesthetic order is to be created by the very negation of its traditional modes.

It could be, and probably should have been, argued that much of Greenberg's later writing on the 1950s, including the famous '"American-Type" Painting' essay and his move to authorize colour field painting, would have been inconceivable without, or at least depended critically upon, what Helen Frankenthaler did from 1952 onwards and had thus opened up, and for which he only allowed her to be a 'bridge', not a game-changer in her own right.[82] Hers was a gesture of which he could never fully speak. Its full significance, I would argue, lay not in her 'sex' as a 'woman artist', but in the shifting of alignments within the practice towards what we now, the feminist generation of post-1968, with our psycho-semiotic terms of analysis, might tentatively, and with care, define as a semiotic dimension *in, of and from the feminine*, because we now have the means to theorize and politicize the complex we name sexual differ-ence, which both found a place in, and brought about changes to, New York abstract gestural painting through mobilizing the potentialities of process so that, for some painters, the effects were 'metramorphic' not phallic.

Like Pollock, Frankenthaler seized the key modernist assertion that process was at the heart of what was making this kind of painting 'new' and also truly 'abstract': in the very mode of making, the painting would itself become both the anti-signifying effect and the generator of aesthetic affect, not just Fry's emotion of form. As such, it would, however, neither achieve meaning nor justify interpretation. There would be no fixed sym-bolic equivalent. Associations, fleeting glimpses of possible forms, sugges-tions, prompts for parodic and humorous titles, yes. The paintings did not aim, however, to let what was on the canvas become a signifier for what was not. As other art historians before me have argued around Pollock's work, this project was also an assault on the centrality of *metaphor* that had so long constituted the basis of signification in Western painting.[83]

Identification of painting as both process and project could lead, however, to different affects. To conflate act and art could collapse the painter into the painting, thus making the subject, the producer, merely a part of his/her own object. An expressionist reading would then consider the painting an inscription of its maker, as an individual personality, psy-che or unconscious. Formalist, and later semiotic, readings of art tend more towards an author-decentring direction, reading painting alone as 'text', or in fact, anti-text, describable only by adjectival qualification. On the other hand, this same confusion of artist and practice could make the painting, the object, signify a single necessary dimension for this to be: namely, an author. Artist Mary Kelly argues that such reification and fetishization of the author characterized mainstream modernist criticism in its inevitable collaboration with the dealers, the art market and the exhibiting strategies of the capitalist culture industry.

Modernist criticism, according to Kelly, treated painting as the sup-port for the 'gesture' that serves, as a result of abstraction, to create and guarantee an *artistic subject* that then is provided with an author name for an exchangeable product – 'a Pollock'. *Gesture* in painting comes to be consumed (I am thinking Marx: production–distribution–exchange–consumption) as a *signature* – in the case of Abstract Expressionism the overall marking and making as much as the final verbal flourish of an added name – that confirms the artist's singular subjecthood as the symbolic commodity offered to the art market, a process that is assisted by art history's predominantly monographical writing and exhibition practices (the one-man [sic] show or the solo retrospective) in artist-centred modes.[84] What indeed are most retrospective exhibitions but another episode of this narrative affirmation of a single creative subjectivity through the painted signature of a singular artistic gesture tracing a career as synchronous with a life and a life as art? Authorship dominates scholarship and its constructed function is to predetermine the forms of our cultural consumption of art.[85]

To go beyond modernist criticism is to de-fetishize and de-commodify the modernist gesture/signature/author complex by returning both to the labouring, producing body and to subjectivity – on trial – in history, subjectivity as a condition not an individualized person, whose psychic and social practice the gesture indexes as it works across and within the non-representational space of its unplanned inscription on canvas. Instead of using the painting as a metaphor, a substitution for the artist, rendering 'him' (as this logic demands) the symbol and the subject of art, I propose to explore the practice of painting, in social as well as symbolic space, as a metonymic trace, an index of socially formed, psychically enacted subjectivities at work, both consciously and unconsciously, upon, in this case, painting's materials.

The key is to trace the relations between the gesture (not understood as mere formal device or technique, and not just as a way of putting on paint, but as the overall semiotic process of a specific context of painting as a modernist practice), the surface (not imagined as flat support, but rather as a territory, a field, a mirror, a screen, a psychic territory and an imaginary otherness) and the subject (not as the coherence retrospectively secured by name as author/artist, but as a process, divided, heterogeneous, negotiating difference and the radical instabilities of identity, and as *différance*). This requires us also to rethink *le masculin* more deeply and explore gesture and difference more fully.

Let me return to my opening epigraph by painter Bracha Ettinger. She argues that what artists bring into culture 'from the margins of their consciousness' can transgress the limits of, enlarge or shift the dominant Symbolic order she defines as phallic because it is structured solely by the symbol, Phallus. She also argues that this transgressive, potential transformation 'cannot be detached from ideas, perceptions, emotions, consciousness, cultural meaning' and 'subjective traces of their creators'. Because of the entanglement of subjectivity as process with aesthetic process, there is a possibility of new creation, a genesis of meaning that calls for and desires interpretation so that their novelties can become part of a shifted culture through the hospitality of serious engagement with what such *artworking* is bringing into the world. From this 'analysis of inscriptions' we can 'forge new concepts' (enabling thinking and theory) which indicate and elaborate 'traces of an-other Real' and 'change aspects of the symbolic representation (and non-representation) of the feminine within culture'.

Thus, challenging Greenberg's deafening silence in the face of the transgressive moves of painter-women at this time in the history of modern, abstract painting, we do not, however, *add in some missing names*, but seek *to enlarge the entire frame of our understanding* of both the character of the dominant culture and the potential for its transformation at the level of our understanding of subjectivity and its 'inscriptions' differently. *Differently* means at the level of an expansion of concepts of art and meaning that shifts and supplements, but is not an other to, a currently universalized white, heterocratic masculine norm. The 'feminine' theorized with the Matrix is not 'of women' as defined by the Phallus, and not an attribute of gendered persons. It is a site within the expanded field of subjectivity and creativity, intersecting with the aesthetic sphere and its psycho-somatic processes.

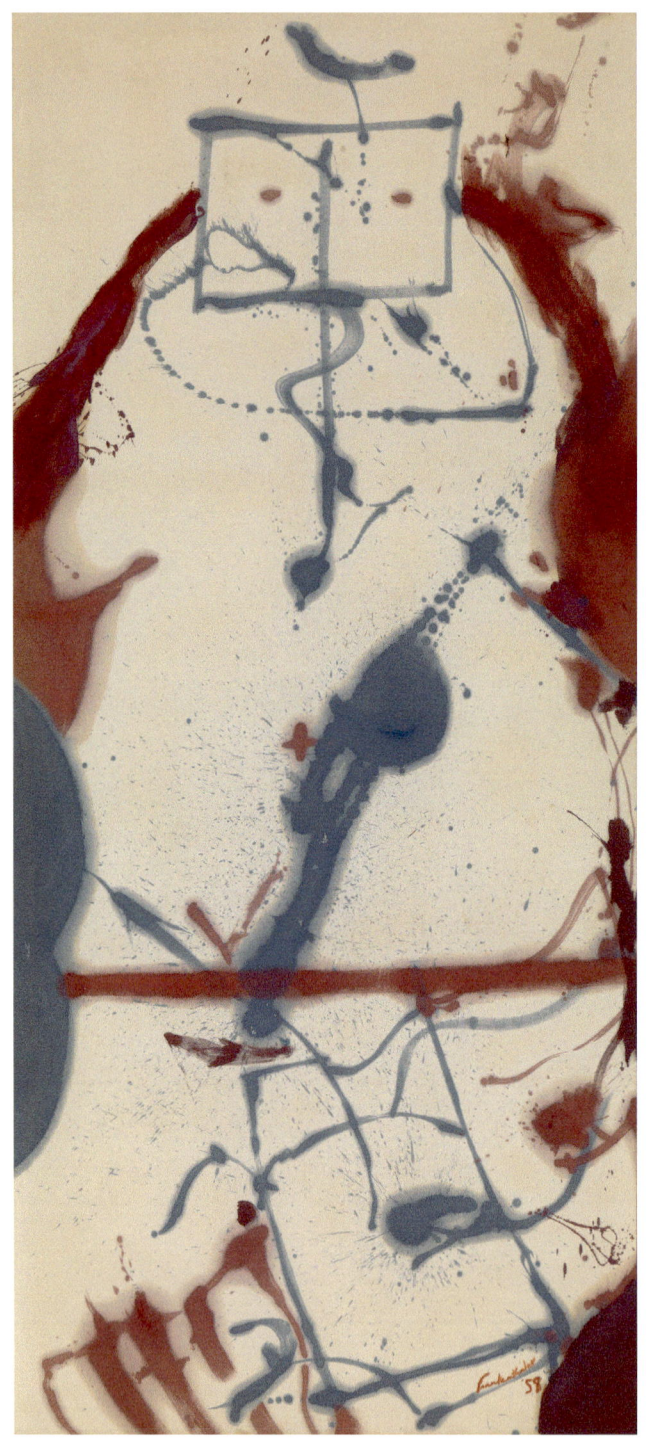

Figure 4.1 Helen Frankenthaler, *Nude*, 1958

Is the gesture male?

Disappearing the mother into symbol or capturing her absence in space

> Woman then stands in patriarchal order as signifier of the male other, bound by a symbolic order in which man can live out his phantasies and obsessions through linguistic command by imposing them on the silent image of woman still tied to her place as bearer of meaning, not maker of meaning.
>
> Laura Mulvey[1]

> That is, once the painting is *there* – painted – and the *immediate* reaction to it (feeling) is passed, it is possible to examine and discuss the whys … There are no flat rules for getting at the workings of a painting, but I feel more than ever that the secrets lie in ambiguity; ambiguity that makes a complete final statement in the painting whole.
>
> Helen Frankenthaler, 1950

> I learned how to look at modern pictures because of old masters, and vice versa.
>
> Helen Frankenthaler, 1989[2]

The painting titled *Nude* (1958, fig. 4.1) is hung on the vertical, portrait not landscape, orientation. Title and orientation incite us to look for a figure, to see a body, to imagine a sexed body, to link title and female, sexual body. Its title places the work in the category of Western art first analysed as a genre by Kenneth Clark in his Warburg-inspired study of the nude as pathos formula in 1956.[3] Yet this work was painted abstractly by the same procedures discovered and enacted in *Mountains and Sea* (fig. 3.5), stain and soak, poured, spread and drawn. What are we seeing? What was the painter finding through her gesture?

My title question, 'Is the gesture male?', knowingly invokes a widely used (and abused) concept arising in feminist film theory, from which, following Laura Mulvey, film theorist E. Ann Kaplan titled an essay introducing a whole series of studies on feminism and cinema: 'Is the gaze male?'[4] Elegant as this formulation is, the term *male* is not accurate. Mulvey posed her investigation into cinema through psychoanalysis, in which the terms *masculine* and *feminine* define psycho-social-linguistic positions, relative and asymmetrical, and always failing – hence the compulsive iteration of the phallic model of sexual difference across an entire, brilliant and entrancing industry. Some feminists have been misled into imagining that we can posit a *female* gaze, a gaze of women. Thus Helen Frankenthaler, a woman, paints a *Nude* that suggests a female body, and we might be tempted to ask is her gaze female as she looks upon the figuration that emerges from her painting gestures being anchored by its art historical self-classification as *Nude*.

What can thinking with psychoanalysis offer to those of us asking questions about both the place of *Woman* in a patriarchal Symbolic and the means of discovering other pleasures, other anxieties, other desires in relation to women 'as makers of meaning' (Mulvey) in this field of abstract, gestural painting? To take us further, I shall introduce artist and theorist Bracha L. Ettinger's concept of *fascinance*. *Fascinance* means prolonged and sustained looking at and learning from a desirable Woman-other on the part of a Girl who will become a woman, but not by internalizing the negative notion of her own castratedness (the Freudian thesis). Instead, she may learn her own desirability through reciprocal gazing (seeing, welcomed, and being seen) – *fascinance* – desirability not being herself as sexual object of a man, but herself as subject of desire and, one might say, as locus of desirable attributes of all kinds necessary for being a full person. My feminist art historical quest to see the works created by women constitutes itself such a *fascinance*.

Many nudes in Western art recline, especially in works by the great Venetians Giorgione and Titian, who effectively elaborated the erotic nude (for example, Giorgione's *Sleeping Venus* [1510, Gemäldegalerie, Dresden] or Titian's *Danae and the Shower of Gold* [1560–65, fig. 4.2]). Titian was a painter much admired and studied by Helen Frankenthaler for his fabulous elaboration of the possibilities of oil painting and colour. Please now turn Frankenthaler's painting (fig. 4.1) horizontally, first to the right and then to the left. What do you see, without the vertical axis? Can we still see the nude female sexual body? I think not. Elements suggestive of breasts or a head with eyes are now seen vertically.

My speculation is that the canvas was begun on the floor and on a horizontal axis. I also suspect that it has been cropped along the top and the bottom edges, on that axis. If viewed by a right-hand turn to the horizontal, I see a central spill or pour of blue paint claiming the canvas as a starting point. Working with that colour, there is one small spill on the left and trails of paint that create a rectangle around it, and there is a rectangle on the right. There is also a double swell of this same colour on the

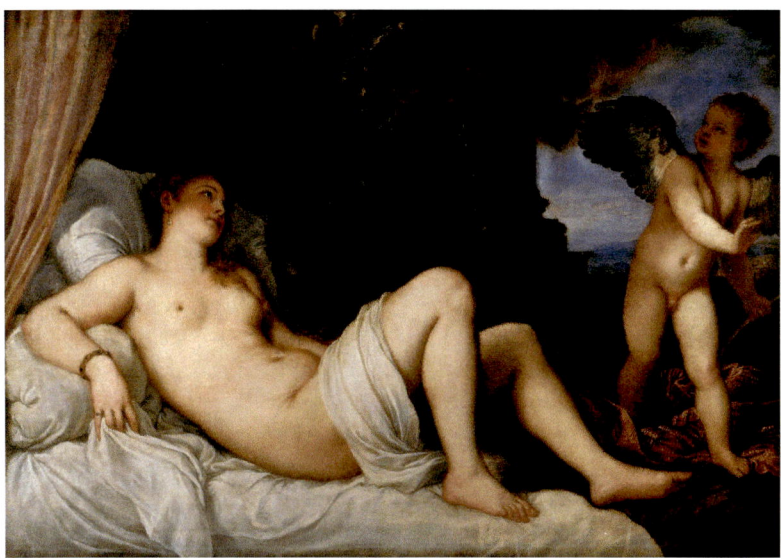

Figure 4.2 Titian, *Danae and the Shower of Gold*, 1544–46

edge that has a tiny halo of oil around it. The rich, earthy reds are introduced to nudge a space into view from the otherwise unmarked area, perhaps initially marked with small spills and shapes. As this occurs, possibilities arise, and when turned to the left on to the vertical or seen from the lower left-hand end as the artist looked from there along the length of the canvas, something else came into view, which could be held in sight by a title that places this painting in conversation with the great machines of historical oil painting. This is one hypothesis as to how this axis, this title and an evocation of the history of art and a sexed figure might have turned up in Frankenthaler's studio as she worked with her materials.

What shall we need to consider to proceed to study this work?

Laura Mulvey opened the case for a feminist analysis of cinema using psychoanalysis as a 'political weapon, demonstrating the way the unconscious of a patriarchal society has structured film form'.[5] Focusing on the visual pleasure offered by the forms in which the feminine other is coded and offered to a *masculinized* spectator through voyeurism (sadistic looking) or scopophilic fetishism (rendering a fearful sight aesthetically beautiful to displace the anxiety incited by lack), Mulvey carefully identified the overlaying of cinematic and psychic mechanisms that *masculinized* the – any – spectator and the process of fascinated looking she termed *the gaze*. The shorthand phrase she used, *only once* in a very subtle and complex argument, was 'the determining male gaze'.[6] I am returning to this over-familiar concept, which has been banalized beyond usefulness, because 'the male gaze' has, unfortunately and incorrectly, become widespread as the simplistic idea that heterosexual men natu-rally like looking erotically at beautiful women and their bodies. Mul-vey's surprising argument revealed quite the opposite. The masculine subject is, she argued, terrified by the *sight* of woman, disarmed by the woman as sight/site of difference, and cinema is an elaborate plea-sure-managing machine for negotiating the deeply contradictory mascu-line psycho-sexual condition *in the field of vision*.

Let me recap Mulvey's precise argument. On the one hand, we all take pleasure in looking. This arises, pre-Oedipally, from both the dou-bling of *scopophilia* – the delight in looking at others – and *exhibitionism* – the delight in being looked at, both characteristic of all infants. Then, as an effect of Oedipal castration anxiety on the masculine subject, terror becomes associated with the sight and image of woman, whose differ-ence appears to confirm a horror of mutilation and the threat of loss of the tiny organ autoerotically offering the child comfort and pleasure. This is castration anxiety. Terror/horror incites defences that engender both Oedipally scopophilic *fetishization* of the female body – building up its aesthetic appearance and/or phallically remodelling the body itself as fetish – and, in narrative form, plays out a sadism enacted by what is done to women, and through the cinematic rendering via the voyeuristic gaze. Mulvey argued that using psychoanalysis provided an analytical tool not only to identify the patriarchal and phallocentric *unconscious* that cinema spectacularized and institutionalized, but also to reveal the missing knowledge in both cinema and conventional psychoanalysis so that we, women as feminists, can inquire into issues for women and a 'female unconscious', such as 'the sexing of the female infant and her relation to the symbolic, the sexually mature woman as non-mother, maternity out-side of signification of the phallus ...'.[7] Mulvey deconstructed the normal-ized pleasures offered by patriarchal Hollywood cinema to enable women's production as filmmakers and viewers to create and experience 'a new language of desire' that would, of course, be written in cinematic forms while negotiating and differencing its component, psychic and aes-thetic mechanisms. It was in this context that Kaplan titled an essay introducing a whole series of studies on feminism and cinema: 'Is the gaze male?'

From the neighbouring territory of New York painting 1940–70, I pun on this question in the same interrogative and theoretically investigative spirit by asking, not entirely ironically, 'Is the gesture male?' What can thinking with psychoanalysis offer when exploring the place of *Woman* in a patriarchal Symbolic and the means of discovering other pleasures, other anxieties, other desires in relation to women 'as makers of meaning' in this field of *gestural* painting?

Theorizing the gesture as site of sexual difference

In her study of sculptor Louise Bourgeois, Hilary Robinson drew on philosopher Luce Irigaray's 'Gesture in Psychoanalysis'.[8] I now draw Irigaray's analysis into an excursus on sexual difference and the role of gesture in the painting practices with which I am here concerned to provoke reflection, while wanting to revoke any suggestion of a simplified absolutism: men paint/gesture like this and women like that.

As both philosopher, linguist and psychoanalyst, and observer of infant play and speech, Irigaray challenged traditional and much feminist philosophy by asserting that sexual difference must be the key question of our age.[9] Her philosophy has often been misread as universalizing and absolute. She has been misinterpreted as 'essentializing' sexual difference in terms of men, women and heterosexuality, partly because she is posing her questions in terms of those forms of human being whose asymmetrical difference has structured Western thought, and certainly corresponds to how many people think of themselves and to the basis on which most societies define the differential and discriminatory treatment of those they regard as men and women.[10] Queer theory has thus critiqued, if never entirely disowned, Irigaray's thought. However, read philosophically, rather than anatomically, and for her specific textual strategies in analysing the gendered metaphorics of Western philosophy and psychoanalysis, her writings can be shown consciously to mimic, parody and revise the declarative assurance of Western, phallogocentric philosophy, which not only tends to think through absolute oppositions, but also metaphorizes its entire system of thought in terms of a gender binary, asserting and sustaining the asymmetrical hierarchy of One and its Other in the forms of the One (and only) sex – masculine – and its Other.

We are not done with the complexities of sexual difference when we hardly understand of what we speak. Psychoanalytical theory has become one way as both a theoretical opening of sexual difference *as an unfinished question* and a historically conditioned institution that has promoted and maintained an ideological interpretation of sexual difference that it has been necessary to challenge, as did many of the feminist writers of the 1960s–1970s. Feminist denunciations of the psychoanalytical institution have, therefore, been challenged with equal force by those for whom psychoanalysis is of immense significance because it explores psychic life – subjectivity – its formations, its deviations, its resources and its traumas, as they interweave with social, economic and cultural modes of subjection and play out across aesthetic practices in art, literature, music, opera, cinema, popular culture and the media.[11]

The gesture in psychoanalysis

'Gesture in Psychoanalysis' is one of Irigaray's assaults on the false neutrality of Western philosophy and psychoanalysis. In her exploration of gesture as an elaborated meaning system involving both bodies in space and intersubjective relations paralleling verbal communication, Irigaray thinks about sexual difference in the analytical scenario. Imagine the bodies and the space: the recumbent, speaking or silent analysand and the unseen, upright, listening analyst behind. The gestures – that is, lying down in a professional space and talking to someone who does not reply about things that memories and associations prompt from formative scenarios with parents, carers, siblings, then falling silent, weeping, raging, discovering – break with social conventions and the relations of signs to language, and to the here and now. Irigaray's question is this: does sexual difference matter to the way this disarming analytical scene is experienced and how it works. Some analysts argue that it cannot matter because the analytic scenario returns analysands, male and female alike, to a childlike state. So, Irigaray asks: is *the child* neuter?

To answer this, Irigaray turns to the game, *fort/da*, already mentioned in the previous chapter, which concerned Freud's interpretation of his grandson, Ernst, playing with his cotton reel when his mother left him. Freud used this episode to introduce his exposition of the theory of repetition and his unexpected discovery of the death drive: an anxiety that leads not to self-killing but a desire to escape the anxiety of being as *being left*: separation.[12]

To deal with his mother's occasional absence intimating the development process of his separation from her body, little Ernst invents and plays three games. In the first, he throws a cotton reel away and accompanies the gesture with the vocalization, *o-o-o*. In the second version, he throws away the reel but draws it back with a string and now utters a second vocalization *a-a-a* when the reel is recalled. These sounds are interpreted by Freud and Ernst's mother, Sophie, as the German words *fort* – gone, and *da* – there as in here. The interpretation is that both reel and words become part of the way the little child is dealing with the anxiety occasioned by separation from his mother and the absence of her once-nurturing body. In a third variation, Ernst kneels before a mirror and makes his image disappear and reappear while expressing now the phrases *bébi ooo* and *bébi aaa*.

Much analytical literature has devoted itself to the discussion of these games and the ways in which they dramatize how maternal absence propels the child towards the use of symbols through play and ultimately words: 1) external object-symbols, such as the toy cotton reel that stands for the disappearing and reappearing mother, as much as for the mastery the boy-child is imaginatively creating for himself in the *play repetition* of away and return; 2) internal, verbal symbols, in which the boy-child masters loss through vocalizations that, according to Irigaray's psycholinguistic interpretation, are significantly varied in their force and position in terms of lips, tongue, teeth, through which we create differentiated sounds as consonants and vowels. Expulsive sounds (*fort*) may mark the phantasy of mastery while others (*da*) may symbolically keep the mother inside where the sounding vibrates in the mouth, shutting the imaginary mother that such sounds evoke behind the teeth: within.

Freud observed and interpreted in his grandson the initiating processes of symbolic substitution that would eventually insert the boy-child and his ambivalent relations to loss and mastery by phantasy into the signifying chain of language and culture. Irigaray pauses to ask if this story could have been told about a girl. She argues not.

> A girl does not do the same things when her mother goes away. She does not play with string and reel that *symbolize* the mother, because the mother is the same sex as she is and cannot have the *object status* of a reel. The mother is of the same *subjective identity* as she is.[13] (my emphases)

This could, for some, be a problematic statement in so far as it might lead us to think that Irigaray assumes an early knowledge on the part of the girl of sexuation or gender identity. We can, however, read it another way, and then it is not at all strange. For, I would argue, there would be no reason for any child to imagine itself different from its mother. It is the culture that invents and imposes sexual differentiation on children, which afflicts the child who has to learn he is a boy; not just that his mother leaves him and that he must gradually lose access to her body, but that he is exiled permanently from being like the figure of nurture who sustains all his needs and desires at this point. It is this trauma that erects the boy's sense of defensive masculinity as an anxiogenic and indeed traumatic realization *of his difference from the mother*; that he is not like the primary human other on whom his life has depended (Mother condenses all caring and nurturing). The game of *fort–da* is one of the mythic moments of that condensation of absence and loss with a prescience of the trauma not of absence, but of the difference of the boy-child from his mother, to cover which anxiety what we call masculinity is formed – with radical repercussions for the girl-child in a system ruled by the Father endowing the boy with a compensatory illusion of future phallic authority that is aligned with aggressive defensiveness.

So, without having to assume that the little girl knows the phallocentric order of sexual *difference* and consciously recognizes that she is *the same as* what the phallocentric order constructs as its difference – the feminine – we can follow Irigaray, who allows femininity to have its own, particular psychic formation and history between girl and mother. She then asks: what will the girl's reactions be to *her* separation from *the/her* mother? When she misses her mother, Irigaray observes, the little girl may throw herself down on the ground in distress. She is lost. She loses the power and the will to live. She neither speaks nor eats. She becomes totally anorexic. Or,

> She plays with a doll, lavishing maternal affection on a quasi-subject, and thus manages to organize a kind of symbolic space; playing with dolls is not simply a game girls are forced to play; it signifies a difference in subjective status in the separation from the mother. For mother and daughter, the mother is a subject that cannot be easily reduced to an object, and a doll is not an object in the way that a reel, a toy car, a gun are objects and tools used for symbolization.[14]

A third defence Irigaray outlines is when a little girl 'dances and thus forms a vital subjective space open to the cosmic maternal world … to the present other'. If she speaks during this play, it will not be the opposing of syllables and phonemes, but something like a litany or a song, tonally modulated, often a humming, which deeply keeps the *mmmmm* within the mouth.

Irigaray analyses the psychic basis of differences arising from the primary psychological formation through the required separation from the primary, the maternal Other, differences often merely sociologically ascribed to the social conditioning of young children according to gendered conventions. In doing so, Irigaray posits structurally *differentiating* post-natal, psychic processes in which the girl-child negotiates separation. What is specifically relevant for this study of a moment in the history of painting practices in the West is Irigaray's focus on the sexual difference at work in the psychic experiences of space, rhythm and the gestures of the body that *psychically* enact the experience of what Ettinger, in her own, radically different theorization of the pre-maternal, pre-natal, proto-psychic formation, the matrixial, elaborates further as *proximity-and-distance*, *relations-without-relating* and a shared *borderspace* between *several* partialized subjects.

Helen Frankenthaler

In *Nude* (fig. 4.1) Helen Frankenthaler poured, stained and spread paint in ways that, clearly, left much of the central area of the canvas blank. This almost empty space makes visible *in the negative* a potential figuration. Titling anchors it as a maternal or mature sexual female nude. With no little humour, the nude appears only as the painter let it emerge from within the canvas into a visibility that cannot, however, detach her from that support. It is through colour and the ambiguous play between the absence and presence of the painted gestures and trailed paint that the artist discovered, and then allowed, something of what I invoke as *Woman/ Mother* to become an intimated presence, never a representation, because it is also formed negatively as where the paint is not.

Neither viciously covered, strangled, trapped nor wrenched into or out of shape as we find in the paintings of *Woman* by de Kooning (fig. 6.1), a reference to a female body has been made visible, and yet 'she' is not there. 'She' is neither absent nor present. The mirage that is titled *Nude* is also made nude by no-paint applied to where a form is created negatively by the paint soaking into the canvas. *Nude* is precisely the effect of where the traces of the artist's gesture-deposited colour have not stained the surface. *Nude* is what *becomes* where the artist has not touched. *Nude* is almost present as where the painter has not been. In this flowing play, the painting dialectically creates an allusive, yet elusive, almost-form.

We have the painter's marks and the pools of paint. We see a possibility created by where paint has not stained. Signs of the painter and the image she has *not* painted coexist and co-emerge in an oscillation that draws attention to the fundamental play in painting, as Alison Rowley explained earlier, between its presence as material and medium and its ability virtually to evoke the impression of an image of something in the world, or to deliver into visibility a phantasm from the imagination.[15] I am tempted to read this form of ambiguity (Frankenthaler named another painting after the book by William Empson, *Seven Types of Ambiguity* [1930]) in terms of Irigarayan exploration of the specificity of a feminine psyche as the evocation of play that does not so much create a symbolic substitute object for the missing mother, but 'dances', making a symbolic *space* in which the Mother – and also perhaps the trace of Ettinger's matrixial *m/Other* – is not lost and substituted and the one does not have to die for the other to be. The field of painting becomes *a dancing space*. Irigaray writes: 'Girls describe a space around themselves rather than displacing a substitute object from one place to another.'[16]

There is, however, a fundamental flaw in this argument as I have presented it so far.

I seem to be setting up the possibility of a painting practice that is not caught up in the logic of *fort–da*. Rowley has suggested that painting cannot but be part of that process. We ask repeatedly: Is it just paint? Is it an image?[17] The very conditions of 'material there/not thereness, the mark/ no mark, form/no form of the paint on canvas' pulls all painting into that 'phallic' on/off field.

In a sustained psychoanalytical analysis of this very artistic/theoretical problem of painting, *The Matrixial Gaze* (1994), painter-analyst Bracha L. Ettinger examines the varieties of theories that struggle to analyse and go beyond *fort–da* to understand aesthetics: philosopher Jean-François

Lyotard proposed an archaic *figure-matrice*, psychoanalyst Pierre Fédida theorized what he termed *objeu* – a wordplay on object (*objet*) and play (*jeu*) in French. These attempts explore the very conditions of meaning and subjectivity in a kind of pulsional scansion of the play of presence and absence that animates a certain kind of gestural painting. Fédida argues: 'It is perhaps *the mother as repetition* […] *repetition as the mother*', and,

> What we call meaning is engendered by the play of absence-presence […] It is not enough to say that the reel play is the active staging of a repetition passively experienced by the child (Freud leads us to this interpretation): there is no play possible without the rupture (disjunction) introduced here in the repetition and aided by the enacting of this repetition … What is important is the discovery of meaning as absence and the play finds its strength in the creation of the effect of absence's meaning.[18]

Ettinger glosses this Freudian reading with her matrixial shift:

> The absence of the mother is painful by what she leaves behind when she is no longer there, that is a repetition wherein even play is impossible because the I finds itself subjected to the mother's active absence and 'it is under these circumstances that the presence-absence scansion – *before it becomes play* – is correlative to a passivity in which the "subject" is activated [*agi*]'. The production of meaning is initiated by the creation of absence, so that 'one might claim that *there is no meaning outside the playing of absence.*' Presence-absence thus connotes the event-moment of meaning when the subject is not only passive but is also active toward the object and the Other.[19]

Ettinger then proposes to explore another possibility for painting as play/ work in this domain. In these negotiations of the limits of absence/presence as the condition of meaning, Ettinger sees what she terms the 'post-natal offspring of the Matrix' and then outlines a supplementary mode of the gaze:

> The matrixial gaze emerges by a simultaneous reversal of with-in and with-out. The matrixial space as encounter does not represent an eternal inside, which is how Fédida suggests we understand the space of the uterus. The matrixial gaze emerges in a transgression of borderlinks manifested in a contact with-in/out an artwork. This subject-object transcendence of the subject-object interval *is not a fusion* because it is based on an a-priori *shareability-in-difference.*[20]

Irigaray suggested that the girl-child has no reason to question that she shares something with the Mother. Ettinger is proposing something more structural in the conditions of human becoming in which the late pre-natal/ pre-maternal matrixial condition already leads all becoming-infants to the intimation of the co-emerging presence of a not-quite-other that Ettinger terms the *m/Other*. We now know that post-natal infants respond to music heard intra-uterine. Thus, late pre-natality is neither fusion nor symbiosis. There is difference but it is a shared space. There is no possibility of not-sharing. This, Ettinger argues, lays downs a proto-subjectivizing track, a primordial archaic track of sensations, intimations and aesthetic effects carried into post-natal life in all born human subjects. The Matrix is the earliest experience of humanizing, subjectivizing otherness that is insepa-rable from a co-emergence. It leaves post-natal tracings in aesthetic pro-cesses and aesthetic responsiveness.

> In the matrixial aesthetic experience, 'relations without relating' transform the unknown Other into a still unknown partial subject with-in an encoun-ter. The subject's relations with the Other do not turn it into a known object, swallowed or fused, rejected or abjected. The *non-I/non-entirely-other as a subject* changes me while *I/non-object* changes the *non-I;* all participants receive and invest libido with-in and with-out through the joint process of change itself – the metramorphosis – with-in and with-out their common borderspace.[21]

The operation by which this encounter happens is not symbolism but *metramorphosis*, which involves the non-traumatic transgression of bor-ders without causing collapse of the partners (what would post-natally be a psychosis). Thus, matrixial sharing of thresholds and transgression of borders and fixed limits is a primordial condition of our becoming, com-ing into being and meaning.

> Transgression becomes an ontogenetic meaning; conversely meaning becomes a matrixial transgression. In metramorphosis, the fluidity of expe-rience places both partial subjects in a *reciprocity without symmetry*, in which they are both *transformed and differently transform each other*, creating *joint eroticized aerials* further shaped by traces of their irradiation, engendering *matrixial desire*.[22] (my emphases)

These expanding theorizations of subjectivity, sexual difference and the matrixial allow us to draw out from this moment of painting the differ-ent psycho-corporeal registers on which they were formed and through which they form us as we view them now. The finished painting is always in the end a symbolic substitution. Its making, however, becomes a site of a replay of the process of negotiating meaning through absence (Fédida). It can, moreover, also be the space for an aesthetic and psychic supple-mentation from another level or stratum such as matrixial subjectivity, that coexists with and swims beneath, shifting the phallic on/off logic, even though phallic culture and its theories of both meaning and the sub-ject have repressed the recognition of such a supplementary level where the sexual difference as *m/f* is not yet in place, while a difference from the matrixial feminine is already-always affecting all and any subject who is born. Matrixial theory allows us to acknowledge the coexistence of both the proposition that, as a phallic activity, painting is ruled by the logic of *fort–da* and that, as a matrixial process, it is open to aesthetic co-affecting transgression of the shared borderspace of partners-in-difference unknown to each other. Some painting may intimate in its very procedures and resulting forms a supplementary negotiation of difference through the shared matrixial borderspace experienced in our earliest, aesthetic, pre-cognitive incitements into human proto-subjectivity. In the aesthetic evocation of the archaic but still active matrixial borderspace of shared becoming within all subjectivities, several partial-subjects almost encounter each other at the moment of the painter's touch at the limits of the visible – even though that gesture, in a phallic prism, enacts the mark/no mark, on/off logic that defines the phallic order of signification and subjectivity.

This theoretically rich – and challenging – investigation into sexual difference and the painting practice of the 1950s and beyond does not end here. Theoretically, there is a division. On the one hand, there is still the necessity to undo the fixities of gender, where gender is understood as a determination of identity and is used as the prejudicial ground for differential treatment of artists by art histories and artworlds when this nomination as man or woman positively or negatively determines their access to exhibition, and frames critical reception and appraisal. On the other hand, from the resources offered by various psychoanalyses from the classic and phallocentric to more recent elaborations including Ettinger's on the matrixial feminine, as well as from cultural theories acknowledging the interlacing of psychic formations, the aesthetic and the semiotic, we have a radically different conceptualization of subjectivity formed through phallocentric and Oedipal processes and also through others. Concepts of the feminine in both psychoanalytically inflected discourses (phallic and matrixial) do not refer to women but 1) *phallically* to post-natal identifications and positionality within a field of triangulated relations (the Oedipal model) and 2) *matrixially* to a constitutive almost-other, *the m/Other*, to whose affects and effects as a co-emerging, co-affecting partner-in-difference in proximity-in-distance all born subjects have been exposed, and whose traces we all carry as an aesthetic, proto-ethical dimension within our subjectivity later, post-natally, impressed into its Oedipal moulds. Now I must return to Irigaray's little Girl and her Mother and introduce, from Ettinger, a third dimension we need to consider. This is the *ffAm*, a site of *fascinance* for the becoming Girl-Woman learning her adult desire and desirability.

Fascinance and *ffAm: femme-fatale-Autre-mère*

Ettinger has developed a theory of a supplementary stratum in the forma-tion of subjectivity, the matrixial, the most archaic dimension shared by all irrespective of later sexualities and gender identifications. The Matrix is archaically formed in the *asymmetric severality of late pre-maternity/ pre-natality*. Its affects and possibilities persist, however, across the trau-matic expulsion of the pre-infant into its post-natal condition, subjected, in classical psychoanalytical theory, to progressive stages of separation: birth, weaning, symbolic 'castration' and the precipitation Oedipally into language. This phallic model never completely obliterates the matrixial, which *expands* our hitherto unitary concept of the Symbolic (the realm of meaning and its signifiers) so that it becomes possible to imagine more than one signifier for the processes and multiple strata within subjectiv-ity.[23] Matrix and Phallus are signifiers. They differentially organize modes of meaning. Subjectivity is thus formed under more than one logic with-out either supplanting or knocking the other out.

In lieu of the monolithic One, established by phallic logic, Ettinger theorizes the stratum of archaic, aesthetic, non-linguistic impressions and affects that arise before the post-natal One/Other binary emerges to structure subjectivity in the dominating phallic mode to which we all accede in order to become speaking, sexuated subjects. Matrixial affects emerge through *aesthetic* dimensions such as sense, sound, movement, breath, rhythm and acoustic resonance on the side of the becoming-in-fant in the later stages of its uterine existence, while the becoming-mater-nal is precipitated by the becoming-infant into reawakenings and carried fantasies of her own matrixial infant co-becoming. Matrix signifies pro-cesses of co-affecting, co-emergence and co-transforming occurring across the shared borderspaces of the matrixial severality through *metramorphosis*.

A symbol, just as the Phallus is a symbol that organizes meaning, the Matrix allows us to acknowledge those aspects of feminine psycho-corporeal specificity that contribute to human subjectivity. Such acknowledgement allows those effects to filter into and enlarge the Sym-bolic, the realm of signified meaning.[24] Acknowledged, the Matrix allows 'the relief of signification' for those meanings that the phallically domi-nated Symbolic currently forecloses (denies signification to), leaving them in the realm of psychosis or mysticism. Matrixial feminine psycho-corporeal specificity is, it must be clear, neither anatomical (Freud) nor morphological (Irigaray). Yet it is undeniably corporeal, and its primary plane is *aesthesis*: aesthetic rather than cognitive. While utterly distinct from Luce Irigaray's theory, Ettinger's Matrix also challenges the denial of sexual difference as an issue of complex significance by formulating a complex theorization of sexual difference. I have elaborated it here because it alone supplies some of the *aesthetic* dimension to the insights Irigaray will offer from her observations of the post-natal girl-child's negotiation of separation from the post-natal Mother.

Irigaray attends to the much later occurrence of the daughter's – feminine – response to the absence of the post-natal Mother through the enactment of 'dancing space', rhythmic sound and non-syntactical vocalization. To this I am adding the negotiation of the loss of psychologically formative, shared matrixial corporeality that also draws attention to *aesthesis*: the registers of movement, pressure, sound, resonance, co-affection. The matrixial tempers the phallic demand for absolute separation from the Mother, which its logic retrospectively reduces to merely a containing body, and the pre-natal maternal as a potentially overwhelming No-Thing. The archaic matrixial feminine that Ettinger terms *m/Other* is jointness-in-difference that gives rise post-natally to positions, not of loss and mourning, but of *wit(h)ness* and *fascinance*. As a durational transforming mode of unsighted gazing and being transformed, *fascinance* is incited archaically but becomes significant in post-natal relations for the infant who is now becoming a Girl. Ettinger explains *fascinance* as the feminine position negotiating difference between the Girl and the woman-*m/Other*.[25]

> I am describing a *transubjective* psychic position that infiltrates these later psychic positions. I suggest that long before and also beside, after and beyond Oedipus, the girl is not jealous of the mother because the father desires the mother instead of herself. This will arrive later. The girl is jealous because she recognizes the difference between a girl and a woman-m/Other.[26]

Ettinger displaces the Freudian thesis that the girl becomes a girl by turning away from the mother in hatred for having born her as a castrated being or through jealous rivalry with the father. For Ettinger, we have to ask how the the girl comes to understand what she will become as an adult woman. She argues that it is by gazing-learning, *fascinance*, at an adult woman, not her mother, in order to situate herself in desirability, to situate herself in desire.

> The girl needs to find ways, and many times she fails again and again to find them, for sharing in the secrets of femininity with a *m/Other* whose fascination she must catch in/for their shareable space. She looks for a Woman-Mother figure whom she might adore and whose secrets she would be able to share on condition that such a *m/Other* would open herself to allow such a sharing and accommodate her gaze. She looks for proofs of the desirability of this figure by images and symbols. Any rejection or betrayal of and by such a figure feels catastrophic for the girl who is trying to become a woman.[27]

Ettinger recognizes this process already registered in literature and psychoanalysis, but not recognized. She refers to and matrixially reinterprets the famous case study study by Freud of a young suicidal woman, code-named 'Dora' (1905), who was caught between her sickly mother and a sexually desirable woman, her father's lover, 'Frau K', to whom she herself drew close, all mediated by her 'fascination' with Raphael's painting of a young mother in *The Sistine Madonna*. Ettinger's other case study is a novel by Marguerite Duras, *The Ravishment of Lol V. Stein* (1964), the tragic story of a young woman seeking to resolve her own becoming as an adult, sexual woman who is traumatically precipitated into psychosis for lack of the time for *fascinance* to perform its transformative psychic work in relation to an adult woman and mother, Anne-Marie Stretter.

Ettinger redefines sexual difference, introducing terms with which to trace the psychic formation of the feminine subject in relation to another woman in *fascinance*. This displaces the phallocentric account of a girl's psychic formation as her turning away in hatred from the mother she discovers to be castrated (Freud's basic thesis), and hence that she too is castrated, lacking vis-à-vis the masculine. Ettinger's radical revision offers the following. (She uses the term 'female' intentionally to insist on corporeality as a layer of any theory of subjectivity, while femininity is a psychic position.)

> The sexual difference of any human being (female or male) is staged with and against a female *m/Other-woman* figure. Even where the maternal post-natal figure is male, the prenatal maternal figure is always female, and the imprints of the contact with this female figure will infiltrate any maternal figure, be it the same or another person. The first corporeal-psychic connection between I and non-I occurs inside the maternal womb where every I is in [real and proto-psychic] linkage with the female invisible corporeality and *is borderlinking to the m/Other's psychic environment.*[28]

This leads to the proposal of new terms for this negotiation of the post-natal formation of femininity and her desire and desirability that moves from the primordial *m/Other* to the *Woman-beneath-the-m/Other* in what Ettinger proposes is *transubjectivity*:

> From then on, *the self-difference and the sexual difference of any human being embodied as female (Girl)* is defined with and in reference to another woman (the *m/Other*) first, and at a later stage also to several other women who can hold the site – time-and-space – of the *Woman-beneath-the-m/Other*, who remains forever enveloped inside the figure of the archaic *m/Other* that dwelt in resonance with the I within the primary relational field of encounter. In post-natal life, this relational field is thought of not in terms of inter-subjective relationships of the *Girl* with *the Woman-m/Other* but firstly in terms of transubjectivity.[29]

Ettinger thus argues that long before and alongside Oedipal formation, there is a feminine sexual difference shaped in matrixial co-emergence: '*the difference of the girl child from another woman – a woman-m/Other figure –* not from men, boys or the father – a difference opened in jointness and inside resemblance', and concludes: 'In other words, the enigma of feminine sexual difference is posed from the start between "woman" subjects and between the *Woman-beneath-the-Mother* and the *Woman-beneath-the-Girl* in non-Oedipal pre-transitional transubjective psychic interweaving.'[30]

Transgression, transubjective, interweaving allow a supplementary vocabulary for analysis of the events I am discerning in painting when 'it happens that the artist is a woman'. I am not seeking her difference, her lack or her essence *in relation to masculinity*. I trace a psychic formation of feminine subjectivity, sexuality, desire that is formed in both an archaic and a post-natal *fascinance* with several modalities of feminine sexual difference, sexual because it does concern bodies, desires, experiences, corpo-realities. These theoretically distinguish between later pre-natal *m/Other*, Mother and Other Woman.

Still within the more strictly Freudian and Lacanian accounts according to which separation from the solely post-natal mother must traumatically occur, Irigaray offers us her still valid insight that acknowledges the deforming force of the phallic order. As a result of a relation to an imagined identity that is, nonetheless, spatially separate – the post-natal mother leaves and must be left – Irigaray's girl does not master such individuation/separation by means of the *fort–da* game. She dances, hums, plays, fails to eat or dies of grief. Thus, something of Ettinger's supplementary sense of a primordial relation is implied but articulated in a physical rather than a psychical form. Irigaray suggests: 'The daughter has her mother *under her skin*, secreted in the *deep damp intimacy of the body*, in the mystery of her relation to gestation, birth and sexuality' (my emphasis).[31] Furthermore, for Irigaray, the proto-sexual movement characteristic of the girl is whirling her own body around rather than throwing and pulling objects back, as does Freud's little boy Ernst. Positing the girl-child's attempt to reproduce, around and within her space, an energetic, circular movement that, both phantasmatically and kinetically, protects her from abandonment, from attack, depression and loss of self, Irigaray invokes the relation of body to body-in-space in distinction from the mastery of space through the relation of subject, child, to object, toy, mediated by syntax and language (*fort/da*).

Irigaray's metaphor of dancing in space opens pathways to thinking about gestural painting practice within the psycho-sexual dimensions of sexual difference. Ettinger leads me to propose also that the otherness of the Other, the space of the canvas, could also, at times, be a space of encounter, for all painters, with the virtual tracings of *m/Other*, a partner in the process, while also evoking the negotiation of the loss of the Mother. This would engender a different modality in the very terms of a painting practice where artist, alone with paint, plays in a space of gesture and movement. The ethos of the resulting painting would require new terms for its elucidation. The key is not identification with the Mother – Freud's theory or even Irigaray's – but '*inclusion in transubjectivity by a com-passionate, generous hospitality* that would emanate from the *fatal woman-m/Other figure*'.[32]

In relation to art, Ettinger elaborates this insight:

> A similar transgression is also the effect of artistic images. Sometimes, this transgressive hospitality is precisely what the psychoanalyst offers. This was not, however, the case of Freud with 'Dora'. This was indeed the case of Jack Hold with Lol (Hold who occupies, in fact, the place of the author, who is, metaphorically, Marguerite Duras herself). To 'Dora', Freud was a phallic mother in transference, and a failing phallic father too. The phallic mother is a screen that blurs the *Woman-beneath-the-Mother* so longed for by the girl. Can a girl discern any desirability in herself if she cannot designate any desirability at all in her own mother or in another woman, thus establishing the desirability of her own archaic *m/Other* as *fascinance* for herself, not for a man? Can a girl become a woman without being co-affected in an encounter of fascination with a *m/Other*? … Can a girl become a woman if she cannot receive admiring recognition of her femininity from another woman-Mother? Can a girl become a woman without aspiring to participate in the missing gaze that will arise from the encounter, will *turn around* the couple and herself and look back at the couple from her future self, a gaze that will envelop her and subjectivize her as a potentially ravishing being, closing the gap between a Girl and a Woman in the establishing of the necessary woman-to-woman difference?[33]

This is a brilliant intervention into our theories of the formation and process of subjectivity that identifies the specificity, the sexual difference of the feminine. Irigaray's and Ettinger's radical extensions of psychoanalytical theory and indeed aesthetics are suggestive for a structural reading of painting – not, I stress again, to produce a reading of men's art versus women's art, but in order to admit and theorize specific tendencies and processes that might tend more towards capturing the unknown, not yet acknowledged possibilities of aesthetic affects not only seen and rendered invisible through the phallic prism. In doing so, these theories of subjectivity and sexual difference make more intelligible the possibilities for touching a relation for artist-women to the matrixial feminine in the space of artistic practice. It might also shift our understanding of the affects underpinning both longing for and killing in the work of masculine psychic life enacted gesturally as well as figuratively in art.

Matrixiality heightens our sense of the damage done by making invisible or dismissing as lacking artworks by artist-women when a solely phallocentric art historical and critical imagination dominates. As *fascinance*, Ettinger elaborates its formative effects and helps to explain my concept – *feminist desire for difference*, the Pandoran feminist desire for knowledge, another *fascinance* – of women as creative artists, writers and thinkers. Their *inscriptions in, of and from the feminine* (matrixial and phallic), deposited unknowingly in art and culture as they participated in avant-garde practices that opened up such possibilities in the era we call modernism, are there, awaiting our reading.

These insights need, however, to be used carefully. I mobilize them to read the artistic moment that art history defined stylistically as Abstract Expressionism. I term it gestural painting that I read as seeking to access and to stage a kind of primal gesturing, an intentionally informal relation between the body of the painter and the materials with which the painter works to create a trace of psychically charged phenomenal being in that body by its movements in space – both literal and mapped on canvas. Many of the artists acknowledged a desire to open up to the Unconscious, but now we can add matrixial non-conscious ways of working.

If, at a certain level, abstract painting took to its logical conclusion, as Greenberg argued, the fundamentals of the activity – paint and surface – and if we add from Harold Rosenberg the proposition of an active, but also *acting* painter, we can read, as Irigaray does, the gesture as index of that process of the iterative formation of subjectivity, which, of course, now we cannot allow to be considered neutral or masculine by default, with the feminine as the other of the masculine.[34] Furthermore, if gesture can be tracked to certain formative moments in the subject's history – and even from the late pre-natal, shared, co-emerging matrixial formation of any subject – heightened and re-evoked in the Surrealist legacy of 'psychic automatism' that Jackson Pollock and his associates embraced as another method of breaking down the conventions embedded in their practice, and if the gesture in this formative moment of any subject's history falls along different axes according to the sexually differentiated child's phantasized relation to both the post-natal Mother and the pre-natal matrixial partner, the *m/Other*, then we must begin to speculate on the sexual difference of the traces in the work that is the product of the gesture on the canvas in the studio in that painting practice.

Hans Namuth's photographs make Jackson Pollock appear to dance (figs 4.19 and 4.20). Frankenthaler herself stressed his 'choreography'. Pollock, however, moves in a regular, repeating pattern. Photographed from above, Pollock appears at times like a whirling figure in the flurry of creative activity as he moves up and down and around the length of his canvas laid out on the floor. His movements are, however, ritualized, dictated by the primary activity of repeatedly throwing the skeins of paint off his stick and on to the supine canvas in recurring patterns, even when stretching into the canvas from its edge. As B. H. Friedman unwittingly revealed, Pollock's work conveys more 'insistent and regular rhythms', pulses, that take no little imagination to relate to masculine sexuality, what T. J. Clark admitted are a 'metaphorics of masculinity'.[35] The shapes of Pollock's canvases reflect this more patterned, syllabic, alternating, spraying movement, distinctly different than the squarer or upright rectangular formats characteristic of Frankenthaler's works. Moreover, Pollock's gestures produce thick skeins of linear paint that eventually cover the blankness of the canvas.

What is the canvas, psychically?

I am tempted to follow the metaphoric licence typical of Irigaray's writing and heretically propose that the canvas is not just a blank surface awaiting his mark. In psychic phantasy, it is a space that evokes the Other. To use the verb *to be* makes an emphatic statement of what is always in the realm of phantasy and thus the overdetermined site of many possible meanings. In phallic terms, the canvas functions as a kind of mirror which, as yet, contains no reflection, signalling either the nothingness of terrifying absence, or the equal terror before the immense self-sufficiency of the Other in relation to which the emerging subject is always being constituted. This Other is not a person. It can be Nothing and Death, or Culture and Language. Yet the complex and evolving relation with the Mother is the mediator of this necessary relation to a non-personified Other, whose purely symbolic place the Name of the Father will later support. At the same time, that indifferent Otherness of the blank canvas threatens to overwhelm, if not wipe out, the emerging subject, its unmarked perfection signifying its indifference to the subject and the subject's absence, even the death of that would-be subject. Recall Ernst's third game of appearing and disappearing in the mirror – a game repeatedly acting out *his own* feared absence/death and its disavowal. Any painting that results from such a staging of the encounter of artist and canvas as a field, as a territory of the Other, is the product of the risk, experienced in that procedure, that what the painter threw from his stick was also part of himself, and that what he covered in layering of skeins or dripped paint was his own absence/non-sense.

At the same time, there is the equal possibility that what Pollock as artist was seeking to touch with that aggressive gesture was also his matrixial partner-in-becoming, the *m/Other*. In the violent act of obliterating this otherness by covering the surface with himself, signified by the dense webs of paint and painted-in gaps, what the Pollock-like painter mastered was for him her dreadful absence; as being a boy-child he was forever exiled. What he, as phallic masculine subject, might be distancing could also be, as Freud more paranoically projected, an engulfing presence, separation from which is, in the phallic story, a necessary, if also agonizing, condition of the would-be phallic subject's existence as a discrete subject, an I. The passage of both self and (*m*)*Other*, Mother, Other into object – the painting – and their negotiated differentiation is the product of this psychic formation when, for art historical reasons, the process of painting is made the exclusive site and form of the practice.

What may be implicit in all painting – from the point of view of this specific interest in psychic deposits in cultural practice – was foregrounded at the moment when 'the law of modernism' exposed the structural demand for painting 'to be steeped in its own cause' (Mallarmé), while releasing, through movement in the act of painting and the extended spatial scale of the gesture made by an entire body, its latent psychic dynamic – loss, death, disavowal.[36] When we confront a painting by Jackson Pollock, we confront the energy of that *couvade*, that relentless pacing, covering, knotting a surface of his own making and a sealing over the awe-ful, even threatening self-sufficiency of blank and infinite surface of the once virgin canvas. Surface becomes lid, the heavily worked covering that overlays the ghost of the corpse in the tomb – a ghost that always threatens to rise up and haunt even the most abstract work with anthropomorphic hallucinations.

I do not imply literal superimposition of cotton reels and strings on to Pollock's painting practice. I note instead the aggressiveness involved in what Freud identified watching his grandson play: it may be said, a little metaphorically, that in mastering through play and investing objects with the potential to cover over a threatening absence, and to disavow lack in order to prevent oneself dying, one could become, symbolically, a 'killing man'. Therein may lie some of the violence and the sadism that so-called Abstract Expressionist painting practices liberated; not in the (un)conscious misogyny of individual men whose mothers messed up their heads – as is implied in many of the Pollock or de Kooning biographies. It lies in a structural condition of modern masculinity to which a certain painting practice opened an aesthetic arena.[37]

Helen Frankenthaler's practice 'played' in and on that same material and psychically charged space – vast sheets of unstretched, unprimed cotton duck on the floor of a large studio – but I also view it through the structural, not biographical, prism of sexual difference (both Irigarayan and Ettingerian matrixial) to allow for a differentiating and thus differentiated relation to the psychic space of the drama of presence and absence, of both phallically ordained loss of, and perpetual matrixial co-emergence with, the primordial maternal feminine. I evoke both the matrixial *m/Other* and, in Irigaray's terms, a sense of a feminine psycho-sexual self *like* the post-natal Mother and the Ettingerian Other Woman, the *femme-fatale-Autre-mère*. We can also reread Frankenthaler's innovation of stain and soak – which generated pleasure through the partial suspension of the material distinction between her mark and the canvas as support by the immersion of the one in the other – as the loosening of boundaries that evoke the matrixial borderspaces of co-emergence (Ettinger's terms) which we, viewers, sense in *fascinance* as our eyes explore these specific paintings, where neither paint nor surface can be separated, while neither is annulled in their difference to produce a third entity. The painting practice works as inscription by movement, staining, not only of the inevitable psychological dimension of loss and separation, but also of matrixial *proximity-in-distance*. To this we might add Irigaray's insight:

> Woman always speaks with the mother, man speaks in her absence. This with her obviously takes different shapes and it must seek to place speech between, not to remain in an indissociable fusion, with the women woven together. This *with* has to try and become a *with* self. Mother and daughter turn around each other, they go up and down while encircling themselves, but they also delineate two entities that they are: in the lips, the hands, the eyes.[38]

Frankenthaler produced paintings that are neither tangled skeins nor webs and tremulous veils of thinned poured paint – that is, whatever the colour field painter Morris Louis took from her and returned to Pollock. However visually entrancing Louis's poured work, these paintings lack the excitement, ambiguity and tension we find in Frankenthaler's work, not only in the 1950s, but consistently over her long career. Veiling and covering the canvas is different from allowing a spectral body its space or its energies and intensities. From Frankenthaler's stained canvases we see emerging, sometimes joyously, humorous and *jouissant* spectres of figures which are, by the artist's retrospective titling, maternally connoted: for instance, *Mother Goose Melody* (1959) as well as *Nude* (1958, fig. 4.1).

With colour and surface oscillating as one and yet other, this painter created space through the ambiguities of colour: saturation, hue and vibration. This introduces the question of colour into the field of gesture. In her reading of Frankenthaler's works of the 1950s, Rowley added an additional layer of psychoanalytical interpretation by considering the *work* that colour is doing in Frankenthaler's painting. She draws into her study literary theorist Julia Kristeva's interpretation, in 'Giotto's Joy', of the dominant blue chromatic in the work of the Italian Renaissance painter Giotto in the Arena Chapel. There Kristeva argues that colour is not part of the language, but becomes the *economy* of painting. This means acknowledging the drives, the erotics and the semiotics of colour in painting.[39]

Kristeva combines a Freudian thesis of the drives (the pulsations that repeatedly flow over, groove and eroticize zones of the infant body in the oscillating states of pleasure and unpleasure, alleviated by the various objects by which the drives seek satisfaction and stasis – the breast, the gaze, skin, voice, and ultimately its own body parts) with semiotics (emerging from rhythm and a space of holding, the chora) to identify three dimensions of colour: 'an instinctual pressure linked to external visible objects; the same pressure causing the eroticizing of the body proper *via* visual perception and gesture; and the insertion of this pressure under the impact of censorship as a sign in a system of representation.'[40]

Drawing also on Matisse's thoughts about colour, Kristeva explains this tripartite understanding of colour in reverse, so that colour in art serves as an undoing of 'our alienation' in the 'codes' and signs of culture, reconnecting us to the primordial processes and, for her, the earliest semiosis of the body's pulsations: the drives.

> Color might, therefore, be the space where the prohibition foresees and gives rise to its own immediate transgression. It achieves the momentary dialectic of law – laying down One Meaning so that it might at once be pulverized, multiplied into plural meanings. Color is the shattering of unity. Thus, it is through color – colors – that the subject escapes its alienation within a code (representation, ideological, symbolic, and so forth) that it, as a conscious subject, accepts. Similarly, it is through color that Western painting began to escape the constraints of narrative and perspective norms (as with Giotto) as well as representation itself (as with Cézanne, Matisse, Rothko, Mondrian). Matisse spells it out in full: it is through color – painting's fundamental 'device' in the broad sense of 'human language' – that revolutions in painting come about.[41]

Frankenthaler was, above all, a colourist (Lee Krasner too, in her equal *fascinance* before Matisse).

For an exhibition of Frankenthaler's work at the Museo di Palazzo Grimani in Venice, shown independently of but during the Venice Biennial in 2019, the art historian and author of a major monograph on the painter, John Elderfield, presented a finely selected chronological sample of her paintings under the title *Pittura/Panorama: Paintings by Helen Frankenthaler 1952–1992*, which was reviewed by Joachim Pissarro and David Carrier:

> How dramatic was Frankenthaler's development and how surprising her willingness to synthesize elegance with marvellous gawkiness. *Open Wall* (1953) [fig. 3.1] opens a wall just right of center into a luscious blue field. *Italian Beach* (1960) with intensely colored irregularly shaped greens, blues and ochres on the white canvas shows her mastery of the aesthetic power of blankness. These earlier works are oils. And *For E. M.* (1981), which uses

acrylic, covers the lower part of the canvas almost entirely with a darkening field of tumultuous colors, set between dark blacks overhead. If the old master Venetians had painted abstractly, they would have done sensuously handsome works like these.[42]

Invoking Walter Pater on Giorgione and the Venetian Titian (fig. 4.2), all beloved of the painter herself and both creators of the erotic nude in Western painting, the adoring critics, nonetheless, move Frankenthaler out of her time and back into the history of *la pittura*: painting, invoking sensuousness, eroticism, fluidity – every stereotypical framing I have sought to suspend in this chapter in order to try and see and acknowledge something deeper, different and more structural to her participation in the project of New York painting in the 1950s through deploying the *fascinance* of Ettinger and colour theory developed by Rowley, and through the proposition that nether the gaze nor the gesture is male, while neither is reversible as female. I suggest that the complexity of the psychic formations of subjectivity are subject to different modes of difference and differentiation that are sites of expanded creativity and necessitate expanded theories of our complex psycho-sexual formations of subjectivities that come into play in the specific arena of this new moment in the history of painting.

But what of masculinity and painting, once we refuse the myth of phallocentric sexual difference?

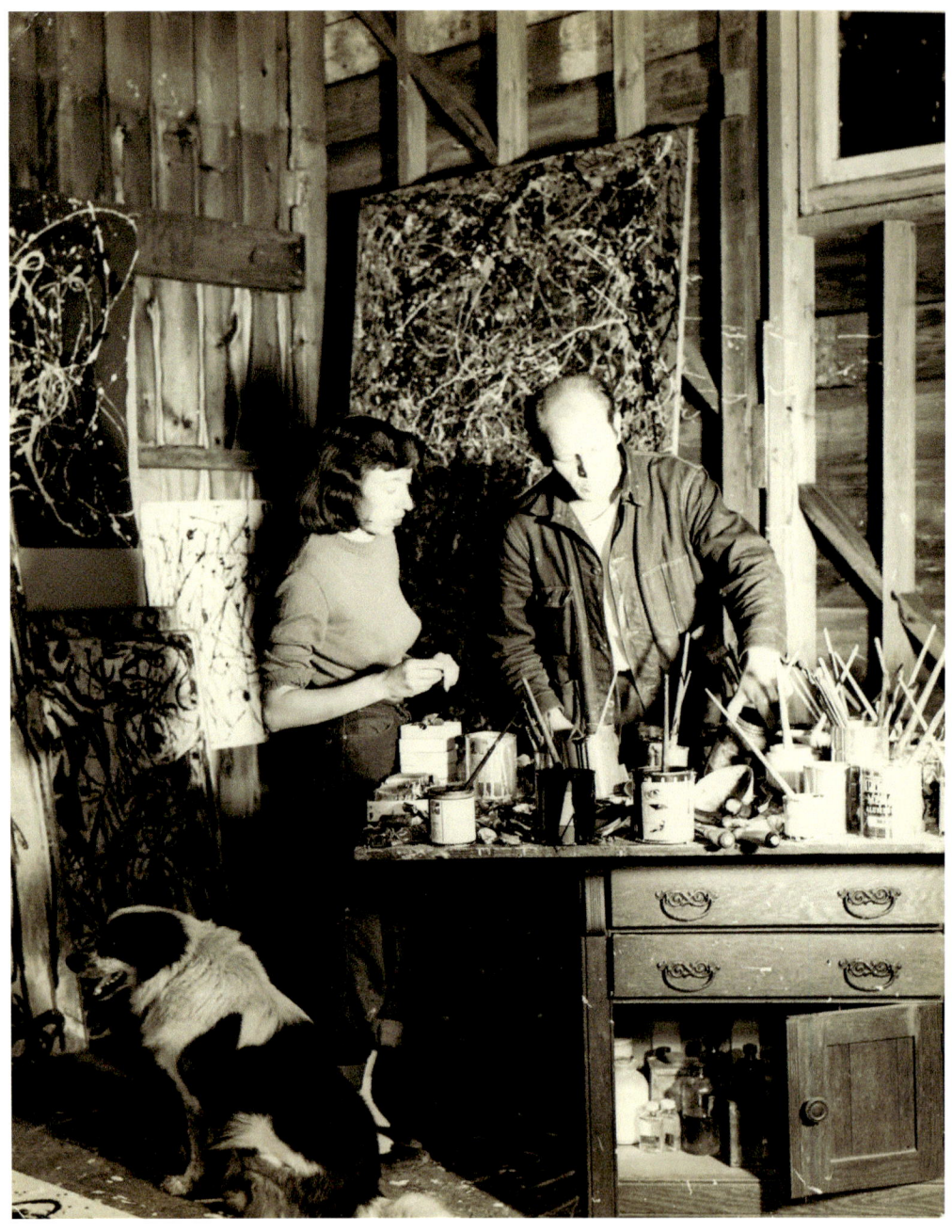

Figure 5.1 Lawrence Larkin, *Jackson Pollock and Lee Krasner in his studio at The Springs, East Hampton*, 1949

5

Is the artist hysterical?

> Not so long ago, art history and in particular the history of literature was not
> yet a science, but rather gossip. It obeyed all the laws of gossip; it moved
> cheerily from one theme to another and the lyrical flood of words on the
> elegance of the form gave place to anecdotes drawn from the artist's life. Psy-
> chological truisms alternated with problems related to the philosophical
> basis of the work and to problems about the social milieu […] Gossip does
> not have a precise terminology […] Thus art history knew no scientific ter-
> minology since it used words from the common everyday parlance without
> first critically screening them.
>
> Roman Jakobson, 1921[1]

In her study of semiotic and psychoanalytic contributions to the analysis
of painting, cultural analyst Claire Pajaczkowska reminds us why we might
need theoretical approaches to historical painting practices by citing linguist Roman Jakobson's critique in 1921 of art history as gossip. Research-
ing painting in the 1950s, I was overwhelmed by the mass of anecdotal
information about the artists, their dealers, their marriages and friends,
their work. So immense is such detail – interviews, oral history and plain
old-fashioned gossip – that I felt I might sink under the unmanageable
weight of all these words that rarely touched on the question of the structures or the affects of *painting* except in lyrical celebrations of the formal
innovations that served to elevate the greatness of the always male artists,
while some authors bravely struggled to provide comparable detail in the
study of artist-women.[2] Like Jacobson, I think we need to push art history
beyond gossip, and to theorize artistic practices in addition to studying
their social and historical conditions of existence.

First, an anecdote. After a day's painting, Jackson Pollock would invite
Lee Krasner into his barn studio, asking her to review his day's work and
to decide: 'Is this a painting?' (fig. 5.1).[3] Why were they uncertain? Or
rather, on what grounds could she answer him affirmatively? What did she
have to know about painting to be able to answer such a question?

In an article published in 1977, the astute critic and art historian Barbara Rose argued that Krasner, of all the artists who formed 'New York
painting in the 1950s', was the most deeply in touch with all the major
sources in early twentieth-century art and the range of art thinking associated with the emergence of abstract art of the entire bunch. A brilliant
student of Hans Hofmann (1880–1966), who was able to pass on a

fruitful understanding of the principles of analytical and synthetic Cubism, Krasner was also a deep analyst of Mondrian's passage from landscape painting to geometric abstraction, as passionately engaged with Matisse and earlier Fauvism, already a member of the American Abstract Artists, and selected to participate in John Graham's *French and American Paintings* show in 1942 alongside de Kooning and Pollock, Picasso, Matisse and Braque, their European mentors. Krasner was profoundly aware of what the current stakes were for the young American artists in New York: understanding and transforming the necessary tensions between surface and depth, colour and line, form and feeling. Alfred H. Barr's schematic focus on formal evolution alone (excluding Surrealism and Dada) in his projection of the trajectory of modern art into geometric or organic abstraction crossed with the 'colour' of expressionism, proposed in his exhibition *Cubism and Abstract Art* (Museum of Modern Art, 1936), offered one route to understanding abstraction. In *Systems and Dialectics in Art* (1937), Russian artist-writer John Graham (1881–1961) advanced a pathway that was spiritual, mystic (not quite Kandinsky's version, however) and emotionally charged. Rose writes of Krasner that she was

> anxious to invest line not only with space-creating potential, but with emotional drive as well. Hofmann taught that colour was the basic means of communicating emotion; but for Graham drawing, and in particular drawing as *the record of physical gesture*, was the principal means of expressing deep emotion.[4]

Rose quotes Graham's text:

> A work of art is neither the faithful nor distorted representation, *it is the immediate, unadorned record of an authentic intellect-emotional REACTION of the artist set in space* … This authentic reaction recorded within the measurable space immediately and automatically in terms of brush pressure, saturation, velocity, caress or repulsion, anger or desire which changes and varies in unison with the flow of feeling at the moment, constitutes the work of art.[5]

The confluence of resources for proposing a deep source for what appears in art as form, colour and line, and is, at its core, the inscription of formless emotion, extended for these early theorists both to 'the spiritual in art' via Theosophy, as in Kandinsky, and to the Freudian or Jungian Unconscious. These inform what Graham termed *the physical gesture* that impresses them into an artwork through processes and materials. I want to gloss these insights by introducing more recent formulations of such insights – semiotics and psychoanalysis – precisely to open up, and at the same time destabilize, the issues of embodiment and sexual difference as explored in the previous chapter, with the more radical instability but equally intense psychic freight of hysteria.[6]

Claire Pajaczkowska introduces French semiotic and psychoanalytical theories about painting that remain little studied within the English-language academic community.[7] The application of semiotics and structuralism to Western painting was initially premised on the model of language, which approached painting like a verbal signifying system. While enabling us to discern in figurative painting an organization of signifieds in a structure similar to that of myth, which Lévi-Strauss identified, such a semiotic treatment of painting fails, according to Pajaczkowska, to address the aesthetic processes and material resources of painting that touch on the non-linguistic, hence the Imaginary and the psycho-somatic dimensions of subjectivity that specific artistic practices may put into play. Social histories of art and structuralist readings of signs ignore *the psychic freight* that art practices not only carry, but which are the driving force behind their emergence into visibility as not only the resource for, but the topic of, the abstract practices of painting in the mid-twentieth century.

Pajaczkowska follows another thread in psychoanalytic theories of modern painting, notably the propositions of Guy Rosolato and Julia Kristeva.[8] In contrast to Freud, who believed that of all the psychic structures, that of neurosis, and particularly hysteria, are relevant to the study of art, Rosolato argued that art might be better understood through the psychic structure of perversion – and a particular form of it, fetishism.[9] Fetishism is not only an arrested erotic activity, it is also a widespread, dynamic psychic process that is to be understood as our fundamental oscillation between knowing and not knowing, between perception and disavowal of threat, between surface and depth. It works between the two poles of meaning: metaphor and metonym. As a metaphor, the fetish stands for that which is absent (or feared to be so) – in Freudian terms this is, for the boy-child fearful of castration, the mother's phantasized penis (that would make her the same as him and hence not introduce the fear of difference as the threat of castration). As metonym, the fetish is erected to veil the discovery of her (seeming) lack of what the boy-child needs to see to reassure himself of his wholeness. The fetish then becomes contiguous with the lack. Paradoxically, just as the fetish disavows absence – standing in for what is missing – it continuously commemorates the site and threat of that lack. Fetishism is the oscillation. It effectively indexes what the psyche is metaphorically trying to disavow by substitution. Taken over into thinking about artistic practice, artwork can be read fetishistically. It displaces absence while the practice of art as repetition (*fort/da*/gone/here) marks its very spot of an eternal anxiety oscillating around loss and lack in both the other and in the self.

What about the pleasures – what Rosolato calls the *jubilation* and *fascination* – of art? For Rosolato, pleasure arises for both artist and spectator in identification, which brings us back to hysteria. Identification is a basic component of the formation of post-natal subjectivity.[10] It is, however, subject to vagaries and instabilities, to cross-, multiple and shifting identifications, which are part of the creativity and anguish of hysteria that signifies the radical instability in identification.

Pleasure in art, argues Rosolato, derives from the point at which an artwork stabilizes the relations of the subject to the Unconscious and, beyond that, to the unsignified and unsignifiable body, a realm of nonsense. This links artmaking to yet another psychic structure: the formation of the ego in the Mirror Phase that Lacan had theorized as a metaphor for the ways in which the infant is drawn into becoming a (potential) ego, a later grammatical subject who will find itself articulated by the linguistic I, or first-person grammatical form.[11] Lacan argued that a subject-to-be acquires the possibility of an ego (that is, the possibility of centring chaotic bodily feelings within an incorporated and territorialized ego and thus taking up in language the I-position) through a complex encounter with an *imago* in the extended cultural, not actual, mirror (namely the encounter with others already formed as culture-bearing subjects).

In this fiction of the repeated encounter with literal or metaphoric mirrors – the mother's face and gaze, the culture's representations to the child, culture itself – there are many threads and paradoxes rather than any simple moment of recognition. (This will constitute the fiction of the subject who can recognize where there is not yet a possibility of recognition.) In the Mirror Phase as a long process of formation, the ego will form through the incorporation of an imagined architecture borrowed from the others in the world, and then internalized, around which to organize the chaotic sensations that flow over the child's unincorporated body as sites of intensity. In so far as the image that the putative subject must embrace and internalize as an imaginary, territorializing container within which to situate an ego – a composed and cohering I – comes from outside, from the place/the space and surface of the Other (culture, the already-subjects of the adult world), the Mirror Phase equally incites aggressiveness towards the alien, the *imago* which the child takes in from elsewhere (culture) as it offers an image for its I.[12] Hence, there is a splitting between the site of the subject and the sight or image that will alone allow the subject to come into being as a fictively territorialized ego-image within which its uncontained drives and sensations will be localized to sustain the possibility of an identity – a difference from and likeness to the other – that will be always precariously stabilized and henceforth haunted by a retrospective phantasy of the body-in-pieces. Hence there is a link between this

Imaginary formation of an ego and the location provided by the linguistic and grammatical 'I'.

Moreover, the Mirror Phase involves misrecognition through the idealization of the *imago* as more complete and more potent than the still motor-incapable proto-subject that the infant senses itself to be because it is still radically dependent on others around it and physically immature in its motor skills. The subject-to-be joyously 'identifies' with that which is other (in the field/space of the mirror), as a more perfect ideal-ego, and takes it *in* as an identification. Since the *imago* is other, there is a certain competitive aggressiveness towards this image that can be turned back on the subject, or against the image, predicting a dynamic struggle at this site – or any site or situation that re-evokes the Mirror Phase, such as the screen of cinema or, even, the expanse of canvas before the artist.[13]

Another layer of Rosolato's analysis of the structure and pleasure of art is the question of authorship. Every time artists sign a painting, they make a claim to authorship. In patriarchal culture, this is a claim to paternity, and thus an insertion of the name into the Symbolic Order which operates under the 'Name of the Father' (Lacan). Authorship is the point at which the person painting makes a claim for a *stabilization of a self in the work* that can sustain the fiction of an author identity, I, so as to be acknowledged an artist. Authorship is thus, paradoxically, a reinvention of that law of the Father.

Yet, for Rosolato, making art is a transformation of rules and representations that up to that point have held authoritative status within the community of culture. Transgression of the rule, however, is always itself also affirmative of the law of the Father. Freud argued in *Totem and Taboo* that killing the primal Father is the very means by which the law of the Father is installed as an effect of the guilt in the son for the envious aggression that incited the dominated sons to revolt against the Primal Father.[14] In the paradox of patriarchal culture founded on what Freud called 'the common crime', the more you kill the Father, the more Symbolic he becomes, the more that killing affirms his authority, or rather, authority and law in the paternal name that sons seek to appropriate. Each signing is a claim for that place in the anxious knowledge of both guilt and envy.

Authorship is linked to the Symbolic Father. Thus, we might also read the modernist avant-garde's creative logic of transgression as a transparent moment of the paradox of phallocentrism in art: the more competitively artist-men kill father-men, the more powerful the latter's Symbolic, phallocentric order becomes, legitimating their succession to the illusory paternal position, which is always at risk of being challenged. Avant-gardist transgression (gambits of reference, deference and difference) is not merely idealist play; and it is certainly not implicitly radical or revolutionary. It conforms to the engine of the Symbolic law which is played out by the Oedipal son on canvas over the Mother: disappeared, retrospectively endowed as phallic, but also a fearfully castrated body beneath his ever-resurrected dead Symbolic Father's gaze. In this sense, the difficulty feminist art historians experience when trying to situate artistic practice by artist-women within a modernism so nakedly driven by, or exposed by, artistic practice itself to this phallocentric logic is revealed as a contest with another, structural sexism, embedded in the very notion of vanguardist rivalry as the engine of artistic progress and the psychic logic of the gender-exclusive, adulatory art historical canon.

Let me backtrack a bit and see how we could insert a different sexual narrative. According to Rosolato, what provides pleasure in art is the way in which painting allows movement between several points: 1) 'the body' – or rather the drives and pulsations of a chaotic, infantile corporeality – which is in a state of non-sense, un- or not-yet-signified; 2) the Unconscious, where meaning is determined through repression (condensation and displacement), and the Imaginary, where it is shaped by images and phantasy; and finally, 3) the realm of symbolically articulated, culturally recognized thought and communicable meaning – language. Painting provides specific and intense pleasures precisely because, notably in its modernist forms, it allowed so precisely for play between these registers through its simultaneous operation as both metaphor and metonym.

For Rosolato, its pleasures derive from the movement which carries the work from the realms of bodily non-sense and unconscious phantasy (Melanie Klein's supplement) towards systematized meaning. A new, historically and aesthetically particular pleasure arises when that movement became so finely balanced between the first two points while trying never to arrive at the final destination of discernible, symbolic meaning. Abstraction is, thus, not just non-figuration. It introduced specific pleasures of psychic play between the body and the Imaginary, the body, its drives and the Unconscious, while avoiding resolution as a production of meaning separable from the operations of the activity of making the work.

In a practice that both aimed to avoid figuration and iconic representation – trying to escape or evade the burden of tradition that tied painting to a metaphoric status with regard to referencing a world or an idea iconographically – and tried to stay closer to the very *physical gestures*, body movements and rhythms, vibrations of colours that are painting's *arche* materials, explaining this as accessing 'the unconscious' or nature, Pollock and Krasner's daily question is genuine and interesting. I read it as follows in Rosolato's terms: does what has happened today on my canvas stabilize at a point that, without becoming metaphoric – *this* expresses *that*; *this* refers to *that* out there – can provide something to hold an imaginary *identification*, and can even offer a *jouissant*, jubilant pleasure in the precarious balance it sustains between stability and flux, between the realm of potential sense, inviting interpretations that are deadly to this pleasure, and the domain of non-sense, that is threatening in its potential slide towards the place where the subject disappears into sheer, abject materiality?

This movement passes through a range of signifying, or rather, to introduce a little prematurely the work of Julia Kristeva, *semiotic* elements, from traces or marks to the early patterning of rhythm, on through to pictograms – archaic sensory images – and fuller pictorialization and finally on to symbolization.[15] This allows us to theorize the gossip around artists such as Jackson Pollock and Lee Krasner about their ambition to use painting to liberate the Unconscious (more Jungian than Freudian). By this vague, somewhat Surrealist invocation, I think they were trying to find a working method that allowed them to operate in the seemingly more open psychic zones, inhibiting pictorialization and symbolization, while privileging those elements of the process of their practice that stayed close to the body-psyche as trace and rhythm, coming closer at times to calligraphy rather than semiosis, but still indexed to the drives and evocative of the way things are later put together in the Unconscious and dreams (for Pollock, this would be a Jungian archetype rather than a Freudian Unconscious of repression of the infantile) and phantasies. These artists were not painting anything external and did not want their paintings to end up being treated as symbols, as metaphors for the Cold War, fear of nuclear disaster, democratic freedom, machismo or the feminine. We could argue that the very process of painting that they invented and practised tried to remain closer to the pole of metonym, that is, of contiguity with the indexicality of the painting body and to the condition of becoming-subjectivity that Kristeva defined as the *subject-on-trial,* in process, precarious, rather than moving towards the level of meaning through metaphor or symbol. [16]

Thus, we seek in vain to say what these abstract paintings mean at the usual level of social historical or even individual psychological *interpretation.* Their meaning operates at what Rosolato insisted was the non-dialectical oscillation that the painters strove to maintain between the metonymic and metaphoric poles characteristic of painting at a structural level that they were discovering and making the practice itself. Such a practice, for which Pollock was recognized in the early 1950s in paintings made from dripped skeins created by the repeating and rhythmic movements of his entire body, read as a process where draw-painting acted as a filter for deposits from the bodily strata of sensate memories and from the Unconscious. These opened the zone of phantasy without forming an image, yet creating the painting as *imago,* an entity that being signed, sustained the painting ego's link to a name, authorship.

The painter, however, participated in a culturally recognized semiotic system, and designated his vanguardist authorship by being able to recognize at what stage such a painting practice could deliver pleasure by aesthetically or formally stabilizing a viewing relation to those bodily and unconscious elements it indexed through its pulsional, rhythmically deposited traces of an embodied subjectivity-in-action. When it would be a painting and not a mess of paint is also the daily experience of finding out how this balance might be sustained in any one performance with paint across the field of the canvas. From the full space of performance, Pollock had to select and cut the final canvas, where its edges form stabilizing limits, a mirror-space: a painting. The viewer, including the artist (or artists, for Krasner and Pollock discussed their work daily) as first viewer, could enjoy a managed identification, not with an image (echoes of the Mirror Phase), but with the field that constantly opens the relay between metaphoric possibilities of stability and metonymic traces of the other scene that promise transgressive, perverse pleasures. This involved, however, the risk of unravelling subjectivity entirely. So, each move towards these pleasures might also need at times to be fetishistically disavowed. Thus, the play of painting as process might need to be ended with the agreed completion and cutting and then *signing* the painting.

At this point, you, the reader, must endure yet one more turn of the theoretical screw. Painting, especially in the traditions of figurative representation in the West, served as a kind of doubling: a repetition of the Mirror Phase that is also the transformed mirror in which the act of mirroring is represented and the ego jubilantly finds itself with an identity through which to stabilize itself by seeing a perspectively organized, delineated and anthropomorphic world. Yet remember the mirror moment of the *fort/da* game played by Freud's little grandson Ernst that Freud related to the death drive, to the problem of separation from the mother which haunts us and lures us with the drive to return to an unanguished state of stasis, inanimate and not so much dead as no longer subject to the anxiety of being alive and sensate – forever longing and forever losing.

The third stage of the game played out between child and mirror was such a play with non-being; not just his mother's through absence, but his own. This game established the separateness of the boy and supplied him with a phantasy of its always dangerous mastery. The forms of the game, however, articulated his expulsion from the mother's space, from her body as both space and limit, by mapping both into an object, a substitute, be it toy or word, modelled, according to Irigaray, on a phallic logic.[17] Being, for a subject construed 'in the masculine', is, therefore, sustained at the price of that expulsion and its fetishization. If Rosolato called abstract art perverse and often fetishistic, his insight indicates the continuing necessity to stall this being-threatened recognition of difference and loss for the child that will be, within the patriarchal order, designated as masculine with the signature that society acknowledges as such.

What, however, of Freud's original suggestion that a different psychic formation – hysteria – offers a model for understanding the artist? Consideration of another possibility might allow a less rigidly phallocentric, masculinist account of art – for it is generally agreed that fetishism is not a major feminine perversion. Hysteria, not solely connected historically with the feminine subject, is, in addition, related to questions of life and death, as cultural analyst Elizabeth Bronfen has shown in her writing on hysteria in general and on the work of American artist Cindy Sherman in particular.[18]

The hysteric poses the very question of subjectivity. The hysteric puts the subject of sexual difference on trial by asking: What am I? Man or Woman? The hysteric also questions: animate or inanimate? Alive or dead? Hysteria would be a way for, and a sign of, a kind of phantasmatic bisexuality, or rather, a suspension of the patriarchal law of *m/f* sex, a momentary refusal of any stabilization of identity as a sexual identity, a possible if anguished place of play and oscillation. For a hysteric 'in the feminine', hysteria is a refusal to be confined within the cipher of the 'feminine' under a patriarchal law, under the terms that patriarchal order specifies for her. For the masculine subject, however, hysteria allows a recovered identification with the mother from which he, as a 'he-to-be', has to be expelled as the price of having an Imaginary relation of possession to the paternal Phallus. Being an artist has to involve some phantasmatic connection with the maternal, creative specificity of the female body. Thus, Claire Pajaczkowska concludes:

> If authorship means paternity, 'being an artist' is a compromise identity forged by the adult male ego as a way of mediating a fantasy of being a woman and of creating, and 'art' is male hysteria institutionalized and contained within representation.[19]

Representation as canonical, masculinized art history has institutionalized, however, a world orchestrated by psychic desires, traumas and drives of various masculine-identified subjects, whatever their sexualities. Made to the measure of masculine phantasy, it has gained hegemonic status. This then determines the very terms within which we are obliged to be creatively male or female. Artist-women have been placed not only in an asymmetrical relation to the artworld/world in representation because of the current ordering of sexual difference and whatever specificity that might imply, but they are positioned asymmetrically both to the figurations of femininity within the culture, and to the figurations of artistic identity which *hysterically appropriate both parental figures*, maternal and paternal – presently on behalf of the masculine subject. The very theory that enables us to see this also allows us to break down the ideological fixing of a binary system of sexual identity – art history's hegemonic attachment and neutralizing universalization of masculinity – so that the masculine process in artistic practice looks less fetishistic and is reconceived as hysterical, identificatory, hence unstable, or rather fluid, in its relation to an imaginary gender position.

This move opens up a gap wherein we can glimpse how a subject 'in the feminine' differentially orchestrates her constitutive gender-transgressing hysteria – her unstable-fluid and creatively destabilizing relations to both maternal femininity and paternal law – into creativity. At the beginning, I proposed an apparently fixed, binary and fetishistic opposition of sex symbol and art symbol: Marilyn Monroe and Jackson Pollock, movie icon and vanguard artist. The suggestion that masculine art is a form of masculine hysteria, that it might contain a destabilizing of the fixity of phallic masculine subjectivity in relation to the maternal and the matrixial *m/Other* in the same move as it inscribes once again the paternal law through avant-gardist rivalry, unfixes sexual identity for us to consider the play around women's bodily and phantasmatic inscriptions in the texts of culture.[20]

We thus discover a way to theorize these practices of painting in their historical and stylistic diversity as a kind of staging of the hysterical drama of the complexity and self-transgressing of any subject. What is produced is not a style or an object, but a moment of opened identity, which, in the male canon, has been achieved only through the encounter with and specific negotiation of sexual difference, that is, with the constituting symbols of sex in Western culture: the Mother/Woman and the Father. If we relate the canvas, the material resources such as colour and the gesture to the framing psychic relations within which subjectivity is shaped – the phantasmatic/Imaginary figures of the Mother and the Father – we can ask what is going on within a matrixially engendered and an Oedipally restructured *feminine* subject-on-trial on this stage.

By including Freud's work on art as hysterical within the larger psychoanalytical framework, it is possible to see the drama of art as the drama of sexual difference through which there will be several possible individual trajectories; indeed, in the end, as many as there are artists. Thus, we can escape the perennial trap, when discussing the impact of sexual difference, of determining all artists as merely exemplars of its asymmetrically polar terms: artist/woman artist. Being an artist 'in the feminine', working in a practice that opens up historical and aesthetic possibilities of 'inscriptions in and from the feminine', does not reduce Helen Frankenthaler or Lee Krasner to 'being women' in the Oedipal register. Their work is instead made legible, as each artist uniquely plays on this historical stage when the semiotics of artistic practice within modernist painting opened up the very questions of subjectivity on trial, pleasure and difference, in which the bodily and the psychic traces of the produced but always unravelling subject of sexual difference could reconfigure their relations *in and through painting to produce other pleasures for themselves and for us, the viewers invited to experience with the paintings.*

Instead of leaving unchallenged and unreconstructed the dominant and still heroizing and gender- and race-exclusive (or at best highly selective) gossipy narratives of Abstract Expressionism in order to make a sideways move off the map of serious art history to consider *women artists*, I hope to have redefined the central playing field on which many artists were engaged. The binary opposition of sex symbol and art symbol is revealed as an ideological fixing of processes, that, in the studios where Abstract Expressionist or American-type painting was being made, may have been far less stable, more transgressive – or at least differently orchestrated. This allows us to understand modernist painter-women's serious and deeply sustained investment in and contributions to the protocols of modernist painting; to grasp their embrace of that extraordinary practice which is painting that artist-women such as Krasner and Frankenthaler and so many others did, day in day out, for a lifetime, right into the twenty-first century. Artist-women of the 1950s were drawn to the practices of painting that structurally opened up spaces for the exploration of what had not yet been inscribed through that process – an invitation existing in the synonymity of *énoncé* and *énonciation*, of what is said and the means of saying of it, non-representation as the process of subjectivity itself.

They practised, however, in an artworld that, shaped in the ideological polarities of the moment, was barefacedly misogynist. Curators, gallery owners, critics and other artists created an ambience that was not only masculinist, but virilist and sexist and actively excluded on grounds of gender much of the creative community making modernist art. Part of the culture in which this happened was imaged through its popular icons, of whom the central sign and symbol was Marilyn Monroe. In her image, *MM* becomes the fetish supreme, all perfected, shiny, glossy, punished surface. We can pierce that carapace both to return her to her body and subjectivity, and return to Lee Krasner, who as a painter was closest to Pollock and was thus – artistically – in mortal danger; and, finally, to get to the maternal body buried in her art that *Prophecy* fearfully presaged and that *Sun Woman I* (figs 1.1 and 1.2) allusively contacted.

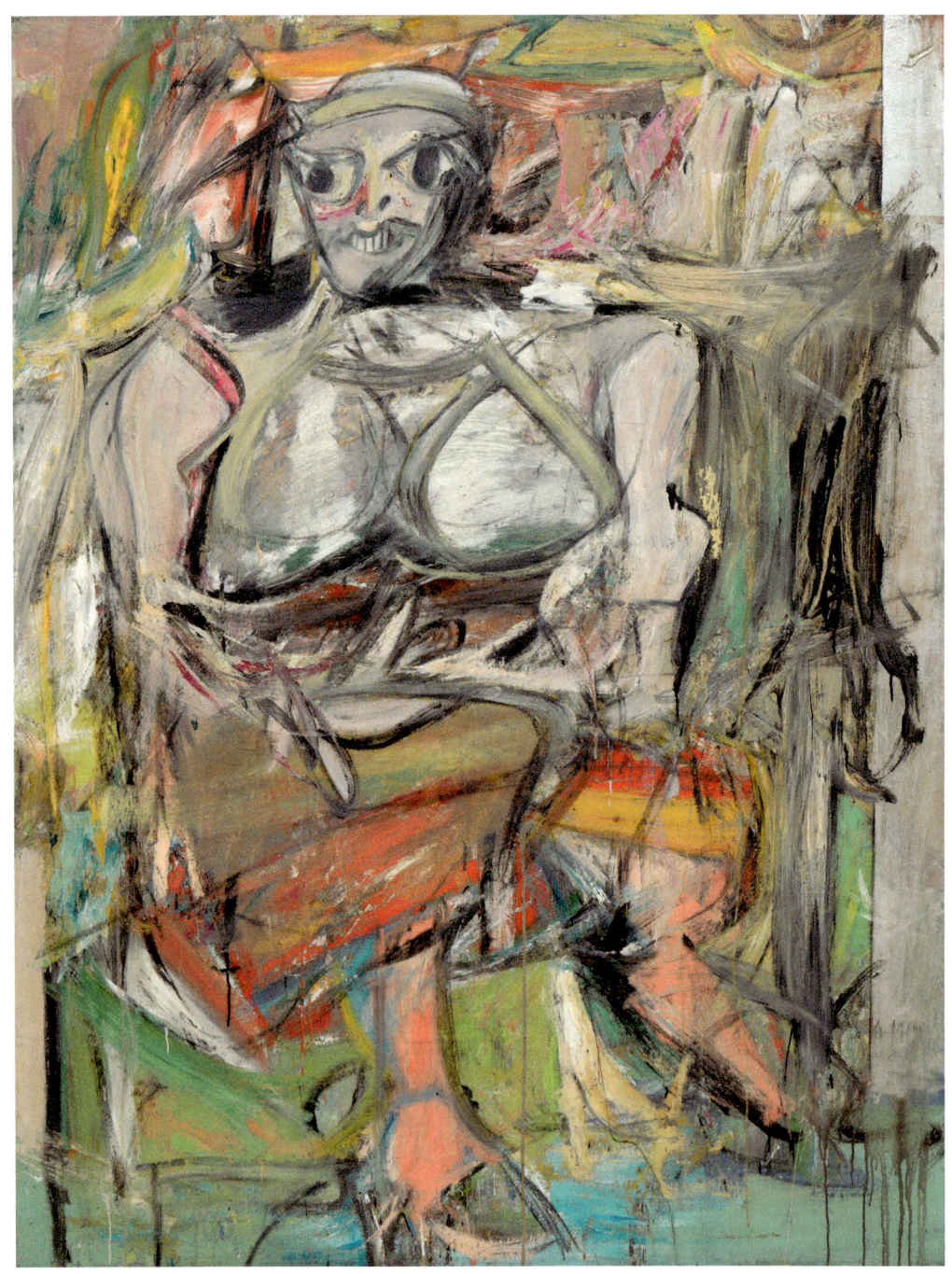

Figure 6.1 Willem de Kooning, *Woman I*, 1950–52

Massacred women do not make me laugh, nor do the agonies of Marilyn Monroe's body

In her essay 'A New Type of Intellectual: The Dissident', first published in 1977, Julia Kristeva identified several types of modern dissidence that stand in opposition to the assimilation of the intellectual to the modern patriarchal, capitalist, conservative establishment of power.[1] The rebel attacks political power. The psychoanalyst wages a contest between death and discourse and finds his archetypal rival in religion. The writer (we might add artist) experiments at the limits of identity, shifting the relations of law and desire by stripping the latter down to its basic structure: Kristeva calls this rhythm, the conjunction of body and music. But from these three spaces of politics, analysis and art/writing, *Woman* is absent because she represents a fourth kind of dissidence. *Woman* does not mean female people in the social sense. *Woman* is a sign within a phallocentric ordering of sexual difference that manages the potentialities of humans as corporeal, psycho-symbolic entities within historically shaped, social and semiotic forms. *Woman*, that is, sexual difference, is a particular instance of historical dissidence because it is as *Woman* that those termed *women* encounter, as artists and writers, analysts or political rebels, the intransigence of patriarchal culture and the phallocentric symbolic ordering of this difference.[2]

As a result of her specific potentialities in sexuality and sometimes through maternity, those under the sign *Woman* are caught up, according to Kristeva, with what she calls divine law, death and religion, in opposition to human law, government, politics and ethics. This results from *Woman* being in touch with the *unthinkable* processes of pregnancy, childbirth and the huge psychic work demanded post-natally by maternity, but also with what Ettinger names the shocks of maternality.[3] These form the maternal feminine that Kristeva theorizes as the fold of life and meaning.[4] From the point of view of human, patriarchal law, *Woman* is thus a kind of exile – who, when captured for its social forms, is made either into the demonic image of the witch (femme fatale, movie star, name her as you wish) or targeted for total assimilation to the existing order as mere reproductive container. We can join in either by trying to be the President or singing Happy Birthday to the President in a

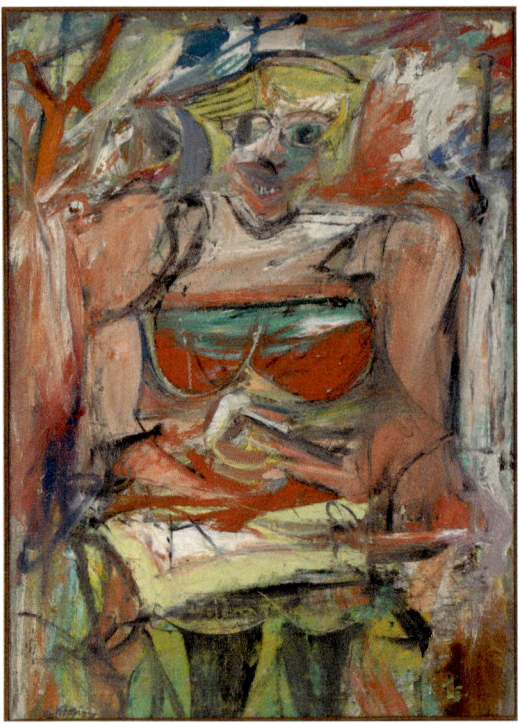

Figure 6.2 Willem de
Kooning, *Woman V*,
1952–53

transparent, glittering dress so tight the singer had to be sewn into it
(fig. 6.3). This tension is a result of the lack of a language in which to speak
of maternity and childbirth, of their psychic complexity that both provides the structure of particular feminine experience and erases all subjectivity in an encounter with an other than is literally within. Thus,
Kristeva concludes, indicating the hysterical identification she recognizes
at work in the creativity of artist-men:

> Under these conditions female 'creation' cannot be taken for granted. It can
> be said that artistic creation always feeds on an identification, or rivalry
> with what is presumed to be the mother's *jouissance* (which has nothing
> agreeable about it). This is why one of the most accurate representations of
> creation, that is, of artistic practice, is a 'series' of paintings by de Kooning
> entitled *Women* [*sic*] savage, explosive, funny, inaccessible creatures in
> spite of the fact they have been *massacred* by the artist. But what if they had
> been *created* by a woman? Obviously, she would have had to deal with her
> own mother, and therefore with herself which is a lot less funny.[5] (my
> emphases)

This passage has fascinated and challenged me for years. Put simply, the
artist as creator, whoever you are, confronts the Mother, but differentially
as an effect of the phallocentric formation of sexuated subjectivities.

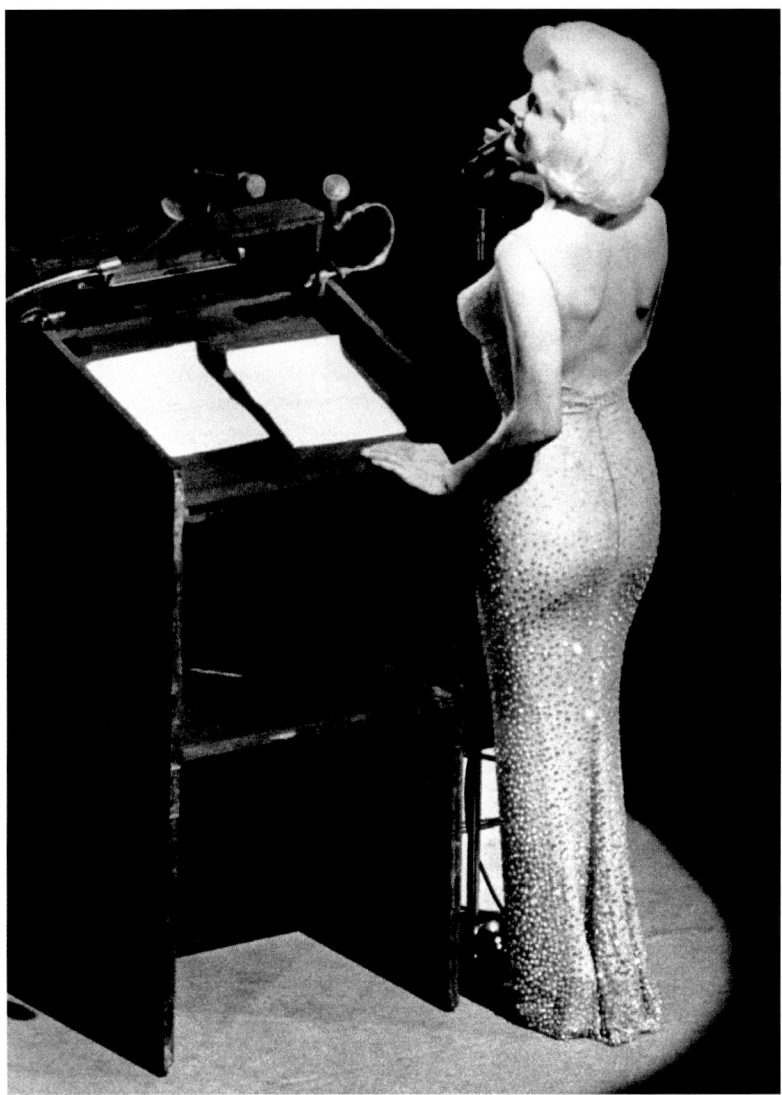

Figure 6.3 *Marilyn Monroe singing Happy Birthday to President Kennedy, 1962*

Hence, we must acknowledge the modalities in which sexual difference is always in play, not from the artist as man or woman, but *flowing across masculine or feminine subjects* in relation to unconscious processes of formation and identification and the place of the self in the potential for play via art with identification and the parental figures. The *massacre*, which is possible for de Kooning the son, would be *suicide* for the artist who is a daughter, as we have already begun to recognize through the writings of Luce Irigaray and Bracha L. Ettinger. While the parent is other to the child *qua* adult, the mother and the daughter are *like* both at the level of the phallocentric ordering of sexual difference and in terms of both Irigarayan and matrixial theories of how a girl-child learns who or what she is. To kill the mother, an element of herself would be killed but also the relation to the mother will be radically different, whether we take a classical or a matrixial psychoanalytical perspective. My reading of Helen Frankenthaler's joyous and humorous paintings of the 1950s, I hope, belies the idea that women cannot deal with the mother or themselves pleasurably. But it's the idea of killing men, of men killing women in their art being funny that I resolutely cannot handle.

De Kooning's paintings stand at the opposite pole to that at which I have tried to situate Pollock's dripped canvases. In the six canvases titled *Woman I–VI* (1950–53, figs 6.1 and 6.2) there is less metonymy and a tendency towards metaphor signalled by explicit titling and internal signifiers, even as the painting method is as deconstructive of the image as it is productive of its emergence. *Woman I* (fig. 6.1) is an image of a seated woman in modern dress with ankle strap high heels merging with/emerging from a gestural field of comparably bold brushwork. The paint conveys its powerful indexicality to the bodily intensity of the artist's energy, his gestures and physical movements as he produced this monumental form with searing, toothy, blood-red smile and staring, stylized, cosmetically enlarged, dead eyes.

In 2014 art historian Richard Schiff countered the historic condemnations of de Kooning's misogyny: 'De Kooning thought that his imagery should cause people to laugh, not in derision, but in appreciation of the ironies and the absurdities of the body as it actually is rather than its static ideal.' He added that the artist was offering 'parodic inversions of the typical advertising image of the all-American girl, where the female body assumed its most culturally sanctified form', concluding:

> Elements of Minnie Mouse, as much as Marilyn Monroe, motivated his art. If there was a politics to his images of *Woman*, we find it in the wilful transformation of the post-war American ideal of everyday beauty. This imagery is not anti-woman but anti-conformist: anti-*Vogue* magazine, if you will; anti-Revlon cosmetics; anti-Breck shampoo and Ivory soap – products laid out for American consumption and a cultivated American beauty.[6]

While radically Americanizing his own long and deeply admiring struggle with Picasso's seated woman *topos*, de Kooning may also have looked with European eyes at the Hollywood manufacture of the cinematic woman, not yet epitomized and self-parodied by Monroe, the huge star, but present in her many early bit parts as much as those of her predecessor, pin-up supreme Betty Grable. Parody, laughter can also be resourced with a violence that certain artist-women perceived, if not in de Kooning's paint-ings, then in what his paintings revealed about the cultural tropes they refashioned through Picasso-inspired energies.[7]

In an interview with Dolores Holmes in 1972, Lee Krasner, a deep admirer of de Kooning's paintings even as she had had to struggle to exor-cize their ghosts when they came to inhabit her imagination and her paint-ing in *Prophecy* (fig. 1.1), made this statement of her feelings about the *Woman* paintings.

> Well, with regard to de Kooning, certainly he is one of the leading forces in the movement. With regard to his 'series' *Woman*, I reject them one hundred percent. I find them offensive in every possible sense; they offend every aspect of me as a woman, as a female.[8]

The US-American feminist art critic Cindy Nemser had a conversation with painter Grace Hartigan about these paintings. To Nemser's expres-sion of straightforward feminist distaste for the violence she felt in de Kooning's paintings, Hartigan responded:

> The violence is in the paint. De Kooning's women are very loving. Since imagery became part of my work, I became closer to de Kooning than to Pollock. I saw most of those women being created in Bill's studio and we were very good friends. When those first women – those fifties women – were shown I had a big argument with Jim Fitzsimmons who is the editor of *Art International*. He said they were destructive, that it was hatred, Kali, the blood goddess. He pointed to one painting that had big palette knife strokes slithering across the chest and said 'Look, De Kooning is wounding her with blood.' So, I went to Bill and I said, 'Jim Fitzsimmons said you stabbed that woman and that is blood.' Bill said 'Blood? I thought it was rubies.'[9]

Nemser wondered about the unconscious impulses behind an artist's actions, but Hartigan would have none of it. 'No one is going to convince me that Bill de Kooning does not love women.'[10] I think one could make a case with the paintings either way. At the same time, to get back to dying women and killing men, I could put forward an argument about men kill-ing the fetish.

Laura Mulvey has argued that Hollywood cinema at its height in the 1950s condensed the fetishism of the commodity (Marx) and the psychic economy of fetishism (Freud) into the spectacle signified by the cosmetic *image* of woman on screen. Woman as spectacle is all surface, appearance. Turn the psychic screw of fetishism, however, and this image is all threat. Marilyn Monroe's exceptional appeal lay in the cosmetically and chemi-cally achieved allaying of that threat by the combination of her enactment of sexuality with delectable goodness: like vanilla ice-cream as Norman

Mailer put it.[11] As comedienne, so often mocked and self-mocking in her brilliantly realized roles in often banal movies, Monroe's characters embodied the funny, inaccessible creature that was repeatedly massacred, film by film, in that movie culture. Among de Kooning's *generic* engagements with *Woman* (used here conceptually and not as a title) in his paintings in the early 1950s, we might want to consider the named painting *Marilyn Monroe* (fig. 2.14). These works bring together the legacy of Picasso's cut-up women (Angela Carter's phrasing) and the iconic objectification of woman in the blood-red lips and kohl-lined eyes that are the displaced and violated sign of her 'wound'.[12] De Kooning uses Picasso to allow him to open up the female body so that out comes, not vanilla ice-cream (Mailer on Monroe), but ruby red jewels. Lipstick or blood? The ambiguity of these images lies precisely in their oscillation between metonymic and metaphoric figuration of female sexuality on the one hand, and of masculine castration fantasies projected and allayed on the other, by imaginary and prophylactic gestural energy enacted through the labour of painting in actions that remain undecidably suspended between forming and deforming.

Yet, in a sense, the shock offered by de Kooning's paintings that so polarizes opinion about them is that they are *so little fetishized*. Even dressed, they expose the female body. They give it so frankly a sex – yet in displaced and disavowed a fashion – rubies? blood? Yet they emerge from massively built-up densities of gesturally applied paint. 'The violence is in the paint.' The signature – the gesture in the paint as well as the name – makes such revelations a violent conjuring up of women dressed in modern fashion. We cannot escape the aptness of Julia Kristeva's notion of a massacre. Killing men/dying women.

Clearly hinged between Marcel Duchamp's *Etant donnés* (1964, Philadelphia Museum of Art) and Picasso's *Demoiselles d'Avignon* (1907, Museum of Modern Art, New York), behind which lurks Paul Cézanne's terrifying *L'éternel féminin* (1877, J. P. Getty Museum, Los Angeles), while also haunted by the anxiety of the cosmetic and the sheer joyous beauty of its 1950s embodiment, Marilyn Monroe, and a million red-lipped, smiling women on Camel cigarette and lipstick advertisements, de Kooning's paintings *Woman* are paradigmatic of modernist creation: namely a creativity that is predicated on a hero-artist generating himself as creator only through the erasure of the maternal-begetter who is, necessarily, disowned and displaced into representation in a dual and paradoxical image in both monumental splendour and bleeding abjection. Anguish, guilt, desire and ambivalence compete and destabilize any one interpretation, creating the force that polarized opinions on these works.[13]

Standing beside Marilyn Monroe

Marilyn Monroe was not only a cinematic icon. She came to embody the type realized in de Kooning's series *Woman*, with their full breasts, smiling red mouths and dazzling white teeth. We need, however, to get beyond such 'covering exposure'. As image traversing the border between art and cinema, 'Marilyn Monroe' was culturally an inescapable presence in the visual landscape of Lee Krasner's journey from *Prophecy* to *Sun Woman* by the mid-1950s, and indirectly as the pin-up, advertising type she came to embody, evoked in de Kooning's *Women*, even as he stated that he was painting from his artist-partner, Elaine de Kooning. I cannot, however, leave Monroe as mere icon, a glossy, manufactured, celluloid image that appears to be the opposite of the genuine, hand-created works of modern art in which, as I have been suggesting, psycho-sexual traces and imprints of the Mother, of the matrixial *m/Other*, of the cultural concept of Woman were so consistently traced both figuratively and in abstract art.

With the painting *Nude* (fig. 4.1), Helen Frankenthaler unexpectedly discovered – and thus acknowledged by the title – a reverse (like an analogue photographic negative) that transformed the Western erotic nude. By upending the canvas and making us see twoness, eyes and breasts, the figure was also maternalized at one level, as adult sexual woman. Its affect arises from the fact it was neither drawn nor painted with violent energy. As non-image, this sense of a mature woman was nudged into visibility only by the central area of the canvas remaining hardly touched. The nude that words tempt us to see *becomes* a female form through what is shaped by the inner edges of abstract areas of poured, applied and brushed paint around the cropped edges of the canvas, troubled only by dribbled lines of paint, a central spill and the two drawn rectangles. The painting is graphic and painterly at the same time. The nude areas of the canvas, the emptiness, is not surface, but both interior and the fullness of a spectral female body. It is this sense of the feminine and sexual difference that I want to consider here.

No woman, I suspect, can look at either the image of Marilyn Monroe, or her replicas such as Jayne Mansfield, without pain. Writing in the introduction to a book of photographs by George Barris, Gloria Steinem recalls: 'For me this book began when, in 1953, as a teenager who loved movies, I still walked out of *Gentlemen Prefer Blondes* in embarrassment at seeing this whispering, simpering, big-breasted child-woman who was simply hoping her way into total vulnerability.' But then she turns this angry statement of disdain into compassion: 'How dare she be just as vulnerable and unconfident as I felt?' Steinem ends by feeling a 'protectiveness explained by the endlessly vulnerable child that looked out of Marilyn's eyes'.[14] Steinem's conversion from embarrassed distaste to compassionate, and later feminist, empathy tracks the change of attitude from which my forthcoming book on Marilyn Monroe itself emerges. Yet it affirms what Monroe scholar Graham McCann also documents, the rejection of the Monroe image by women viewers and commentators during the 1950s.[15]

For all the gloriousness of the dramatic skills and the exceptional beauty as women of movie stars such as Marilyn Monroe, the torturing of their bodies and the total neglect of their souls – to quote Victorian poet Dante Gabriel Rossetti on his wife, the artist Elizabeth Siddall – makes for a profound and contradictory anguish as we watch the fetishistic, corseted, sexually exaggerated distortions that betray – and sometimes knowingly perform to – the sadistic, sexual culture from which Monroe died metaphorically, even if her death was but the unfortunate accident of disastrously poor medical supervision.[16] Monroe is reported as saying, not without bitterness and a terrible frankness:

> The truth is I've never fooled anyone. I've let men sometimes fool themselves. Men sometimes did not bother to find out who and what I was. Instead, they would invent a character for me. I wouldn't argue with them. They were obviously loving someone I wasn't. When they found this out, they would blame me for disillusioning them – and fooling them.[17]

McCann also cites this comment in his sociological study. McCann produces another kind of biography for the star, one that recognizes the author himself as part of the text and part of the problem, while also wanting to allow Monroe – she who was called 'the body' – a voice.[18] Unexpectedly, however, McCann's text also allows Monroe another kind of body, with a specific sexual interiority. McCann chronicles with tenderness Monroe's desire to have a child and the difficulties she experienced in so doing through miscarriage and life-threatening ectopic pregnancy.

> It was at Amagansett that Monroe learned she was pregnant. By six weeks she was in acute pain and Miller rushed to the city, where a doctor diagnosed a tubular pregnancy and operated to save her life. She woke from surgery to be informed that the embryo had been surgically removed. Doctors explained to her the child she had lost would have been a son. She would never entirely recover from this experience and, ironically, she would die five years hence on the anniversary of this miscarriage. The desire to have children was intense for Monroe: her body would at last be her own, since she felt it would exist for the child who belonged to her, a physical exclamation of blood, spirit and soft, warm flesh. As a mother she hoped to have her existence justified by the wants she would supply. She would attend not a man, but a self lost in a fragile and dependent body.[19]

Elaborating on the metaphysical repercussions that seeking to create and losing this new life induced, McCann adds:

Monroe's curiosity turned increasingly to her own body, her pride in it and the urge to win it back for herself; the desire to have a child became more acute, promising her commitment and continuity. She said to Truman Capote: 'I hate funerals. I'm glad I won't have to go to my own. Only, I don't want a funeral – just my ashes castaway by one of my kids, if I ever have any.' (Capote in 1981). Arthur Miller remarked: 'To understand Marilyn best, you have to see her around children. They love her; her whole approach to life has their kind of simplicity and directness.'[20]

Further on, McCann emphasizes her intense mourning in the wake of this loss of her child:

As one of her friends put it, 'Her whole womb was weeping': while she was presented as an image of playful purity, inside she was bruised and broken, increasingly forced to use drugs to assuage her agony. Such was the pain that doctors tried to persuade her to consider a hysterectomy. She flatly refused, explaining: 'I can't do that. I want to have a child. I'm going to have a son.'[21]

I am quoting these passages as they force upon our mental, emotional and psychological lives the living in bodies whose different organs and capacities shape our sense of psychological self and sexuality when we *desire* to engage with them – for instance, wanting to conceive a child – and when they act against our desires – miscarrying a conception. *Miscarriage* is a very bland word for the traumatic experience of losing a wanted baby in early pregnancy. All the hopes and dreams that are released when a desired pregnancy is discovered grow quite out of proportion to the size of the tiny embryo burrowing its way into the cavities of one's loving yet alien and uncontrollable body. The failure of one's physiology to sustain a wanted pregnancy unleashes the pain of a disappointment that is experienced by the woman as her failing in her own deepest fantasies of what she has discovered once she has chosen to activate this dimension of possibility that her body offers. Losing one's imagined, potential motherhood may and does also replay the very loss of the becoming-mother's own mother that, through the becoming-mother's sharing her bodily capacity for child-carrying, pregnancy might phantasmatically repair. In miscarriage, against a woman's will, her body destroys the nestling child that the mother-in-hope has already so richly imagined as her desired and restoring other. Is it a murder of an other – a killing woman or a moment of dying *as a woman*?

In countless stories about pregnancy loss created in a feminist impulse to break the silence about this appalling pain, we learn from women's experiences, and as attested to by this author's own, that losing a pregnancy – which has been initiated in desire and is desperately desired or even elective – is psychically catastrophic. While the medical profession offers statistics about high rates of early miscarriage (1 in 3–5 pregnancies fail) and reassures the woman about trying again, women experience two or more deaths: the death of what has already been imagined as a future child, the death of her own belief in her body's capacity to carry a child, and the re-enactment of any other death this woman may herself be mourning, a previous child, a mother, a love, a friend. The tangle of emotions that is released from Pandora's box of hope once a woman opens herself up to this area of her psycho-corporeal potentiality is massive, intense and devastating if loss occurs.

It is in these situations that we come face to face, as it were, with both *being in a body*, and *being a body* – whose autonomous acts, such as failing to hold or shedding a pregnancy, declare a war on our wills, desires and our deepest sense of self, hitherto unthought, long ignored, but now exposed in all its acute vulnerability. Mortal disease may involve a similar encounter with our powerlessness before the mindless will of corrupting cells. But conceiving, carrying and birthing are not the product of invasion by rogue cells. They are the physical process of an embodied, corporeal psycho-sexuality, a locus of an *experienced* sexual difference. The failure of a foetus or of a womb to sustain a foetus is experienced by the subject in that body as a death so profound that the mourning also never ends, even if a subsequent live birth ensues. Someone never was. No future pregnancy will ever occur without dread and anxiety.

In the context of this study of painting and the question of sexual difference, so complexly explored through psychoanalytical and philosophical theories, I introduce this element of the body and sexual difference not as a corrective to remind us that anatomy is indeed destiny (Freud's much maligned and misread phrase), but to remind us of the corpo-reality of our affective entanglement with the corporeal as medium of our psycho-sexual subjectivity. Fear of such acknowledgement, minimalization of the traumatic significance of what Ettinger names the corpo-real, and indeed feminist policing of any serious thought about this traumatic corpo-reality as reductive, politically unspeakable essentialism bears all the marks of the partial, one-sided phallocentric culture.

Representation

In Western Christianocentric visual art and culture, premised on the central image of the baby as salvation and its mother as the virginal vehicle of a divine conception, the event of procreative loss, and its attendant grief, loss of self and depression, are radically under-represented and ignored. There are almost no representations of it. US-American artist Joanne Leonard (b. 1940) created a moving, courageous, visually subtle but piercingly profound series of 30 photo-collages titled *Journal of a*

Miscarriage 1973, first exhibited in 1974 and completed in 1985, while also being censored by some curators who believed that 'no one wants to know about these experiences', especially via however aesthetically or formally created visualizations.[22] Leonard later discovered the one other artist, the object of recent feminist reclamation, Mexican Frida Kahlo (1907–54), who had forthrightly and visually explored her own pregnancy loss in one striking painting, *Henry Ford Hospital, the Flying Bed* (1932, Dolores Olmeido Collection, Mexico City), and an untitled lithograph (fig. 6.4). Kahlo's graphic surreal vision exteriorizes in phantasmatic forms a female bodily interior as well as an imaginary internal world of objects and images, dividing the body into dark and light spheres, one reaching towards art via a palette, another evoking the

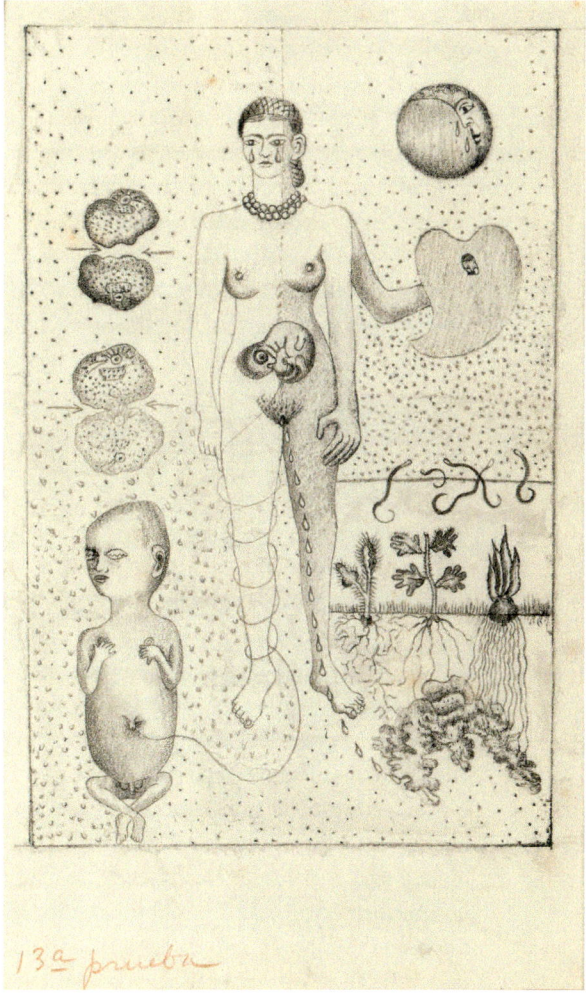

Figure 6.4 Frida Kahlo,
Untitled, 1932

multiplying cells imagined as a full-term child outside but still attached. Both bodies bleed; both weep.

There is a silence as profound among women about pregnancy loss, for it is so devastating a process that it is hardly spoken of for fear of frightening newly pregnant women. Miscarriage turns this culturally endorsed celebration of a function as bearers of new life into a narrative of death, despair and the challenge to deepest identities at the point at which we have chosen to confront, to be open to, or even to open up this sexually specific capacity, a moment for many women when, like lifting the lid on this Pandoran box of our own body-psyches, we discover depths and complexities of feelings about life, sex, bodies, mothers, ourselves that are unanticipated and were hitherto unknown.

Having lived through three miscarriages to tell the deadly tales of shock, grief, prolonged depression and deepest self-doubt, I feel personal empathy for the person behind the icon, Marilyn Monroe, when I read of this other Monroe body, with its briefly living and dying interior. Empathy, whether historically justified or not, breaks through the carapace of the fetishized image to a woman weeping in the hospital bed for yet another wanted child she had lost, for yet another lost chance to repair the psychological loss of her own mentally alienated long-absent mother by the mothering of the baby she might have borne.[23] This narrative of her longings and losses imagines a female body differing from the caricature of female sexual desirability that the costume designers created for her. It forces into shocking conjunction the fetish body of the sex symbol and the body of the would-be mother, the bleeding, miscarrying site of death and mourning.

And worse

In this sense of going beyond the beautiful surface of the closed body, McCann also raised a serious health issue. We also need to acknowledge a woman, Monroe, in the male-dominated film production industry, regularly doubled up with mind-numbing endometrial menstrual pain, which the studios dismissed as malingering and lack of professionalism. Marilyn Monroe suffered badly from a debilitating but under-reported and under-researched condition, endometriosis, whose agonies, physical and mental, are only now becoming more widely known through published testimonies.[24] Endometriosis creates acute, monthly and persistent abdominal and widely dispersed agony. This condition can never be completely successfully medically alleviated, although repeated surgeries can be performed when it becomes unbearably acute.[25] The condition impinges negatively on conception and sustained pregnancy. Any long-term amelioration risks causing permanent damage and infertility.

Writing the foreword to a recent collection of testimonies by women with this condition, Heather Guidone, Program Director at the New York Centre for Endometriosis, points out that this disease afflicts 176 million women worldwide, the population of the eighth largest country on the globe, while being little researched, badly understood and often heartlessly treated, a victim of the fact that 'unrelenting bias enshrouds menstruation and pelvic pain, keeping endometriosis often belittled, ignored, under-diagnosed, medicalized, inadequately treated and marginalized'.[26] She explains its impact:

> Endometriosis exacts a vast and painful toll on lives, including my own: significantly reduced quality of life, compromised academic and professional opportunities, impaired sexual and physical functionality, losses in productivity, 'in your head' diagnoses that can lead to crippling self-doubt, hopelessness and isolation, countless, ineffective medical and surgical treatments and more. In a word: despair.[27]

The disease does not afflict women alone but is intense in women because of menstruation. As the hormonal cycle causes blood-enriched cells in all the sites endometriosis has invaded – rogue cells that usually line the womb can colonize any part of the body, urethra, vagina, bladder, intestines, spinal tissues or brain – to engorge and then be shed, the woman suffers agonizing menstrual pain throughout all the affected areas and for prolonged periods, for, in addition, it aggravates pre-menstrually. Its constant killer is pain. Pain is devastating, exhausting and overwhelms other functions, causing fatigue, mental fuzziness, short-term memory weakness and a multitude of related psychological effects. Beyond conventional pain relief, drugs become addictive and overdosed.

I have been seeking material with which to comprehend the implications of this condition. I found on an internet list of 'The Top Twenty Books on Endometriosis' an unexpected and visceral memoir by multiple Booker Prize winning novelist Hilary Mantel, titled *Giving Up the Ghost*.[28] In Part Five, 'Show Your Workings', which explores her student years and early marriage, Mantel gives a searing account of her suffering at the hands of both her endometriotic body and the sexist, ignorant, dismissive medical profession that gave her drugs that made her mentally ill, submitted her to unhelpful surgery and indignity on the way, and prescribed drug treatments that caused her body to swell. Only reading this text, written in the novelist's inimitable style, will truly convey the power and significance of what she has decided to tell of life with this condition.

I reread the many sensational and often derogatory stories about Marilyn Monroe in the new light of a burden carried and managed since adolescence in a world not yet attuned to sexually specific conditions of women. Monroe's endometriosis is taken up with in-depth research in a clearly feminist study by historian Lois Banner.[29] She points out that you cannot diagnose this disease through palpation. It requires investigative surgery. Banner notes the scar that is visible on the pathologist's schematic drawing of the post-mortem body of Monroe, just above the pubic hair, which suggests that abdominal surgery had been possibly several times performed.[30] Tracing the many gynaecological operations on Monroe during the 1950s, Banner concludes: 'Thus, even Marilyn's magical body, the body of the world's greatest sex queen, was riddled with paradox. Externally flawless, it was flawed in its eternal internal anatomy, requiring surgical procedures to make a whole.'[31]

Age

Yet there is the body, reshaped through time, lived over time, and confronting time: the ageing body.[32] What would an old Marilyn Monroe have been like? She said:

> I want to grow old without face-lifts. They take the life out of a face, the character. I want to have the courage to be loyal to the face I've made. Sometimes I think it would be easier to avoid old age, to die young, but then you'd never complete your life, would you? You'd never wholly know yourself.[33]

I found a photograph of Monroe's mother, Gladys Baker (1902–84), in older age; she lived until she was 82. There is also a video circulating on the internet said to be of Gladys as an older woman wandering in a garden in Florida with her carer.[34] None of this allows us fully to accommodate to the idea of an older Marilyn Monroe, who is forever suspended by premature death at the age of just 36.

While the drunken man Pollock, just eight years older, died in an alcoholic act of self-destruction, and the dyed lady was possibly inadvertently killed by her doctors, 'female creators' (Kristeva's ambivalent term) such as Lee Krasner survived a culture that did its best to kill them by denying them representational support and symbolic acknowledgement. It falls to us to grasp Laura Mulvey's idea of creative curiosity and break open Pandora's box – smashing the fetishized artifice of *Woman* and letting through to the surface of culture's texts our desire to know about femininity – its pleasures, fascinations and, at times, its killing humour.

Why, you may be asking, is this chapter in this book? Neither Helen Frankenthaler nor Lee Krasner 'chose' to have children. Neither were artist-mothers. Here is the rub of another asymmetry. I have a collection of photographs by Hans Namuth I think, that I have used for many years and whose source as a collection I can no longer trace, in which several New York artists appear as family men, often posed with wife and child in attendance on, and as confirmation of, the masculinity of the main man.

Professional artistic life militates against child-bearing. Artist-women who dare to have children are often doubly distanced from being considered candidates for avant-garde status; witness Clement Greenberg's dismissal of the sculptor Anne Truitt that I quoted in Chapter 3. Mother of three sons, Louise Bourgeois only became something other than Mrs Goldwater and a *woman-artist* on the margins of the New York artworld once she was old enough for her maternal deviation to be overlooked. She was 70 when she had a retrospective at the Museum of Modern Art in 1982. Only with the support of the post-1968 Women's Movement have artists such as Mary Kelly (b. 1941) and Susan Hiller (1940–2019) or filmmaker Laura Mulvey (b. 1941) made the psycho-sexual and imaginative topic of motherhood, in culture and personally, a theme for and through radical artistic practice.[35]

Focusing on psychological suffering that is a specific effect of a sexual and sexuated body, I have wanted to ground my often-hesitant question about painting and sexual difference, via bodies in movement, via gesture, via fetishism and then hysteria, with testimony to the body's place in subjectivity. This chapter has, moreover, been about dying, about loss, grief, mourning. What happened on 11 August 1956, when *the dying and killing man* precipitated Lee Krasner into mourning as a psychologically dying woman, into a depth of psychological intensity that would be compounded at the end of that decade by the death of her mother, a *dying woman*? As a member of a generation of Americans introduced to spiritualism via John Graham and psychoanalysis through Surrealist appropriations and actual Sullivanian analysis, Krasner was always frank about her dark nights during the later 1950s. She spoke of them as the companions in her painting, while making painting was the way to work through their worst.

Body, movement, gesture, painting, psychic structures … these we have tracked. *Working through, the work of mourning* and what Bracha L. Ettinger has added to Freud's vocabulary for psychic work as *artworking* are the psychoanalytical terms for a psycho-dynamic rather than cathartic understanding of the psyche that *transforms* rather than merely abreacts to trauma. It is with this in mind that I can address the painting practice of Lee Krasner, which moved from the monstrous body that is *Prophecy* (fig. 1.1) to the painting that is *Sun Woman I* (fig. 1.2) and beyond. Dying? Killing? Neither? Both?

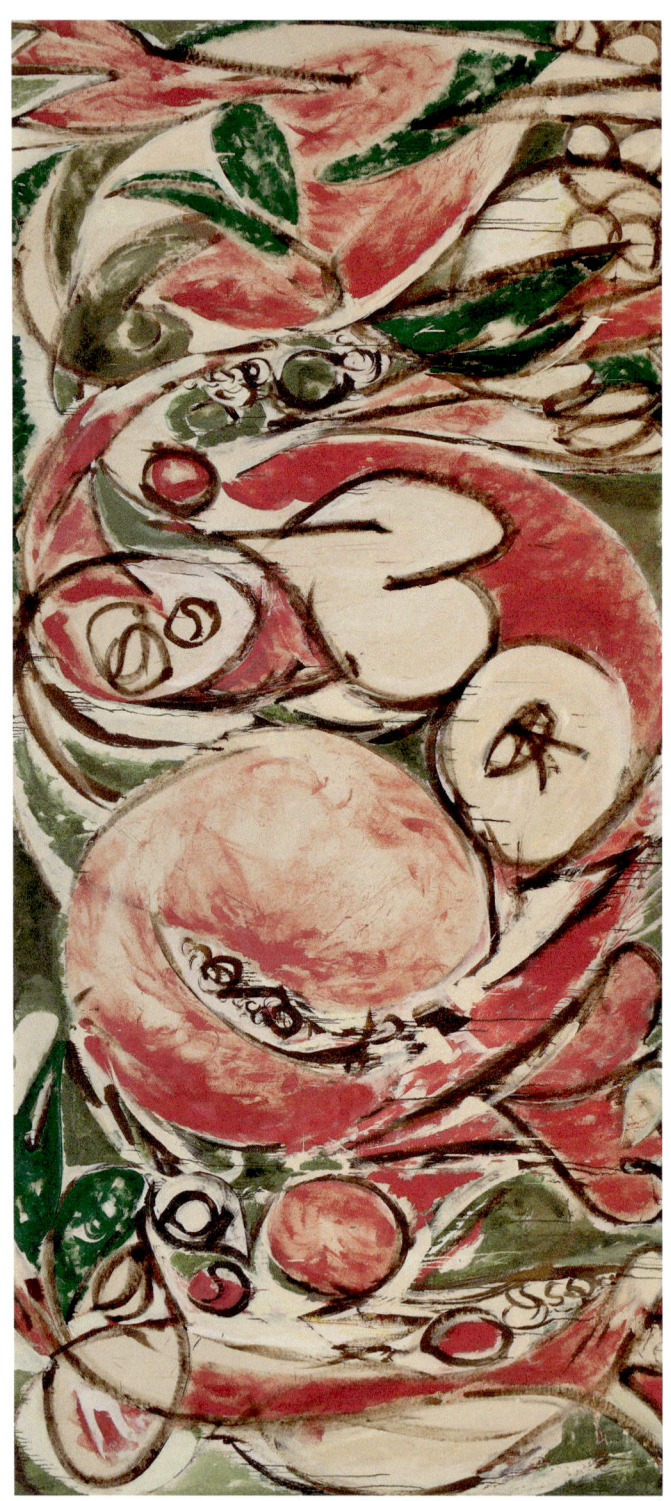

Figure 7.1 Lee Krasner, *The Seasons*, 1957

Dancing space: *Prophecy* to *Sun Woman I*

Visual control begins around the age of eighteen months: in such a case, it is control after-the-fact, since the eye follows the hand without yet guiding it. Only after the age of twenty-four months does the possibility of visual control over marking and gesture appear: the eye no longer follows the hand but guides it. Thus, the earliest drawings are not guided by a visual exploration of space but by an exploration of movement. At its origin, graphic expression is blind. It is guided by muscular, tonic, and plastic sensations.

Serge Tisseron[1]

How did a long-standing abstract artist, Lee Krasner, confront the menacing creature looming into paint in *Prophecy* in 1956 (fig. 1.1) and how did she get to *Sun Woman I* (fig. 1.2) and *The Seasons* (fig. 7.1) by 1957? I add: Why do I think this is a significant question – art historically, culturally, theoretically?

Georges Bataille's thesis on modern art's progression through 'murder' and his notion of painting's surface as tombstone converge in the work of this artist-woman of the 1950s. In that decade, painter-women knew that they wanted to be artists. They wanted to be, and indeed were, part of an exciting modernist project that included the painting of Pollock and de Kooning alongside many other women and men, black and white, straight and queer, Jewish, Catholic, Protestant, Muslim, spiritual or agnostic and neither, working-class, economically privileged, immigrant, born to immigrant families, old country families, urban aristocrats. Some of their fellow artists inspired them, opening new pathways from which all eagerly learned. They would, from time to time, have to be dealt with – when what they were doing was important, interesting, necessary for any artist who wanted to be part of the game in the tiny fraction that formed the self-consciously avant-garde New York art community. Fred Orton and I defined the formation we name the avant-garde as follows:

An avant-garde does not simply emerge 'readymade' from virgin soil to be attributed *à la mode*. It is actively formed, and it fulfils a particular function. It is the product of self-consciousness on the part of those who identify themselves as, and with, a special social and artistic grouping within the intelligentsia at a specific historical conjuncture. It is not a process inherent in the evolution of art in modern times; it is not the motor of spiritual renovation and artistic innovation; and it is more than an ideological concept, one part of a complex pattern of imagery and belief. An avant-garde is a concrete cultural phenomenon that is realized in terms of identifiable (though never predetermined) practices and representations through which it constitutes for itself a relation to, and a distance from, the overall cultural patterns of the time. Moreover, its construction and the definition of its function result from a broader discursive formation that provides the terms of reference by which artists can see themselves in this illusory but effective mode of difference, and by which others can validate what they are producing as somehow fulfilling an avant-garde's function.[2]

Yet how would an artist-woman prevent the publicly acclaimed practices of some artist-men from rendering unrecognizable the resources from which an artist-woman – her identity qualified and enriched by factors of class, family history, lived identity, race and ethnicity, and psycho-sexual specificity – must both create and launch her singular gambit in the avant-garde game of *reference, deference and difference*?[3]

A brief overview of Lee Krasner's painting from the 1940s to the late 1950s reveals that she might be a creative *Baillist*. Like all the artists of her generation and ambition, she had to take on haunting presences, from Cézanne to Picasso to her co-creating contemporaries such as Pollock and de Kooning, and *process* – but not exactly obliterate – them as much as aesthetically *transform* them, right there, on her canvas, precisely because underlying, driving and giving the gestural and psychic force to so much of their work and its violent energies was the powerful shadow of *their* anguished battle with *Woman*, with the *Mother*, with their *Other*, with female bodies that condense desire, death and envied/recast generativity.[4] Krasner had to take *them* on – meaning these artists and their phantoms as well as her own phantasmatic feminine and matrixial *m/Others and Others* – but to such radically different painterly effect and with such different *affects* that it has awaited feminist art history and theory to allow us to read the event of this encounter as differentiating realignment within that artistic moment, rather than her lack or mere diversion from its dominant, phallic trajectory.

Let me elaborate.

Of all the modernizations that have informed the construction and internal radicalization of bourgeois culture since the late nineteenth century, that of *sexual difference* remains profoundly unfinished. Yet how shall we think that difference if not through what alone allows us to specify the source of a difference that is distinctly sexual and sexuating, namely the primordial maternal encounter that 'seduced us into life'?[5] This is not to be confused with saying that woman's destiny is confined to the social role of domesticity and motherhood, or that motherhood is the essential truth of Woman. Such statements reflect the historically, sociologically and ideologically confining concept of gender utterly colonized by the Oedipal and the phallic One sex and its Other, a logic that Luce Irigaray defines as the morpho-logic of the same, *not of difference.* Resisting ideological fixing of the feminine to a patriarchal and reproductionist – Gayatri Spivak names patriarchy a uterine – economy that denies female desire, Bracha L. Ettinger argues that the feminine is a source of a supplementary domain of signification and phantasy that has real repercussions for a rethink of the human, hence the social and the ethical.[6]

When I speak here of the maternal, I am drawing on two, disparate conceptualizations.

For Julia Kristeva, maternity, which all of us encounter in having being born, is, on the maternal side, a *subjective/psychic structure that transforms the violence of individual eroticism into a tenderness that allows the born other to live.* The complexity and fallout of this psychic structure cannot be underestimated, since it flouts so much of what we understand as generalized psychological operations based on individuation, the formation of an ego, and a sense of distinct identity as child/adult. Kristeva argues that, as a structure, this psychic process is not confined to actual maternity. Maternity is *a model* for the ethical, capable of an actual (in child-raising) and symbolic realization (through teaching, friendship and democracy) of an ethics involving the withdrawal of the ego and its own desires to allow the other to live, separate, become itself.[7]

Artist-psychoanalyst-theorist Bracha L. Ettinger re-theorizes both the pre- and the post-maternal as also but very differently a structure or model. Ettinger's theory of the Matrixial, however, undoes Kristeva's perplexity about how the maternalized subject suspends her narcissism and, by massive psychic disinvestment and work, allows the other, the child, to become separate. From its most archaic origins, the matrixial is a *joint psychic encounter-event, a severality* to which every born person has been exposed in the prolonged condition of their human becoming (later pre-natality) and having being born. In the most primordial inklings of subjectivity, we cannot but *co-emerge with the pre-maternal m/Other.* The ethics that flow from this matrixial dimension are *the impossibility of not-sharing the passion, pain and events of the partner-in-difference.* The matrixial is a primordial dimension of co- and trans-subjectivity premised on the *severality* of partial/partialized subjectivities co-emerging, co-affecting, co-disturbing on the basis of a feminine sexual difference – not between men and women but a difference arising *from/with* the sexual body-psyche in/by/with which we are generated and whose psycho-somatic imprints (with its own historical transgenerational matrixial transubjective sharings) initiate the humanizing inklings of proto-subjectivity in the last trimesters of the becoming-infant that is being *carried*, and thus emerges in hospitality and compassion.

The matrixial thesis of *subjectivity-as-encounter* radically pre-dates and then later realigns what we take to be the post-natal phallocentric individuation and sexuation via 'castration' in the Oedipal complex. The Matrix is not a characteristic or essence of women as defined by the phallic division of the sexes into plus and minus, man and not-man, bodily cavity or penis. It forms an originary difference (defined as the originary *carriance* of the becoming-maternal and the becoming-infant *severality*) that is logically sexual (since it occurs within a sexed and sexual body-psyche) based on the conception of subjectivity as always and already an encounter of an I and non-I that are *co-habit(u)ating*.

The condition in which this structure arises in the Real, the term Lacan created for the unthinkable Thing that precedes what is, becomes an object for my drives. The Real pre-exists image or word, being the unthinkable before phantasy (the Imaginary) or language (the Symbolic). Ettinger matrixially introduces a Thing-event. In matrixial terms, the Real of our becoming as event-encounter is *aesthetically*, sensuously registered. The Real in late pregnancy is matrixially defined as the co-affecting, co-emergent 'trauma' of subjective/proto-subjective entities, each shaped (becoming-infant) or reshaped (becoming-maternal, who was once a becoming-infant and is now a full subject temporarily re-partialized) in that state by the sensed/imagined presence of the *unknown* and *unknowable* other, which confronts either *partner-in-difference* as either a full subject or as an object for its drives. That will come much later. These becoming entities share, however, a borderspace of asymmetrically co-affecting and co-subjectivizing events producing resonances that occur on the level of *aesthesis*, not phantasy and not cognition – yet.

The taboo against recognizing the matrixial becoming-mother/ becoming-infant as an encounter in sexual difference remains at the heart of a still virulent *horror feminae*, a phallocentrically induced terror in the face of *female* bodily otherness on the part of the phallic masculine that renders it incautious, ill-advised and theoretically suicidal for any woman theorist to dare to speak of it within the frame of serious intellectual debate. This taboo itself shows how far the feminist question, far from being over as has so prematurely been trumpeted, has hardly begun its transformative work. It is now even more circumscribed by forms of external and self-censorship of what we are allowed to theorize. Emerging in the same moment as the modernizations – *subjectivity*: psychoanalysis; *language*: semiotics; the *physical sciences*: relativity and quantum mechanics; and *metropolitanization*: social living defined by colonial, imperial and global capitalist modernities – the question of *sexual difference*, namely feminism, has played through them all, but disjunctively. We are still at work on the unfinished project.

The modernizing restructuring of sexual difference has, however, followed an interrupted – almost trauma-like – history of *delay* (from the later nineteenth century to the 1920s), *repression* (at the onset of fascism and the internalization of its conservative gender ideologies by the Allied victors in the 1930s–1950s) and repoliticized *reconfiguration* in an anamnesiac re-emergence of feminist consciousness in the 1970s, which delivered both an activist worldwide social movement and – for the first time in history – a sustained international intellectual, theoretical and cultural revolution which we can collectively term feminist theory that has rethought every discipline and epistemology. This fractured feminist temporality challenges both the progressivist, teleological histories of the avant-garde as synonymous with dominant bourgeois culture and the critical histories of the avant-garde as discontinuous eruption and recurring defeat of its critical negativity. We can identify various 'avant-garde moments' in art's modern histories. Those of the late nineteenth century and the 1900–1930s have been addressed by art historical narrative. Other 'moments' – 1870s/1880s, 1920s, 1970s – have not, namely those that are specifically significant in the feminist challenge to the hegemony of a phallocentric, heterosexist and Eurocentric concept of the avant-garde as a particular cultural formation within capitalist modernity.[8] Feminism c. 1968 made possible the emergence of a *feminist* avant-garde moment that was violently delayed by the sexism of twentieth-century modernism, continuing legal, political and economic discrimination, and fascism's defeat of feminism's initial cultural flowering in the 1900–39 period.[9]

Let me now explain the intricate network of links within the avant-garde of social ensemble, semiosis, subjectivity and sexual difference identified by Julia Kristeva that have specific relevance for understanding how Abstract Expressionist painting can be connected with these historical-political moments and with issues of body and psyche and aesthetics. Kristeva argued that the state and the family, institutions respectively of national-social order and patriarchal-sexual ordering, 'hold together a certain type of relation between the unity (*ed:* fixing of meaning and identity) and process (*ed:* the semiotic, drives and the radical instability of subjectivities on trial [i.e. never fixed]) in the economy of the speaking subject, at the same time, being consolidated as a result of this relation.'[10] The state manages the forces and relations of production. The family ensures unity in the face of the process of drives and pleasure associated with sexuality and reproduction. Hence the ideological function of the third component of a trinity – religion.

This unity, of state and family, is achieved at the price of a murder and a sacrifice – that of the soma, the drive and the process. This is recognized by religion, which thus arrogates to itself the privilege of representing (i.e. unifying into the socio-symbolic ensemble the hitherto heterogeneous) and of speaking the infinite element the ensemble oppresses and yet demands to be spoken. Religion is here that discourse […] which knows, as far as is possible, what is at stake in the relation between socio-symbolic homogeneity and the heterogeneity of the drives at work within and upon the homogeneity. Complicit with the state and the family to the extent that it restores their other to them, this religious discourse appears not only as the speculative (and often specular) forms of what is unrepresentable in orgasmic pleasure (*jouissance*) but of what is uncapitalizable in expenditure (of productive forces): it is also the privileged space of speculation … [11]

The concatenation of state, family and religion, far from crumbling with the coming of modernity, was, according to Kristeva, consolidated precisely by the triumph of the bourgeois revolution in the later nineteenth century. Here lies her striking novelty – not to see secularization as the dissolution of an age of Christianity, but to grasp the bourgeois order of the nineteenth century in the West as the contradictory moment of *its social sublimation*. This moment of a religiosity that manages, on behalf of the socio-symbolic unity, the excess of drives and phantasies not allowed into representation in the tightening economies of production and reproduction – Victorian values, if you will – was, however, simultaneously contested by a new formation – art, which had been progressively seeking its independence from the very discourses and institutions upon which it was founded. We are talking about a radical rupture – an *avant-garde* – that Kristeva poses as a breach with what had been hitherto either an overt or a subliminal *religious* foundation for art.

This complicity of family, state and religious discourse appears for the first time in the second half of the 19th century, following the triumph of the bourgeois revolution, the consolidation of capitalism, and the accompanying fulfilment of the Christian religion. At the same time, there also appears the subversive function of 'art' – subversive because of the way it cuts through and reworks the frontiers of the socio-symbolic ensembles. [12]

What happened with the coming, and becomes the characterization, of the avant-garde in art, literature and music, as well as the many related intellectual trends such as psychoanalysis, constituted a break with fundamental concepts of what these practices were. Since the Renaissance, Western art shared an intimacy with Christianity that shaped not just the content but the very plastic and aesthetic *representational* character of and impulse for its artistic ideologies and figurative practices. The Christian theology of the Incarnation and of the 'word made flesh' provided the deepest drive towards the conquest of mimetic-expressive representation of the body in pictorial narrativization of the specular human figure in composition and the development of gesture and pose to incite the appropriate affective reception of the key theological propositions through imaginary identifications with an anthropomorphic illusionism. The Renaissance direction in the visual arts offered theological incarnation a figurative but also formally and aesthetically sustained visualization in representation.

To the tension between theological metaphorics and a kind of visual picturing that worked iconically, the seeds of the avant-garde revolt against religion can be traced. Religion here stands for a metaphoric discourse in so far as it must accept that it seeks to speak in linguistic or visually iconic terms of that which defies those terms, while it yet can only be imaginable within them – that is, except for the excess which religious practice, ritual and experience allows into, but manages on behalf of, the socio-symbolic ensemble and the social order – affectivity, intensity, mysticism, (dis)possession of the self.

In defying, not as Clement Greenberg argued, the visual arts' servitude to literature, but its function as the representational screen for incarnation theology, the increasingly multi-ethnic, sometimes atheistic and partially secularizing Western avant-garde tried to force into productive acknowledgement both the bodily materiality and the psychic excess that underpin (and threaten as they energize) any signifying system. The project of the avant-garde is to deal with the irreparable dislocation between signifier and referent where the latter term itself has lost the transcendent meaning that was guaranteed by Christian religious discourse. In passing from religious to mundane subjects of everyday modernity, and ultimately towards the abstract, the Western visual arts were opened specifically to artists from Protestant and Jewish culture or background, the latter recently emancipated under a different aspect of modernity. Modernism's materialism and formalism reminds us endlessly that what we are encountering are but signifiers, that then enjoy, or give pleasure through, materiality *infused with displaced* aesthetic, semiotic affects, evocative of both the bodily and the ineffable. The avant-garde seeks to get back to the condition of most of the rest of the world's art that did not take Christian incarnation deviation to heart. Much of the world's art has always been 'abstract' or rather affective-semiotic, even as Western art historians condescendingly dismissed so much of world art that is non-figurative as mindlessly geometric, decorative and, in their most arrogantly racist terms, primitive.

Even in its semiotic nakedness, the play of signifiers affects us, touching something beyond the signifying system that tries to harness it for meaning. In coming to know that, art, however, lost its faith in its ability as well as its need to provide the visualization of an incarnated subject.

Avant-garde art is, structurally if never ideologically, both atheist and aniconic. Instead of trying to provide the representation of God as a Body, Kristeva argues that the avant-garde sought to register what had been sacrificed in Christianocentric culture, the *soma* (Greek: body) – or rather the psyche-soma, the drives and pleasures of the endlessly unravelling subject. Ironically, but inevitably, this took the avant-garde *in its predominantly masculinist character* back to the lost maternal body and to envy of her *jouissance* (see Chapter 5). Hence the massacred feminine Kristeva recognized in de Kooning's *Woman* paintings that replaced the idealized but perpetually melancholy *Madonna* she sees in the maternally bereaved painter Giovanni Bellini's Virgins and Child.[13]

Kristeva's theory of the avant-garde assists my return to a secular Jewish artist Lee Krasner in 1956 and what she was able to paint in 1957. We must, however, first track back sixteen years.

In the very early 1940s, Russian-Jewish but American-born Krasner (Leonore Krassner as she still signed herself) was photographed in her apartment studio surrounded by works created while studying with Hans Hofmann (fig. 7.2). Her paintings affirm her elaboration of a post-Cubist mode of semi-abstract art in a way that remained true to Hoffmann's strong sense that abstract art arises from engagement with objects in the world, be that figures or still lives. Her works enliven her confident knowledge of Cubist de-re-composition and de Stijl's grids with playful, coloured, abstracted linear compositions.

The photo dates from the early 1940s by which time Krasner had produced a mural for the Works Progress Administration and designed abstract shop windows, and had joined the Association of Abstract Artists of America. Her paintings in this idiom are very accomplished structurally as well as being intense in colour, and already exhibiting energy and formal rhythm. They reveal her understanding of the vocabularies of the still influential School of Paris that was increasingly fertilizing New York painting both through forced migration of artists from Nazi-dominated Europe and the exhibitions that Alfred Barr had organized at the Museum of Modern Art throughout the 1930s and early 1940s, such as *Cubism and Abstract Art* (1936), *Fantastic Art, Dada and Surrealism* (1936), *Vincent van Gogh* (1937), *Georges Rouault* (1938), *Picasso: Forty Years of His Art* (1939–40), *Modern Masters from European Collections* (1940), *Masterpieces by Picasso* (1941), *Van Gogh: Starry Night* (1941) and *Paul Klee* (1941). We also need to note the singular impact of one painting by Picasso, *Guernica* (1937, Centro de Arte Reina Sofia, Madrid), sent specially by the artist to New York for a benefit exhibition for Spanish refugees held at the Valentine Dudensing Gallery in New York in 1939, and then in Boston. Krasner recalled her shocked encounter with *Guernica*: 'It knocked me right out of the room … I circled the block four or five times and then went back to

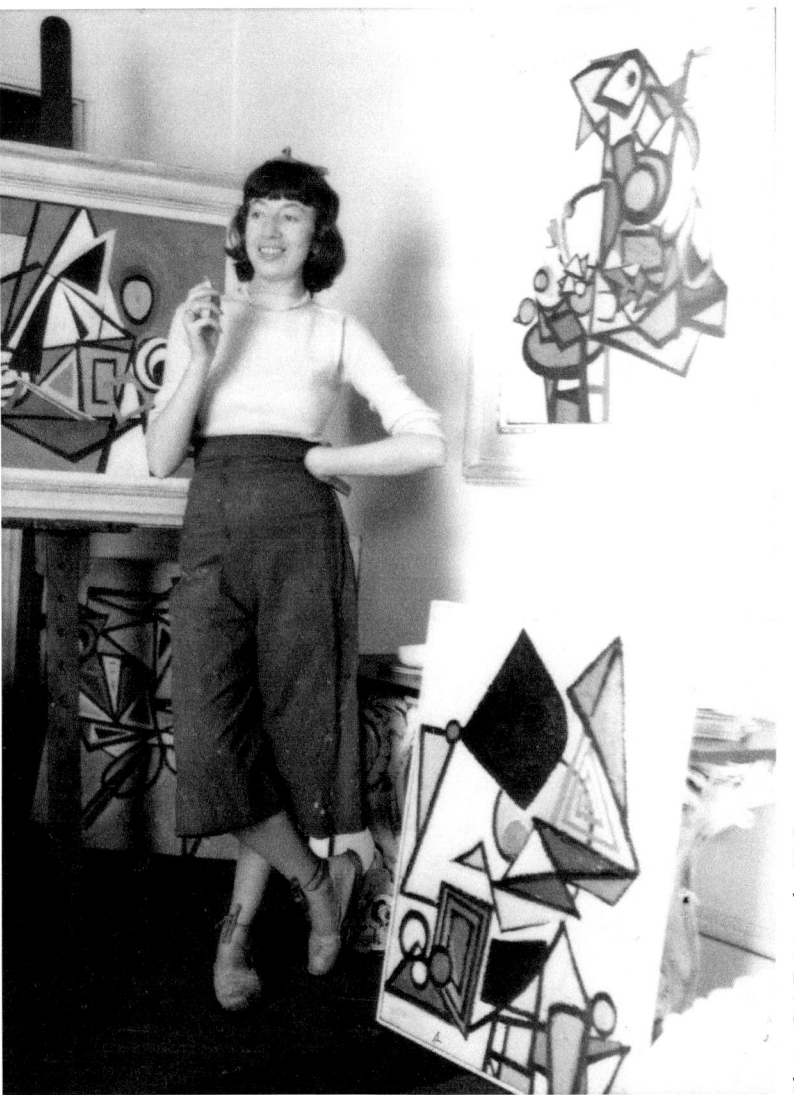

Photo: © A.E. Artworks, LLC

Figure 7.2 Maurice Berezov, *Lee Krasner in her New York studio,* 1939.

have another look at it.' She later explained: 'The presence of a great work of art … does many things to you in one second. It disturbs so many elements in one given second, you can't say "I want to paint like that." It isn't that simple.'[14]

It is equally vital to register the impact of shows at MoMA that extended the histories of art beyond Europe and beyond the twentieth century, such as *Twenty Centuries of Mexican Art* (1940) and *Indian Art in the United States* (1941), which we know had an immense impact on Jackson Pollock as it included First Nations artists demonstrating sand painting, namely changing the position of the body and the nature of the gestures relating to material and unframed space, working on the ground.

In this rich context, Krasner retrospectively described her first encounter with Pollock in November 1941 in interesting ways. They had both been invited take part in an exhibition, *French and American Painting*, at the McMillen Gallery, organized by Russian-American artist John Graham, author of *System and Dialectics of Art* (1937), a book that Krasner had read intently on publication. Graham's hermetic view of abstraction was completely opposed to Hoffmann's insistence that abstraction was grounded in and derived from the perceptible world and Western art's traditional genres. Graham argued in a more mystical way that art is a process; it is always a process of abstraction. 'Art has nothing to do with representation, impersonation, interpretation, decoration, compromise, character, caricature, or psychological problems. It contains psychological problems but deals with them in terms of form not subject matter.'[15] Like the art historian Herbert Read in Britain, Graham was not theorizing art as a practice or its objects, but rather as a condition – creativity – as it articulated emotions or mental states in objective and subjective forms, and which was as much present in the most ancient records of human marking as in the most elaborated of artistic modes defined in the European West as 'art'.[16]

Pollock's then current work was apparently unknown to the older and already established abstract painter Lee Krasner. Some think this a mythic version of the first meeting story told in retrospect, since Krasner was so deep in the close-knit New York subculture of avant-garde art that she knew or must have known of everyone, and there is evidence that she had met and danced with Pollock in the late 1930s. In the tale of the first meeting, on discovering they were both to be in the Graham show and lived quite near each other, Krasner called on the younger man (born in 1912 to her 1908 birthdate). She reports that when she first saw Pollock's works in his studio, she was impressed, moved, overwhelmed, blasted, stunned, bowled over. Once she said that 'she almost died'.[17] *A dying woman meets a killing man?*

Art historians have argued that Krasner was initially uncertain about what to make of Pollock's work. She was a much more mature, advanced and thoughtful abstract painter at the time than this recent student of regionalist figurative painter Thomas Hart Benton (1889–1975). Pollock was just discovering Surrealism and the art of First Nations, and was already an afflicted alcoholic previously institutionalized for his illness. Such an account, however, of the mythic moment when their relationship began can be read in terms of a wider context of artists absorbing what was coming in from Europe, what they themselves were doing with it and with the arts of the first and earlier settler nations of their own continent. In a small coterie of artists constantly mixing and examining each other's work and those that they saw in new shows, Krasner's response to what she saw in the studio of the little-known youngest Pollock brother (Charles and Sandford Pollock [who renamed himself McCoy] were also artists) expresses her astute judgement and her excitement at witnessing what, in part under her influence, would become a major dynamic force in New York painting by the end of the decade, if only for a brief moment. What she was seeing was precisely not Cubism, but the loosening up by Surrealism of a visual imagination trained in figuration. Benton's flowing and rhythmic compositions of figures were being abstracted by Pollock from finished hypernaturalism, and Pollock's work was becoming mythic in subject matter. It was violent in painterly terms, intense in psychic terms. Such paintings prompted Krasner to make a break in her own work with what had been excellent, but not yet transformative.

> What did I think? I saw all those marvellous paintings. I felt as if the floor was sinking … I must have made several remarks on how I felt about the paintings. I remember remarking on one, and he said, 'Oh I'm not sure I'm finished with that one.' I said, 'Don't touch it!' Of course, I don't know whether he did or not. He was not a big man, but he gave the impression of being big about 5 foot 11 … His hands were fantastic powerful hands. I wish there were photographs of his hands. All told he was physically-powerful.[18]

She later added in her unpublished text titled *Pollock*: 'It was a force, a living force, the same sort of thing I responded to in Matisse, in Picasso, in Mondrian. Once more I was hit that hard with what I saw.'[19] In her monumental study *Originals: American Women Artists*, Eleanor Munro records the following:

> I was confronted with something ahead of me. I felt elation. *My God there it is*. I couldn't have felt that if I had not been trying for the same goal myself. You just wouldn't recognise it. What he had done was much more important than just line. He has found a way to merge abstraction with Surrealism.[20] (my emphasis)

This seems to me to be the key.

The strongly Protestant Christian thinker and first director of the Museum of Modern Art Alfred H. Barr had divided his history of modern art between a Cubism-to-Abstraction telos and what was, for him, the problematic engagement with modern media (Dada) or figuration and the Unconscious (Surrealism); he named both *Fantastic Art*. From his different, Jewish cultural formation, Greenberg also disdained Surrealism. So, what was it that Krasner saw in Pollock's surreal psycho-dramatic aberration from the official MoMA line and what Greenberg had already articulated in his influential essays in *Partisan Review* in no uncertain terms: 'Avant-Garde and Kitsch' and 'Towards a Newer Laocoon'? I suggest that she saw the impact of theosophist John Graham's counter-vision for all art as inherently *spiritually* abstract, thus allowing for *the image* in a radically different understanding of composition from that which Cubism and de Stijl had first destroyed and then recreated as a formal synthesis.[21] Perhaps this makes sense of another account, also recorded by Eleanor Munro, quoting an even more retrospective account of the first encounter, in which Krasner writes of the moment when one artist seems to open a door for the others who live on and work through what that sudden opening made possible.[22] Pollock's ex-centric work, with fluid, rhythmic, semi-figurative derivations from the flowing, entwined compositions of Thomas Hart Benton and exposure to Picasso's often violent recasting of Surrealism in dramatic paintings such as *Guernica*, and armed with Graham's sub-religious and semi-psychic ideas, was such an opening. It was not, however, an influence, but rather a confirmation of a shared sense of possibility.

Krasner's words also convey the risks entailed in being so close to a fire that could either warm or overwhelm her, even as her recognizing it as such a fire signified her attunement to the threshold for change it offered. It could indeed either renew her as an artist, or kill her, because, as an artist, she was subjected externally to what the sexist world would exclusively choose to 'see' – a woman in the shadow of a man. Like Helen Frankenthaler a decade later, Krasner recognized a potentiality in Pollock's *practice* and *project* to which she chose to be close *on her own terms*, probably because of her own maturity as an abstract painter, who had worked for the previous decade through the lessons offered by Hofmann on Cubism, Graham on the non-formal elements of abstract art, and who was acquainted with what Gorky and Mondrian were also offering in radically different ways with regard to line, while she also studied how Matisse and Kandinsky reshaped colour. Her artistic education in modernist developments ran much deeper and more widely than Pollock's.

We must imagine what the fact of being drawn emotionally and sexually into a relationship with the person, Jackson Pollock, meant in terms of an intimate *artistic* relationship with one of the new, if eccentric, live wires of contemporary art at a particularly critical moment of reworking the pressure of earlier European abstract modernism. It is indicative of Krasner's ambition and not submission, as so many biographers of Pollock seek to suggest. It is the risk that artist-women repeatedly take when their artistic intelligence draws them into proximity with a resource that indeed most other artists would eventually also have to deal with, when, as in the case of Pollock, his late 1940s work became *the* avant-garde gambit for ambitious younger artists to figure a way beyond in the game in which they were all equal players. Even his contemporaries, like the older Krasner, would both want to know it and yet need to 'kill it' creatively for there to be, not an *after* 'Pollock', but a *beside*, or *with* 'Pollock' that was 'Krasner', a *with-self*. Neither partnership nor master–pupil, might there not be a *matrixial* moment of co-becoming, a creative covenant between two painters different and differentiating in their very proximity where creative rivalry does not entail the artistic death of either one?

During the first half of the 1940s, however, Krasner apparently found her painting 'still born'. The paintings she was making refused to resolve into the abstract 'image' she hoped would emerge in the new painting process to which she had committed herself. Instead, her paintings built up layer by layer only to become *entombed*; she talked of ending up with slabs of grey. Colour became muddied and 'image' was never 'delivered'. No image (and I do not mean this figuratively) would emerge from this crisis of shifting from the derived mode of abstraction via reduction of the world to structure to a synthesis that would emerge only in the drama of materials and subjectivity happening in the process of painting.

Some have been tempted to see the years of blockage, 1942–45, as the dire if not deadening effect of her killing exposure to the brilliant light of the painter and difficult man Jackson Pollock, whom Krasner married in 1945. While this is a possibility, I also want to argue that we can acknowledge her act of artistic recognition, which translated into so material a support for the ex-alcoholic Pollock in the few years in which he came to produce the remarkable work for which art history hails him between 1948 and 1951. This support meant more than the mundane back-up of domestic chores. No one should underestimate the importance of domestic order, companionship, removal of alcohol, shared lifestyle and good food, much of which they cultivated themselves, in the relative poverty in which they were obliged to live when they moved out of New York City to The Springs, East Hampton. Krasner also provided the first level of what is called a social representation for the work, namely, the mirror of intelligent criticism in which that artistic personality we call 'Pollock' could daily gauge the character of his own novel activity as a painter. Just as the mother forms the third look in the Mirror Phase, the point to which the child looks to confirm that 's/he' is both *what* 's/he' has seen and *where* what 's/he' has been looked at and been seen from, on the surface of the mirror, and that she is the Other who has seen her/him, so Krasner's intelligent, artistically advanced eye was there to confirm that what the artist Pollock saw in his paintings was *painting*, was *art*, was good or dead, one painting event by each agonizing painting event.[23] For her own practice, however, the early and mid-1940s coincided with artistic stalemate: a block, a phenomenon that occurs in the artistic biographies of a number of artist-women trying to negotiate their specific space in modernist practices within a sexist culture where their sex, their humanity and their artistic identity are so hard to coordinate.[24]

Art historian and curator Robert Hobbs has, however, argued that this dark period for Lee Krasner in the mid-1940s can be situated. The nightmare that obstructed her creativity was both personal and historical and related to the event we now name the Shoah/Holocaust. Hobbs argues that the deadliness of her paintings registered the profound impact of a traumatizing realization of current events, not just a world at war, but the horrifying mass genocide of the Jewish people of Europe, up to two million of whom came from Soviet territories, including the very villages and towns where members of her family lived in Soviet Ukraine. Hobbs writes: 'A possible explanation for these dense and turgid works of the mid-1940s is that they were subliminal reactions to the mass murder of Jews in Nazi-occupied Europe.'[25]

Following Operation Barbarossa, the German invasion of the Soviet Union on 22 June 1941, between 1.5 and 2 million Jewish people were killed in mass shootings by the *Einsatzgruppen* (mobile killing squads), who destroyed Jewish populations village by village across the Ukraine, Belarus, Latvia and Lithuania in the wake of the conquering German forces.[26] Hobbs also mentions the public acknowledgement in the United States of America on 2 December 1942 of what was happening in Europe, when industrial murder by gassing began at secret sites in Poland. On that day in 1942, over half a million people in New York, Jews and non-Jews alike, stopped work for 10 minutes in commemoration of the murdered Jews and to incite public awareness of the horrors taking place in Europe. CBS anchor Edward R. Murrow announced to the American world: 'The phrase "concentration camp" is obsolete. It is now possible only to speak of extermination camps.'[27]

To grasp the impact of these revelations on the American Jewish communities, many of whom had relatives in the regions where direct mass murder was being carried out, as well as in the five dedicated exterminations camps on Polish soil (Chełmno, Sobibor, Bełżec, Treblinka and Auschwitz-Birkenau), Hobbs also explores the complex crisis of identities among the Jewish liberal members of the avant-garde community, who distanced themselves, by willed assimilation to modern American identity, from European Jewish tradition and religious observance, but were now obliged to confront an identification with and personal connection to atrocious events that had to be accepted, despite assimilation and rejection of religious affiliation.[28] Hobbs explores Krasner's double bind of kinship and disaffected modernism. He sees her work at this time as confronting another kind of dilemma that played this historical personal crisis out upon the canvas itself. She was suspended in

> a deadlock between literal and figurative levels...liquidating themselves in the process of being realized...Whatever the reasons for this series of efforts – and there were no doubt many in addition to the Holocaust – Krasner was unable to transcend the difficulty she was experiencing and take comfort in art's transfigurative or redemptive powers. She was lost in an irrepresentability, caught up in a phase in which conventional visual language was inadequate to the level of intuition she wished to achieve. Rather than being able to subordinate her imagery to the good of art, she found art inadequate to convey her feelings, and so she left the un-visualisable in a turgid state.[29]

Writing in the wake of the emergence after 1989 of 'trauma studies', which forms the belated register in cultural theory, philosophy, historiography and sociology of the trauma that the Holocaust/Shoah was, Hobbs references the work of Shoshana Felman and Dori Laub when concluding: 'Her [Krasner's] reactions may be understood in terms of recent efforts to distinguish between the codes of memory and those of trauma in which the former follows well-rehearsed scenarios while the latter remains caught up in the moment and never achieves the distance necessary to attain rational form.'[30] Hobbs judiciously and historically situates this 'crisis of witnessing' for Lee Krasner. It was the moment when one hitherto minimalized aspect of her subjectivity and identity, her Jewishness, was made historically inescapable by an egregious assault upon the entire Jewish world. The seeping knowledge of the horror of the Shoah/Holocaust not only impacted the artist as a Jewish person. It interpellated her as Jewish, just as she was electively reconfiguring her practice as an abstract painter, newly premising her practice on interiority, affect, gesture and her subjective resources. Her own aesthetic battleground was canvas and paint.

Hobbs offers a subtle and compelling analysis of these 'unborn' or 'dead' paintings:

> Contemporaneously with these acts of communal mourning and public acknowledgement of atrocities on a heretofore unheard-of scale, Krasner found herself face-to-face with the mounting resistance of the grey slabs she was creating. Although she characterized her difficulty as an inability to discover an intuitive self in her work, she may in fact have been far closer to her goals than she realised. The unbelievable horror of the Holocaust that is heightened by the clinical means with which it was carried out was so profoundly unsettling that many Jews were at a loss as to how they should react. They became truly speechless, words and images seeming to be inadequate

responses to the situation these bureaucratically administered killings represented. Krasner's grey slabs might be considered the first of a series of reactions that culminated in Newman's and Rothko's evocations of the Sublime under the aegis of Nietzsche's Dionysian realm, Edmund Burke's 'danger at a distance', and Emanuel Kant's abject inferiority, indicating the failure or inability of reason to deal with certain overwhelming ideas.[31]

Krasner's agonizing struggle with painting in this unique conjuncture leads Hobbs to reject the cheap psycho-biographical reading of her loss of self in the presence of Pollock's overwhelming genius. Furthermore, he argues that what she was doing in this profound and historically significant moment of aesthetic negativity may well have had its own impact on Pollock and farther afield:

> The grey slabs can be regarded as tarpits of futile invention, barricades established by the conscious mind against intuitive understandings, and sublime events in which the mind collapses in the face of the unsayable and the unrealisable. This liquidation of the world into resistant fields of grey paint, no doubt, had a profound effect on Pollock's work, becoming a possible basis for his use of this colour to establish the recalcitrant middle grounds in such words and works as *Guardians of the Secret* 1943, *She Wolf* 1943, *Totem Lesson One* 1944 and *Totem Lesson 2* 1945. In addition, these unyielding grey slabs need to be acknowledged in discussions of Pollock's decided preference in 1947 for aluminium paint in such paintings as *Full Fathom Five, Cathedral Alchemy* and *Comet.* And they should also be taken into consideration when considering pieces by German painter Anselm Kiefer who, in the 1980s, used lead to evoke the profound melancholy of the Holocaust.[32]

It is impossible, therefore, not to re-invoke Bataille's prescient concept of the surface of a painting as a kind of tomb. Yet, in the face of a history that he was also witnessing differently in his writings, Bataille's metaphorics are shattered by an unthinkable historical reality that would shape some of the major writings in the wake of the catastrophe in the works of poet Paul Celan and playwright Samuel Beckett. Writing of the latter, Theodor Adorno explains:

> This could be shown in Beckett's works. These enjoy what is today the only humanly respectable fame: everyone shudders at them, and yet no one can persuade himself that these eccentric plays and novels are not about *what everybody knows and no one will admit* ... They deal with a highly concrete historical reality: the abdication of the subject.
>
> ... Beckett 's *Ecce Homo* is what human beings have become. As though with eyes drained of tears, they stare silently out of his sentences. The spell they cast, which also binds them, is lifted by being reflected in them. However,

the minimal promise of happiness they contain, which refuses to be traded for comfort, cannot be had for a price less than total dislocation, to the point of wordlessness.[33]

Closer to home but late in his career, Jewish American playwright Arthur Miller wrote a play in 1994, *Broken Glass*, the title evoking the pogrom in Germany on 9–11 November 1938 and its the nights of violence and murder that was named in Nazi celebration *Kristallnacht*, from the shattered glass of shops, homes and synagogues, and is now termed by the Jewish world *Pogromnacht*. The play's central character is a sensitive, middle-aged Jewish woman from Brooklyn who is traumatized by reading daily newspaper reports about *Kristallnacht* and the Nazi brutalization of Jews in Germany and Austria. Becoming hysterically paralysed from the waist down, she ponders: If this can occur in Berlin, how easily could such outrages against Jews occur on the streets of New York? The striking aspect of the play is, in this context, the manner in which it registers, perhaps from Miller's own memories of his mother, the effect of their learning about the assault on European Jewry, commencing with the pogrom of 1938 and the reports of humiliation and cruelty enacted on the streets by fellow citizens, as it resonated through the seemingly safe streets of New York. Miller's play, starting with this powerful and affecting portrait of Sylvia, typically moves from his subdued meditation on the meaning of the Holocaust for American Jewry into his primary concern, the tragic study of masculinity on trial.

If the lid of the surface that is the painting remained firmly slammed shut in her slab paintings, never yielding any intuitive register of a self, Lee Krasner looked back to explain that this struggle was the result of her double realization that what she had been doing and doing well no longer had integrity, rooted as it was in a world *before this horror*. She also knew that what she needed to do could not yet reveal itself. So, she continued to paint each day. It was a genuine creative battle in a moment without words to grasp it – not a loss of direction. It demonstrated extraordinary willingness to risk radical change, and in this case, to be open to what she discerned was new in Pollock's Surrealist abstraction, even as the road to a new opening for her would resolve only via a historically created trauma-tomb of no-meaning that was prescient, if yet without the terms to explain it as traumatic mourning for the destruction of Europe's Jewish world, which was so intimately linked to her own family and childhood world in New York.

> I began feeling the need to break with what I was doing and to approach something else. It wasn't clear what I was moving into. I went into my own black out period which lasted two or three years where the canvases would simply build up until they'd get like stone and it was always a grey mess. The

image wouldn't emerge, but I worked pretty regularly. I was fighting to find I knew not what, but I could no longer stay with what I had.[34]

In interviews about the period 1946–49, Krasner reported that eventually an image began to 'break through'. The 'image' was not drawn, figured or applied. A kind a restless graphism emerged on to the surface as if from the painting's own depths. Coming through from beyond or from an imaginary interiority, her abstractly *touching* that borderline with paint seemed both to allegorize and enact a self through mark and energy. These paintings formed a series called *Little Images* (fig. 7.3). They combine a grid-like, all-over order and infrastructure, each unit of which is animated by calligraphic, linear playfulness enlivened by vibrating colour. No reproduction can adequately convey the eventful density, sensuous colour and dynamic surfaces of these micro-worlds on canvas, roughly two-foot square, made on the floor or a table with paint of a thick, pouring quality. The idea of an image does not imply a figuration, but rather an ordering of non-signifying semiotic elements that lure the travelling eye to the surface and sustain its exploratory pleasures over a non-hierarchical surface of oscillating depth and visual incident. The image's 'breakthrough' suggests a specific topography of the image coming from behind the surface, a borderline of the visible, a threshold between the emerging subjectivity of the painter painting and the other, fantasized part-subject with which painting symbolically plays.

Thus, the surface now functions as a system, a structuration (in Rosolato's terms) which renders it more than the blank site of inscription. Surface becomes the plane of a movement or a moment of opening between surface and depth, between image – the pole of metaphor – and its (re)sources that index rather than articulate or figure some aspect of the fantasizing, painting body, closer to the pole of metonym. In the *Little Images* paintings, the surfaces are worked but ordered, pictogrammic rather than pictorial, calligraphic but non-syntactical.

After the success of her first one-person show at Betty Parsons Gallery in 1951 with work she later destroyed, Krasner began a series of drawings with her artist partner, Pollock. But then she cut them up in disgust. She later did the same to paintings, mostly her own, and sometimes his rejected canvases (that were only paint perhaps?). This violent cutting-up left shards of paper or burlap piled on the floor of her studio in an informal disarray that in turn inspired her move into collage – which Bataille had praised in Miró as the very undoing of painting. Sliced up and relayered, the resultant works use that murderous device in a Bataillean creativity that also breaks open the tomb and devastates notions of surface and covering, behind and on top, image and materiality, so that the elements jostle and realign in a relentless ambiguity defying certainty about the plane

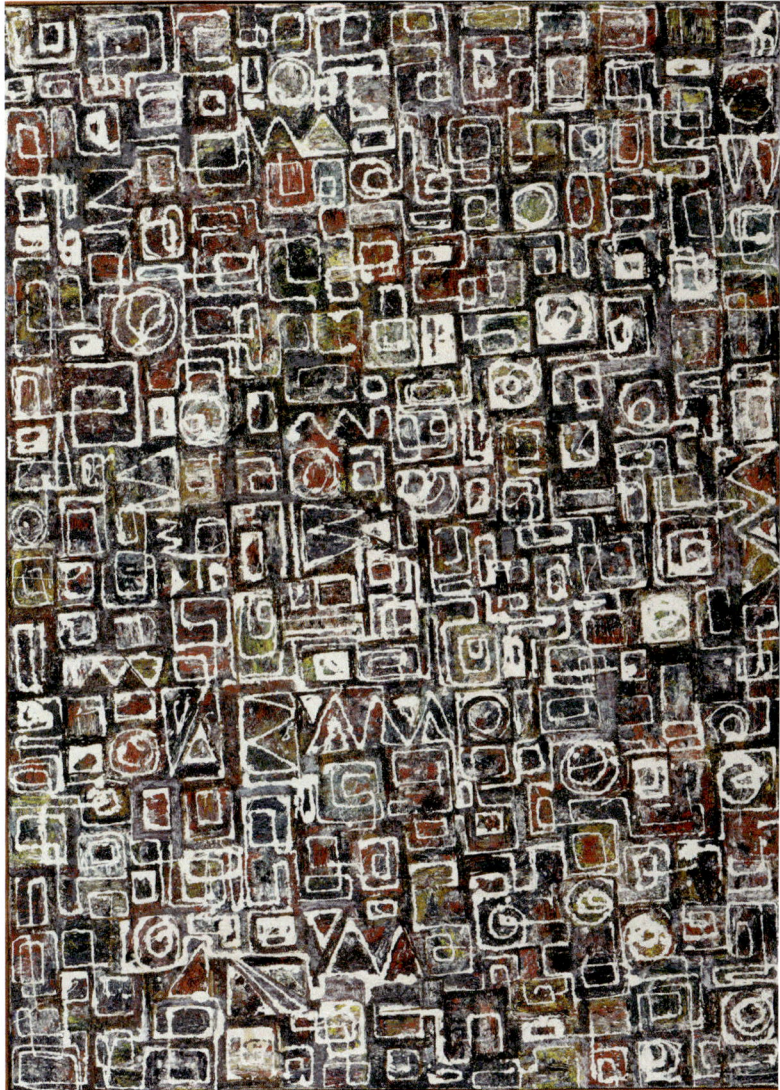

Figure 7.3 Lee Krasner, *Composition*, 1949

and its pictorial space: *City Verticals* (1953, fig. 7.4). Continuing to work with collage into 1955, when she again had a major one-person show at the Stable Gallery to considerable acclaim, Krasner processed the possibilities and dangers offered in the work of many other artists who formed the community of her activity, while in a sense returning to her own artistic identity as a brilliant abstract composer (fig. 7.5).

This all-too-brief survey of Krasner's work from the mid-1940s to the mid-1950s serves to underline the radical shock represented by the

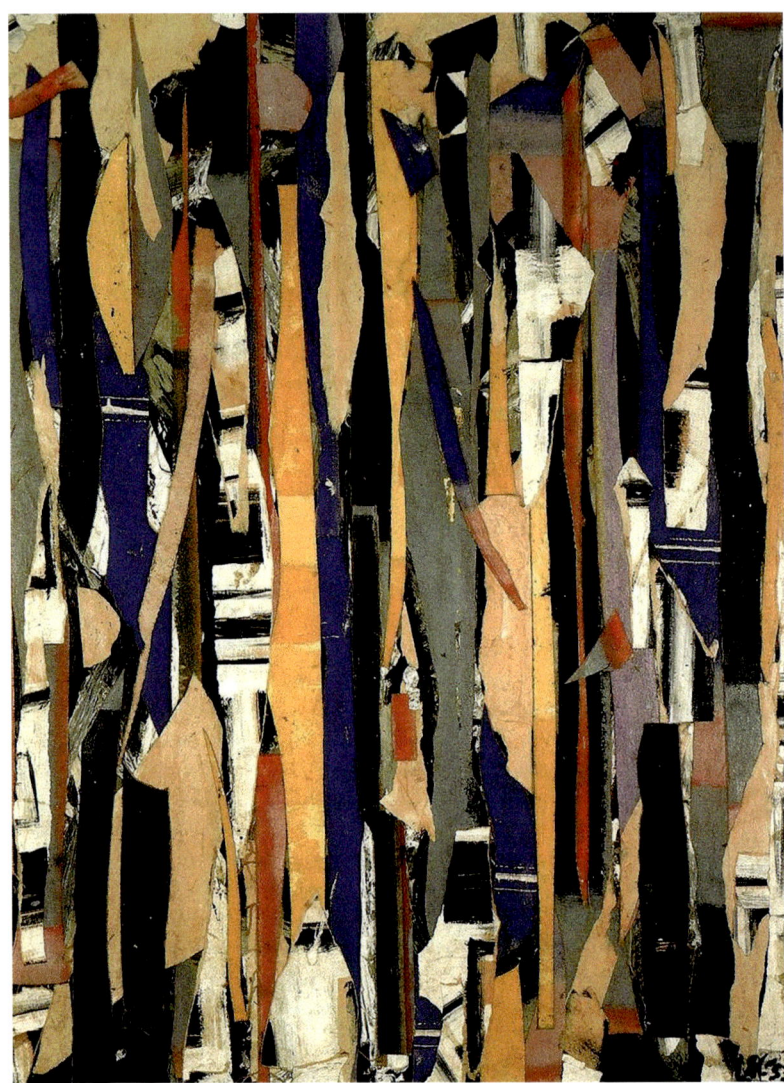

Figure 7.4 Lee Krasner, *City Verticals*, 1953

emergence in the early summer of 1956 of a figurative *image* in *Prophecy* (fig. 1.1). It must have felt like a disaster. The artist could not but be morti-fied. Amid all the other factors bringing this work into being, a new men-acing presence – de Kooning's recent work – broke through all censorship, demanding its own price: life or death. De Kooning was not just the other big name on the current New York scene to be dealt with. He was the painter of *Woman* and *Marilyn Monroe* (figs 6.1 and 2.14). For an artist of her, namely his, generation, that dominance inscribed the violent if ambiv-alent mythemes of artistic masculinity and its tortured relation to

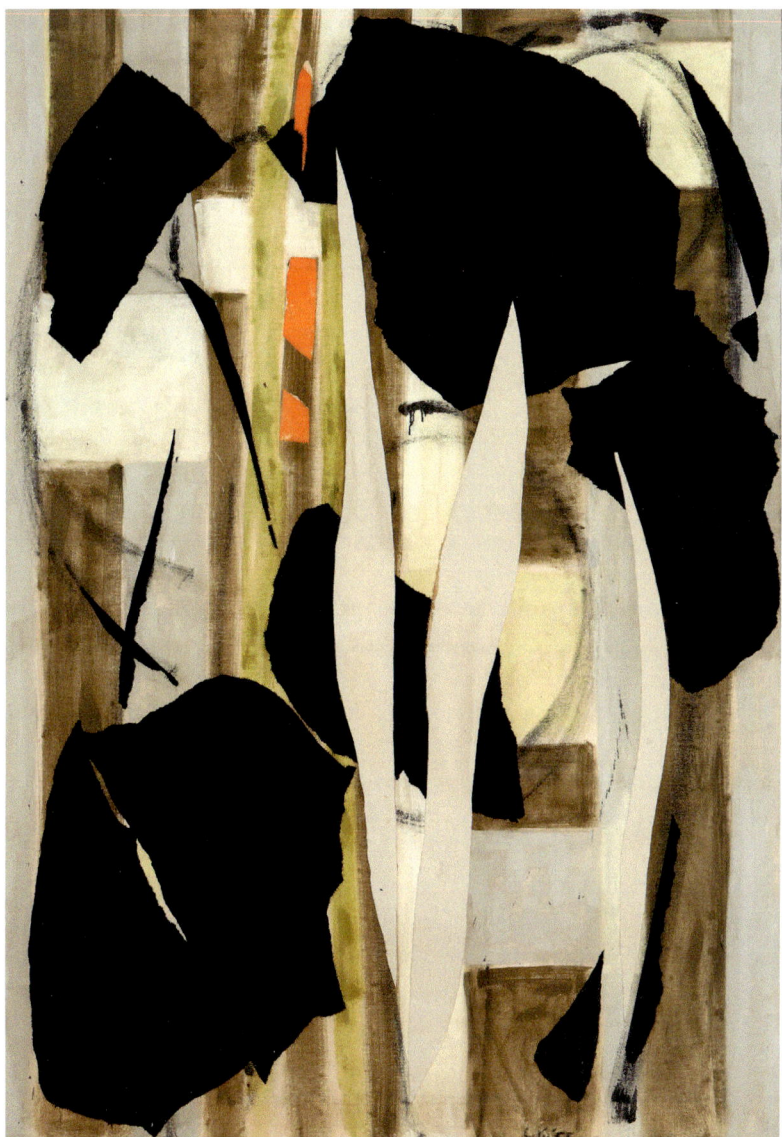

Figure 7.5 Lee Krasner, *Milkweed,* 1955

femininity into the heart of current modern American painting. As such, it could not be avoided. Even more so was it inevitable for a painter such as Lee Krasner to take it on in her canvas.

Krasner's creative practice echoes Bataille on hybridity and decomposition in modernism, rather than Greenberg's teleological and all-male, Oedipally murderous law of avant-garde succession and internal formal purification of the medium. Seeing her exhibition at the Stable Gallery with the new collage paintings in 1955, Greenberg, speaking in 1965, named it 'a major addition to the American art scene of that era'.[35] Yet he included no reference to Lee Krasner in his definitive essay '"American-Type" Painting', published in 1956, even though her latest move was perfectly consonant with his argument about the progress of modern art as the flattening of illusory space in honesty to the medium of painting as paint on canvas.[36] By 1965 it was ten years too late, for Greenberg's version of the story – modernism as a formalist evolution and confrontation with Cubism's shallow space – was becoming hegemonic, cast in the concrete of museal and academic histories of modernism that had only men in its annals. The archive would only record his deafening silence and her non-presence.

Bataille's interest in decomposition and destructive reworking permits a way to relate Krasner's knight's moves across the board of New York painting, which could allow Pollock, de Kooning, Rothko, Motherwell and the others their necessary contribution to what was interesting in making paintings at this moment, while also creating the space for her own decisive reconfiguration of the project of painting. Yet *Prophecy* stands shockingly outside this model at this point, traumatically revealing monsters.

Surfacing into view bodies, fleshy and plant-like with animal paws, and sightless eyes dislocated on the watch, the phantoms that followed *Prophecy* in 1956 confront the viewer like the great sphinxes of Egypt, or even perhaps hide within them the naked, hollow-eyed survivors of concentration camps shown on newsreels. A series of seventeen works (fig. 7.6) created in the eighteen months after Pollock's sudden death in August 1956 were clearly about Pollock ('Pollocks' of the early 1940s perhaps), and killing him again – reliving the very crux of their relationship as a mythic competition between the sexes, killing men and dying women. It cannot be without significance that this painting (fig. 7.7), made soon after that death, was titled *Birth*, sharing its name with the work by Pollock seen in his studio in 1941 when Krasner first introduced herself to him. The dead man – the dead Father that a canonized Pollock would soon become for that generation – could not be killed openly. He had been killed by a disease: alcoholism. Pollock had to be included in the work, but *transfigured*, there and then on the canvas through the work of *undoing* not only painting, but a new threat to the artist's painting self that would again have to break out of the ordering she had rediscovered after the grey slabs, first through the *Little Images* series and then the Bataillean creativity via collage during the early 1950s.

A deadly other with whom the painter had to struggle was also the much-admired painter and friend de Kooning, from whom the woman as artist must reclaim her body, the body he had used, the sexuality he had

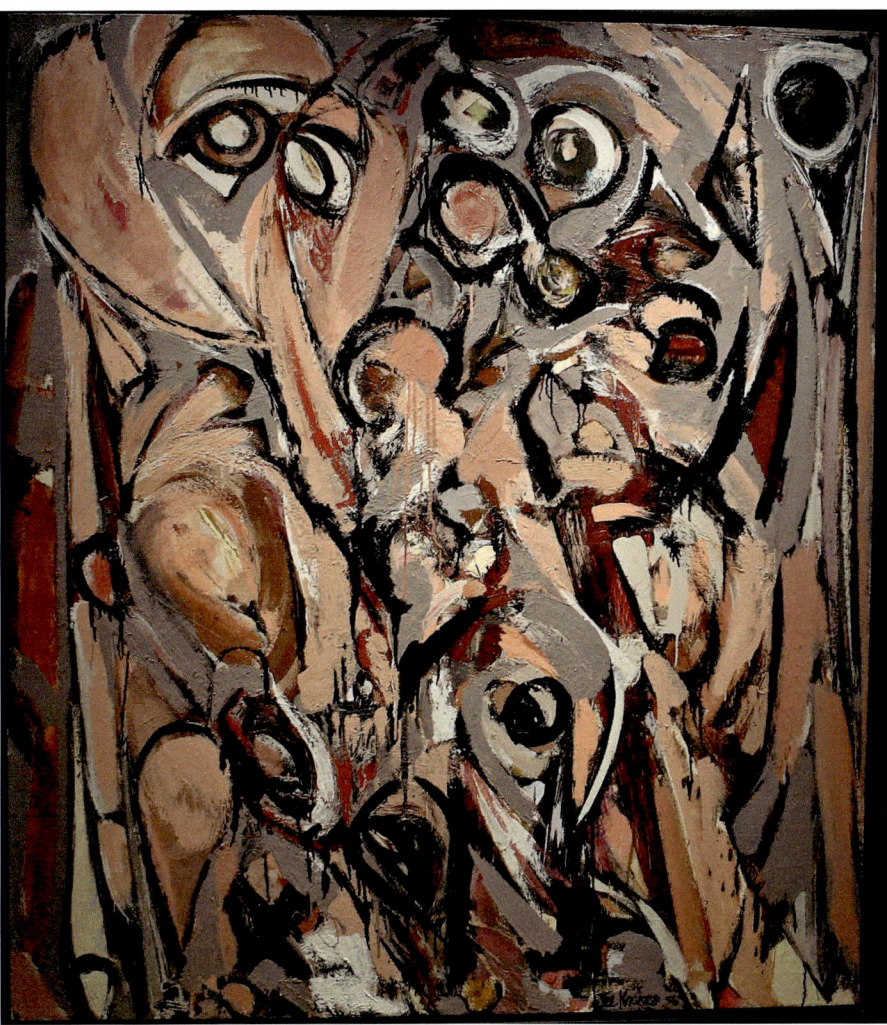

Figure 7.6 Lee Krasner, *Embrace*, 1956

either celebrated or prostituted, the interior he had filled with rubies or torn open and covered up with his grandiose gesturing in paint. Sadism must be released and then creatively sublimated to avoid being just another dying woman – and to reach 'the creative woman's body'.[37]

Out of this struggle emerged *Sun Woman I* (1957, fig. 1.2) – painted a year before Helen Frankenthaler's *Nude* (fig. 4.1). The explosive ebullience of the centrifugal composition, the lightness of the painted touch with its deep reds and yellows, the repeating circularity of gesture that tempts us to read a face or two, with half-closed laughing eyes and open, singing mouths, a breast, a belly – this seems a liberated universe away from the clogged surfaces and desultory colours of paintings such as *Birth* (fig. 7.7)

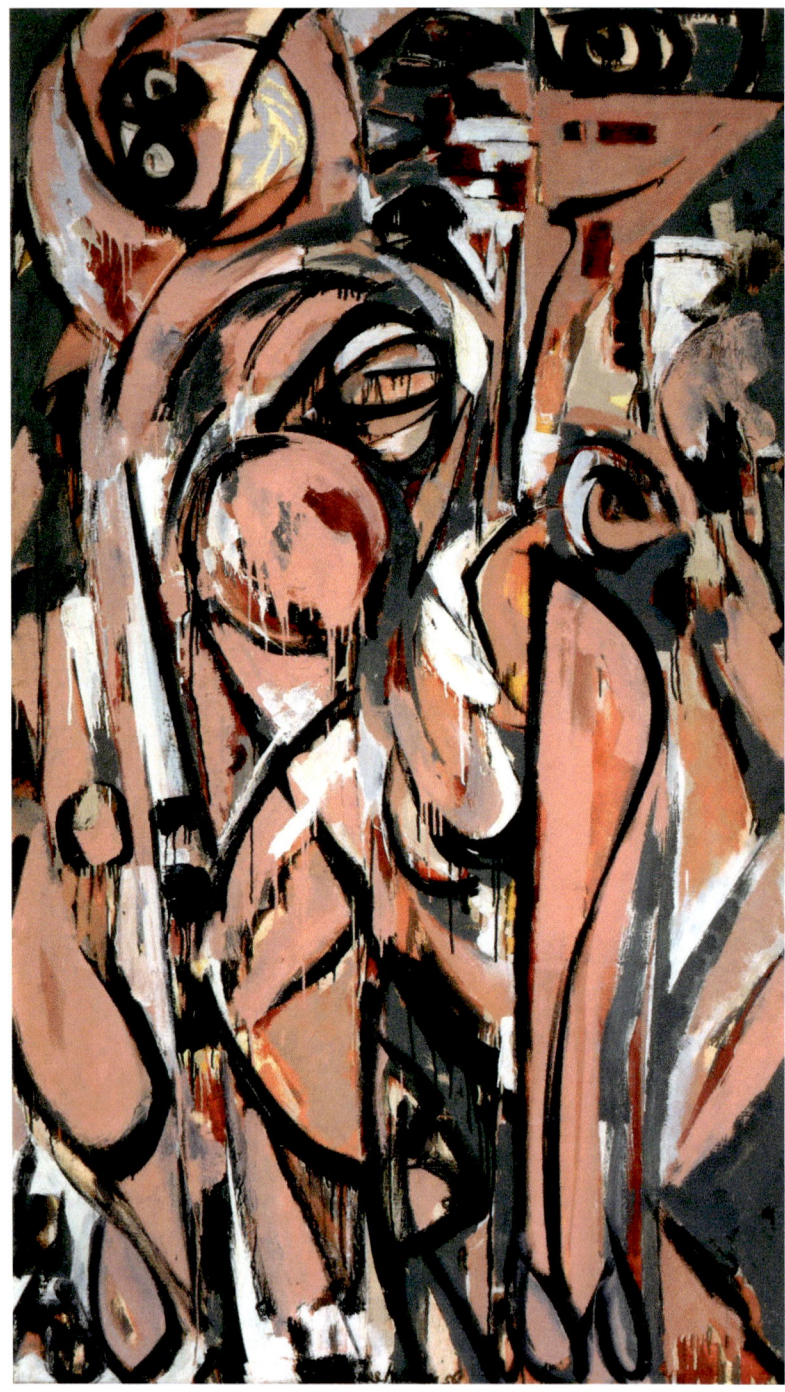

Figure 7.7 Lee Krasner, *Birth*, 1956

or *Embrace* (fig. 7.6) or *Three in Two* (1956, private collection) that followed *Prophecy*. Not a massacred yet sometimes a funny creature, these
clearly gynomorphic forms belie Julia Kristeva's doubts about the possibility of laughter in 'female creation'.

Kristeva argued that for a woman to paint pictures such as de Kooning's that index the problem and significance of the dissidence of *Woman*,
of sexual difference, the woman as artist would have to deal with her own
mother and thus herself as woman, as the like, like herself, of his founda-
tional Other. At no point have I assumed that a woman *is*, that is, that
Woman is on the plane of being, an ontological, given entity. I work with
the difficult notion of being both inside and outside a designated social
space and a semiotic sign system, both shaped by the complex configurations of psyche, phantasy and concept that constitute a Symbolic order
and a psychic regime that produces sexual difference. Both are disrupted,
however, by the excess that remains beyond Symbolic ordering and the
Oedipal hierarchy of sexual difference it generates. Yet I feel more and
more compelled to allow that excess as well as that ordering to include
a psycho-corpo-real schema, an image or sensation that phenomenology
terms *bodilyness* and that Bracha L. Ettinger psychoanalytically theorizes
as *corpo-reality*.

Without falling right back into the trap of a founding anatomical basis
to the difference of the sexes, via both Irigarayan morpho-logic and Ettingerian matrixiality, I embrace the possibility that our psychic and symbolizing experience of the corporeal – filtered through its aesthetic and
psychic representatives and our symbolic signifying systems – will be
always marked by bodily specificity as a resource for affects, sensations
and meanings. Our particular, phallocentric Symbolic order might fore-
close certain bodily specificities from representation, forcing them on to
the plane of hallucination, the uncanny and apparition. The pulsational
rhythms of the masculine experience of sexuality mark a different possibility of what is never just *the* body's repertoire of sensations and meanings. Bodies are always my body, his body, her body, and even that is not
simple, for hers may be a lesbian body, a black lesbian mother's body, a
marked body, a trans body and so on.

With *Sun Woman I* and *The Seasons* (figs 1.2 and 7.1) I am now picking
up on movement and moving towards the possibility of recognizing in the
space of this painter's actions, gestures, processes, meditations, responses,
decisions, desires, ambitions, distress, a moment of what a phallically
ordered culture does not allow us to see, let alone name, but that via other,
matrixial routes I can finally enjoy, even with some anguish: *jouissant* pleasures in the jubilant identification of a difference that the language of even
sympathetic formal analysis will kill. There is a jubilation and a joy that is
not of a body depicted but a corporeality enacted, given a liveliness and

expressivity by both line and colour within the consciously managed frame of a composition that refuses to be framed and contained.

A modest proposal is on offer, after a lengthy theoretical and historical journey to lay in the conditions of one painting's visibility – for me at least. My working-through prompts me to see a joyous revelation of a *body schema* on a canvas, an opened surface, incorporating the calligramic signature encountered in the *Little Images* series. It escapes the linguistic boxing of residual Hebrew alphabets in the latter. The painting leaves evident the traces of the circular movements of the artist's generous arms encircling space, which produces the possibility of an image that is a corporeal schema invented for projective identification – a moment of stabilization that structures the viewer's visual tourism within the elaborated surface. Then there is the measured play of absence and presence, of paint and canvas, of painting and not painting, of colour and ground. These create what I must call in gratitude to Luce Irigaray *a dancing space*.

This is not like the literal, repetitive movements performed by Pollock along or around his supine canvas and mythicized in photo-session and film by Hans Namuth. It is a created effect, a produced illusion, made through the play of colour, the energy of line, the ebullient fullness of the *riant*, singing central evocations of laughing lips/eyes on the canvas. The viewer perceives the canvas optically but experiences it empathetically as a dancing space, a play around presence and absence that is pleasurable because it does not index an obsessive repetition of mastery (Pollock) or the need for violence (de Kooning), however much disowned as love.

I have tracked a pathway through several psychoanalytical theories of the subject with the art critical and art historical discourses of and on painting. Hingeing the discourse of sexual difference in popular culture – where it is so visible – to the formalist text of high art – where it is virtually denied – moving from 'Marilyn' to 'Jackson' and back, opens up a space in which to read 'Lee' as a 'female creation' (Kristeva) that was ecstatic, funny, intellectually intense, artistically acute, lined with energy, thus revealing the semiotic possibilities and historical conditions of a relation between creativity and femininity that did not involve massacre.

Once posed at the theoretical level through a psychoanalytical aesthetics that, at least, allows me to frame such a question, do we need a sociohistorical base of practices with which to probe it, let alone answer it? That is what I have been hoping to do. The paradox of feminism's interest in the repressed question of sexual difference addressed to the social history of art's apparent indifference to anything but what is framed by gender-indifferent dialectical materialism or actively sexist heroic formalism is played out in a historical archive that was structured by its historically formed version of that contradiction. High modernism, according to Greenberg, outlawed questions of the social, that is, all ideological baggage that prevented art from saving itself within and yet, on behalf of, a capitalist system. Gender, like class and race, was irrelevant and dangerous to the ambitious pursuit of the self-denying ordinances of modernism. Diverse women and other others paid the price.

Lee Krasner, like Helen Frankenthaler and the many women active on this American scene of modernist painting and sculpture, had comparable ambitions and agendas: to push painting down that modernist trajectory and to create a major event within it. To do this, they wanted to be considered merely painters, but were consistently *only* perceived as women. Yet our readings can both empathize with their renunciation of stereotyping, gendered readings and acknowledge our desire to recognize specificity with difference that we can otherwise theorize. Krasner was often eloquent about just how sexist the actual art community was – the critics who did not review the shows, the dealers who would not buy and exhibit, the curators who did not collect and historicize. Gender bias was as active in the modernist community as it was in the rest of the conservative, post-war culture of Eisenhower's hegemonizing Cold War America. Yet the very conditions of the painting practices that she and other artist-women embraced were premised on a wilful disrobing of the self, seeking to work closer to psyche and from subjectivity that could not but inscribe imprints or impressions *in, of and from* each unique and socially situated as well as psychically charged experience of 'the feminine'.

The feminist writer faces the challenge of naming sexism, while simultaneously unpacking the practices of painters who, as women, were 'disappeared' from their historical moment because it has been allowed to continue as and become 'good', gender-free art history. I seek to discover terms for their visibility in the actual historical moment of production. This is not a feminist return to formalism. Rather, feminism intervenes in a historical discourse to tease out possibilities already struggled for by those who painted knowingly within its orbit. Yet those painters, such as Krasner, worked from a position that opposed the ideological straitjacket of gender socially and within formalist criticism. Nonetheless, they engaged with a process in painting that opened their practice up to unsignified dimensions of what must be named and claimed as aesthetically elaborating a space for sexual difference(s). Traversing modernist painting, they created a space for access to an alignment of relations of subjectivity that I theorize as 'the feminine'. Modernist language and feminist desire converge in a moment of shocking necessity. Feminism, however, effects a movement within the paradigm, an internal shifting of its elements.

I am part of a project that makes Lee Krasner's work more visible, seriously debated and freely admired. The desire is not, however, to integrate 'women artists' within the dominant, and often dismal, narrative of the art history of the New York School or Abstract Expressionism. As Julia

Kristeva has argued in 'Women's Time', this would only mean assimilation to the time of nations, their histories, and phallocentric misrecognition. Equally we need to guard against the opposite tendency, which turns to culture and insists absolutely on women's difference in an almost religious counter-idealization of a femininity that had been so violently abjected under phallocentrism. Kristeva argues that an aesthetic-cultural experimentation, an avant-garde, complements the agitation for political reforms on behalf of women that have formed the basis of women's social movements since the nineteenth century:

> Essentially interested in the specificity of female psychology and its symbolic realizations, these women seek to give a language to the intra-subjective and corporeal experiences left mute by culture in the past. Either as artists or writers, they have undertaken a veritable exploration of the *dynamic of signs*, an exploration which relates this tendency, at least at the level of its aspirations, to all major projects of aesthetic and religious upheaval.[38]

It would be an anachronism to place Krasner and her contemporaries already in the cultural generation of 1968 and imagine that they could ever conceive their work in terms of such a 'dynamic of signs' – or a *peinture féminine*. Yet, as abstract painters, they were already within it even as they thought about and accounted for their work in the then current, if diversified, modernist terms.

It would, however, be self-defeating *not* to allow the insights created by this post-1968 generation of psychoanalytically inspired artists and writers to reread their moment and reframe the questions we ask about all artistic practices by women. For there is an excess in the work of the painter-women of the 1950s that is not legible through the art historical discourses that typically account for its production. Hence Greenberg's symptomatic silences. This excess is not *Woman*, in any essentializing way. It has to do with 'the feminine' conceived theoretically and defined via semiotics and feminist readings in both phallocentric and matrixial psychoanalyses. Equally, it was determined by the actual social coding and cultural representations of gender that I have suggested can be tracked across the major myths of that culture – there in the iconic images of 'Marilyn Monroe' on screen and canvas. The social history of art opened up modernist criticism and art history to historical and ideological analysis. Yet when, in turn, its gender-indifferent discourse is expanded by the philosophical and theoretical elaborations of feminism, an even playing field is produced on which the image of 'Jackson Pollock', made across the spaces of studios, galleries, art magazines, films, museums, art history books, postcards and jokes, can be tracked in the same way as we chart the making of the icon 'Marilyn Monroe' to enable us to encounter Lee Krasner.

While identifying the mythic faces, bodies and styles of a polarized culture of gender, I have also deployed theories of subjectivity, corporeality and gesture to destabilize the very binary of gender that bourgeois myth tries to naturalize, in order to represent artistic practice as a site of psychic and semiotic negotiation, a drama of the will towards subjective stabilization through identification and metaphor, and a drama of the drives that plays with the pleasures of staying closer to metonymy, to an indexicality of the bodily, to the archaic alternations of presence and absence, becoming, living and dying, upon which the very possibility of embodied subjectivity is predicated. This is what I mean by introducing the concept of sexual difference: a tricky space where both subjectivity and sexuality are precariously produced, while always deforming, destabilizing, undoing whatever cultures and societies try to do with/to them.

Yet even in the remotest reaches of the constantly occurring process of subjectivity, we encounter its framing within the problem of sexual difference. The subject comes into existence in a structure that casts the major players in its psycho-drama in both sexed and sexualizing roles. Artistic practices of the kind that emerged in studios in New York in the 1940s, and that were elaborated in mature statements during the 1950s, historically and aesthetically lifted the lid and opened the pathway to an aesthetic engagement with the elements of that journey. Whether through personal encounters in analysis or therapy, or through popularized notions of 'working from the unconscious' and automatism inherited from Surrealism or John Graham's ideas, the moment of the 1950s cannot be studied without taking the indirect cultural presence and impact of psychoanalysis into account: the artistic practices themselves staging a shifting sense of subjectivity and artistic activity which was historically conditional upon the psychological modernism that was psychoanalysis. Embarrassing as the attempts to read Pollock psychoanalytically may sometimes be, they at least try to breach the censorship of formalism. They remain, however, caught in individualistic expressionism. I am not interested in psychological interpretation of the paintings or psycho-biographical readings of the man or the woman as artist. Post-1968 feminist interest in psychoanalysis does not address individuals. It reads culture, society and its institutions through the texts, myths, images and subjectivities they produce, while wanting to resist total anti-humanism by retaining the destabilizing concept of the divided *subject-in-process-on-trial.*[39]

Yes, art history has to learn how to read paintings by Lee Krasner and Helen Frankenthaler as works by painters who were American, Jewish, New Yorkers, immigrant, working-class or bourgeois women. No, that women bit does not say it all. The real struggle is for us to be singular in our femininities – to demassify what sexual difference might mean *for women* from the term that in effect negates its very articulation: *Woman*. Each artist I am interested in is unique, particular, historical – yet each practice provokes questions about the semiotics of *the feminine* in generative differencing in culture, articulated through the prisms of multiple differentiating factors that make it heterogeneous. Kristeva argues:

> This process could be summarized as an *interiorization of the founding separation of the socio-symbolic contract*, as an introduction of its cutting edge into the very interior of every identity whether subjective, sexual, ideological, or so forth. This in such a way that the habitual and increasingly explicit attempt to fabricate a scapegoat victim as foundress of a society or counter-society may be replaced by the analysis of the potentialities of victim/executioner which characterize each identity, each subject, each sex.[40]

To speak of the feminine is neither to idealize artist-women nor to scapegoat them as victims of a discriminatory sexist society. Killing/ Dying – art as a play around sadism, creativity, passivity, activity, loss and displacement – these are the thematics that have to be tracked in artistic practices for each practitioner who has, in order to be a subject, to negotiate the sacrifices demanded by the socio-symbolic bond. To 'aesthetic practices' such as painting, Kristeva then attributes the possibility of supporting, even staging, such an adventure. Not only will art stand in opposition to the ever-more extensive massifications of hegemonic multinationalism, with its totalizing use of a false community of language. Aesthetic practices – working on the very semiotic and subjective materials of identity and culture – bring out the 'singularity of each person, the multiplicity of every person's possible identifications ... *the relativity of his/her symbolic as well as biological existence*, according to the variation of his/her specific symbolic capacities'. Here we confront my theme and Kristeva's defection: 'And the responsibility which all will immediately face of putting fluidity into play against the threats of death which are unavoidable whenever an inside and an outside, a self and an other, one group or another, are constituted.'[41]

Killing and dying/men and women/surface and depth/insides and outsides. I have played with these terms – undone their apparent oppositions – in order to confront violence, sadism, aggression and creativity; to link making art and not dying even while the death of the subject, non-being, is always the stake in art. At this point in her theory, however, Kristeva's resolution is undermined by a rapid descent into phallic binaries of self versus other. Irigaray's tentative suggestions that the feminine offers ways to be with the imaginary maternal other while also separate and creative – to dance with death (loss, absence) – take us one stage away from an exclusively phallic model. This is radically expanded by Ettinger's concept of the Matrix: 'a feminine dimension of the symbolic order dealing with asymmetrical, plural, and fragmented subjects composed of the known as well as the not-rejected and not-assimilated unknown, and to unconscious processes of change and transgression in borderlines, limits, and thresholds of I and non-I emerging in co-existence'.[42]

I neither assimilate Krasner to these theories nor consolidate one theory through appeals to Krasner's painting. The project is to create a covenant – a kind of productive exchange – between two moments of femininity, modernity and representation, hers and mine. One is a historical moment of artistic practice and gender politics in the 1950s, the other a moment of politico-philosophical revolution and gender politics after 1968. The unfinished business of twentieth-century feminism is the precipitating force that bridges these two moments of women's history and offers ways to allow the feminine visibility through a gesture – in art and in theory.

I turn to two photographs of Lee Krasner at work, one by Ernst Haas from 1981 (fig. 7.8). The artist has been painting, standing up at a large table.

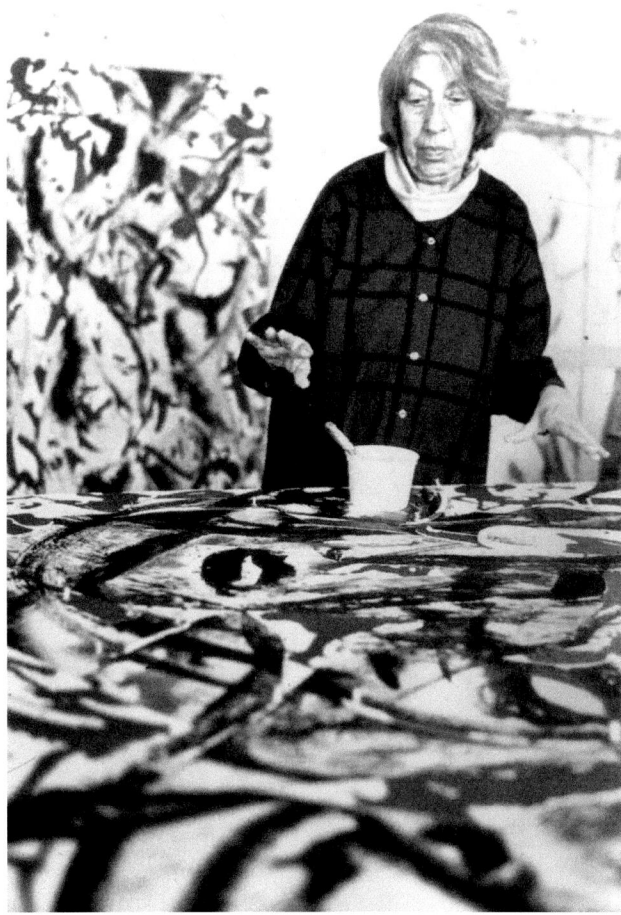

Figure 7.8 Ernst Haas, *Lee Krasner at work,* 1981

She is now thinking about what she has done. She is reading her own work, with her eyes but also with her hands. The gesture is captured in the photograph. Yet the gesture is nothing so literal as the action that made the painting. Her hands describe an imaginary space, prompted as well as indexed by what she has done on the canvas. Those hands, circling above the canvas as an unconscious bodily response to the energies of the painting at that moment, provide a visual clue, a glimpse beyond the visible sign, beyond the object that is an index, to what this practice offers: much less dramatic than Pollock's elaborate choreography; more detached than Frankenthaler's pouring and stroking. The photograph holds in view the complex sense of gesture in painting: a woman's mind body in the studio space, creating, thinking, dancing with death but also with life as the act of determined resistance to real, encountered, mourned dying.[43]

The second photograph (fig. 7.9) shows Krasner a decade after *Prophecy*. She is working on *Portrait in Green* (1966, Pollock–Krasner Foundation). She paints upright with the canvas on the wall. She is moving too quickly for the shutter speed. It is an image of the artist in action, the painter as action artist.[44] Her body is involved in its movement and in its gestures. In broad, body-opening movements, the painting hand forms curving, rounded, circular, intersecting shapes, creating internal and interstitial space by leaving so much canvas blank. To action itself, I must now, finally, turn.

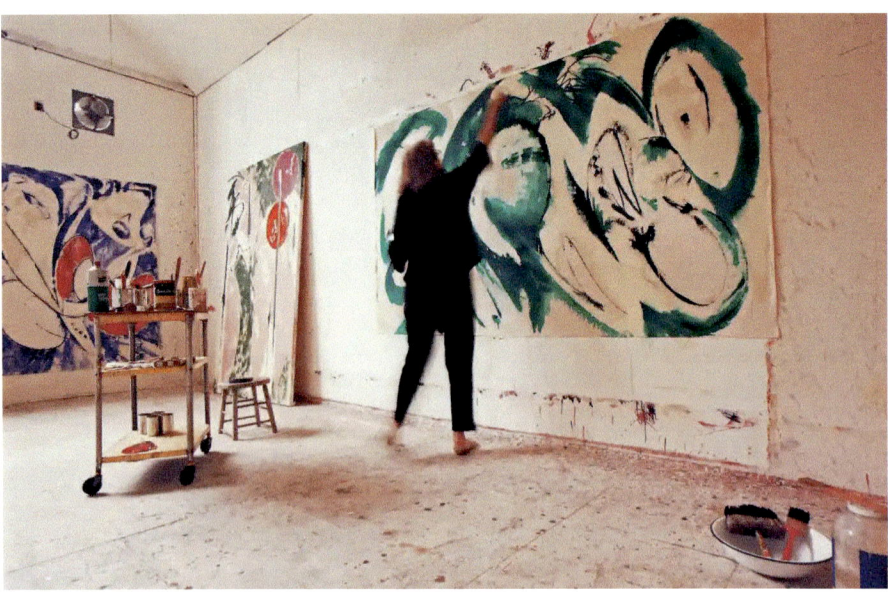

Figure 7.9 Mark Patiky, *Lee Krasner painting in her studio working on* Portrait in Green, *The Springs, Long Island*, 1969

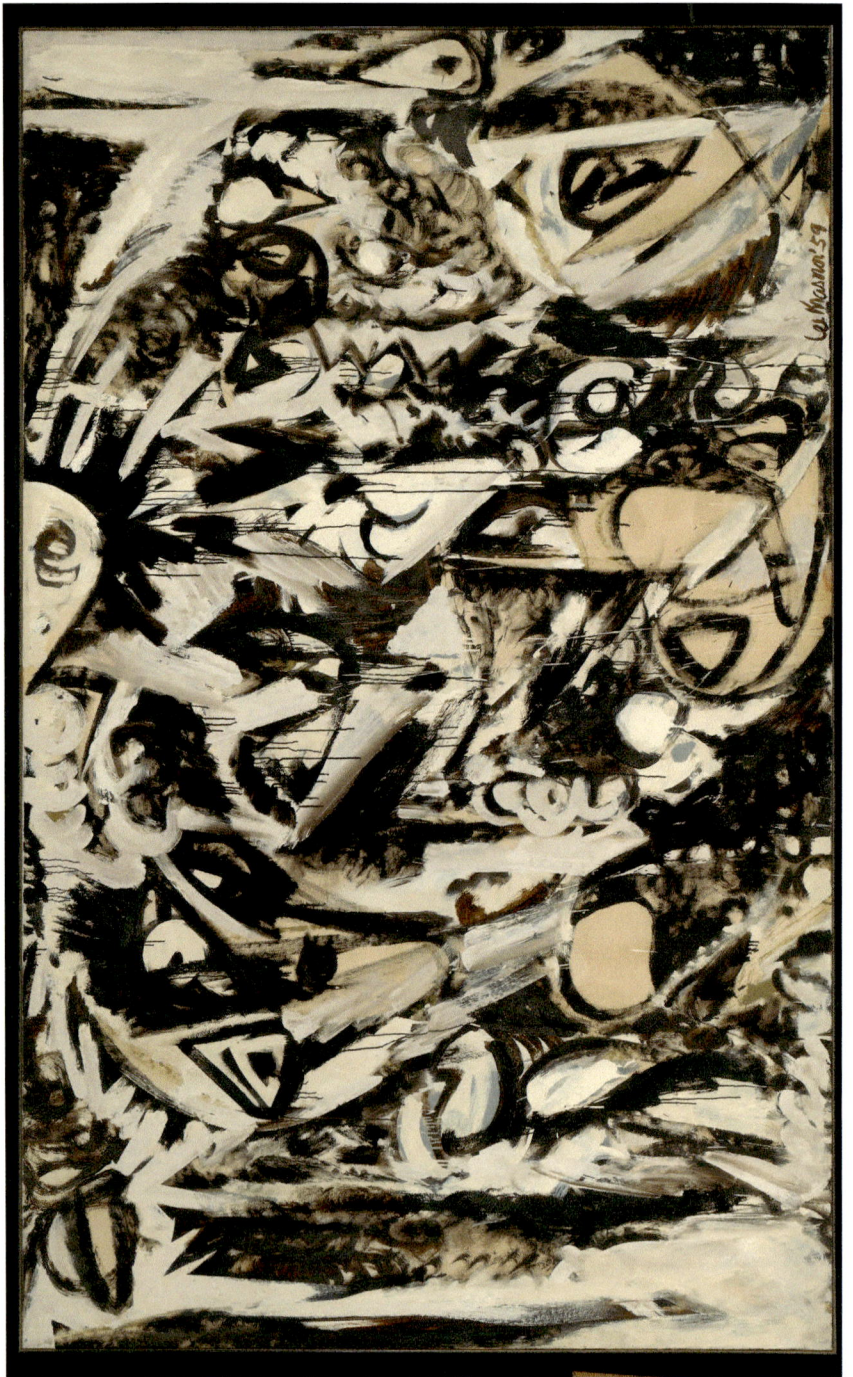

Figure 8.1 Lee Krasner, *Cool White*, 1959

Three memories: Rosenberg and Monroe

I Canberra

In 1986 I was Visiting Scholar at the University of Queensland, Brisbane, and had to give lectures at other universities in Australia. I was visiting Melbourne when my brother phoned from England to alert me to my father's deteriorating health. My father might not live to see me again when I returned a month hence. I was also then weaning my six-month-old daughter. Yet I was due to go – alone – from Melbourne to Canberra for a day and overnight to give a lecture at the Australian National University before flying back to Brisbane. Heavy with shock and anxiety, I arrived in Canberra to spend some hours in the National Gallery before the lecture. I wandered through its cavernous galleries and wonderful collection. There, I had a rare experience.

I encountered the gallery's most famous acquisition, Jackson Pollock's last great painting, *Number 11 (Blue Poles)* (1952, fig. 8.2); and there also, hanging obliquely – the paintings were suspended in space – was *Cool White* (1959, fig. 8.1) by Lee Krasner, purchased in 1978. Painted during a period of insomnia when the artist worked at night, the monochrome series includes both gestural forms traced with energetic movements of her arms and biomorphic shapes that some read as eyes. A drama is enacted with the elements of the painting, its materiality, its dynamics and its tension between all-over rhythms and recurring evocations: eyes and mouths. Radically different, Pollock's is a horizontal density of woven skeins of industrial paint sustained by repeating verticals, while Krasner's is more open, with unmarked areas of canvas unexpectedly creating a sense of interiority – all-over creating a dynamic 'world' in itself.

They withstood each other.

It was enchanting to encounter these two artists in such intimate dialogue hanging obliquely amid their companions in the Abstract Expressionist project. So different as psychically charged, aesthetic economies, they shared much in exploring gesturality as abstraction. Neither following nor continuing, every element of Krasner's generous artistic language is utterly different from the iterative linearity of Pollock's. Visual effects and resulting affects are incomparable. Each has its own integrity. I

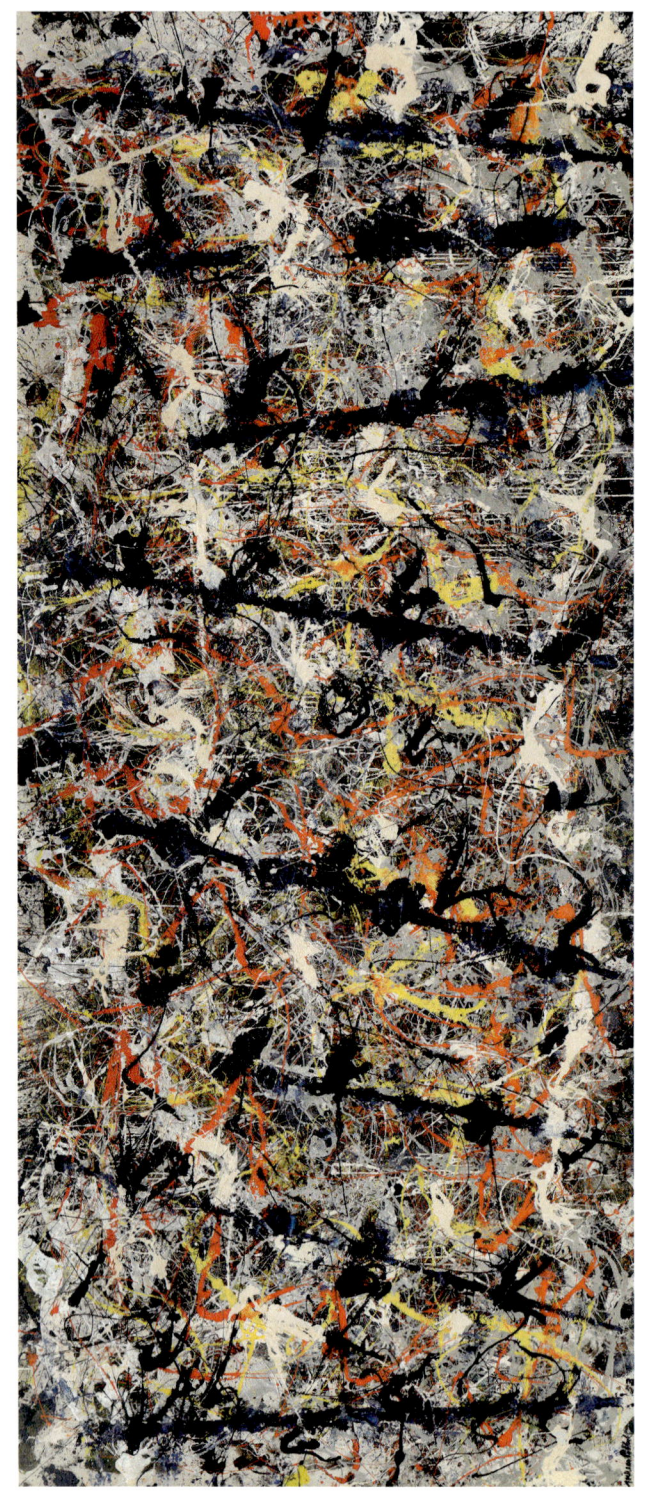

Figure 8.2 Jackson Pollock, *Blue Poles* (*Number 11*), 1952

was solaced in my loneliness by being in this space with them both, knowing the darkness from which *Cool White* had been made.

II London

In 1999 the Tate (only one institution then) in London mounted a retrospective of Jackson Pollock. Not unexpectedly, the galleries were packed. We queued to get in, and, given the crowds, it was hard to see the works on the walls. I pushed my way slowly through the galleries, unable to spend time either to gain distance or to study any painting closely. I was alternatively unimpressed or distressed by Pollock's works of the 1940s. He was certainly no colourist and many of the surfaces seemed clogged and overwrought. I was resistant to the entire atmosphere of undiluted and obligatory awe in the presence of everything signed *Jackson Pollock*.

I soon escaped from the bustle and wandered into the relatively empty galleries of the Tate's American rooms. There, I found their one painting by Lee Krasner, *Gothic Landscape* (1961, fig. 8.3), acquired in 1982. It was hanging in the space that, until the big show next door, had been the location of the Tate's prized *Summertime Number 9A* (1948, fig. 8.4) by Pollock, purchased in 1988. It seemed that Krasner's work came out of the

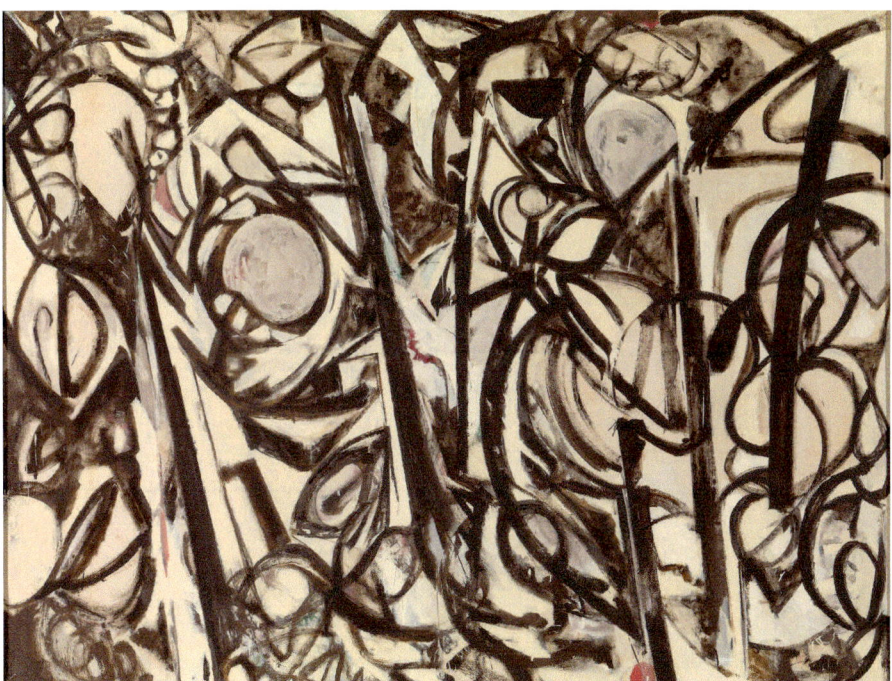

Figure 8.3 Lee Krasner, *Gothic Landscape*, 1961

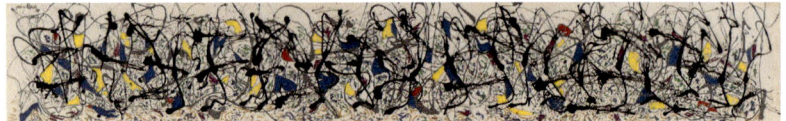

Figure 8.4 Jackson Pollock, *Summertime (No. 9A)*, 1948

stacks only when Pollock's work was not on show in this gallery. This was
the counter-move to the Australian National Gallery. At the Tate, it was
one or the other.

III Brooklyn

Early in January 2001 I found myself in in the Brooklyn Museum, then
hosting a retrospective exhibition of Lee Krasner curated by the art historian Robert Hobbs. The show was just about to complete its four-venue
tour, which had started at the Los Angeles County Museum on 10 October
1999. I visited the show early on a Saturday morning. My abiding, and
melancholy, memory is the sound of my own solitary footsteps on the
wooden floors, echoing through the otherwise empty galleries. (It was
the last few days of a show that had opened there on 6 October 2000, and
it was the tail end of the winter holiday, and it was early on a Saturday
morning.) The stark contrast between the stifling crush at the Tate for
Pollock and the desultory silence for Krasner made audible the blatant
sexism of art history and the artworld, and the public they had shaped,
against which I had struggled for so long. It was, however, wonderful to be
with this extended body of work in a space that allowed long and slow
study, uninterrupted vistas for retrospect and comparison, as I retraced
Krasner's steps so as to assimilate decisive and radical changes of direction
while discerning deep continuities in her artistic project. Krasner so constantly challenged herself, relentlessly opening new possibilities for painting over a sustained practice across fifty years before her death on 19 June
1984, aged 75. No signature style emerged to be repeated. No late decline
witnessed a loss of creative invention. Yet there were also continuities – in
colour, in the dynamics of internal, formal relations daringly sustaining
surface tension while evoking sensations of volume and movement.

This was my first opportunity to see so many paintings by Lee Krasner
together in the flesh for myself. I was impressed by the judicious selection
for a chronological hang that took the viewer through her entire career.
The phenomenological experience of the scale, materiality and facture
conveyed an energy and intensity in the making that is so different from
purely visual impressions gained by flicking through illustrated catalogues
or seeing one work alone. A monumental catalogue raisonné of Krasner's

works compiled by art historian Ellen Landau (who completed her PhD on Krasner in 1981) was published only in 1995, finally allowing scholars like myself an overview of her immense production and its different focal points. It could not, however, set me in relation to the physical entities through phenomenological confrontation.

My encounter in the Brooklyn Museum was profound and joyous. Made anxious that 'feminist desire' for the work of artist-women might have tipped me towards unjustified enthusiasm – that hateful sexist whisper in my head: were the men-critics right after all? – I worked my way slowly and systematically through each room. Each space was a revelation. Here was an artist at work, always expanding her scope while remaining faithful to the *riant* innovations that constituted the diverse but shared projects of swiftly shifting modes of modernist art, in whose arc and transformations she had been involved since the mid-1930s. Krasner came across as fearless, constantly questioning her own practice, reinventing, experimenting, renewing and moving abstract painting in new directions, underlying all of which was a constancy of purpose: the examination of painting itself. While most of the 'famous boys' arrived slowly at a signature 'image' – Barnett Newman's zips, Mark Rothko's colour-saturated rectangles, Ad Reinhardt's all-over monochromes, Clyfford Still's jagged caverns of impasto-rich paint, Jackson Pollock's dripping – Lee Krasner refused a signature. Her inventiveness continued decade after decade.

Yet I felt I could discern a recurring dialectic that made sense of the two key moments of her career. The first was the early 'classical' Hoffmann period through which the artist absorbed what had happened in Europe since 1907. Hoffmann taught his students an academic Cubism by which to discern, beyond yet from within observed forms, deep structure so as to produce abstracted, armatured and flattened surfaces holding interest through his famous concept of the push and pull dynamic: an inner compositional tension. The second period involved exposure to and absorption of the Surrealist 'action' moment that emerged chaotically in New York in the 1940s as a distillation of figurative imagery through reduction to material process. This released the artist, encouraging a spontaneity of gesture through which psycho-bodily energies might create a rhythmically charged spatiality that found resolution of its tensions only through the long battle with the painting as an emerging, internally generated and materialized 'event'.

The curator of the Brooklyn exhibition, the theoretically informed art historian Robert Hobbs, sought to understand Krasner's painting practice as an evolving discourse on the self that stretched from the ideas of the Marxist existentialist Harold Rosenberg to the then-contemporary postmodern theories of the decentred subject.[1] In a later article, Hobbs would elaborate this argument.[2] By suggesting that the Abstract Expressionist moment (rather than being an stylistic or formal *-ism*) was centrally concerned with the issue of *subjectivity* – understood as both the subject of action and the locus of thought, imagination and an unconscious – Hobbs could distinguish Krasner's practice from her masculine contemporaries' more Romantic, expressive concepts of the self. He characterized the latter as metaphorical – they considered art forms as constituting or realizing, symbolically, a whole self. Krasner, he argues, exhibited a more open-ended view of the self, played out across series and renewed searching. He characterizes her practice as one that

> plays on metonyms in which she and her related attributes are connected through a chain of signifiers without being hypostasised as their essence. By relying on metonym as opposed to metaphor, Krasner breaks away from Abstract Expressionist claims of autonomy and transcendence as she embraces the countering ideas of contingency and fragmentation. Looking at Krasner's work in this manner allows one to see how both her postmodern works made for the first 1976–1977 Pace Gallery exhibition entitled *Eleven Ways To Use The Words To See*, and those created subsequent to it, are not radical departures from her earlier work, but instead are far more self-conscious developments of attitudes and practices appearing in it since the 1940s when she began viewing the self as other.[3]

The Brooklyn exhibition was my first encounter with *Eleven Ways To Use The Words To See* (1976–77, fig. 8.5). I had hitherto focused on work of the 1950s. *Eleven Ways…* are eleven canvases made by Krasner's return to long-stored, somewhat smudged charcoal drawings from her Hoffman period in the late 1930s, when, drawing from the model, she was working through the reconstitution of figure and space by learning to use an analytical Cubist-derived methodology in which the traditional language of Western art – figure drawing with its deep humanist identification with and through the human body, pose and gesture – was rationally deconstructed in order to discern and bring to the surface an abstracted infrastructure of uni-dimensional relations of parts forming a purely formal unity on the flattened surface of paper or canvas.[4] In the early 1960s, visiting her studio for research for the first retrospective of Krasner that he was organizing in London, British curator Bryan Robertson discovered these drawings in a cupboard, unframed and many unfixed. The charcoal on some drawings had smudged or imprinted its ghostly trace on the blank backs of their neighbours in storage. The artist put them aside and had again forgotten them for another decade, until she was selecting work for several shows about her early drawings and collages.[5] She thus re-encountered this historical body of work, using those she could not exhibit to create a totally new body of work titled with tenses of see: *Imperative* (i.e. See!), *Imperfect Subjunctive*, *Present Conditional*, *Imperfect Indicative*, *Past Continuous*. The new form coupled with these titles

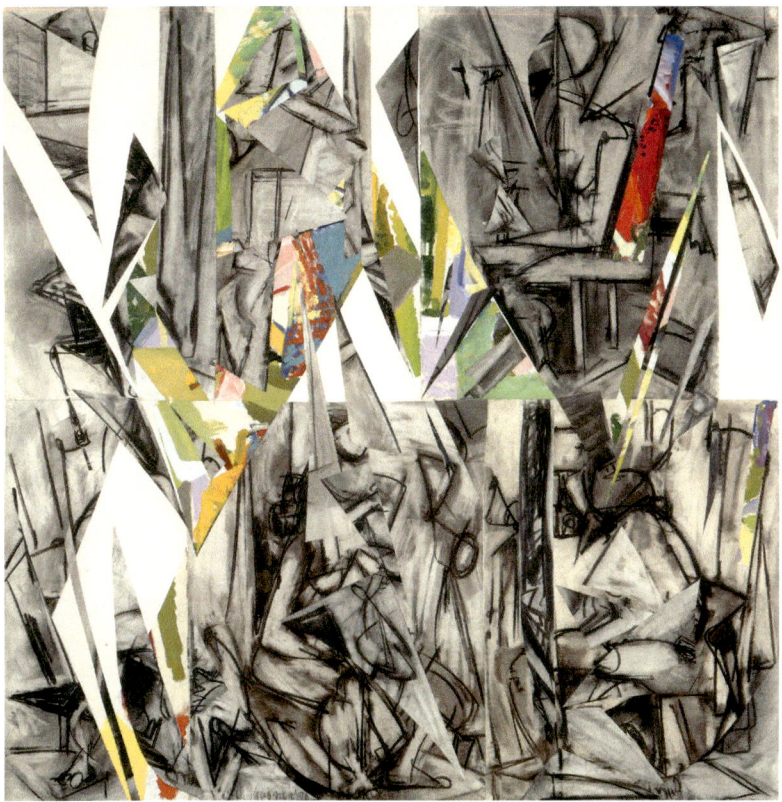

Figure 8.5 Lee Krasner, *Imperative* from *Eleven Ways To Use The Words To See*, 1976

performed a sardonic commentary on Greenbergian criticism, current engagements with opticality in art and generic historical critical blindness to the work of artists such as Krasner herself. Time was also inscribed in the several tenses (I saw, I was seeing, I am seeing) as well as moods such as conditional (I would see) and subjunctive (were I to see). Cut with precision into strips and shapes, the severed elements of damaged drawings were collaged on to a large canvas, with added shaped sections of colour, or counterposed to uncovered areas of canvas that act as counter-forces to the acute angles of the sliced fragments of once unified drawings.

Writing in her catalogue raisonné of Lee Krasner's oeuvre, Ellen Landau draws our attention to the residual content of Krasner's Hoffman-nesque figure studies, which remain visible in these large works. Discerning the still intact, if formalized or abstracted, female bodies of the model that remain recurring presences, Landau wonders if Krasner ever knew of a collection of staggered photographs taken by Rudolph Burkhardt in 1950–52 recording the six stages in the development of the painting *Woman*

I (1950–52, exhibited 1953) by Willem de Kooning, or of his collaged canvases he made in the early works in the *Woman* works (1949–50, Weatherspoon Art Museum, University of Carolina, Greensboro).[6] It is unlikely. Do collaged female bodies rouse the haunting spectre of de Kooning's massacred women? I want to use such speculation to open a path back to the two paintings at the centre of this book: *Prophecy* and *Sun Woman I* (figs 1.1 and 1.2).

Just as the *Woman* paintings emerged from de Kooning's knowing confrontation with, and struggle to emerge from, the overwhelming presence of Picasso and the latter's obsessive if varying confrontation with *Woman* in his work, so I might find myself arguing that at certain points in her career, Krasner's work was knowingly dealing as much with this long, challenging masculinist-modernist legacy of a refigured and often disfigured female body as she was herself, as painter, exploring another kind of *being-in-the-creative-woman's-body* through both Grahamian psychic play and Rosenberg's model of gestural action painting that she shared with Pollock for a few years. The challenge of, and the distress caused by, the canonized but ambivalently violent and impassioned paintings of *Woman* in the lineage back from de Kooning and Picasso to Cézanne were a constant phantom, compromising any artist-woman's sense of self. They had to be worked through, and with, to find for herself other relations between painting and a body, *in, of and from the feminine*, that could, in painting itself, register not man's Other, but a singular creative woman's body-mind. In doing so, this would also invoke and recast the meanings of any female body that might be residually figured or abstractly obliterated (her early drawings from the model) as well as unconscious evocations of the maternal that lie behind all such figurations (either as image or as the expanse of canvas), for this painter as much as for her male peers. Close analysis of compartments collaged into new combinations reveals repeats of her own drawings of a female body in the art room – anonymous, naked, studied – whose modernized, urbanized, mediatized incarnation in modern painting – de Kooning's cosmetic, dressed and fashionably high-heeled *Women* – she had had to confront in their monstrous emergence in *Prophecy* (fig. 1.1) and reclaim for *jouissant* dancing space in *Sun Woman I* (fig. 1.2) or *The Seasons* (fig. 7.1).

The monumental *Eleven Ways To Use The Words To See* reads as much as a speaking back to her own historical modernisms – of the 1930s through the 1950s – as a declaration, in her maturity, to both de Kooning and Greenberg of both her artistic presence and her *presentness*, now set out in her own, verbally ironic and visually sharpened – but not killing – and witty terms. The collaged drawings reclaim, recast and recreate the past. Krasner had, we need to recall, a long history of work with paper and collage, as well as with doing creative violence to her own older work. The major moment occurred in the early 1950s with works such as *The City* (1953) and *City Verticals* (fig. 7.4) and, in another phase, two years later in 1955: *Milkweed* (fig. 7.5), *Shooting Gold, Lame Shadow, Blue Level, Stretched Yellow, Desert Moon*. Greenberg thought them 'a major addition to the American art scene of that era'.[7] Looking smooth and even in reproduction, these works are very physical entities to encounter, especially when torn, rough-edged strips of burlap or canvas are included with the oil and paper collage on canvas or paper.

This recuperation of cutting and collage and the haunting by art's female body – the nude model – are necessary digressions from my memory of astonishment in 2001 at the fertility of Lee Krasner's pictorial imagination and painterly practice. She regularly deconstructed and reconstructed the elements of her ever-vivid painterly discourse on surface, gesture, material and making, while realigning these elements again and again in relation to her dialectic of painting as a site of tension, canvas as a holding surface and a dynamization of space as an energy field tied closely to the body at work and the unconscious being indirectly allowed to shape and trace the body's gestures that, carefully and critically read and worked by the artist herself, produced complex paintings.

Against my response, I want now to set a cruel review in 2001 of both Hobbs's curatorial argument and the work of Lee Krasner that he exhibited, penned by an art historian David Anfam, who would emerge decades later, for instance in 2018, as the authoritative voice in the reconsideration of Abstract Expressionism as a movement. In his version, almost no woman holds a significant place. Writing in the British *Burlington Magazine*, Anfam casually situated Krasner on the margins of a canon *being redrawn to include its outer edges*. He argued, moreover, that Hobbs's strategy for such a theoretically informed redrawing of the canon to include Krasner was misconceived. Iterating her 'subjection' to Pollock and indeed other painter-men in different ways throughout his review, Anfam categorically writes: 'That Krasner was not her own woman and worked in Pollock's shadow has long been a truth that dare not speak its name in the wake of feminist art historical revisionism.'[8] Such an assertion – Pollock swamping Krasner – is, in fact, not censored at all; it is the commonplace opinion most regularly asserted by men-writers. Moreover, the nature of feminist critique is not to be condescendingly dismissed as wishful revisionism.

Feminist analysis identifies and deconstructs the recurring imperative to reproduce a male/female hierarchy unable to imagine co-creation or allow difference in the making of art, and, in doing so, misinforming the public about historical actuality. Co-creation is not collaboration. It signals the historical fact of diverse women and men making modern art, often side by side or in close-knit artistic communities. Thus, Hobbs's admittedly somewhat forced attempt to link the shifts within Krasner's oeuvre to her undoing the unifying concept of a 'self', in prescient accordance with postmodern theory that posits an inherently unfixed subject, may miss the historically specific discourse on the subject that was emerging during the 1950s, to which I will shortly return. I want, however, to commend Hobbs's attempt to allow Krasner a multi-threaded 'identity' and, consciously or unconsciously, the creation of artistic space for a subjective articulation of her early Orthodox, immigrant, European Jewish heritage when she was confronted in the 1940s with the horror of the industrially murderous destruction of European Jewry to which she was still connected, irrespective of religious affiliation. Hobbs argues, in a feminist-inflected manner, for a nuanced sense of the complexity of any one subjectivity as it is played out across artistic activity on the one hand, and, on the other, the impact of sociohistorical events that shape culturally significant senses of self. This analysis allows us to come to Krasner's work in its *singularity*. In contrast, the rigidly art historical Anfam allows Krasner to have created one or two good works, while for the rest, he insists that she was always 'a couple of beats behind someone else's tunes' in 'an uneven and derivative career'.[9]

Reading his review in the aftermath of my revelatory encounter with Krasner as a dynamically artistic mind at work across her long, sustained and inventive career, the casual assurance of Anfam's damning judgement alarmed me. Why did he *need* to negate this American artist? As I reflected on the troubling inconsistencies I had perceived (at the Tate exhibition in 1999) in Jackson Pollock's short career, from his vicious and violent Surrealist fantasies such as the terrifyingly explicit example of a killing man – *Man with a Knife* (1938–40, Tate Gallery, London, donated by Frank Lloyd Wright), his overtly Jungian evocation and destruction of archetypal male/female sexual and generative bodies *Birth* (c. 1941, also Tate Gallery, and one of the early works seen by Krasner when she first visited his studio), to the brief period of drip paintings such as *Full Fathom Five* (1947, Museum of Modern Art, New York) and *Blue Poles* (1952, fig. 8.2), which were followed by a loss of direction and almost no work at all in the last two years of his shortened life – inconsistencies and brief breakthroughs that unquestionably constitute his unchallenged but temporary brilliance – I can only draw attention to the radical difference in the tone, language and lack of openness to the possibility of extending critical hospitality to an artist such as Lee Krasner.

My response to key encounters with Krasner's work is, I admit, coloured by my wish to *difference the canon* with 'feminist desire' – an openness to seeing art without patriarchal eyes and voices predetermining my immediate viewing or art historical response to the simple questions. What am I seeing? What is going on here?[10] Feminist desire means seeing or encountering difference differently, and not negatively. This is radically distinct from attempts to supplement the existing, masculinized, white canon by elevating a compensatory, fixed idea of 'women's art' and 'women artists' so as to comfort me in my patriarchally wounded narcissism engendered by the selective canon that implies that women have never created anything worth valuing. Admittedly a catachresis, crossing conscious political intent with unconscious desire, feminist desire addresses an elective orientation towards discovering what is not already known, familiar, understood, and what could be learned if difference was not only 'different from the all-male canon', merely the opposite of the given, the masculine, white, Euro-centred, heterosexual, abled positions of canonized normativity. Difference becomes a process in the present continuous – *differencing* – opening us to complexity and to more possibilities that implicate each of us in transgressing the binaries without a resulting loss of positionality. We know very well that a self is already complexly formed of many aspects and open to many identifications. In the encounter with difference, it becomes fragile and receptive, prepared to be affected beyond its own familiar contours. As a feminist, I desire to imagine and think beyond the racist, phallocentric asymmetry and patriarchal hierarchies that limit our imaginations to a stark and value-laden logic of plus/minus. *Differencing* undoes the slashed opposition to find complex negotiations and diverse solutions in shared artistic adventures, a gain all round.

Rosenbergian action and the traces of Monroe in Irigaray's dancing space

Anfam disdained his fellow art historian Robert Hobbs's rather formal case for Krasner as a postmodern *avant la lettre* in terms that allowed him to use the latter to beat Krasner back into the only place in his own art history or his version of the event that was Abstract Expressionism that he would allow her. The phallic rigidity showed itself even as it was armed with its own unexplained judgements as to what was and was not a 'good' or 'innovative' painting.

What does not surface enough in the writing on Krasner's work is the impact of a writer she knew well and personally, Harold Rosenberg, whose Marxism generated the major counter-argument to Clement Greenberg's hegemonic and Kantian determination of what makes for a 'good' modernist work (fig. 8.6). Close to both Harold and May Rosenberg, who were witnesses at her wedding to Pollock and long known to her through their shared political debates and leftist activism during the 1930s, Krasner's

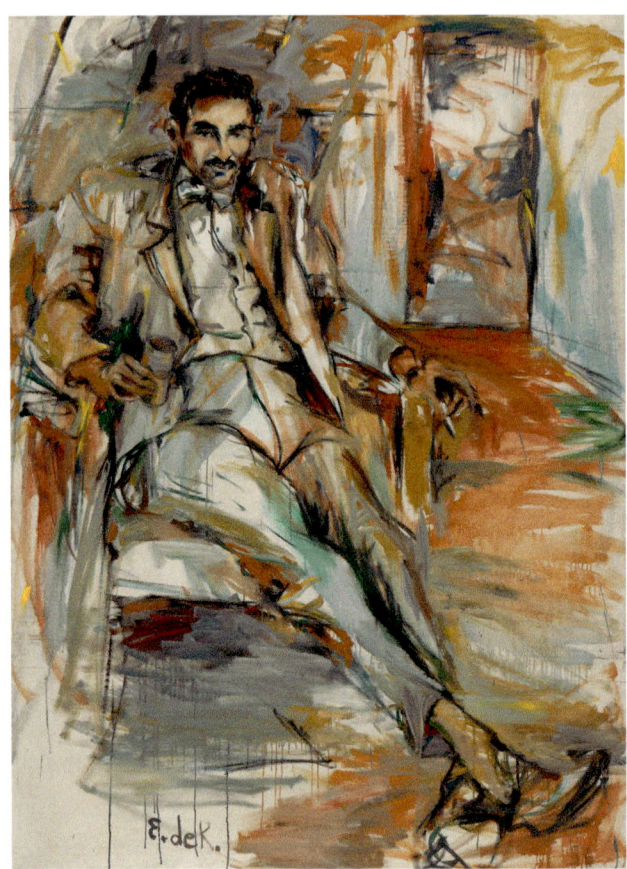

Figure 8.6 Elaine de Kooning, *Portrait of Harold Rosenberg no. 3,* 1956

repeated statements about reading her work as biography invite us to recognize life as a source for art, and echo the premises of Rosenberg's famous, but often misunderstood, arguments about the artist and the work in 'The American Action Painters', first published in *Art News* in 1952. Fred Orton's insightful exposition of the Marxist underpinning of Rosenberg's text is vital and illuminating.[11] Rosenberg displaced the formal approach to interpreting the stakes in modern painting with what Orton has identified as his Marxist concept of *action*, whose outcome is not an art object but an *event*. Rosenberg wrote:

> At a certain moment the canvas began to appear to one American painter after another as an arena in which to act – rather than as a space in which to reproduce, redesign, analyse or express an object, actual or imagined. What was to go on the canvas was not a picture but an *event*.[12]

Equally suspending distinctions between abstraction and figuration, as variations of what remains in effect content, Rosenberg liberated paint and canvas as the material and space for action rather than as purified medium and surface. The outcome is an 'image' that arrives through interaction – encounter – between agent and material.

> The painter no longer approached his easel with an image in his mind. He went up to it with material in his hand to do something to that other piece of material in front of him. The image would be the result of this encounter.[13]

What these statements propose, Orton argues, can be understood in terms of Rosenberg's Marxist diagnosis of the historical moment. The political avant-garde for a revolution in *society* had been stalemated and the concurrent artistic avant-garde consciousness of *art* as a form of revolution had become formalized. In terms of immediate aims, in this non- or post-revolutionary condition, *society* and *art* are confronted with nothingness, nothing but action, which makes all areas of art arenas for action itself in the face of the loss of former goals and the apparent victory of anti-revolutionary capitalist settlement. Conventional art critical and art historical discourse – judgement and naming – become irrelevant. Art's purpose is neither to be part of modern art whose story the museum of that name lays out in a teleological narrative. Nor is it to pursue the Greenbergian idea of art's modern telos of purifying each medium of extraneous elements – literature, religion – or content, as even Bataille also proposed. Referencing Cézanne and the shibboleths of the apologists for modern art's trajectory, Rosenberg explains: 'Call this painting "abstract" or "expressionist" or "Abstract Expressionist", what counts is *its special motive for its extinguishing the object*, which is not the same as in other abstract or expressionist phases of modern art.'[14] Again a killing, this time of bourgeois art as object.

'American' is not a nationalizing adjective but marks an event in history and painting, as Rosenberg counters Greenberg's idealist aestheticism with the focus on the act of painting, not the production of a painting, and no more the artist's sensibility or intention.

> The new American painting is not 'pure art', since the extrusion of the object was not for the sake of the aesthetic. The apples weren't brushed off the table [Rosenberg is referring to Cézanne and Picasso] in order to make room for perfect relations of space and colour. They had to go so that nothing would get in the way of *the act of painting* [my emphasis]. In this gesturing with materials, the aesthetic, too, had to be subordinated. Form, colour, composition, drawing are auxiliaries, any one of which – or practically all, as has been attempted, logically, with unpainted canvases – can be dispensed with. What matters is always *the revelation contained in the act* [my emphasis]. It has to be taken for granted that in the final effect, the image, whatever be or not be in it, will be a *tension* [original emphasis].[15]

For Rosenberg, action is located in the agent, the one who acts by painting, and is inevitably entangled in every way with what we might name life: social, psychological, historical, imaginative, symbolic, political. Biography is thus not reducible to an individual and the personal; subjectivity is elevated to political significance. Echoing and offering a specific reading of the phrase Lee Krasner herself repeated – one that has so often been read reductively in the case of artist-women to link their art to their life-story – Rosenberg raises the action of each artist to both political commitment (in the widest sense) and ethical practice in the face of the nothingness that defined the post-war, post-Holocaust political landscape. Biography means being situated in history and society through the prism of each person's action in the world. Thus, art is not life nor life art. Yet they intersect indistinguishably in a politico-ethical-aesthetic entanglement:

> A painting that is an act is inseparable from the biography of the artist. The painting is itself a moment in the adulterated mixture of his life – when the moment means in one case the actual minutes taken up with spotting the canvas or, in another, the entire duration of the lucid drama conducted in sign language. The act-painting is of the same metaphysical substance as the artist's existence. The new painting has broken down every distinction between art and life.[16]

Identity does not precede but *proceeds from* action. The action is nothing but the decision just to paint. Not to paint something but to engage with the unforeseen that will reveal what painting does. Orton thus explains the paradox. 'Action painting is, in Rosenberg's account of it, painting at the point of formation, when everything has to be redone; it is *Ur-painting* at the moment of thematization; but it is not yet, and may never become, painting as art.'[17]

Orton footnotes philosopher Richard Wollheim's massive study, *Painting as an Art*, as the source for the ideas of *Ur-painting* and thematization, which I understand as the process by which such elements as mark, surface and gesture, with subsequent aspects of the painting process, move from being the component facts to becoming the means by which something called painting emerges in the making, and then, into the recognition of what these elements produce as effects, for the viewer, when they first encounter, begin to look and puzzle out what they are seeing – before and beside any recognition of 'art' or a specific 'meaning'. This may also help to make sense of Rosenberg's follow-up to the inseparability of biography from painting and life from art.

> It follows that anything is relevant to it. Anything that has to do with action – psychology, philosophy, history, mythology, hero worship, anything but art

criticism. The painter gets away from Art through his act of painting; the critic can't get away from it. The critic who goes on judging in terms of schools, styles, form, as if the painter was still concerned with producing a certain kind of object – the work of art – instead of living on the canvas, is bound to seem a stranger.[18]

Rosenberg's text distilled his earlier political activism and hope into a non-art historical but deeply situated historical understanding of the kind of painting that emerged in the 1940s from a small coterie of artists in New York. He provides a contemporaneous language with which to consider Lee Krasner's reply when asked what she did: 'I paint.' Painting constitutes living and each set of works constitute something other than stylistic evolution or a new competitive gambit in the avant-garde game of reference, deference and difference. They mark liveliness, still living, being alive, restlessly examining painting itself as a way of life and a way of being in the face of events that must be lived through and with.

Rosenberg's statements, admittedly vulnerable to glib recitation rather than textual and theoretical examination such as Orton offered, counter precisely the kind of judgement of Anfam and even those who attempt to centralize Krasner the artist around modern and postmodern concepts of the self. Anfam, like the critic situating art in schools and styles, remains a stranger to painting as action in Rosenberg's terms. Yet Rosenberg's terms are indifferent. His subject defaults to *he*. That masculine pronoun can include some of the African American painters of the School such as New York-based Bermudan painter Norman Lewis (1909–79). It cannot fully accommodate, by its own lights, the artist-women of any community. If we read that 'A painting that is an act is inseparable from the biography of the artist. The painting is itself a moment in the adulterated mixture of…' and change the ending to '*her* life', we have to ask, beyond the Marxist underpinnings and privileging of class relations, what is a life when it is *hers*? This is *the* feminist question, itself constantly interrogated because there is no homogeneous *her*. Race, class, sexuality, social and geopolitical location qualify gender creatively as well as negatively. What is a subjectivity when such a diverse *she* is a subject in action? Such questions prompt the search for ways theoretically and analytically to think about both gender as a social axis and sexual difference as a dimension of language, subjectivity and creativity. This *she* is not *Woman* and her life is not a *Woman*'s life in the language and symbolic universe in which Man is the Subject and Woman his Other, in which the Artist is Jackson Pollock and Woman is the image of Marilyn Monroe.

Kerry Filer Harker's prints of the mark of *mm Mark 1* (fig. 00.1), based on the 'dancing' as well as the posed, nude and dressed Marilyn Monroe recorded in the photoshoot with Bert Stern in July 1962, postdate Krasner's 1957 discovery and realization on canvas of a *jouissant* figuration of the feminine sexual body emerging from a battle against the powerful masculine conflations of woman, monstrosity and death among her masculine avant-garde contemporaries in both abstract and figured forms. Looking through Stern's contact prints there is a string I can pull to remake the connection with which I began, with a difference now.

Setting a sacralizing *cordon sanitaire* around art blinds us to the fact that artists participate in culture in its extended forms. Krasner, Pollock and Mondrian loved jazz and dancing. Artists go to the movies, read newspapers and savour comics. The impact of Marilyn Monroe in the year after her *annus mirabilis* of 1953 was visible in all sites of visual culture, from the lofts of New York painters to music, literature and her imitators in cinema. To promote *The Seven Year Itch*, premiering in New York on 1 June 1955, Sam Shaw's image of Monroe featured on a massive billboard above New York cinemas in the iconic pose holding down her white billowing dress in a gesture of smiling ecstasy (fig. 8.7). None of us has ever been able to grasp and name what this actor was able to project before a camera. In my text on gesture in cinema, I analysed the failed photoshoot and filming of Monroe taking this pose on Lexington Avenue. The iconic image on the billboard was, however, recreated away from the hooting crowds in the privacy of the Hollywood back lot. The result is an action-image that I place in the Warburgian genealogy of the *Nympha* rather than what might be expected – *Venus*. It was not as sex symbol that Monroe made her mark, but as life and joy.[19] Her iconic ubiquity would become more evident as post-abstract painters turned towards an engagement with popular American cultural forms, but darkly when she had died, in Warhol's mourning paintings of *Marilyns* in 1962. These would recycle her image of obvious celebrity and make her stilled iconicity visible had it not already become so, but without the 'mark' that I am suggesting surfaces, unacknowledged, in some of 1950s New York painting – in 1957, in Lee Krasner's paintings *Sun Woman I* (fig. 1.2) or *The Seasons* (fig. 7.1). Here we might glimpse a painterly resonance, anti-iconic and non-conscious, with the creative work of 'Marilyn Monroe' as image of life. I am not referring to the woman but to her aesthetic production, which was a singular loveliness that Monroe worked to perform on screen and in still images. Krasner's paintings emerged from the action of one creative-artist-woman's body as it reconfigured the feminine image for herself and endowed this spirit of Monroe's often cinematically 'abused' body with a liveliness and lovely joyousness that we glimpse in Monroe's own action before the camera of Sam Shaw (fig. 8.8), and sense in Kerry Filer's recasting of the Stern photo-session. 'Monroe' iconized a model of sexualization that her own performances – in skilled impersonation – exceeded by joyous parody. In the infamous moment of

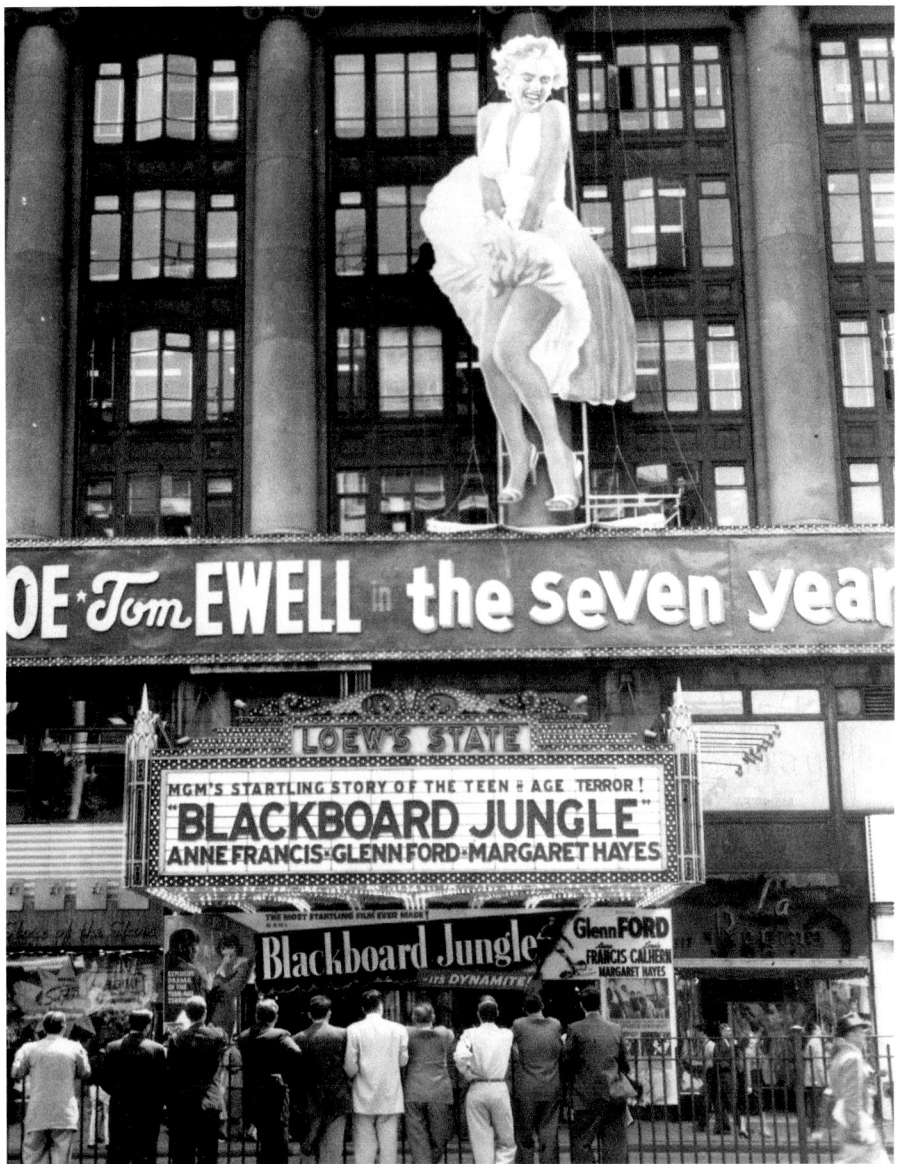

Figure 8.7 Sam Shaw, *photograph of Marilyn Monroe on a New York cinema billboard for*
The Seven Year Itch, 1955

the billowing dress, the image projected joy, or even a *jouissance* that
I have dared to find echoing through another project of a creative woman in
New York in the 1950s, though *Sun Woman* is neither killing nor dying, not
massacre but life.

Coda

Via this last image, I return to de Kooning's *Marilyn Monroe* (fig. 2.14). If Monroe was a brilliant comic actress, she was neither laughable nor comic, whatever idiotic role she had to play. What she created on screen or for the still camera was a word I found in Julia Kristeva's writing about infantile laughter and the mother's laughing face: 'The inaugural sublimation, in most cases visual, brings us not only to the foundations of narcissism (specular gratification) but to the *riant* well-springs of the imaginary' (fig. 2.16).[20] The aura of Monroe's face calls for this term: *riant* (laughing) loveliness that I relate as affect to the *pathos formel* of the *Nympha*, encoding a life force, a liveliness that I borrow from Aby Warburg's conception of images as mnemonic carriers of primary affects.

What unique affective quality did this performer embody and project into the lens and on to the screen that has sustained an unsurpassed and persistent fascination with her still image, despite the desolate quality of the films in which she starred in embarrassing, limited and commodified roles? What was it about her cinematic face that Roland Barthes completely missed when, in 1955, he plotted a history of the cinematic face from Garbo to Audrey Hepburn? Monroe offered neither the face of Garbo's cold beauty nor cheap sexualization. She *created* and *projected* the face of joy that was figured by half-closed eyes and mouth open in laughter – irrespective of the state of mind or life experience of the person (fig. 8.8).

Proposing Marilyn Monroe as a *riant pathos formel*, the *Nympha* figure of life and loveliness, I escape the deadly triangulation Pollock, Monroe, Krasner that I posed at the start. If, as a *lively* articulation of 'the feminine', *Monroe-ness* is indirectly discoverable and inscribed by the one painter who might answer back to Julia Kristeva's scepticism about laughter in women's creation in what Lee Krasner, painting her way through grief and beyond what *Prophecy* (fig. 1.1) had allowed to surface, I need to write another book. It will come from the other side of this coin where Monroe and Krasner might align, as creative women enabling us to image and to imagine difference in 1950s New York painting.[21]

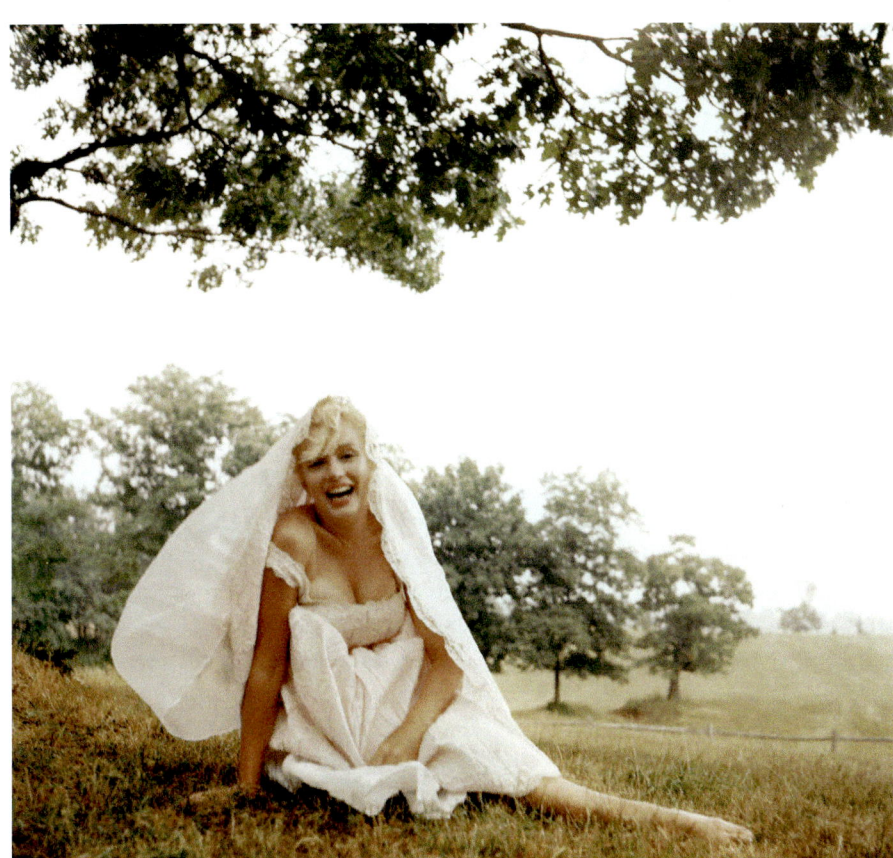

Figure 8.8 Sam Shaw, *Marilyn Monroe at Amagansett*, 1957

Appendix

Sexual difference

Feminist theory proposes that our minds, thoughts, memories, phantasies and embodied sensations are shaped by the *psycho-linguistic* and *psycho-sexual* formations that constitute *subjectivity*. *Psycho-linguistic* formation links psychoanalytical theory to literary and cultural theory in the structuralist and poststructuralist moment of the 1960s–1990s. *Psycho-sexual* formation follows Freud's theory of the psyche, an agency incited by human pre-maturity at birth. The infant is born into a dependency that directs its life-oriented drive towards the world, others and things, ultimately grooving iterative pathways across its body's points of contact, entry and exit – eyes, mouth, skin, anus, genitals – shaped in the see-saw of displeasure (lack of food, discomfort, tension, etc.) and pleasure (satisfaction). To Freud's bodily model, psychoanalyst Jacques Lacan added a *psycho-linguistic* focus on language, tracing the passage from initial inklings of subjectivity and psychic life into culture, whose instrument and territory he identified with, and as, the Symbolic order.[1]

For some, subjectivity is the opposite of objectivity. Being subjective implies seeing something from one's own point of view, rather than taking a distanced, rational or disinterested stance. In cultural theory, however, subjectivity is the condition of becoming-being a thinking, feeling, acting person: a subject. Both a philosophical and a psychoanalytical concept, it signifies how we experience ourselves as thinking, feeling, experiencing and situated beings. This can be related to specific areas of life, such as political subjectivity, social subjectivity or artistic subjectivity. In philosophy, *the subject* refers to agency, consciousness, personhood, and as such corresponds to the grammatical position of the subject, I think, I feel, I act, I suffer. This meets the first sense of subjectivity as a located and personal way of thinking and feeling, while objectivity tries to set aside these *colouring* factors in pursuit of disinterested knowledge. Sociology of knowledge, however, discounts that possibility to argue that all knowledge is situated because we cannot escape class, gender, race, colonial, heteronormative and other inflections of our subjectivity even when we think.

Psychoanalysis theorizes the unconscious processes involved in the formation of *subjectivity*: the psychological condition created by its formation under the laws of culture. Subjectivity is not the object of its analysis, but how do we *become* subjects psychically? What are the stages, registers, vagaries of that process of the formation of a psyche? What are the legacies of our formation? The answer is that we are split subjects. We are divided between conscious/pre-conscious (ego and superego) and unconscious dimensions. Hence, we cannot fully know ourselves. Our personal histories and structural formation imposed by the law and language shape us, while that formation process itself forms the Unconscious, repressed while constantly impressing itself upon the conscious subject through dreams and symptoms. In its uses in art history and cultural theory, and notably in feminist theory, the formation subjectivity is sexuating, creating sexual difference while, as a phallocentric Symbolic order, feminine subjectivity and sexuality become unknowable to those it subjectifies and sexuates as feminine subjects.[2]

Subjectivity is complex. In grammar, the subject, the grammatical *subject* in a sentence, is an agent of a verb: doing, feeling, acting, speaking, etc. Paradoxically, *subject* can also signify the opposite, 'being a subject of the Crown' or 'subject to attacks of anxiety'. These imply being subject(ed) to an authority, a condition or a system: subjection. Being a subject as agent is, however, lined with *being subjected* to a phallocentric Symbolic order, implanted as the Unconscious and articulated in Language itself. The system speaks as us as we use its grammar and words.

For psychoanalysis, we are not born as subjects. We have to become a subject through a tortuous, complex and even traumatic process at whose heart is a series of losses. Becoming a subject is subjectivization.

The formation of psychological subjectivity takes place within existing social, cultural and symbolic orders – orders of meaning, systems of practice that are historically and sociopolitically inflected. The Symbolic is continuous with language since language uses symbols in place of actual things. Symbolic orders have different histories and durations. For the last 3–4 millennia, a culturally patriarchal and psycho-linguistically phallocentric order has prevailed in many but not all societies, and certainly in the West since archaic, pre-classical times. The phallocentric Symbolic order demands every subject's submission or subjection to an always-already, and yet constantly renegotiated, logic of what we theorize as *sexual difference*, which divides and installs human subjects as masculine or feminine. Becoming a subject in the masculine or the feminine is an effect of psycho-linguistic-cultural formation, not natural inclination or natal condition. Formation of subjectivity within psycho-symbolic and cultural systems and laws engenders both a *psycho-sexual* position – a relation to sexuality and desire – and a *psycho-linguistic* position in grammatical language. Sexual difference refutes any given difference between two existing sexes. Anatomy does not define us, even as our bodies and their diversity are critical in very profound ways to how we live as embodied subjectivities. The very premise of these theories is that sexual difference, which we might better express as the psycho-sexual differentiation or sexuation of the born person into grammatically and psychically pre-given positions – masculine and feminine – is an effect of the psycho-sexual (Freud) and psycho-linguistic (Lacan) process not only of subjectivization – becoming a speaker, sexual and sexed subject – but also of subjectification within a phallocentric Symbolic order.

Sexual difference here refers to what psychoanalysis usefully *revealed* to us as a complex constitution of asymmetrical differentiation imposed on the born-human-becoming-a-subject that produces the asymmetrical relation of masculinity and femininity as *hierarchically different positions* in subjectivity and language. Freud identified the mechanism that obliges a child to adopt one or other position proposed to it by the society and culture into which it is being inducted. He called the key mechanism the Oedipus complex. We do not *have* a complex, as bad jokes about boys loving their mothers too often suggest. ('Oedipus Schmoedipus, he's OK as long as he loves his mother' circulated on TV in my North American childhood.) Complex refers to prolonged psychological processes in which we contend with impossibly conflicting infantile wishes. *Infant says:* I want everything – but what I want is in conflict with the law of the culture into which we are born. *Law replies*: you cannot have what you want. There is a price for all subjects to pay, a sacrifice that must be made at the gates of culture – unhelpfully termed 'castration', which means symbolic castration by language. Through our entry into the Symbolic order, we are symbolically (i.e. by the signifiers of language) severed from our pre-linguistic infantile corporeal intensities, while the signifiers from culture's signifying system nestle in their place, *alienating* the subject from the infantile passions that are then repressed to form the Unconscious.

In his studies of the rules of kinship – how cultures and societies manage relations to each other and relations between the generations, hence family and sexual relations – which are expressed in the rules about marriage and the distribution of property down maternal and paternal lineages created to manage human procreativity and social relations, structural anthropologist Claude Lévi-Strauss argued that the foundation of culture/society and its symbolic orders lie in relations and laws of *exchange*. Exchange facilitates social bonds that traverse families to form social groups: kins, tribes, communities, societies. For exchange to operate, Lévi-Strauss discerned a universal rule: the incest taboo.

This is not a law against adult sexual abuse of children, which is a horrifying crime. It is a cultural law that obliges *all children* to separate from their primary attachments to their carers and become available, through exchange, as partners of non-family members in order to reproduce their society with others of their own generation outside the group defined as their kin. This law is, however, the means by which children are designated sexually, not just as potential partners, but as future *husbands* or *wives*. Each term has a different meaning, a hierarchical one in terms of who receives a 'wife' in the exchange and who is exchanged as a 'wife': wife translating *woman*, which signifies: 'to be exchanged'. In this division of children under laws that are not about sexuality as desire, but manage and determine socially regulated reproductive sexual activity as culturally necessary, to be a husband is *not to be exchanged* but to receive; to be a wife is *to be exchanged* and hence not to have ownership of your own body or desire. Thus, the terms *man* and *woman* are not symmetrical, but asymmetrical and hierarchically so.

In the oldest, still living societies that Lévi-Straus studied, this kinship system is visible, as it were, on the outside. Highly ritualized, it is backed up by real force or violence under the authority of the male elders with the compliance of older women enforcers. In more modern and seemingly less visibly socially policed societies, I suggest, kinship structuring persists, however, and is increasingly internalized, ideologized and circulated through cultural iteration. It operates not through paternal authority but by means of ideological inculcation and socialization, and both artistic and popular cultural representation places before us and demands conformity to images of each society's ideological terms. The Oedipus complex, theorized by Freud at the beginning of the twentieth century, and borrowing its name from the myths and literature of fifth-century BCE Greek culture, identifies a mechanism for *the internalization of these archaic kinship rules as psychological structures*. A complex is thus a pattern of emotions, conflicts, unbearable demands for a sacrifice that have to be negotiated and resolved in order for us to take a predestined place in society and in the linguistic terms that signify its social rules.

The Oedipus complex lasts for many years (between the second and sixth year of a child). First, there is a *dyadic pair* – the androgynous child and the mixed adult world, structurally expressed as the needy child and *Nurture*, later linguistically resignified as Mother, *whomsoever does the caring and keeping the child alive, fed etc.* Then we all encounter *a triadic structure*. During this process, the *one*, the child, is confronted with a splitting of *Nurture*, with two others, two positions, represented as two forms of the adult world signified *Mother* and *Father*. The position-figures do not, however, have the same power. Nurture, the infant–carer dyad, is fractured by an Oedipal triangle, demanding the child's alignment with one or other of these positions. These positions are signified by Language (Symbolic order) and in language, actual words, as asymmetrical pairs: he or she, son or daughter, brother or sister, man or woman, father or mother, etc. They are so not because of nature or anatomy, but because of culture, the formation of societies, for whom their own perpetuation has always been a central operation (exchange for procreation) alongside the work of existing day to day (production).

The triadic Oedipal phase inducts the child not only into an alignment with certain, already loaded and culturally predetermined ways to name and speak of itself. It inserts the child into the Symbolic, the realm of Language, which is also the unconscious treasury of the laws of Culture. To become a subject, the child is thus *subjected* and *sexuated*. There is a price for becoming a subject.

All that the child, up to this point, in reality and phantasy, had wanted, needed, felt it could possess as a necessity to ward off its infantile helplessness has been invested in the *place and persons* representing *Nurture*. This is not a woman necessarily but typically so, and not a biological parent necessarily, and so, to avoid confusion, I name this primary Other *Nurture*: the array of adults who keep the helpless infant alive. *Nurture* signifies life and all that comforts. But, as it grows, the child has also begun to discover forms of comfort in its own body parts, its tiny genitals, its own mouth, or comforters, objects. It would also fear to lose these auto-erotic substitutes.

The Oedipus complex is the sociocultural method that forcibly detaches all children from their primary dyadic relation with *Nurture*/the maternal as the price of entry into Culture as a speaking subject. The force that imposes this is the symbolic Father, not the real dad or any person, but what Lacan identified as the *Name of the Father*, the cultural law that must negate the infant's passionate attachment to the older generation who gave birth to it, with one word: No! You cannot have what you want.

We all desire to hold on to the sustaining body and presence signified as *Nurture*/the maternal. In the interests of its own future existence, Society and Culture will not permit this. The child's desire, initiated in its need to be nurtured, with needs addressed to the adults that sustain its life, must be redirected by the paternal negation to later substitutes for its primary attachments and thus to others of its own generation. Need becomes *desire*. The mechanism for this is the Oedipus complex.

Castration acquires its threatening horror as a phantasized terror of mutilation of our imagined, auto-erotic wholeness that runs along a series of losses the child has undergone – of proximity to the maternal body; weaning – of the breast (real or substitute); and of its own body contents in learning to defecate. *Castration* catches all these losses to merge into the haunting anxiety of *not-being*. The price of entry into Culture is submission to castration – sacrificing the Mother to the Law of the Father and thus sacrificing all the infantile pleasures, the origins of sexuality itself, associated with infancy.

There is one further effect. Since that Law is the Law of Culture, the once all-powerful *Nurture*/the maternal is abruptly rendered symbolically powerless before the No!/Name of the Father, whose symbolic prohibition invests the paternal position with the fullness that the infant and *Nurture* now *appear* to lack. The symbolic Father is why we call this a *patriarchal* culture or society. The signifier associated with the symbolic Father is what Lacan defined as the symbolic Phallus.[3] The Phallus not an organ. It is signifier of the power of the *No!* Thus, we speak of a *phallocentric* order in culture. Because it is so organized, as having the power to say No!, creating the proto-subject's powerlessness before that negation, the difference the Phallus orchestrates is sexual difference, and that difference is asymmetrical. Phallocentrism offers those who align with the Father an illusory masculine position; s/he who takes on the feminine subject position must internalize both a different relation to the Father and an alignment with the position that has now been dethroned, abjected, devalued – the Mother; hence *the feminine* now signifies not-power (paradoxical as it may seem that such a demotion of the maternal-generator Other could occur). That's phallocentrism for you.

In this passage, moreover, sexual orientation is not determined, even as sexual desire is incited and directed towards things and others. Desire, in this theory, is an *effect* produced by the resolution of the Oedipus complex. Desire emerges from the complex as the endless and fruitless pursuit, via future substitutes, for what has, in effect, been lost in the passage to subjectivity. Looking to the future for a lost satisfaction, desire is, in fact, always unconsciously retrospective, desiring a lost world without the Law and seeking to escape the loss it demanded of us. What has been lost is our primary attachment to *Nurture*/the maternal, both pre-natal and post-natal, now phantasized as the primal bulwark against paternal Law and loss. Substitutes can, however, never satisfy because the hidden element is the desire to return to an infantile condition before the awful sacrifice demanded by culture's Law, engineered by the Oedipus complex. This process of impossibly awful options distributes the one, the child, into the dual, differentiated, pre-existing cultural positions that Language pre-names *men* and *women*, and precipitates us into Language that codes these positions and predetermines the range of their real, social, cultural and psychological meanings, in advance, for all who are its subjects. The child who emerges from the Oedipus complex is now 'sexuated': a desiring boy or girl. This traumatic process has compensations for some *boyed* subjects, but few for those children who are now *girled*. The psyche of the now *girled* child must submit to the Law, but under terms that produce her as always already having been 'castrated', that is, lacking, secondary, the best she can do being to make herself desirable to the father-boys.

There is no innate, pre-given, psychological sexual difference that is based on their tiny anatomical reproductive organs, despite much auto-erotic pleasure. Yet this phallocentric formation has effects on how subjects imagine and live in their future, adult bodies, psychically mapped as *empowered* (+) or *lacking* (−). For instance, the feminine subject is never identical with the femininity that phallocentrism constructs. She who becomes the *girled*, feminine subject suffers a kind of profound narcissistic damage, for it appears she lacks what it would take to align with the power of the Phallus and the Father. She is cast as an internal exile, for what she is obliged to name herself, a woman, is the term for a *what* – an object of desire, not a *who* – a subject of desire. She has to internalize the devaluation of her like, *Nurture*, now termed Mother, the very femininity with which she must align.

In its many forms over the centuries, feminism has been a revolt not of women who want to be men, but of feminine subjects who wish to *become women-subjects in their own, as yet uncharted ways, beyond the subjectivities offered under the phallocentric regime*. If women want to be someone and so have access to possibilities and activities, it is not *as men* that they wish for this (even though Freud and his followers could logically only think that it was that women wanted to be masculine, suffering envy symbolically for the organ that seemed to approximate to the Symbolic Phallus). Women contest patriarchy and phallocentrism as people who have desires to be active, to experience for themselves, to work and to learn, to relate to others, to create and to lead, *but not only in terms normalized as privileged and masculine*.

If under phallocentrism, the feminine subject has become the disfigured and 'castrated' other of the phallocentric universe, the feminine is also that order's (brutally) suppressed and unknown excess, what that system does not yet know or recognize, since the feminine only functions in this system as a negative, what the Phallus is not, what is missing, an emptiness useful only as a mirroring surface for the Phallus. The feminine signifies a *beyond the phallocentric concept of plus (m) and minus (f)* as the unmapped resource or energy of resistance to the limiting phallic sovereignty over all of human subjectivity and desire. A feminine sexual difference beyond the phallic version is a resource for non-phallic dimensions of subjectivity, and hence for other kinds of ethics (relating to others) and indeed, aesthetics.

M and *F* are thus not identities, categories, gender markers or attributes derived from the body or nature. They are signifiers in a system of asymmetrical and hierarchical difference. Yet the entire point of explaining these theories is not to accept them unconditionally. Psychoanalysis has so far itself unconsciously reproduced its own phallocentrism even as it made legible that this is the character of the existing system that subjectivizes us. What psychoanalysis revealed through its method was that it repressed, to save the narcissism of its masculine inventors, positions that dutiful theoretical daughters internalized as the price of being taken seriously in the work of the fathers that they also brilliantly preserved and elaborated. Thus, I draw upon the proposition of the Matrix developed by artist and psychoanalytical theorist Bracha L. Ettinger, who discerns additional modes of proto-subjectivity that shift the absolute dominance of the phallocentric theory of subjectivity.

The matrixial dimension is not an alternative or a replacement for the Phallus; substitution would still be a product of a binary logic, either/or. The Matrix and its mode of meaning-production, *metramorphosis*, are not identified as, or with, the feminine in the phallic sense derived from phallocentric logic: presence/absence, plus/minus, masculine/feminine. They do, however, make another realm of meaning and affects 'of/from the feminine' thinkable, as both a primordial, non-relative feminine sexual difference, and a Symbolic that is not defined in negative relation to the Phallus. Ettinger's theorization leans on the Lacanian distinction between the Real (unthinkable corporeal intensity, trauma), and the pair Imaginary (the realm of image and phantasy) and Symbolic (the realm of words and thought), to which she adds the 'corpo-real' of the pre-maternal who, as subject not as object, informs all human subjectivity, irrespective of later sexual or gender alignments.

Thus, the Matrix, like the Phallus, is to be understood as a Symbol, a signifier and not just a signified. The matrixial organizes aspects of subjectivity and meaning. Neither is it a body part, however much the very conditions of our thinking bear the continuing imprints of primary corporeal intensities and *aesthetic* registrations of sensations, as well as phantasmatic images of the body's eroticized components (sensed as touch, sight, perceived via aurality, orality, anality, erogeneity). 'The Matrix, whose primary meaning [in Latin] is womb/uterus, is not an organ but a Symbol and a concept related to a feminine Real and to Imaginary structures.'[4] Its conceptualization, however, does indicate and underline the significance of a female and maternal phenomenological and affective contribution to human subjectivity, as well as modes of sublimation from female corporeality that generate aesthetic and imaginative possibilities for the imprinting of this primordial dimension in post-natal, post-phallic creativity and psychological experience.

The Matrixial refers to the original, archaic operations of the late pre-natal event-encounters, shared unevenly and without mutual knowledge, between the becoming-infant in its final pre-birth trimester and the becoming-mother who is humanizing and subjectivizing her partner-in-difference in conditions of proximity-in-distance, even as the becoming-infant is maternalizing her. The event-encounters are transubjective not intersubjective (the infant is not yet a full subject and the becoming-mother is partialized in this condition of *pregnance* (Ettinger's neologism) – a psycho-corporeal, shared event not a medical condition.

They occur asymmetrically across a shared borderspace. The Matrixial is radically displaced by birth when the matrixially becoming-infant is precipitated brutally into its post-natal precarity. Yet traces of this prolonged *fascinance* and intimacy with the unknown but aesthetically sensed *m/Other* persist, may re-emerge, are particularly activated in aesthetic processes and encounters, in artworking.

Metramorphosis is the Matrix's aesthetic-affective meaning-engendering process that refers both to sharing and dispersing affect-events across borderlines, limits, margins, fringes, thresholds and links, and to transformations of the *I* and *non-I(s)* in the Matrix. Metramorphosis is the aesthetic process of the Matrixial and generates aesthetic affects. Metramorphosis is to the Matrixial as metaphor (substitution) and metonymy (contiguity) are to phallic meaning. The metramorphic is closely related to the matrixial gaze, which is distinct from the voyeurism, sadism and fetishism that define the phallic gaze, with Oedipalized mastery at one end (the eye of power) and annihilating anxiety before the lost *object a* at the other. The components of a matrixial gaze are awe, wonder and compassion. A post-natal modality is *fascinance*.

Ettinger identifies several dimensions of post-natal feminine subjectivities – *Woman-beneath-the-Girl, the Girl-beneath-the-Woman, the m/Other-beneath-the-Woman* and *the Woman-beneath-the-Mother* – in matrixial encounter and transformation, opening up feminine subjectivities that are not defined by Oedipal sexual difference (masculine/feminine, plus/minus) but co-emerge in *fascinance* and asymmetrical relations between the different elements. Ettinger proposes that a feminine subject becomes an adult through *fascinance*: 'Fascinance is an aesthetic affect that operates in the prolongation and delaying of the time of encounter-event and allows a working-through of Matrixial differentiating-in-jointness and co-poiesis.'[5] *Fascinance* enacts a woman-to-woman matrixial feminine difference whose figure, pronounced in its French original, is *ffAm, femme-fatale-Autre-mère*. *FfAm* thus signifies 'the desiring/desirable woman–m/Other' encountered in parallel with, but shifting the post-natal feminine subject's confrontation with, Oedipal phallic difference. Instead of a woman as different from a man, Ettinger is posing the Girl as different from but becoming *ffAm*.

Because the terms *femininity* and *the feminine* become very contested, misunderstood and theoretically complex, let me clarify my usage. There are three definitions of *femininity* to be clarified: social-behavioural, psychological and feminist. The first refers to what different cultures and societies deem as proper or necessary for women's behaviour, dress, roles, attributes etc. The second derives from psychoanalytic theory, which identified how masculine and feminine subjects are formed in the crises following birth-dependency and separation from the mother and entry into culture as sexed, speaking subjects. Femininity is a psychological position, not a natural attribute. Feminist theory challenges the naturalness of social-behavioural concepts of femininity (perhaps we might call this gender identity) as much as it has challenged the dominant Freudian and Lacanian theories of psychological formation of the feminine subject as relative to the masculine in a phallocentric +/– formula, with masculinity as the plus and femininity as the minus, that is, lacking. But it is also deeply interested in 'the feminine' precisely as the unrecognized, unknown otherness beyond both the conventional social and phallocentric definitions. Is the feminine the negative force for renewal precisely as the excluded other of the phallocentric order? Is the feminine the as yet unwritten desire and pleasure of the phallocentrically repressed and abused female body and psyche? Is the feminine a distinct and supplementary dimension in subjectivity, ethics and aesthetics? These are the research questions we pose and explore with great difficulty and internal debate even as the very words, the feminine and femininity, cause consternation and are even repudiated entirely in some sections of feminist thought because they are heard only in the first two senses, which seem conventional, essentialist or psychologically compromised. Yet if the difficulty is abandoned, women, as feminine subjects, are left in silenced exile in a phallocentric universe and at risk in patriarchal cultures.

Ettinger's proposition that there are more dimensions to subjectivity than the phallocentric has universal implications, notably for understanding aesthetics and its affects, and for ethics, for non-phallic relations we might enact towards our others. It has especial significance for women, for subjects in the feminine, who are exiled in the desert of phallocentrism. The feminine subject needs ways to grasp theoretically and affectively their archaic arousal into subjectivity in the matrixial rapport with the unknown partner-in-difference, the *m/Other*. They also need to be able to recognize the role post-natally of the desirable Woman, whom Ettinger articulates as *ffAm*, *femme-fatale-Autre-mère* (desiring/desire Other mother), which sounds like *femme*, the French word for woman, when spoken. The *ff* refers to a woman perceiving herself as desiring and perceived as an object of desire; the *Autre*, Other, so not the girl's actual mother; and *mère* marks her as an adult sexual woman. While classic psychoanalysis only allows a place for the mother as castrated, abjected, lacking, damaging feminine narcissism and sexuality, the feminine in the phallic system can only imagine herself as becoming the object of phallic desire, becoming the Phallus for the masculine other. Matrixial theory argues that the girl becomes a woman through *fascinance*, a prolonged, durational, non-scopic gazing and wondering process at and with the *ffAm*, learning and being transformed in the process, which itself replays the primordial *fascinance* of pre-natal becoming. By introducing the psychic significance of late pre-natality, Ettinger does not play into patriarchal control of women's bodies and fertility. The reverse is the case, because matrixiality is always several. Women's bodies are not reduced to being the biological ovens that men control as carriers of their property. The matrixial severality makes the becoming-maternal the solely responsible Subject of the events of her body.

Finally, matrixiality redefines sexual difference. Every born subject is the effect of and thus bears the imprints of the corporeal sexual difference of the sexual *female* body aesthetically (sound, movement, rhythm, breathing, resonance) and proto-ethically (sensing a partner-in-difference and aroused in wonder in this pairing of compassion and hospitality). Thus, Ettinger argues that in a phallic world under a solely phallocentric order, we are all in danger and lack the non-phallic psychic resources to act ethically towards others, be that people, animals, nature, the planet.

The French term *le féminin* is not easily translated by the English words feminine or femininity, to which have accrued connotations more typically disowned by feminists. *Le féminin* does not refer merely to prescribed ideas of what is proper to patriarchally defined women's normalized, gendered behaviour. Understood philsophically as the negated other that consolidates the singular selfhood of the masculine One (de Beauvoir) or as a psycho-symbolic position in language, *le féminin* is defined by Julia Kristeva as 'that which is not'. *Le féminin* cannot *be* in the ontological sense of defining the being of someone, as for example stating that woman is. Rather it functions positionally as a radical negativity (in the Hegelian sense) that generates renovation and sometimes revolution in the Symbolic, which, ruled by a phallocentric logic, places *le féminin* as its outside/ excess. While I resist the absoluteness of Kristeva's radical positioning of *le féminin* as only a semiotic radicality in phallocentric logic, I would want to propose that it is both *what is not yet known* (for lack of its signifiers in phallocentric language) and *what has inevitably and already been, often unconsciously, inscribed into culture* precisely by avant-gardist women artists and writers. As self-conscious avant-gardists, they participated in material, semiotic and creative dissidence with regard to the patriarchal, bourgeois Symbolic. Yet while the avant-gardist experimentation allowed the space or process for such 'other' inscriptions, the artist-women might not have themselves fully recognized what had been inscribed in culture through their aesthetic practices. The otherness of *le féminin*/the feminine in phallocentric culture remains obscured for lack of terms with which to recognize its difference, except as what does not immediately make sense to it. If, up to now, we lacked the appropriate terms to acknowledge *le féminin* as the haunting excess of a limiting phallocentrism, as a result of feminist work on language, art, theory and so forth, we can now both *desire to know* and *frame such difference(s)* via terms of analysis and recognition

developed by feminist theory, itself an intellectual avant-garde intervention: that is, a disturbance of radical significance to the existing orders of
meaning. Feminist theory and practice during the 1970s paid deep attention both to *the body* and to *language*, to both *embodiment* and *affect*. The
intersecting aesthetic and theoretical moves that composed the feminist
avant-garde moment necessarily raised to the level of representational and
philosophical significance the 'excess' within patriarchal bourgeois society that had been formerly managed on the latter's behalf by religion, but
which now self-consciously radical women – feminists – took on. Kristeva
stressed that it was religion that was contested by the avant-garde. Only
once feminism articulated the issues of gender, sexuality and sexual difference, theoretically *and* aesthetically, could the full potential of that contest
be staged.

By the very same token, feminist dissidence can do more than elaborate the psychoanalytical explanation of women's masochism and penis
envy. We can use its resources to explore what might be suppressed for
lack of signifiers, rendered invisible for lack of imagination, and policed
into silence for lack of courage to ask what aspects of a feminine difference
might yet have been impressed into cultural forms, often unknowingly,
but always intensely, by women. What might have been impressed, carved,
painted into culture when certain artistic practices themselves both
embraced psychoanalytical understanding of subjectivity and created
forms of artistic practice uniquely open to the workings of the unconscious, speaking its energies and pressures through the gestures of the
body at work, unfettered by existing systems of representation, figuration
and imagery? I am referring to abstract art and especially the topic of this
case study, abstract gestural painting.

Might linking artistic practice with *the feminine* undermine the concern with simply good art, which should escape all social inscription,
being the very privileged locus of an unmarked individual? I do not think
so. I do not know the final answer. I firmly believe that we need to spend
more time with the issue, openly exploring and questioning difference as
it is and has been enacted transformatively in artistic practice.

Notes

Preface

1   Bert Stern, *Marilyn Monroe: The Last Sitting* (New York: William Morrow, 1982); Bert Stern, *Marilyn Monroe: The Complete Last Sitting* (Munich: Schirmer/Mosel, 2000); Anon., 'Tribute to Marilyn Monroe', *Vogue*, 119.12 (15 September 1962), 72–75. The article included three photographs: Monroe pensive in a black dress (Stern, *The Last Sitting*, 157), mournful in a full-length fur coat (Stern, *The Last Sitting*, 331), and jaunty in a belted overcoat and modified fedora hat (Stern, *The Last Sitting*, 263). Filer Harker's image is based on contact strip 805 negative no. 2. It was used as the cover image of the Stern volume.

2   On the significance of the gesture in modernist art and criticism and its relation to authorship, commodity and the body, see Mary Kelly, 'Re-Viewing Modernist Criticism', *Screen*, 22.3 (1981), 41–52, reprinted in Mary Kelly, *Imaging Desire* (Cambridge, MA: MIT Press, 1997), 80–106.

3   Dorothy Sieberling, 'Is he the greatest living painter in the United States?', *Life*, 27.8 (1949), 42. Hans Namuth's film *Jackson Pollock 51* (10 mins) was first screened at the Museum of Modern Art, New York in 1951. See Caroline A. Jones, 'Filming the Artist/Suturing the Spectator', in *Machine in the Studio: Constructing the Post-war American Artist* (Chicago: University of Chicago Press, 1996), 60–113.

4   Lee Krasner interview with Marcia Tucker in 1973, printed in the catalogue for the Lee Krasner exhibition at the Whitney Museum of Art; reprinted in Barbara Rose, *Lee Krasner: A Retrospective* (New York: Museum of Modern Art, 1983), p. 157. Krasner says to Tucker: 'You know, Jackson used to grab me by the arm, shaking, and show me what he was working on and ask: "Is this a painting?" Not a good or a bad painting – just was it a painting at all. Sometimes, I feel that way, too.'

5   I use the neologism artist-woman/artist-women and artist-man/artist-men throughout in place of the concepts of the apparently neutral *artist*, to belong to which category *women* can only be identified by the qualifier woman (or worse, female) before the word artist, thus disqualifying them as 'artist', which remains masculine by default (and white and straight and Euro-American as well). The identification of gender politics in language was made by Rozsika Parker and Griselda Pollock in *Old Mistresses: Women, Art and Ideology* (London: Routledge, 1981; repr. 1993, 2013; new edn, London: Bloomsbury, 2020), following on from the first use of this label, but still joined with 'women artists', in Ann Gabhardt and Elisabeth Broun, *Old Mistresses: Women Artists of the Past* (Baltimore, MD: Walters Art Gallery, 1972), published as *Walters Art Gallery Bulletin*, 24.7 (1972), 1–24.

6   Griselda Pollock, *Vision and Difference: Feminism, Femininity and the Histories of Art* (London: Routledge, 1988; new edn, 2003).

7   We never completed the manuscript we jointly wrote (I have the handwritten final version), but our collaborative and individual texts were published in Fred Orton and Griselda Pollock, *Avant-Gardes and Partisans Reviewed* (Manchester: Manchester University Press, 1996). This included Fred Orton, 'Footnote One: The Idea of the Cold War', 205–18. Early publications on this topic included Eva Cockcroft, 'Abstract

Expressionism: Weapon of the Cold War', *Art Forum*, 12.10 (1974), 39–41. See Jane De Hart Matthews, 'Art and Politics in Cold War America', *The American Historical Review*, 81.4 (1976), 762–87, for an understanding of the rifts between America First manufacturing interests and internationalist fractions of the capitalist class led by Rockefeller and others seeking to take the lead in reconstructing a war-torn world for their own financial and economic interests. See also G. William Domhoff, *Who Rules America* (Englewood Cliffs, NJ: Prentice Hall, 1970).

8   For instance, only one woman, Grace Hartigan, was included among the 18 selected by Alfred H. Barr for *The New American Painting*, an exhibition organized by the Museum of Modern Art which travelled to eight countries in Europe in 1958–59 before returning 'in triumph' to the New York Museum of Modern Art with the added subtitle: 'as seen in Eight European Countries'; for this idea of triumph, see Irving Sandler, *Triumph of American Painting: A History of Abstract Expressionism* [1970] (New York: Harper and Row, 1976), a book that included none of the artist-women of the first or second generations of New York Abstract Expressionism, despite featuring as the frontispiece a photograph of *The Irascibles* (18 New York painters protesting the conservative collecting and exhibition policy of the Metropolitan Museum of Art in 1950) that at least included Hedda Sterne.

9   *The Bad and the Beautiful* (1952) and *Lust for Life* (1956) starred Kirk Douglas as anguished, creative and self-destructive men. On the artist and the neurotic as the key articulations of Minnelli's vision in his oeuvre, see Thomas Elsaesser, 'Vincente Minnelli', *Brighton Film Review*, 15 (December 1969), 11–13, reprinted in Joe McElhaney (ed.), *Vincente Minnelli: The Art of Entertainment* (Detroit, MI: Wayne State University Press, 2007), 79–96.

10 Griselda Pollock, 'Artists, Media and Mythologies: Genius, Madness and Art History', *Screen*, 21.3 (1980), 57–96.

11 Alfred H. Barr, director of the Museum of Modern Art, was obliged to mount several defences of modern art against a conservative nationalist accusation that it was meaningless and, worse, communistic. Modern art was on the side of freedom and democracy because it was the art that Hitler hated. Van Gogh's *Starry Night* was chosen as Barr's most convincing argument.

12 On *Lust for Life*, see Griselda Pollock, 'Crows, Blossoms and Lust for Death: Cinema and the Myth of Van Gogh', in Tsukasa Kodera (ed.), *Mythologies of Van Gogh* (Amsterdam: John Benjamins, 1993), 217–39; and on the myth, see Pollock, 'Artists, Media and Mythologies'.

13 Orton and Pollock, *Avant-Gardes and Partisans Reviewed*. The co-authored Introduction to this collection is itself testimony both to the amazing years of our close collaboration and to the tensions that arose as we diverged into different theoretical and methodological directions, the split being most acute in my concurrent engagements with feminist and cultural studies.

14 Lisa Saltzman, 'Reconsidering the Stain: On Gender and the Body in Helen Frankenthaler's Painting', in *Friedel Dzubas: Critical Painting* (Medford, MA: Tufts University Press, 1998), 9–24, reprinted in Norma Broude and Mary D. Garrard (eds), *Reclaiming Female Agency* (Berkeley, CA: University of California Press, 2005), 273–83; Ann Eden Gibson, *Abstract Expressionism: Other Politics* (New Haven, CT: Yale University Press, 1997); Anne Wagner, 'Pollock's Nature: Frankenthaler's Culture', in Kirk Varnedoe and Pepe Karmel (eds), *Jackson Pollock: New Approaches* (New York: Museum of Modern Art, 1999), 181–99; Alison Rowley, 'Notes on the Case of *Mountains and Sea*: Helen Frankenthaler: History, Poeisis, Memory', PhD thesis, University of Leeds, 2001, published as *Helen Frankenthaler: Painting History, Writing Painting* (London: I.B. Tauris, 2007); Marcia Brennan, *Modernism's Masculine*

Subjects: Matisse, the New York School, and Post-Painterly Abstraction (Cambridge, MA: MIT Press, 2004).

15   Saltzman, 'Reconsidering the Stain', 374. This and subsequent references are to the reprint version.

16   Griselda Pollock, 'Back to the Twentieth Century: Femininity and Modernism', in Parker and Pollock, *Old Mistresses*, 146/168. This and subsequent citations of *Old Mistresses* give page references both to the original edition and its reprints, and to the new edition.

17   Gabrielle Smith, 'Helen Has a Show', *The New York Magazine*, 2.7 (17 February 1969), 46–49.

18   Pollock, 'Back to the Twentieth Century', 145/167.

19   Pollock, 'Back to the Twentieth Century', 150–51/171–72.

Introduction

1   Bridget Riley, BBC radio conversation between the artist and curator Julian Spalding, no longer available. Abstract painting continues to this day.

2   Double-edged reviews hailing the Barbican show as a revelation were ambiguously titled 'Lee Krasner Retrospective: The Forgotten Genius of Abstract Expressionism – The Barbican show honours a brilliant yet scandalously lesser known painter' (*Financial Times*, 30 May 2019); 'Reframing Lee Krasner, the artist formerly known as Mrs Pollock' (*The Guardian*, 12 May 2019); 'Lee Krasner Hiding in Plain Sight: A major touring show brings her out of the shadow of her famous husband' (*New York Times*, 19 August, 2019). Nadya Sayej headlined her review 'A New Exhibition Reveals Why Lee Krasner Was Not Your Average 1950s New York Artist', following with 'Lee Krasner is famously known as the wife of modern artist, Jackson Pollock. But what art history forgets is that Krasner was an artist, too. Some might even say that Krasner was a better painter than Pollock' (*Forbes*, 15 July 2020).

3   *Alma Thomas: Resurrection Exhibition*, Mnuchin Gallery, 2019; *Alma W. Thomas: Everything is Beautiful*, Chrysler Museum of Art, 2021; *Sonja Sekula and Friends*, Kunstmuseum Luzern (exh. cat., Chicago: University of Chicago Press, 2016); *Perle Fine: The Cool Series*, Gazelli House, London, 3 December 2002–13 March 2021; *The Accordment Series*, Berry Campbell Gallery, New York, 2020; *Perle Fine Retrospective*, Hofstra University, New York, 2009; *Hedda Sterne*, Victoria Miro, London, 2020; *Hedda Sterne: Imagination and Machine*, Des Moines Art Centre, 2020; *The Irascibles: Painters Against the Museum: New York 1950*, Fundación Juan March, Madrid, 2020; *Joan Mitchell: Worlds of Colour*, National Gallery of Australia, Canberra, 2021; *Lee Krasner: Collage Paintings 1938–1981*, Paul Kasmin, New York, 11 March–24 April 2021.

4   Mary Gabriel, *Ninth Street Women: Lee Krasner, Elaine de Kooning, Grace Hartigan, Joan Mitchell, Helen Frankenthaler: Five Painters and the Movement that Changed Modern Art* (New York: Little, Brown, 2019). The TV series is written by Amy Sherman-Paladino.

5   Griselda Pollock, 'Coming late to the party in Bilbao: Lee Krasner's missed place in modern art history', translated as 'La festa tardía de Lee Krasner', *El País*, 28 August, 2020, https://elpais.com/cultura/2020/08/25/babelia/1598369190_378495.html (accessed 7 December 2021).

6   Cindy Nemser, 'Lee Krasner', in *Art Talk: Interviews with Twelve Women Artists* (New York: Scribners, 1975), 81–112. For the Brooklyn exhibition, see Robert Hobbs, *Lee Krasner* (New York: Harry Abrams, 2000).

7   Clement Greenberg avowed his enthusiasm for the work in the Stable Gallery exhibition when interviewed by Bryan Robertson, curator of *Lee Krasner Retrospective*

(Whitechapel Gallery, London, 1965). Greenberg's belated endorsement of Krasner's collages of 1955 is referenced in an interview with feminist art critic Cindy Nemser in 1975 ('Lee Krasner'). Krasner's sardonic response is from a later filmed interview with Barbara Novack in 1979.

8   David Anfam et al., *Lee Krasner: Umber Paintings 1959–1962* (New York: Paul Kasmin Gallery, 2018), essay by David Anfam and reprints of interviews with the artist by Richard Howard (1978) and Barbara Novack (1979). *Lee Krasner: Collage Paintings 1938–1981*, essays by Siri Hustvedt and Saskia Flower (New York: Paul Kasmin, 2021).

9   I return to this exhibition and its criticism in the final chapter.

10 David Anfam, 'Mood Umber', in *Lee Krasner: Umber Paintings 1959–1962*, 10; Harold Bloom, *The Anxiety of Influence: A Theory of Poetry* (Oxford: Oxford University Press, 1973).

11 Ellen G. Landau proposed an 'erotics of influence' as a possible model: 'Jackson Pollock and Lee Krasner: "The Erotics of Influence"', in Bruno Alfieri and Achille Bonito Oliva (eds), *Pollock's America: Jackson Pollock in Venice: "The Irascibles" and the New York School* (Milan: Skira, 2002), 173–78. Landau also writes of 'channeling desire': Ellen G. Landau, 'Channeling Desire: Lee Krasner's Collages of the Early 1950s', *Woman's Art Journal* (autumn 1997/winter 1998), 27–30, reprinted in Alfieri and Oliva (eds), *Pollock's America*, 189–93.

12 On this remarkable body of work, variously analysed as a staged 'castration', imaginative appropriation, working with tropes of dismemberment, excision and transposition – expropriative as well as appropriative techniques, see Landau, 'Channeling Desire', 189.

13 Landau, 'Channeling Desire', 192.

14 Sigmund Freud, 'Mourning and Melancholia' [1915/1917], in *The Standard Edition of the Complete Psychological Works of Sigmund Freud, Vol. XIV, 1914–1916*, ed. James Strachey (London: Hogarth Press, 1957), 243–58. Grief is not a content. As an affective condition, grief requires prolonged psychic *work* to release investment in the lost object or ideal, freeing the libido to be otherwise directed towards life-making. Yet the wound of the loss is permanent. The thin wall between the real and this preserved space of loss can be pierced suddenly and unexpectedly by chance events, sounds or echoes of the lost one or the lost past.

15 On women and mother loss, see Hope Edelman, *Motherless Daughters: The Legacy of Loss* (New York: Da Capo, 1994; new edn, 2007).

16 'Henry Geldzahler: Curator, Influencer, Cultural Svengali', www.christies.com (last accessed 10 April 2020).

17 Henry Geldzahler, *New York Painting and Sculpture 1940–1970* (London: The Pall Mall Press, 1969), 23.

18 Geldzahler, *New York Painting and Sculpture*, 24.

19 Frankenthaler was anything but invisible at this moment. She had in fact just enjoyed the recognition of a mid-career retrospective at the Whitney Museum of American Art in 1969, and would be chosen alongside 51 artist-women for the 1973 Whitney Biennial. She enjoyed a retrospective at the Jewish Museum as early as 1960. Her visibility was maintained by her almost annual exhibitions at the Andre Emmerich gallery. It is not pure invisibility that I highlight here but disproportionate selectivity in the formation of the canon.

20 Linda Nochlin, 'Why Are There No Great Women Artists?', in Vivian Gornick and Barbara Moran (eds), *Woman in a Sexist Society: Studies in Power and Powerlessness* (New York: Basic Books, 1971), 480–510.

21 Asking 'Why *Have There Been* No Great Women Artists?', the essay was reprinted in a shortened version in *Art News* and then in Thomas B. Hess and Elizabeth Baker (eds), *Art and Sexual Politics: Why Have There Been No Great Women Artists?*

(Basingstoke: Macmillan, 1971), 1–43. Hess succeeded Geldzahler at the Metropolitan and had been an editor of the influential *Art News*.

22   I use art history and history of art, available only in English, to make a distinction between the *discourse* of the academic discipline that studies art and its history and the *field* of historical artistic practices that is studied. In this book, I also use the term modernist art history for the main forms of art historical research and writing that attempted to make sense of modern art, which traversed national boundaries and changed very rapidly. Attempts to give coherence to the many tiny factions produced a chronological account of mutually influenced development that posited the telos or direction of art as abstraction. This model privileged a formal approach, defining many new stylistic -isms competing with each other but also influencing each other. The model institutionalized by Alfred H. Barr at New York's Museum of Modern Art was highly influential on other museums, and academic art history was selective in creating the main story of modern art (ignoring many trends and indeed the philosophies underpinning them that did not coincide with this neat line of development). It ignored subject matter, social history and external factors, seeing art as internally driven by formal concerns. While acknowledging the brilliance and theoretical foundations of the formalist art history of modernism as Riegl, Barr and Fry produced it, social histories of art and feminist art histories challenge its many exclusions and its narrowness. It did become the mainstream story circulated in most academic textbooks and museum collections and exhibitions. There is nothing wrong with formalism, clearly part of the way modern artists and critics understood what they were doing. It is only a problem when it becomes the only and exclusive account of the complexity of art made in the modern era.

23   Teresa de Lauretis, *Technologies of Gender: Essays on Theory, Fiction and Film* (Basingstoke: Palgrave Macmillan, 1987), uses Foucault's theses on discourse to demonstrate that the objects of which we speak and write are produced by our speaking and writing; these technologies and cultural apparatuses produce gender – and feminist theory is also a discourse producing gender, even if in contestation with the dominant discourses, challenging what they fold out of sight.

24   Fredric Jameson, *The Political Unconscious; Narrative as a Socially Symbolic Act* (Ithaca, NY: Cornell University Press, 1981).

25   Elisabeth Bronfen, *Over Her Dead Body: Death, Femininity and the Aesthetic* (Manchester: Manchester University Press, 1992); Mieke Bal, *Death and Dissymmetry: The Politics of Coherence in the Book of Judges* (Chicago: University of Chicago Press, 1988).

26   Griselda Pollock, 'Feminism and Language', in Hilary Robinson and Maria Elena Buszek (eds), *A Companion to Feminist Art* (Hoboken, NJ: Wiley-Blackwell, 2019), 261–82.

27   On mythic mystification of history as nature, see Roland Barthes, 'Myth Today', in *Mythologies* [1957], trans. Annette Lavers (London: Jonathan Cape, 1972), 109–59.

28   Situated knowledge is an accepted component of constructivist social theory, and central to Black and feminist critiques. In feminist African-American and Black Studies it is articulated by Audre Lorde, 'The Master's Tools Will Never Dismantle the Master's House' and 'Age, Race, Class and Sex: Women Redefining Difference', in *Sister/Outsider: Essays and Speeches* (Freedom, CA: The Crossing Press Feminist Series, 1984), 110–24; Bettina Aptheker, *Tapestries of Life: Women's Work and Women's Consciousness* (Amherst, MA: University of Massachusetts Press, 1989); bell hooks, *Talking Back: Thinking Feminist, Thinking Black* (Boston, MA: South End Press, 1989). The concept is elaborated by the feminist philosopher of science Donna Haraway, 'Situated Knowledges: The Science Question in Feminism and the Privilege of Partial Perspective' [1988], in *Simians, Cyborgs, and Women: The Reinvention of Nature* (London: Free Association Books, 1991), 183–202, and Lorraine Code,

What Can She Know? Feminist Theory and the Constructions of Knowledge (Ithaca, NY: Cornell University Press, 1991).

29   Joan Scott, 'Gender: A Useful Category for Historical Analysis', *The American Historical Review*, 91.5 (1986), 1053–75.

30   Griselda Pollock, 'Inscriptions in the Feminine', in Catherine de Zegher (ed.), *Inside the Visible: An Elliptical Traverse of Twentieth Century Art in, of and from the Feminine* (Cambridge, MA: MIT Press, 1996), 67–87. For feminine inscription to counter notions of gender as expression, see Mary Kelly, 'On Sexual Politics and Art', in Brandon Taylor (ed.), *Art and Politics* (Winchester: Winchester School of Art, 1977), 66–75, reprinted in Rozsika Parker and Griselda Pollock, *Framing Feminism: Art and the Women's Movement 1970–1985* (London: Pandora, 1987), 303–12, reprinted in Mary Kelly, *Imaging Desire* (Cambridge, MA: MIT Press, 1997), 1–10. Inscriptions or impressions of singular but also structural psycho-corporeal specificity, unknown and unconscious on the part of the artist-women, are deposited as cipher-like inscriptions awaiting our feminist cracking of their unique codes.

31   Bracha L. Ettinger, *Matrixial Subjectivity, Aesthetics, Ethics Vol. 1: 1990–2000*, ed. Griselda Pollock (Basingstoke: Palgrave Macmillan, 2020).

32   Riah Pryor, 'Is Art History under Threat? UK Universities See 28.5% Drop in the Subject in the Past Decade', *The Art Newspaper*, 20 January 2020, www.theartnewspaper.com/news/is-art-history-under-threat (accessed 25 January 2020).

33   Mary Gabriel, 'Want to Get Rich Buying Art? Invest in Women', *New York Times*, 24 September 2018, www.nytimes.com/2018/09/24/opinion/want-to-get-rich-buying-art-invest-in-women.html (last accessed 24 November 2021).

34   Royal Academy of Arts website, 'Abstract Expressionism' exhibition page, www.royalacademy.org.uk/exhibition/abstract-expressionism (accessed 23 September 2021).

35   Gail Levin, *Inside Outside: Selected Works by Janet Sobel* (New York: Garry Snyder Fine Art, 2003), 5–6.

36   Adrian Searle, 'Storms of Colour from a Wild Destructive Genius: Lee Krasner Review', *The Guardian*, 29 May 2019, www.theguardian.com/artanddesign/2019/may/29/lee-krasner-living-colour-barbican-london-review (accessed 25 March 2020).

37   Adrian Searle, 'Abstract Expressionism Review: Crammed in a Room with the Big Men of US Art', *The Guardian*, 20 September 2016, www.theguardian.com/artanddesign/2016/sep/20/abstract-expressionism-review-royal-academy-pollock-rothko (last accessed 25 March 2020).

38   See the publication of the same title with chapters by Joan Marter, Gwen Chanztit, Ellen G. Landau, Robert Hobbs and Susan Landauer: Joan Marter (ed.), *Women of Abstract Expressionism* (New Haven, CT: Yale University Press, 2016).

39   Gibson, *Abstract Expressionism*.

Chapter 1

1   Krasner knew personally and artistically the abstract sculptor Louise Bourgeois, whose 17 carved figures named *Personnages* (1945–55) were first shown in 1949 at the Peridot Gallery. She had another show at the same gallery in 1953.

2   Lee Krasner in Eleanor Munro, *Originals: American Women Artists* (New York: Simon and Schuster, 1979), 116.

3   Sieberling, 'Is he the greatest living painter in the United States?', 42.

4   Any scholar working on Lee Krasner is indebted to the very important analyses by Anne Wagner of Krasner's negotiation of artistic identity in relation both to her own gender and the constructions of it made by the culture in which she worked. I

gratefully acknowledge the importance of her work for this study. See Anne Wagner, 'Lee Krasner as L.K.', *Representations*, 25 (1989), 42–57, reprinted in Norma Broude and Mary Garrard (eds), *The Expanding Discourse* (New York: Harper Collins, 1992), 425–36. See also Anne Wagner, 'Krasner's Presence, Pollock's Absence', in Whitney Chadwick (ed.), *Significant Others: Creativity and Intimate Partnership* (London: Thames and Hudson, 1993), 223–43. Lee Krasner stated: 'I was put together with the wives ... Rosenberg ... never acknowledged me as a painter, but as a widow, I was acknowledged.' Cited in Wagner, 'Krasner's Presence, Pollock's Absence', 223. To see how long a shadow Pollock cast, let me cite a letter complaining to Adrian Searle, the art critic of the London newspaper *The Guardian*, about his review of the newly opened exhibition *Lee Krasner: Living Colour* (Barbican, London, 30 May–1 September 2019): 'Some years ago I was bemused to see that Lee Krasner was labelled as "wife of Jackson Pollock" at the Tate Modern, while in the same room Jackson Pollock didn't seem to require to be anyone's husband. I thought we had moved on from this, but Adrian Searle's review of the new Krasner exhibition at the Barbican in London leaps rather than stumbles into the same trap. Krasner's husband is referred to throughout (including a sole mention in the headline!), as if we can only appreciate Krasner's work through the prism of the husband's life and work'. Richard Ingham, letter to *The Guardian*, 31 May 2019, www.theguardian.com/artanddesign/2019/may/31/lee-krasner-was-an-artist-not-just-a-wife (accessed 24 November 2021).

5   Lee Krasner in Cindy Nemser, 'The Indomitable Lee Krasner', *Feminist Art Journal*, 4 (1975), 9.

6   *Sun Woman I* was auctioned at Sotheby's New York on 14 November 2019, valued at 6–8 million dollars.

7   I want to acknowledge the art historian Bryony Fer, whose subtle and amazing study of abstraction taught me so much, including asking these basic questions about how artists move from one work to another. This counters retrospective narratives of progressive development. Bryony Fer, *On Abstract Art* (New Haven, CT: Yale University Press, 2000).

8   The concept is elaborated in my *Avant-Garde Gambits, 1888–1893: Gender and the Colour of Art History* (London: Thames and Hudson, 1992).

9   See my analysis of Monroe's *jouissant* performance and image as the classical *Nympha*, life force, rather than as Venus: 'Monroe's Gestures Between Trauma and Ecstasy: Reading the Cinematic Gesture "Marilyn Monroe" with Aby Warburg's Venus and Nymph', in Nicholas Chare and Elizabeth Watkins (eds), *Gesture in Cinema* (Abingdon: Routledge, 2016), 99–132.

10 Carol Duncan, 'Virility and Male Domination in Early Twentieth Century Vanguard Art', *Artforum* (December 1973), 30–39, reprinted in Carol Duncan, *The Aesthetics of Power: Essays in Critical Art History* (Cambridge: Cambridge University Press, 1993), 81–108; Carol Duncan, 'MoMA's Hot Mamas', *Art Journal*, 48.2 (1989), 171–78, reprinted in Duncan, *The Aesthetics of Power*, 189–210; Carol Duncan and Alan Wallach, 'Ordeal and Triumph on 53rd Street', *Studio International*, 194.9888 (1978), 48–57; and Carol Duncan and Alan Wallach, 'The Museum of Modern Art as Late Capitalist Ritual: An Iconographic Analysis', *Marxist Perspectives*, 4 (1978), 28–51.

11 Duncan and Wallach, 'The Museum of Modern Art as Late Capitalist Ritual', 28.

12 Duncan and Wallach, 'The Museum of Modern Art as Late Capitalist Ritual', 43.

13 Duncan and Wallach, 'The Museum of Modern Art as Late Capitalist Ritual', 48.

14 I elaborate on Monroe's creative conversations with and resistance to the dominant, even archetypal, phallocentric structuring of gender and fantasies of sexual difference in this decade in post-war US-America's twin cultural capitals in my forthcoming book *Monroe's Mov(i)es*.

15 This is another expression that aims to displace the nightmare of naturalizing phrases such as *female artists* at the same time as it serves to displace the nugatory qualifier 'woman' before artist. 'Woman' or any adjective qualifying the term artist in relation to race, class, sexuality, geopolitical or ethnic origin disqualifies that person from being considered artist *tout court.*

16 Mieke Bal and Norman Bryson, 'Semiotics and Art History', *Art Bulletin*, 73.2 (1991), 174–208, reprinted in Donald Preziosi (ed.), *The Art of Art History: A Critical Anthology* (Oxford: Oxford University Press, 1998), 242–56.

17 Pollock, 'Artists, Media and Mythologies'.

18 See Griselda Pollock, *Differencing the Canon: Feminist Desire and the Writing of Art's Histories* (London: Routledge, 1999), for an analysis drawing on Sarah Kofman's reading of Freud's aesthetic theory to explain the tenacity of the canon in the face of historical documentation and evidence. My question was: What keeps this canon in place? What psycho-subjective interests or even necessity is served by the idealization of the heroic artist-man? How does this also shape the fidelity of so many women, who as scholars and curators continue to service this canon? What other psycho-subjective dynamics produce the 'feminist' art historian, and create 'feminist desire for difference'?

19 On my understanding of the avant-garde as a cultural formation and a specific cultural consciousness, see Fred Orton and Griselda Pollock, 'Avant-Gardes and Partisans Reviewed', *Art History*, 4.3 (1981), 305–27, reprinted in Orton and Pollock, *Avant-Gardes and Partisans Reviewed*, 141–64.

20 *Reference* demonstrates the necessary knowledge of the current state of play and issues in this artistic fraction; *deference* involves an artistic gesture of recognition of who or what is currently a leading player or artistic play; *difference* is the artistic means by which the artist makes her or his play for recognition if not leadership in this competitive but conversational arena of the avant-garde community. See Pollock, *Avant-Garde Gambits*.

21 Rozsika Parker and Griselda Pollock, 'Critical Stereotypes: The Essential Feminine, or How Essential is Femininity?', in Parker and Pollock, *Old Mistresses*, 1–49/1–54. In this chapter, we argue that art historical discourse mentions almost no women as part of historical art movements, periods or styles, but does invoke some women selectively in order to identify signs of weakness and lack, with their definition of femininity. This strategically creates a negative cipher named femininity against which to establish the equation between art and masculinity in such a way that no gendering is apparent in the discussion of 'the artist'; all gendering falls on the women, their function thus being to serve as the negative to the unspoken positivization of solely masculine artists.

22 Lee Krasner in Nemser, 'Lee Krasner', 85.

23 Christine Gledhill (ed.), *Home is Where the Heart is: Studies in Melodrama and the Woman's Film* (London: BFI, 1987); Elisabeth Bronfen, *Home in Hollywood: The Imaginary Geography of Cinema* (New York: Columbia University Press, 2004).

24 Betty Friedan, *The Feminine Mystique* (New York; W. W. Norton, 1963). In 1957 Friedan interviewed her sister graduates from Smith College at a reunion, and her findings of universal discontent – the problem that has no name – led to her expanded research across this age group, the media, contemporary advertising and academic psychology. In its first year of publication over one million copies were sold. My father, travelling to the United States in 1964, bought a copy for my sister and me, thinking it would offer his daughters a guide to femininity. The effect was to make us both instantly ardent feminists. When I went to university in 1967, I so named myself, much to the ribald amusement of both the men I encountered and many of my fellow undergraduates at a women's college in Oxford. When, aged 50, we returned for our reunion with women who graduated one or even two years before

us, we found that very few of them had had careers, whereas almost all of my year or friendship network had taken on the message of Friedan and chosen careers, pursued in many cases with children. The impact of Friedan was immediate in my teens but was clearly flowing across our entire generation.

25   Les K. Adler and Thomas G. Peterson, 'Red Fascism: The Merger of Nazi Germany and Soviet Russia in the American Image of Totalitarianism, 1930s–1950s', *American Historical Review*, 75 (April 1977), 1046–64.

26   I use this date because it marks the culmination of the half-century struggle for the political emancipation of British women, then granted the vote, and it is linked culturally to two key publications in Britain: Virginia Woolf's *A Room of One's Own* and Radclyffe Hall's *The Well of Loneliness*. It also stands for a decade which politically and culturally represents a major moment not just of modernist culture but of the struggle for a 'new woman'. Beyond the false glamour of a slogan, this phrase represents a genuine exploration of modernization of the conditions of sexuality and sexual identity, and was epochal for the attempt to reconstruct the terms of sexual difference. It thus becomes another moment in which we can establish profound historical and philosophical connections between femininity, representation and modernity/modernism. The flowering of visual and literary, theatrical, cinematic and performance culture created by women internationally and in relation to class, gender, race and sexuality was effectively crushed by the emergence of the profoundly anti-feminist counter-revolution represented by fascism. The modernization of women's lives and cultures was stalled by economic disaster, fascism and world war, suspending the feminist revolution for at least two decades before its re-emergence in the later 1960s. Key texts for this period include literary studies such as Sheri Benstock, *Women of the Left Bank: Paris 1900–1940* (Austin, TX: University of Texas Press, 1987); Andrea Weiss, *Paris was a Woman: Portraits from the Left Bank* (London: Pandora, 1995); and in art history, Bridget Elliott and Jo-Ann Wallace, *Women Artists and Writers: Modernist (im)positionings* (London: Routledge, 1994), and Gillian Perry, *Women Artists and the Parisian Avant-Garde: Modernism and 'Feminine' Art 1900–1920s* (Manchester: Manchester University Press, 1995).

27   Friedan, *The Feminine Mystique*. We can read her landmark publication as a mapping of the ideological but also the economic and geographical separation of the spheres. Although Friedan's book was contested, she had delivered into the world 'the problem that has no name', the discontent of white middle-class women who appeared materially and educationally to have privilege but found the ideology of domestic and maternal femininity hollow. This ideology was disseminated in a range of Hollywood meldodramas that struggled to contain the contradictions that it generated between social role and expectation and women's desire. A classic example is *All That Heaven Allows* (dir. Douglas Sirk, 1955). See Gledhill, *Home is Where the Heart is.* In both Friedan's title and critical reviews, it is important to note the use of the term *feminine*, which then had wide currency in the sense of what is proper to women (domestic, passive, maternal), and what is also characteristic of women (in a negative sense: illogical, over-personal, non-objective).

28   See also Thomas Laqueur, *Making Sex: Body and Gender From the Greeks to Freud* (Cambridge, MA: Harvard University Press, 1990); Catherine Gallagher and Thomas Laqueur, *The Making of the Modern Body: Sexuality and Society in the Nineteenth Century* (Berkeley, CA: University of California Press, 1987); Michel Foucault, *La volonté de savoir* (Paris: Gallimard, 1976); Michel Foucault, *The History of Sexuality: An Introduction: Volume 1*, trans. Robert Hurley (London: Penguin, 1978).

29   Denise Riley, *'Am I That Name?' Feminism and the Category of 'Woman' in History* (Basingstoke: Macmillan, 1988), 15.

30 Such views were collected by Cindy Nemser, a post-1968 feminist critic who interviewed many of the major modernist artist-women such as Barbara Hepworth and Sonia Delaunay in the later 1960s and early 1970s. These interviews were published as *Art Talk: Conversations with Twelve Women Artists* (New York: Scribners, 1975). For a longer assessment of the paradox that modernism created for artist-women and why the generation between 1928 and 1968 foreswore feminism and reasonably embraced the modernist stance of indifference to gender, see Griselda Pollock, 'Painting, Feminism and History', in Michèle Barrett and Anne Phillips (eds), *Destabilising Theory: Western Feminism 1970s–1980s* (Cambridge: Polity, 1992), 138–76, reprinted in revised form as 'Feminism, History and Contemporary Practice in the Visual Arts', in Griselda Pollock, *Looking Back to the Future: Essays on Art, Life and Death from the 1990s* (London: Routledge, 1999), 40–52.

31 On modernist criticism suspended between the definition of art as transcendent truth and objective purpose, see Kelly, 'Re-Viewing Modernist Criticism'.

32 The words are by British lyricist Bernie Taupin, set to music by Elton John on the album *Goodbye Yellow Brick Road*, and released as a single in 1974.

Chapter 2

1 According to New York writer Anita Loos in her novella of 1925, *Gentlemen Prefer Blondes*. See also Joanna Pitman, *On Blondes – From Aphrodite to Madonna: Why Blondes Have More Fun* (London: Bloomsbury, 2003).

2 Teresa Podlesney, 'Blondes', in Arthur Kroker and Marilouise Kroker (eds), *The Hysterical Male: New Feminist Theory* (New York: St. Martin's Press, 1991), 7.

3 See Laura Mulvey's analysis of the condensation of spectacle and commodity, 'Close-ups and Commodities', in *Fetishism and Curiosity* (London: BFI, 1996), 40–52.

4 An article on the Abstract Expressionists featuring Jackson Pollock was titled 'The Wild Ones', *Time*, 20 February 1956, 75; Pollock was also posthumously linked with James Dean, whose death preceded Pollock's own by just one year.

5 See Andrew Perchuk, 'Pollock and Postwar Masculinity', in Donald McMahon (ed.), *The Masculine Masquerade: Masculinity and Representation* (Cambridge, MA: MIT Press, 199), 31–43.

6 Podlesney, 'Blondes', 76.

7 Julie Burchill, *Girls on Film* (New York: Pantheon, 1986), 175. The Actors Studio was founded in October 1947 by Cheryl Crawford, a director, and the actor Elia Kazan.

8 The initiating text of a feminist resistance was Friedan, *The Feminine Mystique*. It was an answer to an influential conservative text published in 1947 that inveighed against the dangers to women and men of the modernizing effects of women entering the workplace: Marynia Farnham and Ferdinand Lundberg, *Modern Woman: The Lost Sex* (New York: Harper and Brothers, 1947). 'Rosie the Riveter' was invoked in a song composed in 1942 to celebrate the women who came to work on the assembly lines during the Second World War. Leaving the home, Rosie worked in heavy industry while her boyfriend Charlie was a Marine on active service.

9 Serge Guilbaut, *How New York Stole the Idea of Modern Art: Abstract Expressionism, Freedom and the Cold War* (Chicago: University of Chicago Press, 1983).

10 Sandler, *The Triumph of American Painting*; Cockcroft, 'Abstract Expressionism: Weapon of the Cold War'.

11 Lee Krasner's first major one-person retrospective took place in England in 1965 at the Whitechapel Art Gallery, *Lee Krasner: Paintings, Drawings and Collages*. Marcia Tucker curated *Lee Krasner: Large Paintings* at the Whitney Museum of American

Art in 1974. Significant interventions were made by the writings and research of Ellen G. Landau, Eleanor Munro, Cindy Nemser and Barbara Rose after 1970. In 1995 Landau published the first complete catalogue of Krasner: Ellen G. Landau and Jeffrey D. Grove, *Lee Krasner. A Catalogue Raisonné* (New York: Harry Abrams, 1995).

12   Clement Greenberg, 'Towards a Newer Laocoon', *Partisan Review*, 7.4 (194), 303.

13   Bryony Fer, 'Poussière/peinture: Bataille on Painting', in Carolyn Bailey Gill (ed.), *Bataille – Writing the Sacred* (London: Routledge, 1995), 155. Fer is citing Maurice Raynal, *Anthologie de la peinture en France de 1906 à nos jours* (Paris: Editions Montaigne, 1927), 34, and Tristan Tzara, 'Le papier collé ou le proverbe en peinture', *Cahiers d'Art*, 6 (1931), 2. I am indebted to Bryony Fer's essay for this line of argument.

14   Georges Bataille, *Manet* [1955] (Paris: Skira, 1994), 28, 'une totalité intelligible'. I am grateful to Adrian Rifkin for drawing this text to my attention many decades ago.

15   Bataille, *Manet*, 55. 'Dans l'un et l'autre cas, le texte est *effacé* par le tableau. *Et ce que le tableau signifie n'est pas le texte, mais l'éffacement*' (original emphasis). Bataille uses other metaphors in subsequent paragraphs, such as suppression and pulverization, to define this destructive liberation of painting concluding with the nude painting *Olympia*: 'ce qu'elle est, est "l'horreur sacré" de sa presence – d'une presence dont la simplicité est celle de l'absence' (*Manet*, 55).

16   Newspaper art critic Adrian Searle's review in 2019 of the first exhibition of Lee Krasner's work in Britain since 1965 appeared under the headline 'Storms of Colour from a Wild Destructive Genius'.

17   Bataille, *Manet*, 37.

18   Fer, 'Poussière/peinture: Bataille on Painting', 160.

19   Laura Mulvey, 'Pandora's Box: Topographies of the Mask and Curiosity', in Beatriz Colomina (ed.), *Sexuality and Space* (Princeton, NJ: Princeton Architectural Press, 1992), 53–72.

20   Eight paintings and some photographs were exhibited in *Absent Bodies/Present Lives*, City Art Gallery, Leeds, 1993. The work is in the collection of the artist.

21   John Hoberman, 'Korea and a Career', *Artforum*, 32.5 (1994), 11.

22   These events are briefly mentioned in Podlesney, 'Blondes', 75.

23   *Playboy*, 1.1 (December 1953), 17: 'blonde all over'; 'Monroe is the juiciest morsel to come out of the California hills since the discovery of the navel orange.'

24   Simone de Beauvoir, *The Second Sex* [1949], trans. and ed. H. M. Parshley (London: Jonathan Cape, 1953). I quote from my own copy, acquired in 1964 (London: Four Square Books, 1964), 9. Parshley abridged the original and modified de Beauvoir's philosophical language. In 2011 Constance Borde and Sheila Malovany-Chevallier retranslated the original in its integrity.

25   Simone de Beauvoir, *The Second Sex*, trans. Constance Borde and Sheila Malovany-Chevallier (London: Vintage, 2011), 293.

26   Donald Spoto, *Marilyn Monroe: The Biography* (New York: Harper Collins, 1993), 231.

27   Elizabeth Winder, *Marilyn in Manhattan: Her Year of Joy* (New York: Flatiron Books, 2017).

28   In relation to *Seated Woman* c. 1940, we read: 'While the willful anatomical distortions reflect the influence of Pablo Picasso, the seated figure also recalls the sensuous women painted by the nineteenth-century French artist Jean-Auguste-Dominique Ingres, with their tightly fitted bodices and delicate features.' Philadelphia Museum of Art, https://philamuseum.org/collection/object/69312 (accessed 5 August 2021). For more detailed reference to Picasso's *Woman with a Mandolin* (1910), see David Sylvester, 'The Birth of *Woman I*', *Burlington Magazine*, 37.1105 (1995), 225–29.

29   Sylvester, 'The Birth of *Woman I*', 223.

30 Eve Arnold suggests that Marilyn Monroe was the image behind 'his lively paintings of women', in Eve Arnold, *Marilyn Monroe – An Appreciation* (London: Hamish Hamilton, 1987), 12. We should contest this view since the iconic 'Marilyn Monroe' emerged during 1953, and de Kooning himself was in dialogue with the entire tradition of figurative representations of women from Venus to Manet's *Olympia* and Picasso's *Demoiselles d'Avignon*; see Emilo de Antonio and Mitch Tuchman, *Painters Painting: A Candid History of the Modern Art Scene 1940–1970* (New York: Abbeville Press, 1984), 53–54.

31 Antonio Lara, 'Sensualidad e Inocencia: Las peliculas de Marilyn Monroe [Sensuality and Innocence in the Films of Marilyn Monroe]', *Cuadernos del Norte*, 8.43 (1987), 61–68.

32 Janice Anderson, *Marilyn Monroe: Quote Unquote* (London: Paragon, 1994), 42.

33 Quoted in Hoberman, 'Korea and a Career', 11.

34 Richard Dyer, *Heavenly Bodies: Film Stars and Society* (New York: St. Martin's Press, 1986), 42–43.

35 Dyer, *Heavenly Bodies*, 44.

36 Podlesney, 'Blondes', 72. This idea is listed as one of the four genealogies of the blonde phenomenon that tie it specifically to a moment of production in the 1950s.

37 Dyer, *Heavenly Bodies*, 45.

38 Angela Carter, *The Sadeian Woman* (London: Virago, 1979), 63.

39 Luce Irigaray, 'Women on the Market' and 'Commodities Among Themselves', in *This Sex Which Is Not One* [1977], trans. Catherine Porter (Ithaca, NY: Cornell University Press, 1985), 170–97.

40 Arnold, *Marilyn Monroe*, 27, on cosmetic secrets; 11, on her management of her mouth to reduce the size of her nose in photographs.

41 'Pollock was virtually unknown in 1944. Now his paintings hang in five U.S. museums and 40 private collections. Exhibiting in New York last winter, he sold 12 out of 18 pictures. Moreover, his work has stirred up a fuss in Italy, and this autumn he is slated for a one-man show in avant-garde Paris, where he is fast becoming the most talked-of and controversial U.S. painter.' Sieberling, 'Is he the greatest living painter in the United States?'. On Newman, see 'American Artists Photographed by Arnold Newman', *Art in America*, 53 (1965), 106–13.

42 Cited in Stephen Naifeh and Gregory White Smith, *Jackson Pollock: An American Saga* (New York: Clarkston N. Potter, 1989), 595.

43 For a reading of these photographs, see Fred Orton and Griselda Pollock, 'Jackson Pollock, Painting and the Myth of Photography', *Art History*, 6.1 (1983), 114–22, reprinted in Orton and Pollock, *Avant-Gardes and Partisans Reviewed*, 165–76.

44 Duncan, 'Virility and Male Domination'.

45 See Pollock, 'Painting, Feminism and History'.

46 Thomas Craven and Thomas Hart Benton in 1950 and 1951 accused Pollock of making these drip paintings by eating the paint and then urinating on the canvas. Naifeh and White Smith, *Jackson Pollock*, 631.

47 The major statement of this genealogy is Courbet's *The Painter's Studio: A Real Allegory of Seven Years of My Life* (1855, Paris Musée d'Orsay).

48 Andreas Huyssen, 'Mass Culture as Woman: Modernism's Other', in *After the Great Divide: Modernism, Mass Culture and Postmodernism* (Basingstoke: Macmillan, 1986), 44–62, argues for the historical dialectic between the feminization of mass culture and the masculinization of the modernist project defining itself as the discipline of self-authentication through dedication to the textuality of its own practice.

49 Cockcroft, 'Abstract Expressionism: Weapon of the Cold War'.

50   For Laura Mulvey's analysis of Cindy Sherman, fetishism and femininity and the Eisenhower decade, see 'A Phantasmagoria of the Female Body: The Work of Cindy Sherman', *New Left Review*, 188 (1991), 137–50.

Chapter 3

1   Bracha L. Ettinger, 'Matrix and Metramorphosis', *differences: A Journal of Feminist Cultural Studies*, 4.3 (1992), 195–96, reprinted in Bracha L. Ettinger, *Matrixial Subjectivity, Aesthetics, Ethics, Vol. 1: 1990–2000*, ed. Griselda Pollock (Basingstoke: Palgrave Macmillan, 2020), 118–19. Subsequent references are to the reprint version.

2   This subtitle relates to an article I wrote at the time of Greenberg's death, 'Pollock on Greenberg', *Art Monthly*, 178 (1994).

3   Clement Greenberg, 'Louis and Noland', *Art International*, 4.5 (1960), reprinted in Clement Greenberg, *The Collected Essays and Criticism, Volume 4: Modernism with a Vengeance 1957–69*, ed. John O'Brien (Chicago: University of Chicago Press, 1993), 94–100.

4   Clement Greenberg, 'Changer: Anne Truitt', *Vogue* (May 1968), reprinted in Greenberg, *The Collected Essays and Criticism, Volume 4*, 288–91. The other references to artist-women are passim in the four volumes of Greenberg's criticism edited by John O'Brien.

5   Clement Greenberg, '"American-Type" Painting', *Partisan Review*, 22.2 (1955), reprinted in *Art and Culture: Critical Essays by Clement Greenberg* (Boston, MA: Beacon Press, 1961), 208–29.

6   Pollock, 'Back to the Twentieth Century', 147.

7   It has been said that Pollock reacted tragically to Namuth's photographs and specifically to Namuth's attempt to film him painting outside and on glass with the camera beneath the transparent surface. It was so disturbing to Pollock to be watched in his trance state, in which he had hitherto worked alone, and to be forced to perform his painting practice for the camera, that he subsequently broke from his years of abstinence from alcohol and slipped into the grip of the disease that reclaimed him and disabled him from painting much for the rest of his shortened life.

8   Clement Greenberg, 'The Crisis of the Easel Picture' [1948], in *Art and Culture*, 154–57.

9   For a monumental text on Jackson Pollock's paintings 1947–50 based on such a reading, see T. J. Clark, 'The Unhappy Unconscious', in *Farewell to an Idea: Episodes from a History of Modernism* (New Haven, CT: Yale University Press, 1999), 299–369. 'The studio photographs are a treasure trove. The process of reflection and judgement seems to have been interminable in some cases, and according to Krasner, not something Pollock relished: pictures were set up straight, tried out with more than one orientation, made to dance with others, finessed with brush and finger, conjured away by new layers, sometimes abandoned' (Clark, 'The Unhappy Unconscious', 327).

10   I allude to *écriture féminine*, proposed by Hélène Cixous to suggest a way in which a new form of writing by women might explore the specificities of feminine psychic modalities by drawing on the semiotic resources of the drives and the body's inchoate pleasures. See 'The Laugh of the Medusa', trans. Annette Kuhn, in Elaine Marks and Isabelle de Courtivron (eds), *New French Feminisms* (Brighton: Harvester Press, 1980), 245–64. The phrase *écriture féminine* is translated as 'writing the body'. See Lisa Tickner and Jon Bird, *Nancy Spero* (London: Institute of Contemporary Art, 1987).

11   *Wit(h)ness* is Bracha Ettinger's composite of the term *witness* – both in its legal sense and as used in more recent studies of traumatic events that deliver testimony from the survivors of the Holocaust, for instance – and the word *withness*, a condition of much

more than solidarity. *Wit(h)ness* stands for *the impossibility-of-not-sharing* the other's pain or event. Two subjective modalities coexist in this one word, standing beside to affirm the suffering of another, and being unable to escape being co-affected by and ethically responsive to another whose wound I do not and cannot know. Extended into the condition such as the painter and the world, the painter and her/his passions and pain, the viewer and the painting, *wit(h)ness* posits a non-mastering rapport with an event that remains other but nonetheless affects us and transforms us. It is a thesis on aesthetics and the ethical position of both artist and viewer that gives rise to Ettinger's thesis on 'Art as the Transport Station of Trauma', in *Bracha Ettinger: Artworking 1985–1999*, ed. Brian Massumi (Ghent: Ludion, 2000), 91–116, reprinted in Ettinger, *Matrixial Subjectivity, Aesthetics, Ethics, Vol. 1: 1990–2000*, 325–46.

12   Ettinger, 'Matrix and Metramorphosis', 124.

13   Ettinger proposed this concept in the later 1980s and it was published in texts throughout the 1990s. We know that the makers of the movie of this name, *The Matrix* (1999), were inspired by her texts and concepts.

14   Ettinger, 'Matrix and Metramorphosis', 124.

15   Bracha L. Ettinger, *The Matrixial Gaze* (Leeds: Feminist Arts and Histories Network Press, 1995), reprinted in Bracha L. Ettinger, *The Matrixial Borderspace*, ed. Brian Massumi (Minneapolis, MN: University of Minnesota Press, 2006), 44–92.

16   Rowley, *Helen Frankenthaler*.

17   Luce Irigaray, *Marine Lover of Friedrich Nietzsche*, trans. Gillian Gill (New York: Columbia University Press, 1991).

18   Luce Irigaray, *This Sex Which Is Not One* [1977], trans. Catherine Porter (Ithaca, NY: Cornell University Press, 1985), 109–10.

19   Hilary Robinson, *Reading Art, Reading Irigaray: The Politics of Art by Women* (London: I.B. Tauris, 2006).

20   In French the formulation would be heard as *the mucous-like,* closer to *mucosity*. It is not a thing but a non-solid condition or attribute.

21   Luce Irigaray, 'The Three Genders' [1987], in *Sexes and Genealogies*, trans. Gillian C. Gill (New York: Columbia University Press, 1993), 180.

22   Jardine referencing Luce Irigaray, *The Speculum of the Other Woman* [1974], trans. Gillian C. Gill (Ithaca, NY: Cornell University Press, 1985), in 'Writing as Woman', in *Je, tu, nous: Toward a Culture of Difference*, trans. Alison Martin (London: Routledge, 1993), 58.

23   Irigaray, 'Writing as Woman', 59.

24   Robinson, *Reading Art, Reading Irigaray*, 101.

25   On the importance and meaning of this radical challenge, see Pheng Cheah and Elisabeth Grosz, 'On Being Two: An Introduction', *Diacritics*, 28.1 (2018), 2–18. They quote Irigaray: 'Replacing the one by the two of sexual difference thus constitutes a decisive philosophical and political move, one which gives up a singular or plural being. This is a necessary foundation for a new ontology, a new ethics, a new politics, in which the other is recognized as other and not as the same: bigger or smaller than I, at best equal.' Luce Irigaray, 'The Question of the Other', trans. Noah Guynn, *Yale French Studies*, 87 (1995), 19.

26   Irigaray, *This Sex Which is Not One*, 26.

27   Robinson, *Reading Art, Reading Irigaray*, 104.

28   Robinson, *Reading Art, Reading Irigaray*, 107.

29   Luce Irigaray, 'The Limits of Transference', in Margaret Whitford (ed.), *The Irigaray Reader* (Oxford: Blackwell, 1991), 106.

30   Cheah and Grosz, 'On Being Two: An Introduction', 4.

31   Pollock, 'Inscriptions in the Feminine'. My term was taken over for the subtitle.

32   Alice Jardine, *Gynesis: Configurations of Women and Modernity* (Ithaca, NY: Cornell University Press, 1986). Gynesis is derived from the Greek γυνή gynē, woman, which also gives us gynaecology.

33   Elaine Marks and Isabelle de Courtivron (eds), *New French Feminisms: An Anthology* (Brighton: Harvester Press, 1980); Claire Duchen, *Feminism in France: From May '68 to Mitterrand* (London: Routledge, 1986); Toril Moi, *French Feminist Thought: A Reader* (Oxford: Blackwell, 1987).

34   Jardine, *Gynesis*, 25.

35   Jardine, *Gynesis*, 25.

36   Jardine, *Gynesis*, 25.

37   Alice Jardine and Paul Smith (eds), *Men in Feminism* (London: Methuen, 1987).

38   Jardine, *Gynesis*, 25–26.

39   Shoshana Felman, *What Does a Woman Want? Reading and Sexual Difference* (Baltimore, MD: Johns Hopkins University Press, 1993).

40   Felman, *What Does a Woman Want?*, 3.

41   Felman, *What Does a Woman Want?*, 3.

42   Felman, *What Does a Woman Want?*, 8.

43   Felman, *What Does a Woman Want?*, 11.

44   For a stunning reading of the significance of the Girl in the overall thesis of 'becoming woman', see Elspeth Mitchell, 'The Girl and Simone de Beauvoir's *Second Sex*: Feminine Becomings', *Australian Feminist Studies*, 93 (2017), 269–75.

45   de Beauvoir, *The Second Sex*, trans. Borde and Malovany-Chevallier, 294.

46   Felman, *What Does a Woman Want?*, 14.

47   Felman, *What Does a Woman Want?*, 14.

48   Felman, *What Does a Woman Want?*, 14.

49   Felman, *What Does a Woman Want?*, 14.

50   Saltzman, 'Reconsidering the Stain', 374.

51   Saltzman, 'Reconsidering the Stain', 374.

52   For example, Kelly, 'On Sexual Politics and Art'. Mary Kelly also wrote on modernist criticism in an influential article, 'Re-Viewing Modernist Criticism'.

53   Julia Kristeva, 'La Femme n'est jamais ça' [Woman can never be defined], interview with *psych & po*, *Tel Quel* (1974), reprinted in translation in Marks and de Courtivron (eds), *New French Feminisms*, 137–41.

54   Eva Hesse (1936–70), about a decade younger than the New York modernist painters I am discussing here, read Simone de Beauvoir with great interest in the early 1960s, finding that she offered some way to understand the contradictions Hesse faced being both an artist and woman in New York's artworld. Diary entry 21 November 1964, cited in Lucy Lippard, *Eva Hesse* (New York: New York University Press, 1976), 26.

55   This is how she is referred to by painter Morris Louis in a discussion of her work in an article in 1960 on the colour field painters based in Washington DC, Morris Louis and Kenneth Noland. Greenberg, 'Louis and Noland'.

56   For instance, Lee Krasner came from a working-class, immigrant, Russian Jewish community, while Helen Frankenthaler's family was of German descent and her father was a judge. Anna Chave, 'Frankenthaler's Fortune: On Class Privilege and the Artist's Reception', *Woman's Art Journal*, 37.1 (2016), 29–36. Nell Blaine (1922–96) was born with a serious eye condition that was not corrected until she was in her teens. After a marriage ended, she lived her life as a queer woman. Alma Thomas (1891–1976) was an African American Abstract Expressionist who studied at Howard University in Washington as the first graduate of the Fine Arts Programme in 1924, and was the first African American woman to earn a degree in Fine Arts. She earned her living as a high school teacher, becoming a professional artist only in 1960 when she retired, and having her first retrospective in 1966. An African American

abstract painter of the next generation, Howardena Pindell (b. 1943), graduated in Fine Arts from Yale in 1967 but was obliged to work as a curator for twelve years before she got a teaching post as a professor of Fine Arts. Grace Hartigan (1922–2008) came to painting without formal art education but exhibited under the name George Hartigan in order to gain recognition for her paintings, which sold well and were acquired for the Museum of Modern Art as early as 1953. She was the only artist-woman to be included in *The New American Painting* exhibition that toured Europe in 1958–59. Appearing in *Life* in 1957, she was hailed as 'the most celebrated of the young American women painters'. Cited in William Grimes, 'Grace Hartigan, 86, Abstract Painter, Dies', *New York Times*, 18 November 2008, www.nytimes.com/2008/11/18/arts/design/18hartigan.html (accessed 7 December 2021).

57 Bett Schumacher, 'The Woman Gender: Gender Displacement in the Art of Helen Frankenthaler', *Woman's Art Journal*, 31.2 (2010), 12–21.

58 Schumacher, 'The Woman Gender', 14.

59 Schumacher, 'The Woman Gender', 14–15.

60 Henry Geldzahler, 'Interview with Helen Frankenthaler', *Art Forum*, 4.2 (1965), 37.

61 Geldzahler, 'Interview with Helen Frankenthaler'; Michael Podro '"The landscape thinks itself in me": The Comments and Procedures of Cézanne', *International Review of Psycho-Analysis*, 17.4 (1990), 401–12. The statement was made by Cézanne to Emile Bernard, *Souvenirs sur Paul Cézanne* (Paris: Société des Trente, 1912), 250. Alison Rowley has established the impact of an exhibition of Cézanne's work in New York on Frankenthaler and Greenberg.

62 Rowley, *Helen Frankenthaler*, 21.

63 In the early 1970s, in discussion with Fred Orton who was devising teaching material on New York painting in the 1950s for Fine Art students at Leicester Polytechnic, I boldly challenged his all-male course outline. He replied that I could deliver three lectures for him. I chose to talk about Helen Frankenthaler, Louise Nevelson and Eva Hesse. I tracked the double-speak of critical writing which both reviewed these artists and gender stereotyped them.

64 Roger Fry, *Cézanne: A Study of his Development* (London: Macmillan, 1927).

65 Roger Fry to Robert Bridges, 23 January 1924, in Roger Fry, *Last Lectures* (Cambridge: Cambridge University Press, 1939), 229. Fry began as a connoisseurial specialist in Renaissance painting before becoming interested in recent French art, which he introduced to London with his *Manet and the Post-Impressionists* exhibition at the Grafton Galleries in 1911. He is associated with what is termed formalism.

66 Rowley, *Helen Frankenthaler*, 37.

67 Rowley, *Helen Frankenthaler*, 38.

68 Rowley, *Helen Frankenthaler*, 38. She means that Freud's story concerns a little boy negotiating loss through play, and Woolf's novel and her character are negotiating loss from the feminine position.

69 Maurice Merleau-Ponty, 'Cézanne's Doubt' and 'Eye and Mind' [1960], in Galen A. Johnson (ed.), *The Merleau-Ponty Aesthetics Reader: Philosophy and Painting* (Evanston, IL: Northwestern University Press, 1993), 3–13, 121–50.

70 Rowley, *Helen Frankenthaler*, 70.

71 Rowley, *Helen Frankenthaler*, 70.

72 Rowley, *Helen Frankenthaler*, 70.

73 Ettinger, *The Matrixial Gaze*, 65. This and subsequent references are to the reprinted version in *The Matrixial Borderspace*, ed. Massumi.

74 Rowley, *Helen Frankenthaler*, 70.

75 Ettinger, *The Matrixial Gaze*, 41.

76 Rowley, *Helen Frankenthaler*, 69.

77 Kristeva, 'La Femme n'est jamais ça', 137. There is no positive definition of 'woman' but a constant negation of attempts to fix a meaning for it. This rehearses de

Beauvoir's classic statement that one 'becomes' this creature that is named woman. One is not born so.

78   I am drawing here on Michèle Montrelay, 'Inquiry into Femininity', *m/f*, 1 (1978), 83–102.

79   Jacques Derrida, 'Différance', in *Margins of Philosophy*, trans. Alan Bass (Chicago: University of Chicago Press, 1982), 1–28. I used this Derridean model in my book, *Differencing the Canon*.

80   To give an example of the 'feminine stereotype': 'It was appropriate that she adopted this particular technique. It is free, lyrical and feminine – very different from the more insistent rhythms in the best and most typical Pollocks … Indeed, as this kind of art is completely involved with the physical act of painting (not only with the fingers, or the hand, or the wrist, or the arm, but with the entire body) we recognize a sexual analogy. Her palette, too, is seductive and feminine, often … dominated by pale muted pinks, blues, yellows and greens; rarely harsh or overpowering.' B. H. Friedman, 'Towards the Total Color Image', *Art News*, 65 (1966), 32.

81   Barbara Rose, *Helen Frankenthaler* (New York: Harry Abrams, 1970), 57.

82   Greenberg, '"American-Type" Painting'; 'Louis and Noland'.

83   T. J. Clark, 'Jackson Pollock's Abstraction', in Serge Guilbaut (ed.), *Reconstructing Modernism* (Cambridge, MA: MIT Press, 1990), 229.

84   Kelly, 'Re-Viewing Modernist Criticism'.

85   Griselda Pollock, 'Agency and the Avant-Garde: Studies in Authorship and Art History by Way of Van Gogh', *Block*, 15 (1989), 5–15, reprinted in Orton and Pollock, *Avant-Gardes and Partisans Reviewed*, 315–42.

Chapter 4

1   Laura Mulvey, 'Visual Pleasure and Narrative Cinema', *Screen*, 16.3 (1975), 7, reprinted in Laura Mulvey, *Visual and Other Pleasures* (Basingstoke: Macmillan, 1989), 15.

2   Both quotations are cited in *Pittura/Panorama: Paintings by Helen Frankenthaler 1952–1992*, Museo di Palazzo Grimani, Venice (New York: Gagosian, 2019), 32, from John Elderfield, *Helen Frankenthaler* (New York: Harry Abrams, 1989), 62, and Deborah Solomon, 'Helen Frankenthaler: Artful Survivor', *New York Times Magazine*, 14 May 1989, 63, 76.

3   Kenneth Clark, *The Nude: A Study in Ideal Art* (London: John Murray, 1956).

4   E. Ann Kaplan, 'Is the Gaze Male?', in *Women & Film: Both Sides of the Camera* (London : Methuen, 1983), 23–35.

5   Mulvey, 'Visual Pleasure and Narrative Cinema', 8.

6   Mulvey, 'Visual Pleasure and Narrative Cinema', 11.

7   Mulvey, 'Visual Pleasure and Narrative Cinema', 7.

8   Luce Irigaray, 'Gesture in Psychoanalysis' [1985], in *Sexes and Genealogies*, trans. Gillian C. Gill (New York: Columbia University Press, 1993), 91–104; Robinson, *Reading Art, Reading Irigaray*.

9   'Sexual difference is one of the major philosophical issues, if not the issue, of our age.' Luce Irigaray, 'Sexual Difference', in *An Ethics of Sexual Difference* [1984], trans. Carolyn Burke and Gillian C. Gill (London: Athlone, 1993), 5.

10   For a rigorous exploration of Irigaray's propositions, see Pheng Cheah and Elizabeth Grosz, 'The Future of Sexual Difference: An Interview with Judith Butler and Drucilla Cornell', *Diacritics*, 28.1 (1998), 19–42; Cheah and Grosz, 'On Being Two: An Introduction'.

11   One of the key debates was between American writer Kate Millett (*Sexual Politics* [New York: Doubleday, 1970]) and Juliet Mitchell, whose *Psychoanalysis and*

Feminism (London: Penguin, 1974) mounts the argument for feminist theoretical engagement with psychoanalysis.

12 Sigmund Freud, 'Beyond the Pleasure Principle' [1920], in *The Standard Edition of the Complete Psychological Works of Sigmund Freud, Vol. XVIII, 1920–22*, ed. James Strachey (London: Hogarth Press, 1955), 1–64.

13 Irigaray, 'Gesture in Psychoanalysis', 97. This is a problematic statement because it attributes to the female child an implicit knowledge of an identity in common with the mother at the very point at which separation and loss are only just precipitating the child into a forced sense of its distinctness from the maternal body and world. Obviously all these events hypothesized to explain the trajectory of human entry into language and subjectivity always take place in an already sexually marked world where there is no moment absolutely free of the weight of culturally projected sexual difference. Moreover, we might argue that the girl-child has no need to imagine a sameness because the pre-Oedipal child has no means of imagining a difference from the mother; it is the tragedy of the boy-child to be obliged to admit its unlikeness. The very ambiguity of this moment is important for the subsequent development of my argument about sexual difference and the act of making art. Beyond that point, however, lies the possibility that a non-Oedipal sense of relations of difference between part-subjects is an element of our most archaic formation, which comes before the structures of psychic life that produce the subject–object, the self–other opposition. See Ettinger, 'Matrix and Metramorphosis'.

14 Irigaray, 'Gesture in Psychoanalysis', 97.

15 I am indebted to Alison Rowley for this formulation. See her 'On Viewing Three Paintings by Jenny Saville: Rethinking a Feminist Practice of Painting', in Griselda Pollock (ed.), *Generations and Geographies in the Visual Arts: Feminist Readings* (London: Routledge, 1996), 88–111. This whole argument can be taken much further into a theoretical territory around the borderline visibility and the matrixial *objet a*; that is, another theorization of the specificities of the feminine significations of loss. For her full analysis, see Rowley, *Helen Frankenthaler*.

16 Irigaray, 'Gesture in Psychoanalysis', 99.

17 I am deeply indebted to Alison Rowley for conversations about this issue in particular.

18 Pierre Fédida, *L'Absence* (Paris: Gallimard, 1978), 191–2; translation by Ettinger, *The Matrixial Gaze*, 80–81.

19 Ettinger, *The Matrixial Gaze*, 80, citing Fédida, *L'Absence*, 193, 134.

20 In her theorization of a supplementary dimension in all subjectivity incited in the aesthetic imprints of later prenatal-prematernal co-emergence, Ettinger proposed the symbol of the Matrix, to modify the solely phallocentric accounts of the formation of subjectivity and sexuation in Freudian and Lacanian theory. The Matrix provides a symbol to make thinkable an additional dimension of human becoming. It raises such becoming to the level of symbol and is thus freed from the metaphorics associated with pregnancy and prenatality in phallic culture where the organ, or space, of the womb is treated as either a biological oven, a deadly interior or a utopian inside associated with the relief of death. The Matrix symbolizes an aesthetic and proto-ethical borderspace shared asymmetrically by partial (the pre-infant) and partialized (the prematernal) co-affecting becoming subjects. Its figure for engendering of meaning and affect is metramorphosis, thus displacing the phallic figures of metaphor and metonymy, terms of substitution. It was first elaborated in Ettinger in 'Matrix and Metramorphosis' in 1992, and further situated in cultural and feminist theory by Griselda Pollock, 'Thinking the Feminine: Aesthetic Practice as Introduction to Bracha Ettinger and the Concepts of Matrix and Metramorphosis', *Theory, Culture and Society*, 21.1 (2004), 5–65. Ettinger's 1992 article opens Bracha L. Ettinger, *Matrixial Aesthetics, Ethics and Subjectivity Volume 1*, ed. Griselda Pollock, 93–130.

21   Ettinger, *The Matrixial Gaze*, 82.

22   Ettinger, *The Matrixial Gaze*, 82.

23   The elaboration of Ettinger's theory followed over many papers now collected in the edited volumes of her writings. See Ettinger, *Matrixial Subjectivity, Aesthetics, Ethics, Vol. 1 1990–2000*, ed. Pollock.

24   The Matrix and its figure, metramorphosis, coexist with the Phallus and its figures, metaphor and metonymy. The latter produce figurative meaning through substitution or association, while metramorphosis refers to non-centred, transformative sharing and transgression of limits and borders.

25   The term Other is not used anthropologically to refer to a subject different from the viewing or speaking subject. In Lacanian usage the Other is not a subject but that which structures the subject's coming into existence. It is the place of Law, Language, a position on the grid in relation to which all the various actors in the drama of subjectivity are positioned. At different moments in the process of subject formation, different figures can be assumed to represent the Other for the subject that comes into existence only as an effect of that relation. Feminists intervene to ask how sexual difference is mapped into this other example of neutered language – the Other/the subject. As Lacan argued, the speaking subject, hence the subject, is sexed: the accession to the Symbolic occurs via the Oedipal trauma. The term *m/Other* was introduced by Bracha L. Ettinger, and it marks the trace of the maternal – not the actual mother person but the function and moment of the condition of all our existences as gestated, matured bodies and potentially psychic entities that cohabited the maternal body and passed out of it, but not beyond its sensate memory trace. The Other is not the mother – but equally the Other is not without the maternal as one of its moments and elements, despite what phallocentric culture with its mother-denying, neutral-paternal philosophies try to imply.

26   Bracha L. Ettinger, '*Fascinance*: Girl to M/Other Matrixial Sexual Difference', in Griselda Pollock (ed.), *Psychoanalysis and the Image* (Oxford: Blackwell, 2006), 67.

27   Ettinger, '*Fascinance*', 67.

28   Ettinger, '*Fascinance*', 70.

29   Ettinger, '*Fascinance*', 70.

30   Ettinger, '*Fascinance*', 70.

31   Irigaray, 'Gesture in Psychoanalysis', 98.

32   Ettinger, '*Fascinance*', 66.

33   Ettinger, '*Fascinance*', 66–67.

34   On Rosenberg's Marxist concept of action, see Fred Orton, 'Action, Revolution and Painting', *Oxford Art Journal*, 14.2 (1991), 3–17, reprinted in Orton and Pollock, *Avant-Gardes and Partisans Reviewed*, 177–203. See Chapter 8.

35   Friedman, 'Towards the Total Color Image', 32; Clark, 'Jackson Pollock's Abstraction', 229.

36   'It seems to be a law of modernism – thus one that applies to almost all art that remains truly alive in our times – that the conventions not essential to the viability of a medium be discarded as soon as they are recognized.' Greenberg, '"American-Type" Painting', 208.

37   I approach a reading of Pollock's *bassesse* proposed by Rosalind Krauss in *The Optical Unconscious* (Cambridge, MA: MIT Press, 1993). She argues against the sublimated Pollock, desired and produced by art history's privileging of the hung, exhibited paintings over the moment of their production on the floor, being made by a body with a certain violence.

38   Irigaray, 'Gesture in Psychoanalysis', 99.

39   Julia Kristeva, 'Giotto's Joy', in *Desire in Language: A Semiotic Approach to Literature and Art*, ed. Leon S. Roudiez, trans. Thomas Gora, Alice Jardine and Leon S. Roudiez (Oxford: Blackwell, 1980), 210–36; original *Polylogue* (Paris: Editions du Seuil, 1977), 210–26. See also Rowley, *Helen Frankenthaler*.

40   Kristeva, 'Giotto's Joy', 219.

41   Kristeva, 'Giotto's Joy', 221.

42   Joachim Pissarro and David Carrier, 'Frankenthaler: History Returns to Venice', *Brooklyn Rail*, July–August 2019, https://brooklynrail.org/2019/07/artseen/Fran kenthaler-History-Returns-to-Venice (accessed 5 May 2020), reviewing *Pittura/ Panorama: Paintings by Helen Frankenthaler 1952–1992*, Museo di Palazzo Grimani, Venice (New York: Gagosian, 2019), essay by Pepe Karmel.

Chapter 5

1   Roman Jakobson, 'On Artistic Realism: Theory of Literature' [1921], cited in Claire Pajaczkowska, 'Structure and Pleasure', *Block*, 9 (1983), 5.

2   I do not at all disdain the necessity or the richness of these studies, such as the invaluable and substantial volume by Mary Gabriel, *Ninth Street Women*. I also note two recent publications that are not gossip, but forms of intimate memoir crossed with art writing: Ruth Appelhof, *Lee and Me: An Intimate Portrait of Lee Krasner* (Milan: Officina Libraria, 2020); Alexander Nemerov, *Fierce Poise: Helen Frankenthaler and 1950s New York* (New York: Penguin, 2020).

3   Lee Krasner in an interview with curator Marcia Tucker in 1973, printed in the catalogue for the Lee Krasner exhibition at the Whitney Museum of Art; reprinted in Rose, *Lee Krasner: A Retrospective*, 157.

4   Barbara Rose, 'Lee Krasner and the Origins of Abstract Expressionism', *Arts Magazine*, 77 (1977), 98.

5   Rose, 'Lee Krasner and the Origins of Abstract Expressionism', 98; John D. Graham, *System and Dialectics of Art* (New York: Delphic Studios, 1937), 134.

6   With ancient origins in millennia-old medical manuscripts, the linking of feminine psychological illness with the uterus/womb, Greek υστέρα-*hystera*, and with women's sexual reproduction has bonded woman's psyche to her sexual body and culture's regulation of it. Hysteria became a modern medical condition in the nineteenth century, when certain ailments of a physically incapacitating nature were documented though they had no discoverable physical cause. Women lost the power of speech or mobility and fell into fits and spasms, while organically nothing was wrong. First considered as a neurological disorder that had its own pattern, it was psychologized by Freud at the beginning of his career, when he assisted his paralysed or otherwise afflicted analysands to retrace through language and dreams the traumatic foundation of their condition. This included exposure to extreme situations such as witnessing death, sexual assault or other unassimilable shocks which were displaced on to non-organic bodily symptoms, which revealed to him the intimate link between the powerful force of the mind – what it could not assimilate, what overwhelmed its capacity to process – and the body. This he called the psycho-somatic, which could be helped through the speaking cure. Given that the traumas were often of a sexual nature, hysteria has been understood also as the deflection of the eroticized body into a hystericized body (David-Ménard). Modern forms of hysteria have different sources, for instance war trauma (now termed post-traumatic stress syndrome). Anorexia, bulimia and complaint (lack of direction) are now considered hysterical manifestations. Recent feminist work on hysteria also argues that the trauma at the heart of hysteria is the encounter with mortality (Bronfen) and the anxiety of not-being precipitated by displacement by a new baby (Mitchell).

7   Adrian Rifkin has pointed out the different trajectories of the alliance between semiotics, structuralism and psychoanalysis in France, where painting became the cultural object that was systematically theorized, while in Anglophone communities,

cinema became the focus and thus the paradigm. Cinematic studies have influenced art history through notions of the gaze, the spectator and the mirror, but such theorizations are steadfastly anti-corporeal and take little interest in drives not associated with vision. See Nigel Saint and Andy Stafford (eds), *Modern French Visual Theory: A Critical Reader* (Manchester: Manchester University Press, 2013).

8   Guy Rosolato (1924–2012) was a French psychoanalyst who trained with and then broke away from Jacques Lacan. He was particularly interested in the psychic meaning of sound and the voice, and his work on the maternal voice was taken up by analyst Didier Anzieu and by feminist film theorist Kaja Silverman, who used his term 'acoustic mirror' for her study of the voice in cinema, *The Acoustic Mirror: The Female Voice in Psychoanalysis and Cinema* (Bloomington, IN: Indiana University Press, 1988). Rosolato also recognized that sound is already a dimension in pre-natal incitements towards subjectivity, and across the limit of birth he proposed the maternal as forming a sonorous envelope that contributed to the formation of the body-ego. He was also deeply interested in Freud's thesis in *Totem and Taboo* to which I have referred above, also noting the overlaying of infantile ideas of the phallic mother and primal father.

9   In 'Three Essays on Sexuality' (1905), Freud radically challenged conventional and heterocratic theories of sexuality, completely displacing any notion of normative sexuality with his hypothesis on the formation of human sexuality in a specific phase termed infantile sexuality. Not innate but created, sexuality is, according to Freud, initiated as a human element in infancy, and as a response to the necessity to stay alive when utterly dependent. This infantile sexuality takes the form of the eroticization (associated with pleasurable release from the tension of hunger or separation) of all and any objects and organs relating to this drive for life (and the mitigation of the intense unpleasure of any form of lack). Infantile sexuality is inherently polymorphous and perverse (which means it is not directed to adult reproductive erotic ends by the use of the genitals and that anything can be eroticized and used for relief from tension). Freud then plotted out the impact of the Oedipal complex, which creates the crisis for this perverse and polymorphous infantile sexuality, precipitating the child into latency. With the onset of puberty initiated chemically (hormones were discovered as the key messengers of the body in 1905 also), which reshapes the adult sexual body, social pressures confirm and even enforce certain heterosexual dispositions of boys and girls, and repress other orientations, along the lines of the identifications created in Oedipality (the Father–Mother couple). Some people, however, may remain arrested in infantile pleasures, such as voyeurism (sexual pleasure in looking at another) or those engendered by castration anxiety, such as fetishism. Thus, in Freudian terms, perversion is never a moral judgement on sexual orientation or practice. It is a description of one of the vagaries of non-essential but constituted sexualities. It is part of an expanded understanding of the psycho-sexual production of sexuality in the conditions of human helplessness, dependency and world/other orientation, and the need for release from death anxiety. Perversion in this sense is a specific psycho-sexual negotiation of primary self–world situations that may persist. For a very coherent account of psychoanalytical understandings of perversion, see Claire Pajaczkowska, *Perversion* [*Ideas in Psychoanalysis*] (London: Icon Books, 2000). See also Janine Chassguet-Smirgel, *Creativity and Perversion* (New York: W. W. Norton, 1985).

10   'Identification is the "Psychological process whereby the subject assimilates an aspect, property or attribute of the other and is transformed, wholly or partially, after the model the other provides. It is by means of a series of identifications that the personality is constituted and specified." Identification draws on two senses of the word: both the action of identifying, i.e., recognizing x as identical with y; and the action of becoming identical with another. Psychoanalysis works *largely with the sense*

of identification of oneself with.' Jean Laplanche and Jean-Bertrand Pontalis, *The Language of Psychoanalysis*, trans. Donald Nicholson-Smith (London: Hogarth Press, 1983), 205. The sexuation and sexing, as it were, of the subject occurs, in psychoanalysis, in relation to identification with the adult others, notably the already marked positions of Mother and Father, irrespective of the gender of the parental figure. Identification is one of the planes on which notably feminist film theory developed its analyses; see Laura Mulvey's founding text, 'Visual Pleasure and Narrative Cinema'; it features also in Christian Metz, 'The Imaginary Signifier', *Screen*, 16.2 (1975), 14–76.

11   Jacques Lacan, 'The Mirror Phase as Formative of the Function of the I' [1949], in *Ecrits*, trans. Alan Sheridan (London: Tavistock, 1977), 1–7.

12   For some of the complexity of this logic, see Jane Gallop, 'Where to Begin? "The Mirror Stage"', in *Reading Lacan* (Ithaca, NY: Cornell University Press, 1985), 74–95.

13   Jacques Lacan, 'Aggressivity in Psychoanalysis', in *Écrits*, 8–29; Frederic Jameson, 'Imaginary and Symbolic in Lacan: Marxism, Psychoanalytical Criticism and the Problem of the Subject', *Yale French Studies*, 55/56 (1977), 338–95.

14   Sigmund Freud, 'Totem and Taboo' [1919], in *The Standard Edition of the Complete Psychological Works of Sigmund Freud, Vol. XIII, 1913–1914*, ed. James Strachey (London: Hogarth Press, 1955), 1–162.

15   The concept of the pictogram was advanced by French psychoanalyst Piera Aulagnier in *La Violence de l'interprétation – du pictogramme à l'énoncé* (Paris: Presses Universitaires de France, 1975); *The Violence of Interpretation: From Pictogram to Statement*, trans. Alan Sheridan (Abingdon: Routledge, 2001). Aulagnier was seeking to understand the most archaic formations of subjectivity, and the pictogram forms a link between body zones and sensory experiences and the first mental representations. She insisted on recognizing the bodily and non-verbal processes in the formation of subjectivity. Pictograms form a primary mode of sense making. Ettinger's *proximity-in-distance* or *partners-in-difference* might be considered in relation to Aulagnier, with whom Ettinger was in training analysis in Paris.

16   This phrase is from Julia Kristeva, who framed the subject as *en procès* – reading in English as both 'in process', constantly being formed and undone, and 'on trial', being tested and interrogated. Kelly Oliver comments: 'Her notion of the subject-in-process, however, challenges Lacanian psychoanalysis, with its emphasis on the mirror stage and the Name of the Father as the initiation into subjectivity. For her, subjectivity is a process that begins with the material body before the mirror stage. It is a process that has its beginnings in the maternal function rather than the paternal function. The maternal body is itself a primary model of the subject-in-process; its unity is called into question by the other-within, an other-in-process. In addition to the discourses of psychoanalysis and maternity, poetic language is another discourse that calls the subject into crisis, puts the subject on trial. Undeniable within poetic language, the semiotic element disrupts the unity of the Symbolic and thereby disrupts the unity of the subject of/in language.' Kelly Oliver, *Reading Kristeva* (Bloomington, IN: Indiana University Press, 1993), 13.

17   'The *fort-da* is not their [girls'] move into language. It is too linear, too analogous with the to-and-fro of the penile thrust or its manual equivalent, with the mastery of the other by means of an object. It is too angular also.' Irigaray, 'Gesture in Psychoanalysis', 99.

18   Elizabeth Bronfen, 'The Knotted Subject: Hysteria, Irma and Cindy Sherman', in Griselda Pollock (ed.), *Generations and Geographies* (London: Routledge, 1996), 42–57; Bronfen, *The Knotted Subject: Hysteria and its Discontents* (Princeton, NJ: Princeton University Press, 1998).

19 Pajaczkowska, 'Structure and Pleasure', 9, drawing on Guy Rosolato, 'Fonction du père et créations culturelles', in *Essais sur le Symbolique* (Paris: Gallimard, 1969), 172–84.

20 A short digression will confirm this. Julia Kristeva used some of Rosolato's insights in her writing on Italian painters of the fifteenth century. She shows the differences between various artists in the ways that they negotiate the structural role of painting, which she sees as a 'representation of a psychic relation to the maternal body'. Each biographically distinct male subject has a different narrative of separation from his mother which will inflect the signifying economy he produces. Thus, for Kristeva, Leonardo's psychic relation to the maternal body is revealed to be fetishistic; in contrast, Bellini uses light and colour to articulate maternal *jouissance*. In her reading of Giotto, Kristeva suggests that we get closer to the pre-linguistic instances of what she calls the semiotic, rhythm and colour being the signifying registers that undo the fixity of symbolic meaning to allow a play that runs back to Ernst and the game, to the bodies and the spaces that gestures, sounds and marks began to map out. See Julia Kristeva, *Desire in Language: A Semiotic Approach to Literature and Art*, ed. Leon S. Roudiez, trans. Thomas Gora, Alice Jardine and Leon S. Roudiez (Oxford: Blackwell, 1980).

Chapter 6

1 Julia Kristeva, 'A New Type of Intellectual: The Dissident', *Tel Quel*, 74 (1977), 3–8; trans. Séan Hand, in *The Kristeva Reader*, ed. Toril Moi (Oxford: Blackwell, 1986), 292–300.

2 Patriarchal is an anthropological term used to describe societies ruled by fathers, as in ancient nomadic communities. The term was appropriated in feminist theory to define social and cultural systems, ancient and contemporary, in which men are privileged across a range of axes of power – economic, political, social and sexual – which anthropologist Claude Lévi-Strauss defined as being based on exchange. In this context 'women' are defined as what is exchanged between men, while men are defined as those who are not exchanged, do not become symbolic currency. Thus, patriarchal is used to refer to social practices and their overall cultural systems, ways of thinking and social processes. The term *phallocentric* arises from the inclusion in some feminist theorizing of psychoanalysis, which attends not to social formation but to the formation of subjectivity. Psychoanalysis theorizes subjectivity while also showing how social formation is installed within us as the interior architecture of the psyche – as sexual difference. Language and the unconscious are the locations of this formation and continuous work.

3 Julia Kristeva terms this work de-passioning; see Julia Kristeva, 'Motherhood Today', www.kristeva.fr/motherhood.html (accessed 30 April 2021); Bracha L. Ettinger, 'From Proto-Ethical Compassion to Responsibility; Besidesness and Three Primal Mother Fantasies', *Athena*, 2 (2006), 105.

4 This is explained in her conversation with Catherine Clément; Catherine Clément and Julia Kristeva, *The Feminine and the Sacred* [1998], trans. Jane Marie Todd (Basingstoke: Palgrave MacMillan, 2001). It runs through her writing on the psychological complexity of maternity as a primary ethical relation to the other. See 'Motherhood according to Giovanni Bellini', in *Desire in Language*, 237–70. 'It happens but I am not there.' 'I cannot recognize it but it goes on.' 'Motherhood's impossible syllogism' (237).

5 Kristeva, 'A New Type of Intellectual', 297. De Kooning's paintings featuring the female figure are not a series and are not formally titled as a group even though they are conventionally discussed as his *Woman* paintings. Some have Woman in the title,

alone or with an attribute such as *Woman and Bicycle* (1952–53). I am grateful to the Willem de Kooning Foundation for guidance on this matter as they seek to clarify art historical referencing and de Kooning's own titling or references to the subjects of his paintings.

6   Richard Schiff, 'The Kick, The Twist, The Woman, The Rowboat', *Australian and New Zealand Journal of Art*, 14.1 (2014), 16–17.

7   For discussion of de Kooning's relation to Picasso in these works, see Sylvester, 'The Birth of *Woman I*'.

8   Dolores Holmes, 'Oral History Interview with Lee Krasner' (1972), 5, in the Pollock–Krasner Papers in the Smithsonian Archives of American Art.

9   Cindy Nemser, 'Interview with Grace Hartigan', in *Art Talk; Conversations with Twelve Women* (New York: Scribners, 1975), 158.

10   Nemser, 'Interview with Grace Hartigan', 158.

11   'She was our angel, the sweet angel of sex, the sugar of sex that came up from her like a resonance of sound in the clearest grain of a violin.' Norman Mailer, *Marilyn: A Biography* (New York: Grosset and Dunlap, 1973), 1.

12   There is a Man Ray photograph of a woman in black and white, putting on lurid red lipstick, titled *Red Badge of Courage*.

13   A study of these paintings' genesis, see Sylvester, 'The Birth of *Woman I*'. On the stop-start making of the painting over two years, see Thomas B. Hess, 'De Kooning Paints a Picture', *Art News* (March 1953), 30–32, 64–67.

14   Gloria Steinem and George Barris, *Marilyn* (New York: Henry Holt, 1986), 3.

15   Graham McCann, *Marilyn Monroe* (Cambridge: Polity, 1988).

16   I follow those who suggest that through lack of consultation between the various physicians and psychiatrists treating Monroe's insomnia, she accidentally dosed herself with two kinds of sleeping drugs whose swift action brought her within half an hour to the verge of death. Her last desperate phone call – the phone was found in her hand – was too late to halt the effects.

17   Marilyn Monroe, *My Story* [1974], co-written with Ben Hecht (Lanham, MD: Taylor Trade Publishing, 2007), 133.

18   On Marilyn as social and political body, see S. Paige Baty, *American Monroe: The Making of a Body Politic* (Berkeley, CA: University of California Press, 1995).

19   McCann, *Marilyn Monroe*, 148.

20   McCann, *Marilyn Monroe*, 149, citing Truman Capote, *Music for Chameleons* (London: Hamish Hamilton, 1981), 211. No attribution is given for the Miller quote. We need to remark, however, on a critical slippage from a woman wanting a child to Miller's ambiguous notion of this woman being like or aligned with children in simplicity and directness.

21   McCann, *Marilyn Monroe*, 149.

22   Joanne Leonard, *Being in Pictures: An Intimate Photo Memoir* (Ann Arbor, MI: University of Michigan Press, 2008).

23   Edelman, *Motherless Daughters*: an extensive study of the profound psychological effects of 'motherless daughters'. Edelman includes under motherlessness daughters who are bereaved, abandoned and abused. Monroe was a complex instance of this trauma, which would, I suggest, have overdetermined her own ambivalence about having a child, being a child, being a mother and experiencing repeated intended and unintentional procreative loss.

24   Sylvia Young (ed.), *FemTruth: Endometriosis Edition: A Collection of Stories from Courageous Women* (independently published, 2019); Abby Norman, *Ask Me About My Uterus: A Quest to Make Doctors Believe in Women's Pain* (New York: BoldType Books, 2018).

25   Biographer Donald Spoto typically dismisses it as a 'minor but uncomfortable health problem' (*Marilyn Monroe: The Biography*, 297). On unacknowledged pain experienced by women, see Norman, *Ask Me About My Uterus*.

26   Heather Guidone, 'Foreword', in Young (ed.), *FemTruth: Endometriosis Edition*, 16.

27   Guidone, 'Foreword', 10.

28   Hilary Mantel, *Giving Up the Ghost: A Memoir* (London: Fourth Estate, 2005).

29   Lois Banner, *Marilyn: The Passion and the Paradox* (London: Bloomsbury, 2012).

30   Banner, *Marilyn*, 81.

31   Banner, *Marilyn*, 82.

32   Kathleen Woodward, *Figuring Age: Women, Bodies, Generations* (Bloomington, IN: Indiana University Press, 1999); Lynne Segal, *Out of Time: The Perils and Pleasures of Ageing* (London: Verso, 2013); Germaine Greer, *The Change: Ageing and Menopause* (London: Bloomsbury, 1991).

33   McCann, *Marilyn Monroe*, 80.

34   www.youtube.com/watch?v=oVhI2auXk_k (accessed 10 April 2020).

35   Griselda Pollock, 'Femininity, Modernity and Representation: The Maternal Image, Sexual Difference and the Disjunctive Temporality of the Avant-Garde', in Cornelia Klinger and Wolfgang Müller-Funk (eds), *Das Jahrhundert der Avant-Garden* (Munich: Wilhelm Fink, 2005), 97–120.

Chapter 7

1   Serge Tisseron, 'All Writing is Drawing: The Spatial Development of the Manuscript', *Yale French Studies*, 84 (1994), 29–42.

2   Orton and Pollock, 'Avant-Gardes and Partisans Reviewed', 141.

3   Pollock, *Avant-Garde Gambits*.

4   I have explored this greater detail in my chapter, 'Fathers of Modern Art/Mothers of Invention', in *Differencing the Canon*, 65–97. See also Sigrid Weigel, 'From Gender Images to Dialectical Images in Benjamin's Writings', *New Formations*, 20 (1993), 21–32.

5   Bracha L. Ettinger, 'Demeter–Persephone Complex, Entangled Aerials of the Psyche and Sylvia Plath', *ESC*, 41.1 (2004), 123–54.

6   The term 'negativity' comes from Hegelian dialectics and is also used by Julia Kristeva with regard to the feminine as a revolutionary force. It means we do not attribute an essence to difference (i.e. men and women are different) but a dynamic force as negating what exists. It is not that, nor that, nor that. This means feminist thought is not proposing to invert patriarchal order and replace it, which would confirm its *m* versus *f* model. Instead, the force of feminist or indeed avant-garde negation is disruption of any such order in pursuit of the limitless unknown. The dialectic predicts that the overthrow of one order will constantly generate or expose further energies that produce change beyond the imagination of the existing order. For Kristeva, the feminine is thus not the distorted image – the monstrous or the idealized, the mother or the whore – created in a phallocentric culture; it is resource that incites transformation without itself having a content. The source of that transformative 'negativity' the not-this, not-that, not-yet does, however, lie in its most distinctive 'condition': the unique relation sustained between the body and language, the somatic and the semiotic, in her terms. The reference to Spivak is Gayatri Chakravorty Spivak, 'French Feminism in an International Frame', *Yale French Studies*, 62 (1981), 184. Uterine refers to the colonizing and harvesting of the reproductive female body while suppressing its clitoral sexuality. It is for this emphasis on

sexual pleasure that Spivak accords a place to Cixous and Irigaray in her international feminist curriculum.

7   This formulation appears in Griselda Pollock, 'Dialogue with Julia Kristeva', *parallax*, 8 (1998), special issue, 'Aesthetics. Politics. Ethics. Julia Kristeva 1966–1996', 5–16. See also Kristeva's later work on the psychic work of motherhood as *de-passioning* in order to allow the child to separate (Kristeva, 'Motherhood Today').

8   Pollock, 'Inscriptions in the Feminine'. On the avant-garde as 'moments', see Orton and Pollock, 'Avant-gardes and Partisans Reviewed'.

9   Griselda Pollock, 'Still Working on the Subject: Feminist Poetics and the Avant-Garde Moment', in Sabrine Breitwieser (ed.), *Rereading Mary Kelly Post-Partum Document* (Vienna: Generali Foundation, 1999), 237–63; Pollock, 'Moments and Temporalities of the Avant-Garde "in, of, and from the feminine"', *New Literary History*, 41 (2011), 795–820; Pollock, 'To Inscribe in the Feminine: A Kristevan Impossibility? or Femininity, Melancholia and Sublimation', *parallax*, 8 (1998), 81–11; Pollock, 'Femininity, Modernity and Representation'.

10   Julia Kristeva, 'Signifying Practice and the Mode of Production' [1975], trans. Geoffrey Nowell-Smith, *Edinburgh Magazine*, 1 (London: BFI, 1976), 64.

11   Kristeva, 'Signifying Practice and the Mode of Production', 65.

12   Kristeva, 'Signifying Practice and the Mode of Production', 65.

13   On Bellini and maternal loss, see Kristeva, 'Motherhood according to Giovanni Bellini'.

14   Cited in Gail Levin, *Lee Krasner: A Biography* (New York: William Morrow, 2012), 135.

15   Graham, *System and Dialectics of Art*, 14. See also Elizabeth Langhorne, 'The Magus and the Alchemist: John Graham and Jackson Pollock', *American Art*, 12.3 (1998), 46–67.

16   Herbert Read, *The Meaning of Art* (London: Faber and Faber, 1931).

17   Francine du Plessis and Cleve Gray, 'Who was Jackson Pollock?', *Art in America*, 55 (1967), 49. The various phrases used by Krasner to describe the meeting are compiled in Naifeh and White Smith, *Jackson Pollock*, 392–93.

18   Lee Krasner, Pollock, unpublished, undated notes, series 1.3, box 2, folder 41, Jackson Pollock and Lee Krasner papers AAA-S1, 2; cited in Gabriel, *Ninth Street Women*, 85.

19   Lee Krasner, Pollock, unpublished, undated notes, series 1.3, box 2, folder 41, Jackson Pollock and Lee Krasner papers AAA-S1, 6; cited in Gabriel, *Ninth Street Women*, 85.

20   Munro, *Originals: American Women Artists*, 112.

21   Clement Greenberg, 'Avant-Garde and Kitsch', *Partisan Review*, 6.6 (1939), 34–49; Greenberg, 'Towards a Newer Laocoon'.

22   Munro, *Originals: American Women Artists*, 112.

23   For a corrective view that documents how much of advanced art and its related ideas Krasner revealed to Pollock in these years, see Ellen G. Landau, 'Lee Krasner's Early Career: Part Two: The 1940s', *Arts Magazine*, 56.3 (1981), 80–89.

24   I am thinking here of Meret Oppenheim, who left Paris shortly after her immense success with the *Déjeuner en Fourrure* in 1936 and reported suffering a creative block for twelve years. I am also thinking of Nancy Spero, a young artist from Chicago who tried New York in the later 1950s before leaving for Paris. She produced a series of almost black paintings in which vague images were either buried or struggling to emerge – indexing a degree of struggle that echoes what Lee Krasner endured with what she called her grey slab paintings of the mid-1940s.

25   Hobbs, *Lee Krasner*, 65.

26   A major record of this is provided by Ilya Ehrenberg and Vassily Grossman, *The Complete Black Book of Russian Jewry* (Livingston, NJ: Transaction Publishers, 2003; London: Taylor and Francis, 2017).

27   Cited in Deborah Lipstadt, *Beyond Belief: The American Press and the Coming of the Holocaust 1933–1945* (New York: The Free Press/Simon and Schuster, 1986), 187–88.

28   The mass murders in the Ukraine, Latvia and Lithuania were carried out by shooting. This dimension of the Third Reich's extermination policy, which impacted on the Jewish immigrant communities from the Russian-dominated lands, has been less acknowledged under the rubric of the Holocaust. See, for example, Timothy D. Snyder, *Bloodlands: Europe Between Hitler and Stalin* (New York: Basic Books, 2010).

29   Hobbs, *Lee Krasner*, 69.

30   Hobbs, *Lee Krasner*, 69; Shoshana Felman and Dori Laub, *Testimony: Crises of Witnessing in Literature, Psychoanalysis and History* (London: Routledge, 1992). I choose the date 1989 for Zygmunt Bauman, *Modernity and the Holocaust* (Cambridge: Polity, 1989).

31   Hobbs, *Lee Krasner*, 66.

32   Hobbs, *Lee Krasner*, 69.

33   Theodor W. Adorno, 'Commitment', trans. Francis McDonagh, *New Left Review*, 87/88 (1974), 75–89, reprinted in Andrew Arato and Eike Gebhardt (eds), *The Essential Frankfurt School Reader* (New York: Urizen Books, 1978), 314.

34   Nemser, 'Lee Krasner', 86–87.

35   Nemser, 'Lee Krasner', 95.

36   Greenberg, '"American-type" Painting'.

37   Pollock, 'Painting, Feminism and History'.

38   Julia Kristeva, 'Women's Time' [1979], trans. Alice Jardine and Harry Blake, in *The Kristeva Reader*, 194; 'Le temps des femmes', *Cahiers de recherche de sciences des textes et documents* 5 (winter 1979), 5–19; translated and reprinted in *Signs*, 7.1 (1981), 13–35.

39   The clearest statement of this calibrated balance is Julia Kristeva, 'The System and the Speaking Subject' [1973], in *The Kristeva Reader*, 25–33. She coins the phrase 'semanalysis'.

40   Kristeva, 'Women's Time', 210.

41   Kristeva, 'Women's Time', 210.

42   Ettinger, 'Matrix and Metramorphosis', p. 99.

43   See also Claire Pajaczkowska, 'Art as a Symptom of Dying', *New Formations – Psychoanalysis and Culture*, 26 (1996), 74–88. Pajaczkowska explores a Kleinian reading of the relations between art and dying that may add a further dimension to the arguments explored in my work.

44   For a film about the making this image, see www.youtube.com/watch?v=nKBxON QX01Q (accessed 24 November 2021).

Chapter 8

1   Harold Rosenberg, 'The American Action Painters', *Art News*, 51.8 (1952), 22–23, 48–50, reprinted in Harold Rosenberg, *The Tradition of the New* (Chicago: University of Chicago Press, 1982). Subsequent page references are to the 1952 version.

2   Robert Hobbs, 'Lee Krasner's Skepticism and Her Emergent Postmodernism', *Woman's Art Journal*, 28.2 (2007), 3–10.

3   Hobbs, 'Lee Krasner's Skepticism and Her Emergent Postmodernism', 3.

4   Bryan Robertson, the British curator of Krasner's first UK retrospective in 1965 at the Whitechapel, had found these oil and charcoal drawings in the barn at East Hampton. Some she had saved, and the rest were to be destroyed, but they were later found by the artist in her New York apartment.

5   *Lee Krasner: Collages and Works on Paper, 1933–1974*, curated by Gene Baro at the Corcoran Gallery of Art, Washington, DC (1975), and *Lee Krasner: Works on Paper 1937–39* at the Marlborough Gallery, New York.

6   On the emergence of the *Woman* series, see the significantly titled study by Sylvester, 'The Birth of *Woman I*'.

7   Nemser, 'Lee Krasner', 95.

8   David Anfam, 'Lee Krasner: Brooklyn', *Burlington Magazine*, 143.1177 (2001), 244.

9   Anfam, 'Lee Krasner: Brooklyn', 244.

10 Pollock, *Differencing the Canon*.

11 Orton, 'Action, Revolution and Painting'.

12 Rosenberg, 'The American Action Painters', 22.

13 Rosenberg, 'The American Action Painters', 22.

14 Rosenberg, 'The American Action Painters', 23. My emphasis.

15 Rosenberg, 'The American Action Painters', 23.

16 Rosenberg, 'The American Action Painters', 23.

17 Orton, 'Action, Revolution and Painting', 193. Orton footnotes philosopher Richard Wollheim, *Painting as an Art* (Princeton, NJ: Princeton University Press, 1987), 19–25, 359 n. 9.

18 Rosenberg, 'The American Action Painters', 23.

19 Pollock, 'Monroe's Gestures Between Trauma and Ecstasy'.

20 *Riant*, from the French *rire*, to laugh. Julia Kristeva, 'Place Names', *Tel Quel*, 68 (1976), reprinted in *Desire in Language*, 283.

21 Griselda Pollock, *Monroe's Mov(i)es: Nation, Gender, Performance*, forthcoming.

Appendix

1   Sexual difference theories differ from theories of gender. So let me clarify. In common parlance, there are two genders and we regularly have to tick boxes to indicate which of two we are, *m/f*, male/female. Gender is assumed to be derived from the sex of our bodies or from a gender identification. Some think sex is natural, and that gender terms, man or woman, are based on natural sex. This has been challenged at three levels. Gender has been distinguished from sex by being defined as the *social or cultural definitions of the meanings attributed to masculine or feminine behaviour.* Ideas of gender vary culturally and historically. Gender is distinguished from sex psychologically by understanding that *a person may identify as masculine or feminine* against the attributed *sex* based on features of their bodies. A person can thus change gender. Feminism redefined gender as a *key theoretical concept, akin to class and race*, with two levels of meaning. Gender is *an axis of power in social relations* that creates a hierarchy between those designated men and women, and that creates an asymmetry of power between them. Gender is also the foundation for a range of *symbolic meanings and metaphors for any asymmetrical hierarchies of power, status, value and meaning*. Sun and moon, day and night, strong and weak, active and passive. Aligned, the opposing pairs reinforce a differential between the terms man and woman, masculine and feminine. Gender has become a critical term for deciphering and denouncing patriarchal social relations and for analysing cultural texts and images. Most recently, further undoing the sex–gender–sexuality alignment, gender theory, developing into queer theory, has been recast as a theory that radically challenges heteronormativity.

2 Phallocentrism was first coined by British Freudian psychoanalyst Ernest Jones when he and Karen Horney contested Freud's over-emphasis on the phallic phase in childhood development. In calling upon psychoanalysis to recognize the role of language in subjectivity, French psychoanalyst Jacques Lacan in 1958/59 published a text titled 'Signification of the Phallus', in which he, *contra* Freud and the general public, argued that the Phallus is neither the organ nor an imaginary object, but a signifier in the symbolic system: language. This position led to both a critique of phallocentrism as an ideology and the use of the concept to challenge that ideology. If the Phallus is the sole signifier around which meaning and subjectivity is organized, culture and language themselves become normatively and inescapably phallocentric. Feminist theorists thus denounced the predominant phallocentrism of Western thought while using Lacan as a theoretical resource to identify its operations and analyse the negative implication of the Phallus for women in a phallocentric universe of meaning in which femininity is defined only as 'lack' and other.

3 The Phallus is a key term in Lacan's revisions to Freud's residual anatomism. The Phallus is not a body part or sexual organ. It is a Symbol, the signifier without signified that holds in place the Symbolic order and system of meaning termed phallocentric, in which the Phallus as Symbol articulates a plus/minus binary. Whereas Freud tried to avoid equating psychic elements with real bodies, he struggled to negotiate the relations between imagining children observing differences between male and female genitals and his building a system of psycho-symbolic responses to difference (presence/absence) on the basis of sight, seeing and observation. For Lacan, the Phallus is not visible but is the symbolic behind-the-scenes orchestrator of the logic of on/off, plus/minus, presence/absence that engenders the fear of loss of any narcissistically invested element of the self. Under the Phallus we are all castrated, since its system, language, severs us all from infantile bodily intensities and re-orchestrates our subjectivity via its signifiers.

4 Ettinger, 'Matrix and Metramophosis', 121.

5 Ettinger, '*Fascinance*', 60.

Bibliography

Adler, Les K., and Peterson, Thomas G., 'Red Fascism: The Merger of Nazi Germany and Soviet Russia in the American Image of Totalitarianism, 1930s–1950s', *American Historical Review*, 75 (April, 1977), 1046–64.

Adorno, Theodor W., 'Commitment', trans. Francis McDonagh, *New Left Review*, 87/88 (1974), 75–89; reprinted in Andrew Arato and Eike Gebhardt (eds), *The Essential Frankfurt School Reader* (New York: Urizen Books, 1978), 300–18.

Alfieri, Bruno, and Bonito Oliva, Achille (eds), *Pollock's America: Jackson Pollock in Venice: The Irascibles and the New York School* (Milan: Skira, 2002).

Anderson, Janice, *Marilyn Monroe: Quote Unquote* (London: Paragon, 1994).

Anfam, David, 'Lee Krasner: Brooklyn', *Burlington Magazine*, 143.1177 (2001), 243–44.

— et al., *Lee Krasner: The Umber Paintings 1959–1962* (New York: Paul Kasmin Gallery, 2018).

Anon., 'Tribute to Marilyn Monroe, *Vogue*, 119.12 (15 September 1962), 72–75.

Appelhof, Ruth, *Lee and Me: An Intimate Portrait of Lee Krasner* (Milan: Officina Libraria, 2020).

Aptheker, Bettina, *Tapestries of Life: Women's Work and Women's Consciousness* (Amherst, MA: University of Massachusetts Press, 1989).

Arnold, Eve, *Marilyn Monroe – An Appreciation* (London: Hamish Hamilton, 1987).

Aulangier, Piera, *La Violence de l'interprétation – du pictogramme à l'énoncé* (Paris: Presses Universitaires de France, 1975).

— *The Violence of Interpretation: From Pictogram to Statement*, trans. Alan Sheridan (Abingdon: Routledge, 2001).

Bal, Mieke, *Death and Dissymmetry: The Politics of Coherence in the Book of Judges* (Chicago: University of Chicago Press, 1988).

— *Travelling Concepts in the Humanities: A Rough Guide* (Toronto: University of Toronto Press, 2002).

Bal, Mieke, and Bryson, Norman, 'Semiotics and Art History', *Art Bulletin*, 73.2 (1991), 174–208; reprinted in Donald Preziosi (ed.), *The Art of Art History: A Critical Anthology* (Oxford: Oxford University Press, 1998), 242–56.

Banner, Lois, *Marilyn: The Passion and the Paradox* (London: Bloomsbury, 2012).

Baro, Gene, *Lee Krasner: Collages and Works on Paper, 1933–1974* (Washington, DC: Corcoran Gallery of Art, 1975).

Barr, Alfred, *The New American Painting as Shown in Eight European Countries 1958–59* (New York: Museum of Modern Art, 1959).

Barthes, Roland, 'Myth Today', in *Mythologies* [1957], trans. Annette Lavers (London: Jonathan Cape, 1972), 109–59.

Bataille, Georges, *Manet* [1955] (Paris: Skira, 1994).

Baty, S. Paige, *American Monroe: The Making of a Body Politic* (Berkeley, CA: University of California Press, 1995).

Bauman, Zygmunt, *Modernity and the Holocaust* (Cambridge: Polity, 1989).

Belasco, Daniel, 'See Us Now: The Feminist Positions of Helen Frankenthaler and Grace Hartigan, 1957–1962', *Konsthistorisk Tidskrift/Journal of Art History*, 83.2 (2014), special issue, 'On the Cusp of Feminism: Women Artists in the Sixties', 67–81.

Benstock, Sheri, *Women of the Left Bank: Paris 1900–1940* (Austin, TX: University of Texas Press, 1987).

Bernard, Emile, *Souvenirs sur Paul Cézanne* (Paris: Société des Trente, 1912).

Berry, Ian, and Hayes, Lauren, *Alma Thomas: A Retrospective of Paintings* (Fort Wayne, TX: Fort Wayne Museum of Art and Pomegranate Communications, 1998).

— *Alma Thomas* (Munich: Prestel, 2015).

Betterton, Rosemary, 'Louise Bourgeois; Ageing and Maternal Bodies', *Feminist Review*, 93 (2009), 27–45.

— *Maternal Bodies in the Visual Arts* (Manchester: Manchester University Press, 2014).

Bloom, Harold, *The Anxiety of Influence: A Theory of Poetry* (Oxford: Oxford University Press, 1973).

Brennan, Marcia, *Modernism's Masculine Subjects: Matisse, the New York School, and Post-Painterly Abstraction* (Cambridge, MA: MIT Press, 2004).

Bronfen, Elisabeth, *Over Her Dead Body: Death, Femininity and the Aesthetic* (Manchester: Manchester University Press, 1992).

— 'The Knotted Subject: Hysteria, Irma and Cindy Sherman', in Griselda Pollock (ed.), *Generations and Geographies* (London: Routledge, 1996), 42–57.

— *The Knotted Subject: Hysteria and Its Discontents* (Princeton, NJ: Princeton University Press, 1998).

— *Home in Hollywood: The Imaginary Geography of Cinema* (New York: Columbia University Press, 2004).

Burchill, Julie, *Girls on Film* (New York: Pantheon, 1986).

Carter, Angela, *The Sadeian Woman* (London: Virago, 1979).

Chave, Anna, 'Pollock and Krasner: Script and Post-script', *Res: Anthropology and Aesthetics*, 24 (autumn 1993), 95–111.

— 'Frankenthaler's Fortune: On Class Privilege and the Artist's Reception', *Woman's Art Journal*, 37.1 (2016), 29–36.

Chasseguet-Smirgel, Janine, *Creativity and Perversion* (New York: W. W. Norton, 1985).

Cheah, Pheng, and Grosz, Elizabeth, 'The Future of Sexual Difference: An Interview with Judith Butler and Drucilla Cornell', *Diacritics*, 28.1 (1998), special issue, 'Irigaray and the Political Future of Sexual Difference', 19–42.

— 'On Being Two: An Introduction', *Diacritics*, 28.1 (1998), special issue, 'Irigaray and the Political Future of Sexual Difference', 2–18.

Cixous, Hélène, 'The Laugh of the Medusa', trans. Annette Kuhn, in Elaine Marks and Isabelle de Courtivron (eds), *New French Feminisms* (Brighton: Harvester Press, 1980), 245–64.

Clark, Kenneth, *The Nude: A Study in Ideal Art* (London: John Murray, 1956).

Clark, T. J., 'Jackson Pollock's Abstraction', in Serge Guilbaut (ed.), *Reconstructing Modernism* (Cambridge, MA: MIT Press, 1990), 172–242.

— 'The Unhappy Unconscious', in *Farewell to an Idea: Episodes from a History of Modernism* (New Haven, CT: Yale University Press, 1999), 299–369.

Clément, Catherine, and Kristeva, Julia, *Le féminin et le sacré* (Paris: Stock, 1998; new edn 2021).

— *The Feminine and the Sacred*, trans. Jane Marie Todd (Basingstoke: Palgrave Macmillan, 2001).

Cockcroft, Eva. 'Abstract Expressionism: Weapon of the Cold War', *Art Forum*, 12.10 (1974), 39–41.

Code, Lorraine, *What Can She Know? Feminist Theory and the Constructions of Knowledge* (Ithaca, NY: Cornell University Press, 1991).

Collins, Bradford, Fontán del Junco, Manuel, Vallejo, Ines, and Cordero, Beatriz (eds), *The Irascibles: Painters Against the Museum, New York, 1950* (Madrid: Fundación Juan March, 2020).

David-Ménard, Monique, *Hysteria from Freud to Lacan: Body and Language in Psychoanalysis*, trans. Catherine Porter (Ithaca, NY: Cornell University Press, 1989).

De Antonio, Emilo, and Tuchman, Mitch, *Painters Painting: A Candid History of the Modern Art Scene 1940–1970* (New York: Abbeville Press, 1984).

De Beauvoir, Simone, *Le deuxième sexe* (Paris: Librairie Gallimard, 1949).

— *The Second Sex*, trans. and ed. H. M. Parshley (London: Jonathan Cape, 1953).

— *The Second Sex*, trans. Constance Borde and Sheila Malovany-Chevallier (London: Vintage, 2011).

De Hart Matthews, Jane, 'Art and Politics in Cold War America', *American Historical Review*, 81.4 (1976), 762–87.

De Lauretis, Teresa, *Technologies of Gender: Essays on Theory, Fiction and Film* (Basingstoke: Palgrave Macmillan, 1987).

Derrida, Jacques, 'Différance', in *Margins of Philosophy*, trans. Alan Bass (Chicago: University of Chicago Press, 1982), 1–28.

Domhoff, G. William, *Who Rules America* (Englewood Cliffs, NJ: Prentice Hall, 1970).

Duchen, Claire, *Feminism in France: From May '68 to Mitterand* (London: Routledge, 1986).

Duncan, Carol, 'Virility and Male Domination in Early Twentieth Century Vanguard Art', *Artforum* (December 1973), 30–39; reprinted in Carol Duncan, *The Aesthetics of Power: Essays in Critical Art History* (Cambridge: Cambridge University Press, 1993), 81–108.

— 'MoMA's Hot Mamas', *Art Journal*, 48.2 (1989), 171–78; reprinted in Carol Duncan, *The Aesthetics of Power: Essays in Critical Art History* (Cambridge: Cambridge University Press, 1993), 189–210.

Duncan, Carol, and Wallach, Alan, 'The Museum of Modern Art as Late Capitalist Ritual: An Iconographic Analysis', *Marxist Perspectives*, 4 (1978), 28–51.

— 'Ordeal and Triumph on 53rd Street', *Studio International*, 194.9888 (1978), 48–57.

Du Plessis, Francine, and Gray, Cleve, 'Who was Jackson Pollock?', *Art in America*, 55 (1967), 48–51.

Dyer, Richard, *Heavenly Bodies: Film Stars and Society* (New York: St. Martin's Press, 1986).

Edelman, Hope, *Motherless Daughters: The Legacy of Loss* (New York: Da Capo, 1994; new edn, 2007).

Ehrenberg, Ilya, and Grossman, Vassily, *The Complete Black Book of Russian Jewry* (Livingston, NJ: Transaction Publishers, 2003; London: Taylor and Francis, 2017).

Elderfield, John, *Helen Frankenthaler* (New York: Harry Abrams, 1989).

Elliott, Bridget, and Wallace, Jo-Ann, *Women Artists and Writers: Modernist (Im)positionings* (London: Routledge, 1994).

Elsaesser, Thomas, 'Vincente Minnelli', *Brighton Film Review*, 15 (December 1969), 11–13; reprinted in Rick Altman (ed.), *Genre: The Musical* (London: Routledge and Kegan Paul, 1981), 8–27; in Christine Gledhill (ed.), *Home is Where the Heart is* (London: BFI, 1987), 217–22; and in Joe McElhaney (ed.), *Vincente Minnelli: The Art of Entertainment* (Detroit, MI: Wayne State University Press, 2007), 79–96.

Ettinger, Bracha L., 'Matrix and Metramophosis', *differences: A Journal of Feminist Cultural Studies*, 4.3 (1992), 176–208; reprinted in Bracha L. Ettinger, *Matrixial Subjectivity,*

Aesthetics, Ethics, Vol. 1: 1990–2000, ed. Griselda Pollock (Basingstoke; Palgrave Macmillan, 2020), 93–130.

— *The Matrixial Gaze* (Leeds: Feminist Arts and Histories Network Press, 1995); reprinted in Bracha L. Ettinger, *The Matrixial Borderspace*, ed. Brian Massumi (Minneapolis, MN: University of Minnesota Press), 41–92.

— 'Art as the Transport Station of Trauma', in *Bracha Ettinger: Artworking 1985–1999*, ed. Brian Massumi (Ghent: Ludion, 2000), 91–116; reprinted in Bracha L. Ettinger, *Matrixial Subjectivity, Aesthetics, Ethics, Vol. 1: 1990–2000*, ed. Griselda Pollock (Basingstoke: Palgrave Macmillan, 2020), 325–45.

— 'Demeter–Persephone Complex, Entangled Aerials of the Psyche and Sylvia Plath', *ESC*, 41.1 (2004), 123–54.

— 'Weaving the Woman Artist with-in The Matrixial Encounter-Event', *Theory, Culture and Society*, 21.1 (2004), 69–94; reprinted in *The Matrixial Borderspace*, ed. Brian Massumi (Minneapolis, MN: University of Minnesota Press), 173–200.

— '*Fascinance*: Girl to M/Other Matrixial Sexual Difference', in Griselda Pollock (ed.), *Psychoanalysis and the Image* (Oxford: Blackwell, 2006), 60–93.

— 'From Proto-Ethical Compassion to Responsibility; Besidesness and Three Primal Mother Fantasies', *Athena*, 2 (2006), 102–35.

— *Matrixial Subjectivity, Aesthetics, Ethics, Vol. 1: 1990–2000*, ed. Griselda Pollock (Basingstoke: Palgrave Macmillan, 2020).

— *Matrixial Subjectivity, Aesthetics, Ethics, Vol. 2: 2000–2010*, ed. Griselda Pollock (Basingstoke: Palgrave Macmillan, 2022).

Farago, Jason, 'Lee Krasner: Hiding in Plain Sight', *New York Times*, 19 August 2019, www.nytimes.com/2019/08/19/arts/lee-krasner-barbican-schirn-kunsthalle.html (last accessed 25 March 2020).

Farnham, Marynia, and Lundberg, Ferdinand, *Modern Woman: The Lost Sex* (New York: Harper and Brothers, 1947).

Fédida, Pierre, *L'Absence* (Paris: Gallimard, 1978).

Felman, Shoshana, *What Does a Woman Want? Reading and Sexual Difference* (Baltimore, MD: Johns Hopkins University Press, 1993).

Felman, Shoshana, and Laub, Dori, *Testimony: Crises of Witnessing in Literature, Psychoanalysis and History* (London: Routledge, 1992).

Fer, Bryony, 'Poussière/peinture: Bataille on Painting', in Carolyn Bailey Gill (ed.), *Bataille: Writing the Sacred* (London: Routledge, 1995), 154–71.

— *On Abstract Art* (New Haven, CT: Yale University Press, 2000).

Foucault, Michel, *La volonté de savoir* (Paris: Gallimard, 1976).

— *The History of Sexuality: An Introduction: Volume 1*, trans. Robert Hurley (London: Penguin, 1978).

Freud, Sigmund, 'Three Essays on Sexuality' [1905], in *The Standard Edition of the Complete Psychological Works of Sigmund Freud, Vol. VII, 1901–1905*, ed. James Strachey (London: Hogarth Press, 1953), 125–243.

— 'Mourning and Melancholia' [1915/1917], in *The Standard Edition of the Complete Psychological Works of Sigmund Freud, Vol. XIV, 1914–1916*, ed. James Strachey (London: Hogarth Press, 1957), 243–58.

— 'Totem and Taboo' [1919], in *The Standard Edition of the Complete Psychological Works of Sigmund Freud, Vol. XIII, 1913–1914*, ed. James Strachey (London: Hogarth Press, 1955), 1–162.

— 'Beyond the Pleasure Principle' [1920], in *The Standard Edition of the Complete Psychological Works of Sigmund Freud, Vol. XVIII, 1920–22*, ed. James Strachey (London: Hogarth Press, 1955), 1–64.

Friedan, Betty, *The Feminine Mystique* (New York: W. W. Norton, 1963).

Friedman, B. H., 'Towards the Total Color Image', *Art News*, 65 (1966), 67–68.

Fry, Roger, *Cézanne: A Study of his Development* (London: Macmillan, 1927).

— *Last Lectures* (Cambridge: Cambridge University Press, 1939).

Gabhardt, Ann, and Broun, Elisabeth, *Old Mistresses: Women Artists of the Past* (Baltimore, MD: Walters Art Gallery, 1972); catalogue published as *Walters Art Gallery Bulletin*, 24.7 (1972), 1–24.

Gabriel, Mary, *Ninth Street Women: Lee Krasner, Elaine de Kooning, Grace Hartigan, Joan Mitchell and Helen Frankenthaler: Five Paintings and the Movement that Changed Modern Art* (New York: Little, Brown, 2018).

— 'Want to Get Rich Buying Art? Invest in Women', *New York Times*, 24 September 2018, www.nytimes.com/2018/09/24/opinion/want-to-get-rich-buying-art-invest-in-women.html (last accessed 24 November 2021).

Gallagher, Catherine, and Laqueur, Thomas, *The Making of the Modern Body: Sexuality and Society in the Nineteenth Century* (Berkeley, CA: University of California Press, 1987).

Gallop, Jane, 'Where to Begin? "The Mirror Stage"', in *Reading Lacan* (Ithaca, NY: Cornell University Press, 1985), 74–95.

Geldzahler, Henry, 'Interview with Helen Frankenthaler', *Art Forum*, 4.2 (1965), 36–38.

— *New York Painting and Sculpture 1940–1970* (London: The Pall Mall Press, 1969).

Gibson, Ann Eden, *Abstract Expressionism: Other Politics* (New Haven, CT: Yale University Press, 1997).

— 'Lee Krasner and Women's Innovations in American Abstract Painting', *Woman's Art Journal*, 28.2 (2007), 11–19.

Gledhill, Christine (ed.), *Home is Where the Heart is: Studies in Melodrama and the Woman's Film* (London: BFI, 1987).

Gohari, Sybil E., 'Gendered Receptions: There and Back Again: An Analysis of the Critical Reception of Helen Frankenthaler', *Woman's Art Journal*, 35.1 (2014), 33–39.

Graham, John D., *System and Dialectics of Art* (New York: Delphic Studios, 1937).

Green, Ellen, *John Graham: Artist and Avatar* (Washington, DC: Phillips Collection, 1987).

Greenberg, Clement, 'Avant-Garde and Kitsch', *Partisan Review*, 6.6 (1939), 34–49.

— 'Towards a Newer Laocoon', *Partisan Review*, 7.4 (1940), 296–310.

— 'The Crisis of the Easel Picture' [1948], in *Art and Culture: Critical Essays by Clement Greenberg* (Boston, MA: Beacon Press, 1961), 154–57.

— '"American-Type" Painting', *Partisan Review*, 22.2 (1955); reprinted in *Art and Culture: Critical Essays by Clement Greenberg* (Boston, MA: Beacon Press, 1961), 208–29.

— 'Louis and Noland', *Art International*, 4.5 (1960); reprinted in *The Collected Essays and Reviews, Volume 4: Modernism with a Vengeance, 1957–1969*, ed. John O'Brien (Chicago: University of Chicago Press, 1993), 94–100.

— 'Changer: Anne Truitt', *Vogue* (May 1968); reprinted in *The Collected Essays and Criticism, Volume 4: Modernism with a Vengeance 1957–1969*, ed. John O'Brien (Chicago: University of Chicago Press, 1993), 288–91.

Greer, Germaine, *The Change: Ageing and Menopause* (London: Bloomsbury, 1991).

Grimes, William, 'Grace Hartigan, 86, Abstract Painter, Dies', *The New York Times*, 18 November 2008, www.nytimes.com/2008/11/18/arts/design/18hartigan.html (accessed 7 December 2021).

Grosz, Elisabeth, *Jacques Lacan: A Feminist Introduction* (London: Routledge, 1990).

Guilbaut, Serge, *How New York Stole the Idea of Modern Art: Abstract Expressionism, Freedom and the Cold War* (Chicago: University of Chicago Press, 1983).

Hall, Radclyffe, *The Well of Loneliness* (London: Jonathan Cape, 1928).

Haraway, Donna, 'Situated Knowledges: The Science Question in Feminism and the Privilege of Partial Perspective' [1988], in *Simians, Cyborgs, and Women: The Reinvention of Nature* (London: Free Association Books, 1991), 183–202.

Hardman, Andrew, 'Making Visible Lee Krasner's Occupation: Art Historiography and the Pollock–Krasner Studio', in Victoria Horner and Lara Perry (eds), *Feminism and Art History Now* (London: I.B. Tauris, 2017), 87–103.

Hess, Thomas B., *Abstract Painting: Background and the American Phase* (New York: Viking, 1951).

— 'De Kooning Paints a Picture', *Art News*, 52 (1 March 1953), 30–32, 64–67.

Hobbs, Robert, *Lee Krasner* (New York: Harry Abrams, 2000).

— 'Lee Krasner's Skepticism and Her Emergent Postmodernism', *Woman's Art Journal*, 28.2 (2007), 3–10.

Hoberman, John, 'Korea and a Career', *Artforum*, 32.5 (1994).

Holmes, Dolores, 'Oral History Interview with Lee Krasner' (1972), Pollock Krasner Papers, Smithsonian Archives of American Art, www.aaa.si.edu/download_pdf_transcript/ajax?record_id=edanmdm-AAADCD_oh_214196 (accessed 24 November 2021).

hooks, bell, *Talking Back: Thinking Feminist, Thinking Black* (Boston, MA: South End Press, 1989).

Huyssen, Andreas, 'Mass Culture as Woman: Modernism's Other', in *After the Great Divide: Modernism, Mass Culture and Postmodernism* (Basingstoke: Macmillan, 1986), 44–62.

Ingham, Richard, 'Lee Krasner was an artist, not just a wife', *The Guardian*, 31 May 1989, www.theguardian.com/artanddesign/2019/may/31/lee-krasner-was-an-artist-not-just-a-wife (last accessed 24 November 2021).

Irigaray, Luce, *The Speculum of the Other Woman* [1974], trans. Gillian C. Gill (Ithaca, NY: Cornell University Press, 1985).

— *This Sex Which Is Not One* [1977], trans. Catherine Porter (Ithaca, NY: Cornell University Press, 1985).

— 'Sexual Difference', in *An Ethics of Sexual Difference* [1984], trans. Carolyn Burke and Gilllian C. Gill (London: Athlone, 1993), 116–32.

— 'Gesture in Psychoanalysis' [1985], in *Sexes and Genealogies*, trans. Gillian C. Gill (New York: Columbia University Press, 1993), 91–104.

— 'The Three Genders' [1987], in *Sexes and Genealogies*, trans. Gillian C. Gill (New York: Columbia University Press, 1993), 167–84.

— 'Writing as Woman', in *Je, tu, nous: Toward a Culture of Difference* [1990], trans. Alison Martin (London: Routledge, 1993), 51–60.

— 'The Limits of Transference', in Margaret Whitford (ed.), *The Irigaray Reader* (Oxford: Blackwell, 1991), 105–17.

— *Marine Lover of Friedrich Nietzsche*, trans. Gillian Gill (New York: Columbia University Press, 1991).

— 'The Question of the Other', trans. Noah Guynn, *Yale French Studies*, 87 (1995), 7–19.

Jameson, Fredric, 'Imaginary and Symbolic in Lacan: Marxism, Psychoanalytical Criticism and the Problem of the Subject', *Yale French Studies*, 55/56 (1977), 338–95.

— *The Political Unconscious: Narrative as a Socially Symbolic Act* (Ithaca, NY: Cornell University Press, 1981).

Jardine, Alice, *Gynesis: Configurations of Women and Modernity* (Ithaca, NY: Cornell University Press, 1986).

Jardine, Alice, and Smith, Paul (eds), *Men in Feminism* (London: Methuen, 1987).

Jones, Caroline A., 'Filming the Artist/Suturing the Spectator', in *Machine in the Studio: Constructing the Post-war American Artist* (Chicago: University of Chicago Press, 1996), 60–113.

Kaplan, Ann E., 'Is the Gaze Male?', in *Women and Film: Both Sides of the Camera* (New York: Methuen, 1983), 23–35.

Kelly, Mary, 'On Sexual Politics and Art', in Brandon Taylor (ed.), *Art and Sexual Politics* (Winchester: Winchester School of Art, 1977), 66–75; reprinted in Rozsika Parker and Griselda Pollock, *Framing Feminism: Art and the Women's Movement 1970–1985* (London: Pandora, 1987), 303–12; reprinted in Mary Kelly, *Imaging Desire* (Cambridge, MA: MIT Press, 1997), 1–10.

— 'Re-viewing Modernist Criticism', *Screen*, 22.3 (1981), 41–52; reprinted in Mary Kelly, *Imaging Desire* (Cambridge, MA: MIT Press, 1997), 80–106.

Kleeblatt, Lee, and Brown, Stephen, *From the Margins: Lee Krasner and Norman Lewis 1945–1952* (New York/New Haven, CT: Jewish Museum/Yale University Press, 2014).

Krauss, Rosalind, *The Optical Unconscious* (Cambridge, MA: MIT Press, 1993).

Kristeva, Julia, 'La Femme n'est jamais ça' [Woman can never be defined], interview with *psych & po*, *Tel Quel* (1974); reprinted in translation in Elaine Marks and Isabelle de Courtivron (eds), *New French Feminisms* (Brighton: Harvester Press, 1980), 137–41.

— 'Signifying Practice and the Mode of Production', from *La traversée des signes* (Paris: Editions du Seuil, 1975), trans. Geoffrey Nowell-Smith, *Edinburgh Magazine*, 1 (London: BFI, 1976), 64–75.

— 'Place Names', *Tel Quel* 68 (1976); reprinted in *Desire in Language: A Semiotic Approach to Literature and Art*, ed. Leon S. Roudiez, trans. Thomas Gora, Alice Jardine and Leon S. Roudiez (Oxford: Blackwell, 1980), 271–94.

— 'A New Type of Intellectual: The Dissident', *Tel Quel*, 74 (1977), 3–8; trans. Séan Hand, in *The Kristeva Reader*, ed. Toril Moi (Oxford: Blackwell, 1986), 292–300.

— 'Women's Time' [1979], trans. Alice Jardine and Harry Blake, in *The Kristeva Reader*, ed. Toril Moi (Oxford: Blackwell, 1986), 187–213.

— 'Le temps des femmes', *Cahiers de recherche de sciences des textes et documents* 5 (winter 1979), 5–19; translated and reprinted in *Signs*, 7.1 (1981), 13–35.

— 'Giotto's Joy', in *Desire in Language: A Semiotic Approach to Literature and Art*, ed. Leon S. Roudiez, trans. Thomas Gora, Alice Jardine and Leon S. Roudiez (Oxford: Blackwell, 1980), 210–36.

— *Desire in Language: A Semiotic Approach to Literature and Art*, ed. Leon S. Roudiez, trans. Thomas Gora, Alice Jardine and Leon S. Roudiez (Oxford: Blackwell, 1980).

— 'Motherhood according to Giovanni Bellini', in *Desire in Language: A Semiotic Approach to Literature and Art*, ed. Leon S. Roudiez, trans. Thomas Gora, Alice Jardine and Leon S. Roudiez (Oxford: Blackwell, 1980), 237–71.

— 'Motherhood Today' (2005), www.kristeva.fr/motherhood.html (last accessed 24 November 2021).

Kroker, Arthur, and Kroker, Marilouise (eds), *The Hysterical Male: New Feminist Theory* (New York: St. Martin's Press, 1991), 80–90.

Lacan, Jacques, 'The Mirror Phase as Formative of the Function of the I' [1949], in *Écrits*, trans. Alan Sheridan (London: Tavistock, 1977 [1966]), 1–7.

— 'Aggressivity in Psychoanalysis', in *Écrits*, trans. Alan Sheridan (London: Tavistock, 1977 [1966]), 8–29.

Laqueur, Thomas, *Making Sex: Body and Gender from the Greeks to Freud* (Cambridge, MA: Harvard University Press, 1990).

Landau, Ellen G., 'Lee Krasner's Early Career, Part One: Pushing in Different Directions', *Arts Magazine*, 56.2 (1981), 110–22.

— 'Lee Krasner's Early Career, Part Two: The 1940s', *Arts Magazine*, 56.3 (1981), 80–89.

— 'Lee Krasner's Past Continuous', *Art News*, 83.2 (1984), 68–77.

— 'Channeling Desire: Lee Krasner's Collages of the Early 1950s', *Woman's Art Journal* (autumn 1997/winter 1998), 27–30; reprinted in Bruno Alfieri and Achille Bonito Oliva (eds), *Pollock's America: Jackson Pollock in Venice: The Irascibles and the New York School* (Milan: Skira, 2002), 189–93.

— 'Jackson Pollock: The Body and Nature', in Bruno Alfieri and Achille Bonito Oliva (eds), *Pollock's America: Jackson Pollock in Venice: The Irascibles and the New York School* (Milan: Skira, 2002), 73–90.

— 'Jackson Pollock and Lee Krasner: The Erotics of Influence', in Bruno Alfieri and Achille Bonito Oliva (eds), *Pollock's America: Jackson Pollock in Venice: The Irascibles and the New York School* (Milan: Skira, 2002), 173–78.

— *Reading Abstract Expressionism: Context and Critique* (New Haven, CT: Yale University Press, 2005).

— 'Willem and Elaine de Kooning', in *Artists and Lovers* (London: Ordovas Gallery, 2016), 98–99.

— 'Jackson Pollock and Lee Krasner', in *Artists and Lovers* (London: Ordovas Gallery, 2016), 104–05.

— 'Biographies and Bodies', in *Self and Other in Portraits by Elaine and Bill de Kooning* (New Haven, CT: Yale University Press for the Denver Art Museum, 2016), 30–41.

— '"What a Picture Should Mean": Lee Krasner, Hans Hofmann and the Role of Drawing in Modernism', in *Lee Krasner Charcoals* (New York: Kasmin Gallery, 2019), 4–21, 74–77.

— 'When Vision Became Gesture: Hans Hofmann in the 1940s', in *Hans Hofmann: The Nature of Abstraction* (Berkeley, CA: Berkeley Art Museum and Pacific Film Archive/ University of California Press, 2019), 64–85.

Landau, Ellen G., and Grove, Jeffrey D., *Lee Krasner: A Catalogue Raisonné* (New York: Harry Abrams, 1995).

Langhorne, Elizabeth, 'The Magus and the Alchemist: John Graham and Jackson Pollock', *American Art*, 12.3 (1998), 46–67.

Laplanche, Jean, and Pontalis, Jean-Bertrand, *The Language of Psychoanalysis*, trans. Donald Nicholson-Smith (London: Hogarth Press, 1983).

Lara, Antonio, 'Sensualidad e Inocencia: Las peliculas de Marilyn Monroe [Sensuality and Innocence in the Films of Marilyn Monroe]', *Cuadernos del Norte*, 8.43 (1987), 61–68.

Lee Krasner: Collage Paintings 1938–1981, essays by Siri Hustvedt and Saskia Flower (New York: Paul Kasmin, 2021).

Leonard, Joanne, *Being in Pictures: An Intimate Photo Memoir* (Ann Arbor, MI: University of Michigan Press, 2008).

Levin, Gail, *Inside Outside: Selected Works by Janet Sobel* (New York: Garry Snyder Fine Art, 2003).

— *Lee Krasner: A Biography* (New York: William Morrow, 2012).

Lippard, Lucy, *Eva Hesse* (New York: New York University Press, 1976).

— 'Sweeping Exchanges: The Contribution of Feminism to the Arts of the 1970s', *Art Journal*, 40.1–2 (1980), 362–65.

Lipstadt, Deborah, *Beyond Belief: The American Press and the Coming of the Holocaust 1933–1945* (New York: The Free Press/Simon and Schuster, 1986).

Liss, Andrea, *Feminist Art and the Maternal* (Minneapolis, MN: University of Minnesota Press, 2009).

Lorde, Audre, *Sister/Outsider: Essays and Speeches* (Freedom, CA: The Crossing Press Feminist Series, 1984).

Mailer, Norman, *Marilyn: A Biography* (New York: Grosset and Dunlap, 1973).

Mantel, Hilary, *Giving Up the Ghost: A Memoir* (London: Fourth Estate, 2005).

Marks, Elaine, and de Courtivron, Isabelle (eds), *New French Feminisms: An Anthology* (Brighton: Harvester Press, 1980).

Marter, Joan (ed.), *Women of Abstract Expressionism* (New Haven, CT: Yale University Press, 2016).

McCann, Graham, *Marilyn Monroe* (Cambridge: Polity, 1988).

Merleau-Ponty, Maurice, 'Cézanne's Doubt' [1960], in Galen A. Johnson (ed.), *The Merleau-Ponty Aesthetics Reader: Philosophy and Painting* (Evanston, IL: Northwestern University Press, 1993), 3–13.

— 'Eye and Mind' [1960], in Galen A. Johnson (ed.), *The Merleau-Ponty Aesthetics Reader: Philosophy and Painting* (Evanston, IL: Northwestern University Press, 1993), 121–50.

Metz, Christian, 'The Imaginary Signifier', *Screen*, 16.2 (1975), 14–76.

Micale, Mark S., *Hysterical Men: The Hidden History of Male Nervous Disorders* (Cambridge: Cambridge University Press, 2008).

Millett, Kate, *Sexual Politics* (New York: Doubleday, 1970).

Mitchell, Elspeth, 'The Girl and Simone de Beauvoir's *Second Sex*: Feminine Becomings', *Australian Feminist Studies*, 93 (2017), 269–75.

Mitchell, Juliet, *Psychoanalysis and Feminism* (London: Penguin, 1974).

— *Mad Men and Medusas: Reclaiming Hysteria* (London: Penguin, 2000).

Mitchell, Juliet, and Rose, Jacqueline, *Feminine Sexuality: Lacan and the école freudienne* (Basingstoke: Macmillan, 1985).

Moi, Toril (ed.), *French Feminist Thought: A Reader* (Oxford: Blackwell, 1987).

Monroe, Marilyn, *My Story* [1974], co-written with Ben Hecht (Lanham, MD: Taylor Trade Publishing, 2007).

Montrelay, Michèle, 'Inquiry into Femininity', *m/f*, 1 (1978), 83–102; reprinted in Parveen Adams and Elizabeth Cowie (eds), *The Woman Question* (London: Verso, 1990), 253–73.

Mulvey, Laura, 'Visual Pleasure and Narrative Cinema', *Screen*, 16.3 (1975), 6–18; reprinted in Laura Mulvey, *Visual and Other Pleasures* (Basingstoke: Macmillan, 1989), 16–26.

— 'A Phantasmagoria of the Female Body: The Work of Cindy Sherman', *New Left Review*, 188 (1991), 137–50.

— 'Pandora's Box: Topographies of the Mask and Curiosity', in Beatriz Colomina (ed.), *Sexuality and Space* (Princeton, NJ: Princeton Architectural Press, 1992), 53–72; reprinted in Laura Mulvey, *Fetishism and Curiosity* (London: BFI, 1996), 53–70.

— 'Close-ups and Commodities', in *Fetishism and Curiosity* (London: BFI, 1996), 40–52.

Munro, Eleanor, *Originals: American Women Artists* (New York: Simon and Schuster, 1979).

Naifeh, Stephen, and White Smith, Gregory, *Jackson Pollock: An American Saga* (New York: Clarkston N. Potter; 1989).

Nairne, Eleanor, *Lee Krasner: Living Colour*, exh. cat., Barbican, 30 May–1 September 2019 (London: Thames and Hudson, 2019).

Nemerov, Alexander, *Fierce Poise: Helen Frankenthatler and 1950s New York* (New York: Penguin, 2021).

Nemser, Cindy, 'The Indomitable Lee Krasner', *Feminist Art Journal*, 4.1 (1975), 4–9.

— 'Interview with Grace Hartigan', in *Art Talk; Conversations with Twelve Women Artists* (New York: Scribners, 1975), 149–18.

— 'Lee Krasner', in *Art Talk: Interviews with Twelve Women Artists* (New York: Scribners, 1975), 81–112.

Newman, Arnold, 'American Artists Photographed by Arnold Newman', *Art in America*, 53 (1965), 106–13.

Nochlin, Linda, 'Why Are There No Great Women Artists?', in Vivian Gornick and Barbara Moran (eds), *Woman in Sexist Society: Studies in Power and Powerlessness* (New York: Basic Books, 1971), 480–510.

— 'Why Have There Been No Great Women Artists?', in Thomas B. Hess and Elizabeth Baker (eds), *Art and Sexual Politics: Why Have There Been No Great Women Artists?* (Basingstoke: Macmillan, 1971), 1–43.

Norman, Aby, *Ask Me About My Uterus: A Quest to Make Doctors Believe in Women's Pain* (New York: Bold Type Books, 2018).

Oliver, Kelly, *Reading Kristeva* (Bloomington, IN: Indiana University Press, 1993).

Orton, Fred, 'Action, Revolution and Painting', *Oxford Art Journal*, 14.2 (1991), 3–17; reprinted in Fred Orton and Griselda Pollock, *Avant-Gardes and Partisans Reviewed* (Manchester: Manchester University Press, 1996), 177–203.

— 'Footnote One: The Idea of the Cold War', in David Thistlewood (ed.), *American Abstract Expressionism* (Liverpool: Liverpool University Press and Tate Gallery, 1993), 179–92; reprinted in Fred Orton and Griselda Pollock, *Avant-Gardes and Partisans Reviewed* (Manchester: Manchester University Press, 1996), 205–18.

Orton, Fred, and Pollock, Griselda, 'Avant-Gardes and Partisans Reviewed', *Art History*, 4.3 (1981), 305–27; reprinted in *Avant Gardes and Partisans Reviewed* (Manchester: Manchester University Press, 1996), 141–64.

— 'Jackson Pollock, Painting and the Myth of Photography', *Art History*, 6.1 (1983), 114–22; reprinted in *Avant-Gardes and Partisans Reviewed* (Manchester: Manchester University Press, 1996), 165–76.

— *Avant-Gardes and Partisans Reviewed* (Manchester: Manchester University Press, 1996).

Pajaczkowska, Claire, 'Structure and Pleasure', *Block*, 9 (1983); reprinted in Tim Putnam, Melinda Mash, Jon Bird, Barry Curtis and George Robertson (eds), *The Block Reader in Visual Culture* (London: Routledge, 1996), 31–49.

— 'Art as a Symptom of Dying', *New Formations – Psychoanalysis and Culture*, 26 (1996), 74–88.

— *Perversion* [*Ideas in Psychoanalysis*] (London: Icon Books, 2000).

Parker, Rozsika, and Pollock, Griselda, *Old Mistresses: Women, Art and Ideology* (London: Routledge, 1981; repr. 1993, 2013; new edn, London: Bloomsbury, 2020).

— *Framing Feminism: Art and the Women's Movement 1970–1985* (London: Pandora, 1987).

Paticky, Mark, *Photographing Lee Krasner*, 1969 (2020), www.youtube.com/watch?v=nKBxONQX01Q (last accessed 4 January 2021).

Perchuk, Andrew, 'Pollock and Postwar Masculinity', in Donald McMahon (ed.), *The Masculine Masquerade: Masculinity and Representation* (Cambridge, MA: MIT Press, 1995), 31–43.

Perry, Gillian, *Women Artists and the Parisian Avant-Garde: Modernism and 'Feminine' Art 1900–1920s* (Manchester: Manchester University Press, 1995).

Pissarro, Joachim, and Carrier, David, 'Frankenthaler: History Returns to Venice', *Brooklyn Rail*, July–August 2019, https://brooklynrail.org/2019/07/artseen/Frankenthaler-History-Returns-to-Venice (accessed 5 May 2020).

Pitman, Joanna, *On Blondes – From Aphrodite to Madonna: Why Blondes Have More Fun* (London: Bloomsbury, 2003).

Pittura/Panorama: Paintings by Helen Frankenthaler 1952–1992, Museo di Palazzo Grimani, Venice (New York: Gagosian, 2019).

Podlesney, Teresa, 'Blondes', in Arthur Kroker and Marilouise Kroker (eds), *The Hysterical Male: New Feminist Theory* (New York: St. Martin's Press, 1991), 80–90.

Podro, Michael, '"The landscape thinks itself in me": The Comments and Procedures of Cézanne', *International Review of Psycho-Analysis*, 17.4 (1990), 401–12.

Pollock, Griselda, 'Artists, Media and Mythologies: Genius, Madness and Art History', *Screen*, 21.3 (1980), 57–96.

—— 'Back to the Twentieth Century: Femininity and Modernism', in Rozsika Parker and Griselda Pollock, *Old Mistresses: Women, Art and Ideology* (London: Routledge, 1981; repr. 1993, 2013; new edn, London: Bloomsbury, 2020), 134–69/ 155–94.

—— *Vision and Difference: Feminism, Femininity and the Histories of Art* (London: Routledge, 1988; new edn, 2003).

—— 'Agency and the Avant-Garde: Studies in Authorship and Art History by Way of Van Gogh', *Block*, 15 (1989), 5–15; reprinted in Fred Orton and Griselda Pollock, *Avant-Gardes and Partisans Reviewed* (Manchester: Manchester University Press, 1996), 315–42.

—— *Avant-Garde Gambits, 1888–1893: Gender and the Colour of Art History* (London: Thames and Hudson, 1992).

—— 'Painting, Feminism and History', in Michèle Barrett and Anne Phillips (eds), *Destabilising Theory: Western Feminism 1970s–1980s* (Cambridge: Polity, 1992), 138–76.

—— 'Crows, Blossoms and Lust for Death: Cinema and the Myth of Van Gogh', in Tsukasa Kodera (ed.), *Mythologies of Van Gogh* (Amsterdam: John Benjamins, 1993), 217–39.

—— 'Pollock on Greenberg', *Art Monthly*, 178 (1994).

—— 'Inscriptions in the Feminine', in Catherine de Zegher (ed.), *Inside the Visible: An Elliptical Traverse of Twentieth Century Art in, of and from the Feminine* (Cambridge, MA: MIT Press, 1996), 67–87.

—— 'Dialogue with Julia Kristeva', in *parallax*, 8 (1998), special issue, 'Aesthetics. Politics. Ethics. Julia Kristeva 1966–1996', 5–16.

—— 'To Inscribe in the Feminine: A Kristevan Impossibility? or Femininity, Melancholia and Sublimation', *parallax*, 8 (1998), special issue, 'Aesthetics. Politics. Ethics. Julia Kristeva 1966–1996', 81–11.

—— *Differencing the Canon: Feminist Desire and the Writing of Art's Histories* (London: Routledge, 1999).

—— 'Fathers of Modern Art/Mothers of Invention', in *Differencing the Canon: Feminist Desire and the Writing of Art's Histories* (London: Routledge, 1999), 65–97.

—— 'Feminism, History and Contemporary Practice in the Visual Arts', in *Looking Back to the Future: Essays on Art, Life and Death from the 1990s* (London: Routledge, 1999), 79–112.

—— 'Still Working on the Subject: Feminist Poetics and the Avant-Garde Moment', in Sabrine Breitwieser (ed.), *Rereading Mary Kelly Post-Partum Document* (Vienna: Generali Foundation, 1999), 237–63.

—— 'Feminist Theory: the Visual', in Mary Eagleton (ed.), *Feminist Theory* (Oxford: Blackwell, 2003), 173–94.

—— 'Femininity, Modernity and Representation: The Maternal Image, Sexual Difference and the Disjunctive Temporality of the Dissident Avant-Garde', in Cornelia Klinger and Wolfgang Müller Funk (eds), *Das Jahrhundert der Avantgarden* (Munich: Wilhelm Fink, 2004), 97–120.

— 'Thinking the Feminine: Aesthetic Practice as Introduction to Bracha Ettinger and the Concepts of Matrix and Metramorphosis', *Theory, Culture and Society*, 21.1 (2004), 5–65.

— 'Femininity, Aporia or Sexual Difference', in Bracha Ettinger, *The Matrixial Borderspace*, ed. Brian Massumi (Minneapolis, MN: University of Minnesota Press, 2006), 1–40.

— 'Moments and Temporalities of the Avant-Garde "in, of, and from the feminine"', *New Literary History*, 41 (2011), 795–820.

— 'The Male Gaze', in Mary Evans and Carolyn H. Williams (eds), *Gender: The Key Concepts* (Abingdon: Routledge, 2013), 141–48.

— 'Writing from the Heart', in Jacqueline Stacey and Janet Wolff (eds), *Writing Otherwise* (Manchester: Manchester University Press, 2013), 19–33.

— 'Monroe's Gestures Between Trauma and Ecstasy: Reading the Cinematic Gesture "Marilyn Monroe" with Aby Warburg's Venus and Nymph', in Nicholas Chare and Elizabeth Watkins (eds), *Gesture in Cinema* (Abingdon: Routledge, 2016), 99–132.

— 'Feminism and Language', in Hilary Robinson and Maria Elena Buszek (eds), *A Companion to Feminist Art* (Hoboken, NJ: Wiley-Blackwell, 2019), 261–82.

— 'Coming late to the party in Bilbao: Lee Krasner's missed place in modern art history', translated as 'La festa tardía de Lee Krasner', *El País*, 28 August, 2020, https://elpais.com/cultura/2020/08/25/babelia/1598369190_378495.html (accessed 7 December 2021).

Pryor, Riah, 'Is Art History under Threat? UK Universities See 28.5% Drop in the Subject in the Past Decade', *The Art Newspaper*, 20 January 2020, www.theartnewspaper.com/news/is-art-history-under-threat (accessed 25 January 2020).

Read, Herbert, *The Meaning of Art* (London: Faber and Faber, 1931).

Riley, Denise, *'Am I That Name?' Feminism and the Category of 'Woman' in History* (Basingstoke: Macmillan, 1988).

Robertson, Bryan, *Lee Krasner: Paintings, Drawings and Collages* (London: Whitechapel Art Gallery, 1965).

Robinson, Hilary, *Reading Art, Reading Irigaray: The Politics of Art by Women* (London: I.B. Tauris, 2006).

Rosalato, Guy, 'Fonction du père et créations culturelles', in *Essais sur le Symbolique* (Paris: Gallimard, 1969), 172–84.

Rose, Barbara, *Helen Frankenthaler* (New York: Harry Abrams, 1970).

— 'Lee Krasner and the Origins of Abstract Expressionism', *Arts Magazine*, 51 (1977), 96–100.

— *Lee Krasner: The Long View* (film, dir. Barbara Rose, 1978).

— *Krasner–Pollock: Artworld Relationships* (New York: Grey Gallery, 1981).

— *Lee Krasner: A Retrospective* (New York: Museum of Modern Art, 1983).

Rose, Jacqueline, *Sexuality in the Field of Vision* (London: Verso, 1986).

Rosenberg, Harold, 'The American Action Painters', *Art News*, 51.8 (1952), 22–23, 48–50; reprinted in Harold Rosenberg, *The Tradition of the New* (Chicago: University of Chicago Press, 1982).

— *The Tradition of the New* [1959] (Chicago: University of Chicago Press, 1982).

Rowley, Alison, 'On Viewing Three Paintings by Jenny Saville: Rethinking a Feminist Practice of Painting', in Griselda Pollock (ed.), *Generations and Geographies in the Visual Arts: Feminist Readings* (London: Routledge, 1996), 88–111.

— 'Notes on the Case of *Mountains and Sea*: Helen Frankenthaler: History, Poeisis, Memory', PhD thesis, University of Leeds, 2001.

— *Helen Frankenthaler: Painting History, Writing Painting* (London: I.B. Tauris, 2007).

Saint, Nigel, and Stafford, Andy (eds), *Modern French Visual Theory: A Critical Reader* (Manchester: Manchester University Press, 2013).

Saltzman, Lisa, 'Reconsidering the Stain: On Gender and the Body in Helen Frankenthaler's Painting', in *Friedel Dzubas: Critical Painting* (Medford, MA: Tufts University Press, 1998), 9–24; reprinted in Norma Broude and Mary D. Garrard (eds), *Reclaiming Female Agency* (Berkeley, CA: University of California Press, 2005), 273–83.

Sandler, Irving, *The Triumph of American Painting: A History of Abstract Expressionism* (New York: Harper and Row, 1976).

Schiff, Richard, 'The Kick, The Twist, The Woman, The Rowboat', *Australian and New Zealand Journal of Art*, 14.1 (2014), 5–20.

Schumacher, Bett, 'The Woman Gender: Gender Displacement in the Art of Helen Frankenthaler', *Woman's Art Journal*, 31.2 (2010), 12–21.

Scott, Joan, 'Gender: A Useful Category for Historical Analysis', *The American Historical Review*, 91.5 (1986), 1053–75.

Searle, Adrian, 'Abstract Expressionism Review: Crammed in a Room with the Big Men of US Art', *The Guardian*, 20 September 2016, www.theguardian.com/artandde sign/2016/sep/20/abstract-expressionism-review-royal-academy-pollock-rothko (last accessed 25 March 2020).

— 'Storms of Colour from a Wild Destructive Genius: Lee Krasner Review', *The Guardian*, 29 May 2019, www.theguardian.com/artanddesign/2019/may/29/lee-krasner-living-colour-barbican-london-review (last accessed 25 March 2020).

Segal, Lynne, *Out of Time: The Perils and Pleasures of Ageing* (London: Verso, 2013).

Sieberling, Dorothy, 'Is he the greatest living painter in the United States?', *Life*, 27.8 (1949), 42–43.

Silverman, Kaja, *The Acoustic Mirror: The Female Voice in Psychoanalysis and Cinema* (Bloomington, IN: Indiana University Press, 1988).

Smith, Gabrielle, 'Helen Has a Show', *The New York Magazine*, 2.7 (17 February 1969), 46–49.

Snyder, Timothy D., *Bloodlands: Europe Between Hitler and Stalin* (New York: Basic Books, 2010).

Solomon, Deborah, 'Helen Frankenthaler: Artful Survivor', *New York Times Magazine*, 14 May 1989.

Spivak, Gayatri Chakravorty, 'French Feminism in an International Frame', *Yale French Studies*, 62 (1981), 154–84.

Spoto, Donald, *Marilyn Monroe: The Biography* (New York: Harper Collins, 1993).

Steinem, Gloria, and Barris, George, *Marilyn* (New York: Henry Holt, 1986).

Stern, Bert, *Marilyn Monroe: The Last Sitting* (New York: William Morrow, 1982).

— *Marilyn Monroe: The Complete Last Sitting* (Munich: Schirmer/Mosel, 2000).

Stone, I. F., *The Haunted Fifties* (New York: Merlin Press, 1963).

Sylvester, David, 'The Birth of *Woman I*', *Burlington Magazine*, 37.1105 (1995), 220–32.

Tickner, Lisa, and Bird, Jon, *Nancy Spero* (London: Institute of Contemporary Art, 1987).

Tucker, Marcia, *Lee Krasner: Large Paintings* (New York: Whitney Museum of American Art, 1972).

Tufts, Eleanor, *Our Hidden Heritage: Five Centuries of Women Artists* (New York: Paddington Press, 1974).

Wagner, Anne, 'Lee Krasner as L.K.', *Representations*, 25 (winter, 1989), 42–57; reprinted in Norma Broude and Mary Garrard (eds), *The Expanding Discourse* (New York: Harper Colllins, 1992), 425–36.

— 'Krasner's Presence, Pollock's Absence', in Whitney Chadwick (ed.), *Significant Others: Creativity and Intimate Partnership* (London: Thames and Hudson, 1993), 223–43.

— *Three Artists (Three Women): Modernism and the Art of Hesse, Krasner and O'Keeffe* (Berkeley, CA: University of California Press, 1996).

— 'Pollock's Nature: Frankenthaler's Culture', in Kirk Varnedoe and Pepe Karmel (eds), *Jackson Pollock: New Approaches* (New York: Museum of Modern Art, 1999), 181–99.

Walz, Jonathan Frederick, et al. (eds), *Alma W. Thomas: Everything Is Beautiful* (New Haven, CT: Yale University Press, 2021).

Weigel, Sigrid, 'From Gender Images to Dialectical Images in Benjamin's Writings', *New Formations*, 20 (1993), 21–32.

Weiss, Andrea, *Paris was a Woman: Portraits from the Left Bank* (London: Pandora, 1995).

Williams, Raymond, *Marxism and Literature* (Oxford: Oxford University Press, 1977).

Winder, Elizabeth, *Marilyn in Manhattan: Her Year of Joy* (New York: Flatiron Books, 2017).

Wollheim, Richard, *Painting as an Art* (Princeton, NJ: Princeton University Press, 1987).

Woodward, Kathleen, *Figuring Age: Women, Bodies, Generations* (Bloomington, IN: Indiana University Press, 1999).

Woolf, Virginia, *A Room of One's Own* (London: Hogarth Press, 1928).

Wright, Elizabeth, *Feminism and Psychoanalysis: A Critical Dictionary* (Oxford: Blackwell, 1992).

— *Lacan and Postfeminism* (Cambridge: Icon Books, 2000).

Young, Sylvia (ed.), *FemTruth: Endometriosis Edition: A Collection of Stories from Courageous Women* (independently published, 2019).

Index

Page numbers in *italics* refer to illustrations.